Robert Graves was born in 1895 at Wimbledon, son of Alfred Perceval Graves, the Irish writer, and Amalia von Ranke. He went from school to the First World War, where he became a captain in the Royal Welch Fusiliers. His principal calling is poetry, and his *Selected Poems* have been published in the Penguin Poets. Apart from a year as Professor of English Literature at Cairo University in 1926 he has earned his living by writing, mostly historical novels which include: *I, Claudius*; *Claudius the God*; *Sergeant Lamb of the Ninth*; *Count Belisarius*; *Wife to Mr Milton* (all published as Penguins); *Proceed, Sergeant Lamb*; *The Golden Fleece*; *They Hanged My Saintly Billy*; and *The Isles of Unwisdom*. He wrote his autobiography, *Goodbye to All That*, in 1929. His two most discussed non-fiction books are *The White Goddess*, which presents a new view of the poetic impulse, and *The Nazarene Gospel Restored* (with Joshua Podro), a re-examination of primitive Christianity. He has translated Apuleius, Lucan, and Suetonius for the Penguin classics, and compiled the first modern dictionary of Greek mythology, *The Greek Myths*. He was elected Professor of Poetry at Oxford in 1961, and became an Honorary Fellow of St John's College, Oxford, in 1971. Robert Graves published a new edition of his *Collected Poems* in 1975.

ROBERT GRAVES

I, CLAUDIUS

FROM THE AUTOBIOGRAPHY OF

TIBERIUS CLAUDIUS

EMPEROR OF THE ROMANS

BORN 10 B.C.
MURDERED AND DEIFIED
A.D. 54

PENGUIN BOOKS

Penguin Books Ltd, Harmondsworth, Middlesex, England
Penguin Books, 625 Madison Avenue, New York, New York 10022, U.S.A.
Penguin Books Australia Ltd, Ringwood, Victoria, Australia
Penguin Books Canada Ltd, 2801 John Street,
Markham, Ontario, Canada L3R 1B4
Penguin Books (N.Z.) Ltd, 182–190 Wairau Road, Auckland 10, New Zealand

—

First published by Arthur Barker 1934
Published by Methuen 1939
First published in Penguin Books (in two volumes) 1941
Reprinted 1944
New edition in one volume 1953
Reprinted 1955, 1958, 1960, 1962, 1963, 1964, 1966, 1968, 1969,
1970, 1971, 1972, 1974, 1975, 1976 (twice), 1977 (four times), 1978

—

—

Made and printed in Great Britain
by Richard Clay (The Chaucer Press) Ltd,
Bungay, Suffolk
Set in Monotype Times

I am indebted for the Latin version of the Sibylline verses
mentioned in the first chapter to Mr A. K. Smith, I.C.S.
They are here first printed:

Punica centenos durabit poena per annos:
Res Romana viro parebit caesariato:
Calvus caesarie dominus dominabitur urbi:
Omnibus ille viris mulier mas ille puellis:
Rex equitabit equo bifidis equus unguibus ibit:
Filius imbelli fictus mactaverit ictu.
Imperium hinc alter ficto patre caesariato
Caesariae crinitus habet, qui marmore Romae
Mutabit lateres Non visis vinciet Urbem
Compedibus. Fictae secreto coniugis astu
Occidet ut fictus bona filius occupet heres.
Tertius hinc sumet ficto patre caesariato
Calvus caesarie regnum cui sanguine limus
Commixtus. Victrix penes ilium et victa vicissim
Roma erit. Ille instar gladii pulvinar habebit,
Filius et fictus regni potietur iniqui.
Quartus habet solium ficto patre caesariato
Calvus caesarie invenis, cui Roma ministrae est.
Feta veneficiis Urbs impia serviet uni.
Quo puer ibat equo vectus calcatus eodem
Se iuvenem ferro cecidisse fatetur equino
Caesariatus ad hoc quintus numerabitur hirtus
Caesarie, toti genti contemptus avitae.
Imbecillus iners, aestivas addere Romae
Aptus aquas populo frumenta hiemalia praebet.
Ille tamen fictae secreto coniugis astu
Occidet ut fictus bona filius occupet heres.
Sextus habet regnum ficto patre caesariato.
Flamma pavor citharoedus eunt tria monstra per urbem.
Sanguine dextra rubet materno. Septimus heres
Nemo erit, at sexti busto cruor ibit ab imo.

R. G.

Galmpton, Brixham
1941

... A story that was the subject of every variety of misrepresentation, not only by those who then lived but likewise in succeeding times: so true is it that all transactions of pre-eminent importance are wrapt in doubt and obscurity: while some hold for certain facts the most precarious hearsays, others turn facts into falsehood; and both are exaggerated by posterity.

TACITUS

Author's Note

THE 'gold piece' here used as the regular monetary standard is the Latin *aureus*, a coin worth 100 *sestertii*, or twenty-five silver *denarii* ('silver pieces'): it may be thought of as worth roughly one pound sterling, or five American dollars at pre-war value. The 'mile' is the Roman mile, some thirty paces shorter than the English mile. The marginal dates have for convenience been given according to Christian reckoning: the Greek reckoning, used by Claudius, counted the years from the First Olympiad, which took place in 776 B.C. For convenience also, the most familiar geographical names have been used: thus 'France', not 'Transalpine Gaul', because France covers roughly the same territorial area and it would be inconsistent to call towns like Nîmes and Boulogne and Lyons by their modern names – their classical ones would not be popularly recognized – while placing them in *Gallia Transalpina* or, as the Greeks call it, *Galatia*. (Greek geographical terms are most confusing: Germany was 'the country of the Celts'.) Similarly the most familiar forms of proper names have been used – 'Livy' for Titus Livius, 'Cymbeline' for Cunobelinus, 'Mark Antony' for Marcus Antonius.

It has been difficult at times to find suitable renderings for military, legal, and other technical terms. To give a single instance, there is the word 'assegai'. Aircraftman T. E. Shaw (whom I take this opportunity of thanking for his careful reading of these proofs) questions my use of 'assegai' as an equivalent of the German *framea* or *pfreim*. He suggests 'javelin'. But I have not adopted the suggestion, as I have gratefully adopted others of his, because I needed 'javelin' for *pilum*, the regular missile weapon of the disciplined Roman infantryman; and 'assegai' is more savage-sounding. 'Assegai' has had a 300-year currency in English and acquired new vigour in the nineteenth century because of the Zulu wars. The long-shafted iron-headed *framea* was used, according to Tacitus, both as a missile and as a stabbing weapon. So was the assegai of the Ama-Zulu warriors, with whom the Germans of Claudius's day had culturally much in common. If Tacitus's statements, first as to the handiness of the *framea* at close quarters, and then as to its unmanageability among trees, are to be reconciled, the Germans probably did what the Zulus did – they broke off the end of the *framea*'s long shaft when hand-to-hand fighting started. But it seldom came to that, for the Germans

7

always preferred strike-and-run tactics when engaged with the better-armed Roman infantryman.

Suetonius in his *Twelve Caesars* refers to Claudius's histories as written 'ineptly' rather than 'inelegantly'. Yet if certain passages of the present work are not only ineptly written but somewhat inelegantly too – the sentences painfully constructed and the digressions awkwardly placed – this is not out of keeping with Claudius's literary style as exhibited in his Latin speech about the Aeduan franchise, fragments of which survive. The speech is, indeed, thickly strewn with inelegancies of this sort, but then it is probably a transcription of the official shorthand record of Claudius's exact words to the Senate – the speech of a tired man conscientiously extemporizing oratory from a paper of rough notes. *I, Claudius* is a conversational piece of writing; as Greek, indeed, is a far more conversational language than Latin. Claudius's recently discovered Greek letter to the Alexandrians, which may however be partly the work of an imperial secretary, reads much more easily than the Aeduan speech.

For help towards classical correctness I have to thank Miss Eirlys Roberts; and for criticism of the congruity of the English, Miss Laura Riding.

R. G.

1934

Chapter 1

I, TIBERIUS CLAUDIUS DRUSUS NERO GERMANICUS This-that-and-the-other (for I shall not trouble you yet with all my titles), who was once, and not so long ago either, known to my friends and relatives and associates as 'Claudius the Idiot', or 'That Claudius', or 'Claudius the Stammerer',   A.D. 41 or 'Clau-Clau-Claudius', or at best as 'Poor Uncle Claudius', am now about to write this strange history of my life; starting from my earliest childhood and continuing year by year until I reach the fateful point of change where, some eight years ago, at the age of fifty-one, I suddenly found myself caught in what I may call the 'golden predicament' from which I have never since become disentangled.

This is not by any means my first book: in fact literature, and especially the writing of history – which as a young man I studied here at Rome under the best contemporary masters – was, until the change came, my sole profession and interest for more than thirty-five years. My readers must not therefore be surprised at my practised style: it is indeed Claudius himself who is writing this book, and no mere secretary of his, and not one of those official annalists, either, to whom public men are in the habit of communicating their recollections, in the hope that elegant writing will eke out meagreness of subject-matter and flattery soften vices. In the present work, I swear by all the Gods, I am my own mere secretary, and my own official annalist: I am writing with my own hand, and what favour can I hope to win from myself by flattery? I may add that this is not the first history of my own life that I have written. I once wrote another, in eight volumes, as a contribution to the City archives. It was a dull affair, by which I set little store, and only written in response to public request. To be frank, I was extremely busy with other matters during its composition, which was two years ago. I dictated most of the first four volumes to a Greek secretary of mine and told him to alter nothing as he wrote (except, where necessary, for the balance of the sentences, or to remove contradictions or repetitions). But I admit that nearly all the second half of the work, and some chapters at least of the first, were composed by this same fellow, Polybius

9

(whom I had named myself, when a slave-boy, after the famous historian), from material that I gave him. And he modelled his style so accurately on mine that, really, when he had done, nobody could have guessed what was mine and what was his.

It was a dull book, I repeat. I was in no position to criticize the Emperor Augustus, who was my maternal grand-uncle, or his third and last wife, Livia Augusta, who was my grandmother, because they had both been officially deified and I was connected in a priestly capacity with their cults; and though I could have pretty sharply criticized Augusta's two unworthy Imperial successors, I refrained for decency's sake. It would have been unjust to exculpate Livia, and Augustus himself in so far as he deferred to that remarkable and – let me say at once – abominable woman, while telling the truth about the other two, whose memories were not similarly protected by religious awe.

I let it be a dull book, recording merely such uncontroversial facts as, for example, that So-and-so married So-and-so, the daughter of Such-and-Such who had this or that number of public honours to his credit, but not mentioning the political reasons for the marriage or the behind-scene bargaining between the families. Or I would write that So-and-so died suddenly, after eating a dish of African figs, but say nothing of poison, or to whose advantage the death proved to be, unless the facts were supported by a verdict of the Criminal Courts. I told no lies, but neither did I tell the truth in the sense I mean to tell it here. When I consulted this book to-day in the Apollo Library on the Palatine Hill, to refresh my memory for certain particulars of date, I was interested to come across passages in the public chapters which I could have sworn I had written or dictated, the style was so peculiarly my own, and yet which I had no recollection of writing or dictating. If they were by Polybius they were a wonderfully clever piece of mimicry (he had my other histories to study, I admit), but if they were really by myself then my memory is even worse than my enemies declare it to be. Reading over what I have just put down I see that I must be rather exciting than disarming suspicion, first as to my sole authorship of what follows, next as to my integrity as an historian, and finally as to my memory for facts. But I shall let it stand; it is myself writing as I feel, and as the history proceeds the reader will be the more ready to believe that I am hiding nothing – so much being to my discredit.

10

This is a confidential history. But who, it may be asked, are my confidants? My answer is: it is addressed to posterity. I do not mean my great-grandchildren, or my great-great-grandchildren: I mean an extremely remote posterity. Yet my hope is that you, my eventual readers of a hundred generations ahead or more, will feel yourselves directly spoken to, as if by a contemporary: as often Herodotus and Thucydides, long dead, seem to speak to me. And why do I specify so extremely remote a posterity as that? I shall explain.

I went to Cumae, in Campania, a little less than eighteen years ago, and visited the Sibyl in her cliff cavern on Mount Gaurus. There is always a Sibyl at Cumae, for when one dies her novice-attendant succeeds; but they are not all equally famous. Some of them are never granted a prophecy by Apollo in all the long years of their service. Others prophesy, indeed, but seem more inspired by Bacchus than by Apollo, the drunken nonsense they deliver; which has brought the oracle into discredit. Before the succession of Deiphobe, whom Augustus often consulted, and Amalthea, who is still alive and most famous, there had been a run of very poor Sibyls for nearly 300 years. The cavern lies behind a pretty little Greek temple sacred to Apollo and Artemis – Cumae was an Aeolian Greek colony. There is an ancient gilt frieze above the portico ascribed to Daedalus, though this is patently absurd, for it is no older than 500 years, if as old as that, and Daedalus lived at least 1,100 years ago. It represents the story of Theseus and the minotaur whom he killed in the Labyrinth of Crete. Before being permitted to visit the Sibyl I had to sacrifice a bullock and a ewe there, to Apollo and Artemis respectively. It was cold December weather. The cavern was a terrifying place, hollowed out from the solid rock; the approach steep, tortuous, pitch-dark, and full of bats. I went disguised, but the Sibyl knew me. It must have been my stammer that betrayed me. I stammered badly as a child and though, by following the advice of specialists in elocution, I gradually learned to control my speech on set public occasions, yet on private and unpremeditated ones I am still, though less so than formerly, liable every now and then to trip nervously over my own tongue; which is what happened to me at Cumae.

I came into the inner cavern, after groping painfully on all-fours up the stairs, and saw the Sibyl, more like an ape than a woman, sitting on a chair in a cage that hung from the ceiling, her robes red and her unblinking eyes shining red in the single red shaft of light that struck down from somewhere above. Her toothless mouth was grinning. There was a smell of death about me. But I managed to force out the salutation that I had prepared. She gave me no answer. It was only some time afterwards that I learnt that this was the mummied body of Deiphobe, the previous Sibyl, who had died recently at the age of 110; her eyelids were propped up with glass marbles silvered behind to make them shine. The reigning Sibyl always lived with her predecessor. Well, I must have stood for some minutes in front of Deiphobe, shivering and making propitiatory grimaces – it seemed a lifetime. At last the living Sibyl, whose name was Amalthea, quite a young woman too, revealed herself. The red shaft of light failed, so that Deiphobe disappeared – somebody, probably the novice, had covered up the tiny red-glass window – and a new shaft, white, struck down and lit up Amalthea, seated on an ivory throne in the shadows behind. She had a beautiful mad-looking face with a high forehead and sat as motionless as Deiphobe. But her eyes were closed. My knees shook and I fell into a stammer from which I could not extricate myself.

'O Sib ... Sib ... Sib ... Sib ... Sib ...' I began. She opened her eyes, frowned, and mimicked me: 'O Clau ... Clau ... Clau ...' That shamed me and I managed to remember what I had come to ask. I said with a great effort: 'O Sibyl: I have come to question you about Rome's fate and mine.'

Gradually her face changed, the prophetic power overcame her, she struggled and gasped, and there was a rushing noise through all the galleries, doors banged, wings swished my face, the light vanished, and she uttered a Greek verse in the voice of the God:

> Who groans beneath the Punic Curse
> And strangles in the strings of purse,
> Before she mends must sicken worse.
>
> Her living mouth shall breed blue flies,
> And maggots creep about her eyes.
> No man shall mark the day she dies.

Then she tossed her arms over her head and began again:

> Ten years, fifty days and three,
> Clau – Clau – Clau shall given be
> A gift that all desire but he.

To a fawning fellowship
He shall stammer, cluck, and trip,
Dribbling always with his lip.

But when he's dumb and no more here,
Nineteen hundred years or near,
Clau - Clau - Claudius shall speak clear.

The God laughed through her mouth then, a lovely yet terrible sound - ho! ho! ho! I made obeisance, turned hurriedly and went stumbling away, sprawling headlong down the first flight of broken stairs, cutting my forehead and knees, and so painfully out, the tremendous laughter pursuing me.

Speaking now as a practised diviner, a professional historian and a priest who has had opportunities of studying the Sibylline books as regularized by Augustus, I can interpret the verses with some confidence. By the Punic Curse the Sibyl was referring plainly enough to the destruction of Carthage by us Romans. We have long been under a divine curse because of that. We swore friendship and protection to Carthage in the name of our principal Gods, Apollo included, and then, jealous of her quick recovery from the disasters of the Second Punic War, we tricked her into fighting the Third Punic War and utterly destroyed her, massacring her inhabitants and sowing her fields with salt. 'The strings of purse' are the chief instruments of this curse - a money-madness that has choked Rome ever since she destroyed her chief trade rival and made herself mistress of all the riches of the Mediterranean. With riches came sloth, greed, cruelty, dishonesty, cowardice, effeminacy, and every other un-Roman vice. What the gift was that all desired but myself - and it came exactly ten years and fifty-three days later - you shall read in due course. The lines about Claudius speaking clear puzzled me for years, but at last I think that I understand them. They are, I believe, an injunction to write the present work. When it is written, I shall treat it with a preservative fluid, seal it in a lead casket, and bury it deep in the ground somewhere for posterity to dig up and read. If my interpretation be correct it will be found again some 1,900 years hence. And then, when all other authors of to-day whose works survive will seem to shuffle and stammer, since they have written only for to-day, and guardedly, my story will speak out clearly and boldly. Perhaps on second thoughts I shall not take the trouble to seal it up in a casket. I shall merely leave it lying about. For my experience as a historian is that more documents survive by chance than by intention. Apollo has made the prophecy, so I shall let Apollo take care of the manuscript. As you see, I have chosen to write in Greek, because Greek, I believe, will always remain the chief literary language of the world, and if Rome rots away as the Sibyl has indicated, will not her language rot away with her? Besides, Greek is Apollo's own language.

I shall be careful with dates (which you see I am putting in the margin) and proper names. In compiling my histories of Etruria and Carthage I have spent more angry hours than I care to recall, puzzling out in what year this or that event happened and whether a man named So-and-so was really So-and-so or whether he was a son or grandson or great-grandson or no relation at all. I intend to spare my successors this sort of irritation. Thus, for example, of the several characters in this present history who have the name of Drusus – my father; myself; a son of mine; my first cousin; my nephew – each will be plainly distinguished wherever mentioned. And, for example again, in speaking of my tutor, Marcus Portius Cato, I must make it plain that he was neither Marcus Portius Cato, the Censor, instigator of the Third Punic War; nor his son of the same name, the well-known jurist; nor his grandson, the Consul of the same name, nor his great-grandson of the same name, Julius Caesar's enemy; nor his great-great-grandson of the same name, who fell at the Battle of Philippi; but an absolutely undistinguished great-great-great-grandson, still of the same name, who never bore any public dignity and who deserved none. Augustus made him my tutor and afterwards schoolmaster to other young Roman noblemen and sons of foreign kings, for though his name entitled him to a position of the highest dignity, his severe, stupid, pedantic nature qualified him for nothing better than that of elementary schoolmaster.

To fix the date to which these events belong I can do no better, I think, than to say that my birth occurred in the 744th year after the foundation of Rome by Romulus, and in the 767th year after the First Olympiad, and that the Emperor Augustus, whose name is unlikely to perish even in 1,900 years of history, had by then been ruling for twenty years.

10 B.C.

Before I close this introductory chapter I have something more to add about the Sibyl and her prophecies. I have already said

14

that, at Cumae, when one Sibyl dies another succeeds, but that some are more famous than others. There was one very famous one, Demophile, whom Aeneas consulted before his descent into Hell. And there was a later one, Herophile, who came to King Tarquin and offered him a collection of prophecies at a higher price than he wished to pay. When he refused, so the story runs, she burned a part and offered what was left at the same price, which he again refused. Then she burned another part and offered what was left, still at the same price – which, for curiosity, he paid. Herophile's oracles were of two kinds, warning or hopeful prophecies of the future, and directions for the suitable propitiatory sacrifices to be made when such and such portents occurred. To these were added, in the course of time, whatever remarkable and well-attested oracles were uttered to private persons. Whenever, then, Rome has seemed threatened by strange portents or disasters the Senate orders a consultation of the books by the priests who have charge of them and a remedy is always found. Twice the books have been partially destroyed by fire and the lost prophecies restored by the combined memories of the priests in charge. The memories seem in many instances to have been extremely faulty: this is why Augustus set to work on an authoritative canon of the prophecies, rejecting obviously uninspired interpolations or restorations. He also called in and destroyed all unauthorized private collections of Sibylline oracles as well as all other books of public prediction that he could lay his hands upon, to the number of over 2,000. The revised Sibylline books he put in a locked cupboard under the pedestal of Apollo's statue in the temple which he built for the God close to his palace on the Palatine Hill. A unique book from Augustus's private historical library came into my possession some time after his death. It was called 'Sibylline Curiosities: being such prophecies found incorporated in the original canon as have been rejected as spurious by the priests of Apollo'. The verses were copied out in Augustus's own beautiful script, with the characteristic mis-spellings which, originally made from ignorance, he ever after adhered to as a point of pride. Most of these verses were obviously never spoken by the Sibyl either in ecstasy or out of it, but composed by irresponsible persons who wished to glorify themselves or their houses or to curse the houses of rivals by claiming divine authorship for their own fanciful predictions against them. The Claudian family had been particularly

15

active, I noticed, in these forgeries. Yet I found one or two pieces whose language proved them respectably archaic and whose inspiration seemed divine, and whose plain and alarming sense had evidently decided Augustus – his word was law among the priests of Apollo – against admitting them into his canon. This little book I no longer have. But I can recall almost every word of the most memorable of these seemingly genuine prophecies, which was recorded both in the original Greek, and (like most of the early pieces in the canon) in rough Latin verse translation. It ran thus:

> A hundred years of the Punic Curse
> And Rome will be slave to a hairy man,
> A hairy man that is scant of hair.
> Every man's woman and each woman's man.
> The steed that he rides shall have toes for hooves.
> He shall die at the hand of his son, no son,
> And not on the field of war.
>
> The hairy one next to enslave the State
> Shall be son, no son, of this hairy last,
> He shall have hair in a generous mop.
> He shall give Rome marble in place of clay
> And fetter her fast with unseen chains,
> And shall die at the hand of his wife, no wife,
> To the gain of his son, no son.
>
> The hairy third to enslave the State
> Shall be son, no son, of this hairy last.
> He shall be mud well mixed with blood,
> A hairy man that is scant of hair.
> He shall give Rome victories and defeat
> And die to the gain of his son, no son –
> A pillow shall be his sword.
>
> The hairy fourth to enslave the State
> Shall be son, no son, of this hairy last.
> A hairy man that is scant of hair,
> He shall give Rome poisons and blasphemies
> And die from a kick of his aged horse
> That carried him as a child.
>
> The hairy fifth to enslave the State,
> To enslave the State, though against his will,
> Shall be that idiot whom all despised.

He shall have hair in a generous mop.
He shall give Rome water and winter bread
And die at the hand of his wife, no wife,
To the gain of his son, no son.

The hairy sixth to enslave the State
Shall be son, no son, of this hairy last.
He shall give Rome fiddlers and fear and fire.
His hand shall be red with a parent's blood.
No hairy seventh to him succeeds
And blood shall gush from his tomb.

Now it must have been plain to Augustus that the first of the hairy ones, that is, the Caesars (for Caesar means a head of hair), was his grand-uncle Julius, who adopted him. Julius was bald and he was renowned for his debaucheries with either sex; and his war charger, as is a matter of public record, was a monster which had toes instead of hooves. Julius escaped alive from many hard-fought battles only to be murdered at last, in the Senate House, by Brutus. And Brutus, though fathered on another, was believed to be Julius's natural son. 'Thou too, child!' said Julius, as Brutus came at him with a dagger. Of the Punic Curse I have already written. Augustus must have recognized in himself the second of the Caesars. Indeed, he himself at the end of his life made a boast, looking at the temples and public buildings that he had splendidly re-edified, and thinking too of his life's work in strengthening and glorifying the Empire, that he had found Rome in clay and left her in marble. But as for the manner of his death, he must have found the prophecy either unintelligible or incredible: yet some scruple kept him from destroying it. Who the hairy third and the hairy fourth and the hairy fifth were this history will plainly show; and I am indeed an idiot if, granting the oracle's unswerving accuracy in every particular up to the present, I do not recognize the hairy sixth; rejoicing on Rome's behalf that there will be no hairy seventh to succeed him.

Chapter 2

I CANNOT remember my father, who died when I was an infant, but as a young man I never lost an opportunity of gathering information of the most detailed sort about his life and character from every possible person – senator, soldier, or slave – who had known him. I began writing his biography as my apprentice-task in history, and though that was soon put a stop to by my grandmother, Livia, I continued collecting material in the hope of one day being able to finish the work. I finished it, actually, just the other day, and even now there is no sense in trying to put it into circulation. It is so republican in sentiment that the moment Agrippinilla – my present wife – came to hear of its publication every copy would be suppressed and my unfortunate copying-scribes would suffer for my indiscretions. They would be lucky to escape with their arms unbroken and their thumbs and index fingers unlopped, which would be a typical indication of Agrippinilla's pleasure. How that woman loathes me!

My father's example has guided me throughout life more strongly than that of any other person whatsoever, with the exception of my brother Germanicus. And Germanicus was, all agree, my father's very image in feature, body (but for his thin legs), courage, intellect, and nobility; so I readily combine them in my mind as a single character. If I could start this story fairly with an account of my infancy, going no farther back than my parents, I would certainly do so, for genealogies and family histories are tedious. But I shall not be able to avoid writing at some length about my grandmother Livia (the only one of my four grandparents who was alive at my birth) because unfortunately she is the chief character in the first part of my story, and unless I give a clear account of her early life her later actions will not be intelligible. I have mentioned that she was married to the Emperor Augustus: this was her second marriage, following her divorce from my grandfather. After my father's death she became the virtual head of our family, supplanting my mother Antonia, my uncle Tiberius (the legal head), and Augustus himself – to whose powerful protection my father had committed us children in his will.

Livia was of the Claudian family, one of the most ancient of Rome, and so was my grandfather. There is a popular ballad, still sometimes sung by old people, of which the refrain is that the Claudian tree bears two sorts of fruit, the sweet apple and the crab, but that the crabs outnumber the apples. Among the crab sort the balladist reckons Appius Claudius the Proud, who put all Rome in a tumult by trying to enslave and seduce a free-born girl called Virginia, and Claudius Drusus, who in Republican days tried to make himself King of all Italy, and Claudius the Fair, who, when the sacred chickens would not feed, threw them into the sea, crying 'Then let them drink,' and so lost an important sea-battle. And of the former sort the balladist mentions Appius the Blind, who dissuaded Rome from a dangerous league with King Pyrrhus, and Claudius the Tree-Trunk, who drove the Carthaginians out of Sicily, and Claudius Nero (which in the Sabine dialect means The Strong), who defeated Hasdrubal as he came out of Spain to join forces with his brother, the great Hannibal. These three were all virtuous men, besides being bold and wise. And the balladist says that of the Claudian women too, some are apples and some are crabs, but that again the crabs outnumber the apples.

My grandfather was one of the best of the Claudians. Believing that Julius Caesar was the one man powerful enough to give Rome peace and security in those difficult times, he joined the Caesarean party and fought bravely for Julius in the Egyptian War. When he suspected that Julius was aiming at personal tyranny, my grandfather would not willingly further his ambitions in Rome, though he could not risk an open breach. He therefore asked for and secured the office of pontiff and was sent in that capacity to France to found colonies of veteran soldiers there. On his return after Julius's assassination he incurred the enmity of young Augustus, Julius's adopted son, who was then known as Octavian, and of his ally, the great Mark Antony, by boldly proposing honours for the tyrannicides. He had to flee from Rome. In the disturbances that followed he sided now with this party and now with that, according as the right seemed to lie here or there. At one time he was with young Pompey, at an- 41 B.C. other he fought with Mark Antony's brother against Augustus, at Perusia in Etruria. But convinced at last that Augustus, though bound by loyalty to avenge the murder of Julius, his

19

adopted father – a duty which he ruthlessly performed – was not tyrant-hearted and aimed at the restoration of the ancient liberties of the people, he came over to his side and settled at Rome with my grandmother Livia, and my uncle Tiberius, then only two years old. He took no more part in the Civil Wars, contenting himself with his duties as a pontiff.

My grandmother Livia was one of the worst of the Claudians. She may well have been a re-incarnation of that Claudia, sister of Claudius the Fair, who was arraigned for high treason because once when her coach was held up by a street crowd she called out, 'If only my brother was alive! He knew how to clear crowds away. He used his whip.' When one of the Protectors of the People ('tribunes', in Latin) came up and angrily ordered her to be silent, reminding her that her brother, by his impiety, had lost a Roman fleet: 'A very good reason for wishing him alive,' she retorted. 'He might lose another fleet, and then another, God willing, and thin off this wretched crowd a little.' And she added: 'You're a Protector of the People, I see, and your person is legally inviolable, but don't forget that we Claudians have had some of you protectors well thrashed before now, and be damned to your inviolability.' That was exactly how my grandmother Livia spoke at this time of the Roman people. 'Rabble and slaves! The Republic was always a humbug. What Rome really needs is a king again.' That at least is how she talked to my grandfather, urging him that Mark Antony, and Augustus (or Octavian, I should say) and Lepidus (a rich but unenergetic nobleman), who between them now ruled the Roman world, would in time fall out; and that, if he played his hand well, he could use his dignity as a pontiff and the reputation for integrity which was conceded him by all factions as a means to becoming king himself. My grandfather replied sternly that if she spoke in this strain again he would divorce her; for in the old style of Roman marriage the husband could put his wife away without a public explanation, returning the dowry that had come with her, but keeping the children. At this my grandmother was silent and pretended to submit, but all love between them died from that moment. Unknown to my grandfather, she immediately set about engaging the passions of Augustus.

This was no difficult matter, for Augustus was young and impressionable and she had made a careful study of his tastes: besides which, she was by popular verdict one of the three most beautiful women of her day. She had picked on Augustus as a better instrument for her ambitions than Antony – Lepidus did not count – and that he would stick at nothing to gain his ends and proscriptions he had shown two years before, when 2,000 knights and 300 senators belonging to the opposing faction had been summarily put to death, by far the greatest number of these at Augustus's particular instance. When she had made sure of Augustus she urged him to put away Scribonia – a woman older than himself, whom he had married for political reasons – telling him that she had knowledge of Scribonia's adultery with a close friend of my grandfather's. Augustus was ready to believe this without pressing for detailed evidence. He divorced Scribonia, though she was quite innocent, on the very day that she bore him his daughter, Julia; whom he took from the   38 B.C. birth-chamber before Scribonia had as much as seen the little creature, and gave to the wife of one of his freedmen to nurse. My grandmother – who was still only seventeen years old, nine years younger than Augustus – then went to my grandfather and said, 'Now divorce me. I am already five months gone with child, and you are not the father. I made a vow that I would not bear another child to a coward, and I intend to keep it.' My grandfather, whatever he may have felt when he heard this confession, said no more than 'Call the adulterer here to me and let us discuss the matter together in private.' The child was really his own, but he was not to know this, and when my grandmother said that it was another's he believed her.

My grandfather was astonished to find that it was his pretended friend Augustus who had betrayed him, but concluded that Livia had tempted him and that he had not been proof against her beauty; and perhaps Augustus still bore a grudge against him for the un-lucky motion that he had once introduced in the Senate for reward-ing Julius Caesar's assassins. However it may have been, he did not reproach Augustus. All that he said was: 'If you love this woman and will marry her honourably, take her; only let the decencies be observed.' Augustus swore that he would marry her immediately and never cast her off while she continued faithful to him; he bound himself by the most frightful oaths. So my grandfather divorced her. I have been told that he regarded this infatuation of hers as a divine punishment on himself because once in Sicily at her insti-gation he had armed slaves to fight against Roman citizens; moreover, she was a Claudian, one of his own family, so for these two reasons he was unwilling to show her public dishonour. It was certainly not for fear of Augustus that he assisted in person at her marriage a few weeks later, giving her away as a father would his daughter and joining in her wedding hymn. When I consider that he had loved her dearly and that by his generosity he risked the name of coward and pander, I am filled with admiration for his conduct.

But Livia was ungrateful – angry and ashamed that he seemed to take the matter so calmly, giving her up tamely as if she were a thing of little worth. And when her child, my father, was born three months later she was deeply vexed with Augustus's sister Octavia, Mark Antony's wife – these were my two other grandparents – because of a Greek epigram to the effect that parents were fortunate who had three-months' children: such short gestation had hitherto been confined to cats and bitches. I do not know whether Octavia was truly the author of this verse, but, if she was, Livia made her pay dearly for it before she had done. It is unlikely that she was the author, for she had herself been married to Mark Antony while with child by a husband who had died; and, in the words of the proverb, cripples do not mock cripples. Octavia's was, however, a political marriage and legalized by a special decree of the Senate: it was not brought about by passion on one side and personal ambition on the other. If it be asked how it happened that the College of Pontiffs consented to admit the validity of Augustus's marriage with Livia, the answer is that my grandfather and Augustus were both pontiffs, and that the High Pontiff was Lepidus, who did exactly what Augustus told him.

As soon as my father was weaned Augustus sent him back to my grandfather's house, where he was brought up with my uncle Tiberius, the elder by four years. My grandfather, as soon as the children reached the age of understanding, took their education in hand himself, instead of entrusting it to a tutor, as was already the general custom. He never ceased to instil in them a hatred of tyranny and a devotion to ancient ideals of justice, liberty, and virtue. My grandmother Livia had long grudged that her two boys were out of her charge – though indeed they visited her daily at Augustus's palace, which was quite close to their home on the Palatine Hill – and when she found in what way they were being educated she was greatly annoyed. My grandfather died suddenly while dining with some friends, and it

33 B.C.

22

was suspected that he had been poisoned, but the matter was hushed up because Augustus and Livia had been among the guests. In his will the boys were left to Augustus's guardianship. My uncle Tiberius, aged only nine, spoke the oration at my grandfather's funeral.

Augustus loved his sister Octavia dearly and had been much grieved on her account when, soon after her marriage, he learnt that Antony, after starting out for the East to fight a war in Parthia, had stopped on the way to renew his intimacy with Cleopatra, Queen of Egypt; and still more grieved at the slighting letter that Octavia had received from Antony when she went out to help him the next year with men and money for his campaign. The letter, which reached her when she was half-way on her journey, ordered her coldly to return home and attend to her household affairs; yet he accepted the men and money. Livia was secretly delighted at the incident, having long been assiduous in making misunderstandings and jealousies between Augustus and Antony, which Octavia had been as assiduous in smoothing out. When Octavia returned to Rome, Livia asked Augustus to invite her to leave Antony's house and stay with them. She refused to do so, partly because she did not trust Livia and partly because she did not wish to appear a cause of the impending war. Finally Antony, incited by Cleopatra, sent Octavia a bill of divorce and declared war on Augustus. This was the last of the Civil Wars, a duel to the death between the only two men left on their feet – if I may use the metaphor – after an all-against-all sword-fight in the universal amphitheatre. Lepidus was still alive, to be sure, but a prisoner in all but name, and quite harmless – he had been forced to fall at Augustus's feet and beg for his life. Young Pompey, too, the only other person of importance, whose fleet had for a long time commanded the Mediterranean, had by now been defeated · by Augustus, and captured and put to death by Antony. The duel between Augustus and Antony was short. Antony was totally defeated in the sea-battle off Actium, in Greece. 31 B.C. He fled to Alexandria, and there took his own life – as did Cleopatra too. Augustus assumed Antony's Eastern conquests as his own and became, as Livia had intended, the sole ruler of the Roman world. Octavia remained true to the interests of Antony's children – not only his son by a former wife, but actually his three children by Cleopatra, a girl and two boys – bringing them up with her own two daughters, one of whom, Antonia the younger, was my mother. This nobility of mind excited general admiration at Rome.

Augustus ruled the world, but Livia ruled Augustus. And I must here explain the remarkable hold that she had over him. It was always a matter of wonder that there were no children of the marriage, seeing that my grandmother had not shown herself unfruitful and that Augustus was reported to be the father of at least four natural children, besides his daughter Julia, who there is no reason for doubting was his own daughter. He was known, moreover, to be passionately devoted to my grandmother. The truth will not easily be credited. The truth is that the marriage was never consummated. Augustus, though capable enough with other women, found himself as impotent as a child when he tried to have commerce with my grandmother. The only reasonable explanation is that Augustus was, at bottom, a pious man, though cruelty and even ill-faith had been forced on him by the dangers that followed his grand-uncle Julius Caesar's assassination. He knew that the marriage was impious: this knowledge, it seems, affected him nervously, putting an inner restraint on his flesh.

My grandmother, who had wanted Augustus as an instrument of her ambition rather than as a lover, was more glad than sorry for this impotence. She found that she could use it as a weapon for subjecting his will to hers. Her practice was to reproach him continually for having seduced her from my grandfather, whom she protested that she had loved, by assurances to her of deep passion and by secret threats to him that if she were not given up he would be arraigned as a public enemy. (This last was perfectly untrue.) Now look, she said, how she had been tricked! This passionate lover turned out to be no man at all; any poor charcoal-burner or slave was more of a man than he! Even Julia was not his real daughter, and he knew it. All that he was good for, she said, was to fondle and fumble and kiss and make eyes like a singing eunuch. It was in vain that Augustus protested that with other women he was a Hercules. Either she would refuse to believe it or she would accuse him of wasting on other women what he denied her. But that no scandal of this should go about she pretended on one occasion to be with child by him and then to have a miscarriage. Shame and unslakable passion bound Augustus closer to her than if their mutual longings had been nightly satisfied or

24

than if she had borne him a dozen fine children. And she took the greatest care of his health and comfort, and was faithful to him, not being naturally lustful except of power; and for this he was so grateful that he let her guide and rule him in all his public and private acts. I have heard it confidently stated by old palace officials that, after marrying my grandmother, Augustus never looked at another woman. Yet all sorts of stories were current at Rome about his affairs with the wives and daughters of notables; and after his death, in explaining how it was that she had so complete a command of his affections, Livia used to say that it was not only because she was faithful to him but also because she never interfered with his passing love-affairs. It is my belief that she put all these scandals about herself in order to have something to reproach him with.

If I am challenged as to my authority for this curious history I shall give it. The first part relating to the divorce I heard from Livia's own lips in the year she died. The remainder, about Augustus's impotence, I heard from a woman called Briseis, a wardrobe-maid of my mother's, who had previously served my grandmother as a page-girl, and being then only seven years old had been allowed to overhear conversations that she was thought too young to understand. I believe my account true and will continue to do so until it is supplanted by one that fits the facts equally well. To my way of thinking, the Sibyl's verse about 'wife, no wife' confirms the matter. No, I cannot close the matter here. In writing this passage, with the idea, I suppose, of shielding Augustus's good name, I have been holding something back which I shall now after all set down. Because, as the proverb says, 'truth helps the story on'. It is this. My grandmother Livia ingeniously consolidated her hold on Augustus by secretly giving him, of her own accord, beautiful young women to sleep with whenever she noticed that passion made him restless. That she arranged this for him, and without a word said beforehand or afterwards, forbearing from the jealousy that, as a wife, he was convinced that she must feel; yet everything was done very decently and quietly, the young women (whom she picked out herself in the Syrian slave-market – he preferred Syrians) being introduced into his bedroom at night with a knock and the rattle of a chain for signal, and called away again early in the morning by a similar knock and rattle; and that they kept silence in his presence as if they were succubi who came in dreams – that she contrived all this so thoughtfully and remained faithful to him herself in spite of his impotence with her, he must have considered a perfect proof of the sincerest love. You may object that Augustus, in his position, might have had the most beautiful women in the world, bond or free, married or unmarried, to feed his appetite, without the assistance of Livia as procuress. That is true, but it is true nevertheless that after his marriage to Livia he tasted no meat, as he once said himself, though perhaps in another context, that she had not passed as fit for eating.

Of women, then, Livia had no cause to be jealous, except only of her sister-in-law, my other grandmother, Octavia, whose beauty excited as much admiration as her virtue. Livia had taken malicious pleasure in sympathizing with her over Antony's faithlessness. She had gone so far as to suggest that it had been largely Octavia's own fault in dressing in so modest a way and behaving with such decorum. Mark Antony, she pointed out, was a man of strong passions, and to hold him successfully a woman must temper the chastity of a Roman matron with the arts and extravagances of an Oriental courtesan. Octavia should have taken a leaf from Cleopatra's book: for the Egyptian, though Octavia's inferior in looks and her senior by eight or nine years, knew well how to feed his sensual appetite. 'Men such as Antony, real men, prefer the strange to the wholesome,' Livia finished sententiously. 'They find maggoty green cheese more tasty than freshly pressed curds.' 'Keep your maggots to yourself,' Octavia flared at her.

Livia herself dressed very richly and used the most expensive Asiatic perfumes; but she did not allow the least extravagance in her household, which she made a boast of running in old-fashioned Roman style. Her rules were: plain but plentiful food, regular family worship, no hot baths after meals, constant work for everyone, and no waste. 'Everyone' was not merely the slaves and freedmen but every member of the family. The unfortunate child Julia was expected to set an example of industry. She led a very weary life. She had a regular daily task of wool to card and spin, and cloth to weave, and needlework to do, and was made to rise from her hard bed at dawn, and even before dawn in the winter months, to be able to get through it. And because her stepmother believed in a liberal education for girls, she was set, among other tasks, to learn the whole of Homer's *Iliad* and *Odyssey* by heart.

Julia had also to keep a detailed diary, for Livia's benefit, of what work she did, what books she read, what conversations she had, and so on; which was a great burden to her. She was allowed no friendships with men, though her beauty was much toasted. One young man of ancient family and irreproachable morals, a Consul's son, was bold enough to introduce himself to her one day at Baiae on some polite pretext, when she was taking the half-hour's walk allowed her by the seaside, accompanied only by her duenna. Livia, who was jealous of Julia's good looks and of Augustus's affection for her, had the young man sent a very strong letter, telling him that he must never expect to hold public office under the father of the girl whose good name he had tried to besmirch by this insufferable familiarity. Julia herself was punished by being forbidden to take her walk outside the grounds of the villa. About this time Julia went quite bald. I do not know whether Livia had a hand in this: it seems not improbable, though certainly baldness was in the Caesar family. At all events, Augustus found an Egyptian wig-maker who made her one of the most magnificent fair wigs that was ever seen, and her charms were thus rather increased than diminished by her mischance; she had not had very good hair of her own. It is said that the wig was not built, in the usual way, on a base of hair net but was the whole scalp of a German chieftain's daughter shrunk to the exact size of Julia's head and kept alive and pliant by occasional rubbing with a special ointment. But I must say that I don't believe this.

Everyone knew that Livia kept Augustus in strict order and that, if not actually frightened of her, he was at any rate very careful not to offend her. One day, in his capacity as Censor, he was lecturing some rich men about allowing their wives to bedizen themselves with jewels. 'For a woman to overdress,' he said, 'is unseemly. It is the husband's duty to restrain his wife from luxury.' Carried away by his own eloquence he unfortunately added: 'I sometimes have occasion to admonish my own wife about this.' There was a delighted cry from the culprits. 'Oh, Augustus,' they said, 'do tell us in what words you admonish Livia. It will serve as a model for us.' Augustus was embarrassed and alarmed. 'You mis-heard me,' he said, 'I do not say that I had ever had occasion to reprimand Livia. As you know well, she is a paragon of

27

matronly modesty. But I certainly should have no hesitation in reprimanding her were she to forget her dignity by dressing, as some of your wives do, like an Alexandrian dancing-girl who has by some queer turn of fate become an Armenian queen-dowager.' That same evening Livia tried to make Augustus look small by appearing at the dinner-table in the most fantastically gorgeous finery she could lay her hands on, the foundation of which was one of Cleopatra's ceremonial dresses. But he got well out of an awkward situation by praising her for her witty and opportune parody of the very fault he had been condemning.

Livia had grown wiser since the time that she had advised my grandfather to put a diadem on his head and proclaim himself king. The title 'king' was still execrated at Rome on account of the unpopular Tarquin dynasty to which, according to legend, the first Brutus (I call him this to distinguish him from the second Brutus, who murdered Julius) had put an end – expelling the royal family from the City and becoming one of the first two Consuls of the Roman Republic. Livia realized now that the title of king could be waived so long as Augustus could control the substantial powers of kingship. By following her advice he gradually concentrated in his single person all the important Republican dignities. He was Consul at Rome, and when he passed the office to a reliable friend he took in exchange the 'High Command' – which, though nominally on a level with the consulship, ranked in practice above this or any other magistracy. He had absolute control of the provinces, too, and power to appoint the provincial governors-general, together with the command of all armies and the right of levying troops and of making peace or war. In Rome he was voted the life-office of People's Protector, which secured him against all interference with his authority, gave him the power of vetoing the decisions of other office-holders, and carried with it the inviolability of his person. The title 'Emperor', which once merely meant 'field-marshal' but has recently come to mean supreme monarch, he shared with other successful generals. He also had the Censorship, which gave him authority over the two leading social orders, those of Senators and Knights; on the pretext of moral shortcomings he could disqualify any member of either order from its dignities and privileges – a disgrace keenly felt. He had control of the Public Treasury: he was supposed to render periodic accounts, but nobody was ever bold enough to demand an audit, though it was known that there was constant juggling between the Treasury and Privy Purse.

Thus he had command of the armies, the control of the laws – for his influence on the Senate was such that they voted whatever he suggested to them – the control of public finances, the control of social behaviour, and inviolacy of person. He even had the right of summarily condemning any Roman citizen, from plough-man to senator, to death or perpetual banishment. The last dig-nity that he assumed was that of High Pontiff, which gave him control of the entire religious system. The Senate were anxious to vote him whatever title he would accept, short of King: they were afraid to vote him the kingship, for fear of the people. His real wish was to be called Romulus, but Livia advised him against this. Her argument was that Romulus had been a king and that the name was therefore dangerous, and further that he was one of the Roman tutelary deities and that to take his name would seem blasphemous. But her real feeling was that it was not a grand enough title. Romulus had been a mere bandit-chieftain and was not among the first rank of the Gods. On her advice he therefore signified to the Senate that the title Augustus would be agreeable to him. So they voted him that. 'Augustus' had a semi-divine connota-tion, and the common title of King was nothing by comparison.

How many mere kings paid tribute to Augustus! How many were marched in chains in Roman triumphs! Had not even the High King of remote India, hearing of Augustus's fame, sent am-bassadors to Rome, begging for the protection of his friendship, with propitiatory presents of remarkable silks and spices; and rubies, emeralds, and sardonyx; and tigers, then for the first time seen in Europe, and the Indian Hermes, the famous armless boy, who could do the most extraordinary things with his feet? Had not Augustus put an end to that line of kings in Egypt that went back at least 5,000 years before the foundation of Rome? And at that fateful interruption of history what monstrous portents had not been seen? Had there not been flashes of armour from the clouds and bloody rain falling? Had not a serpent of gigantic size appeared in the main street of Alexandria and uttered an incred-ibly loud hiss? Had not the ghosts of dead Pharaohs appeared? Had not their statues frowned? Had not Apis, the sacred bull of Memphis, uttered a bellow of lamentation and burst into tears? This was how my grandmother reasoned with herself.

Most women are inclined to set a modest limit to their ambitions; a few rare ones set a bold limit. But Livia was unique in setting no limit at all to hers, and yet remaining perfectly level-headed and cool in what would be judged in any other woman to be raving madness. It was only little by little that even I, with such excellent opportunities for observing her, came to guess generally what her intentions were. But even so, when the final disclosure came, it came as a shock of surprise. Perhaps I had better record her various acts in historical sequence, without dwelling on her hidden motives.

On her advice, Augustus prevailed on the Senate to create two new Divinities, namely, the Goddess Roma, who represented the female soul of the Roman Empire, and the Demi-god Julius, the warlike hero who was Julius Caesar in apotheosis. (Divine honours had been offered to Julius, in the East, while he was still alive; that he had not refused them was one of the reasons for his assassination.) Augustus knew the value of a religious bond to unite the province with the City, a bond far stronger than one based merely on fear or gratitude. It sometimes happened that after long residence in Egypt or Asia Minor even true-born Romans turned to the worship of the gods they found there and forgot their own, thereby becoming foreigners in all but name. On the other hand, Rome had imported so many religions from the cities she had conquered, giving alien deities, such as Isis and Cybele, noble temples in the City – and not merely for the convenience of visitors – that it was reasonable that she should now, in fair exchange, plant gods of her own in these cities. Roma and Julius, then, were to be worshipped by such provincials as were Roman citizens and wished to be reminded of their national heritage.

The next step that Livia took was to arrange for delegations of provincials not fortunate enough to possess full citizenship to visit Rome and beg to be given a Roman God whom they might worship loyally and without presumption. On Livia's advice Augustus told the Senate, half-jokingly, that these poor fellows, while obviously they could not be allowed to worship the superior deities, Roma and Julius, must not be denied some sort of God, however humble. At this Maecenas, one of Augustus's ministers, with whom Augustus had already discussed the advisability of taking the name of Romulus, said: 'Let us give them a God who will watch over them well. Let us give them Augustus himself.' Augus-

tus appeared somewhat embarrassed but admitted that Maecenas's suggestion was a sound one. It was an established custom
among Orientals, and one which might well be turned to Roman
profit, to pay divine honours to their rulers; but since it was clearly
impracticable for Eastern cities to worship the whole Senate in a
body, putting up 600 statues in each of their shrines, one way out of
the difficulty, certainly, was for them to worship the Senate's chief
executive officer, who happened to be himself. So the Senate, feeling
complimented that each member had in him at least one six-hun-
dredth part of divinity, gladly voted Maecenas's motion, and shrines
to Augustus were immediately erected in Asia Minor. The cult
spread, but at first only in the frontier provinces, which were under
the direct control of Augustus, not in the home provinces, which
were nominally under the control of the Senate, nor in the City itself.

Augustus approved of Livia's educative methods with Julia and
of her domestic arrangements and economies. He had simple
tastes himself. His palate was so insensitive that he did not notice
the difference between virgin olive oil and the last rank squeezings
when the olive-paste has gone a third time through the press. He
wore homespun clothes. It was justly said that, Fury though Livia
was, but for her unwearying activity Augustus would never have
been able to undertake the immense task he set himself of restoring Rome to peace and security after the long disasters of the Civil
Wars – in which he himself had, of course, played so destructive a
part. Augustus's work filled fourteen hours a day, but Livia's, it
was said, filled twenty-four. Not only did she manage her huge
household in the efficient way I have described, but she bore an
equal share with him in public business. A full account of all the
legal, social, administrative, religious, and military reforms which
they carried out between them, to say nothing of the public works
which they undertook, the temples which they re-edified, the colonies they planted, would fill many volumes. Yet there were many
leading Romans of the elder generation who could not forget that
this seemingly admirable reconstitution of the State had only been
made possible by the military defeat, secret murder, or public execution of almost every person who had defied the power of this
energetic pair. Had their sole and arbitrary power not been disguised under the forms of ancient liberty they would never have
held it long. Even as it was there were no less than four conspiracies against Augustus's life by would-be Brutuses.

Chapter 3

THE name 'Livia' is connected with the Latin word which means Malignity. My grandmother was a consummate actress, and the outward purity of her conduct, the sharpness of her wit, and the graciousness of her manners deceived nearly everybody. But nobody really liked her: malignity commands respect, not liking. She had a faculty for making ordinary easy-going people feel acutely conscious in her presence of their intellectual and moral shortcomings. I must apologize for continuing to write about Livia, but it is unavoidable: like all honest Roman histories, this is written 'from egg to apple': I prefer the thorough Roman method, which misses nothing, to that of Homer and the Greeks generally, who love to jump into the middle of things and then work backwards or forwards as they feel inclined. Yes, I have often had the notion of re-writing the story of Troy in Latin prose for the benefit of our poorer citizens who cannot read Greek; beginning with the egg from which Helen was hatched and continuing, chapter by chapter, to the apples eaten for dessert at the great feast in celebration of Ulysses's home-coming and victory over his wife's suitors. Where Homer is obscure or silent on any point I would naturally draw from later poets, or from the earlier Dares whose account, though full of poetical vagaries, seems to me more reliable than Homer's, because he actually took part in the war, first with the Trojans, then with the Greeks.

I once saw a strange painting on the inside of an old cedar chest which came, I believe, from somewhere in Northern Syria. The inscription, in Greek, was 'Poison is Queen', and the face of Poison, though executed over a hundred years before Livia's birth, was unmistakably the face of Livia. And in this context I must write about Marcellus, the son of Octavia by a former husband. Augustus, who was devoted to Marcellus, had adopted him as his son, giving him administrative duties greatly in advance of his years; and had married him to Julia. The common opinion at Rome was that he intended to make Marcellus his heir. Livia did not oppose the adoption, and indeed seemed genuinely to welcome it as giving her greater facility for winning Marcellus's affection and confidence. Her devotion to him seemed beyond question. It was by her advice that Augustus advanced him so rapidly in rank; and Marcellus, who knew of this, was duly grateful to her.

Livia's motive in favouring Marcellus was thought by a few shrewd observers to be that of making Agrippa jealous. Agrippa was the most important man at Rome after Augustus: a man of low birth, but Augustus's oldest friend and most successful general and admiral. Livia had always hitherto done her best to keep Agrippa's friendship for Augustus. He was ambitious, but only to a degree; he would never have presumed to contend for sovereignty with Augustus, whom he admired exceedingly, and wanted no greater glory than that of being his most trusted minister. He was, moreover, over-conscious of his humble origin, and Livia, by playing the grand patrician lady, always had the whip-hand of him. His importance to Livia and Augustus did not, however, lie only in his services, his loyalty, and his popularity with the commons and the Senate. It was this: by a fiction which Livia herself had originally created, he was supposed to hold a watching brief for the nation on Augustus's political conduct. At the famous sham-debate staged in the Senate, after the overthrow of Antony, between Augustus and his two friends, Agrippa and Maecenas, Agrippa's part had been that of counselling him against assuming sovereign power; only to let his objections be overruled by the arguments of Maecenas and the enthusiastic demands of the Senate. Agrippa had then declared that he would faithfully serve Augustus so long as the sovereignty was wholesome and no arbitrary tyranny. He was thenceforth popularly looked to and trusted as a buttress against possible encroachments of tyranny; and what Agrippa let pass, the nation let pass. It was now thought by these same shrewd observers that Livia was playing a very dangerous game in making Agrippa jealous of Marcellus, and events were watched with great interest. Perhaps her devotion to Marcellus was a sham and her real intention was that Agrippa should be goaded into putting him out of the way. It was rumoured that a devoted member of Agrippa's family had offered to pick a quarrel with Marcellus and kill him: but that Agrippa, though he was no less jealous than Livia had intended him to be, was too honourable to accept such a base suggestion.

It was generally assumed that Augustus had made Marcellus his chief heir and that Marcellus would not only inherit his immense wealth but the monarchy – for how else can I write of it but as that? – into the bargain. Agrippa therefore let it be known that while he was devoted to Augustus and had never regretted his decision to support his authority, there was one thing that he would not permit, as a patriotic citizen, and that was that the monarchy should become hereditary. But Marcellus was now almost as popular as Agrippa, and many young men of rank and family to whom the question 'Monarchy or Republic?' seemed already an academic one, tried to ingratiate themselves with him, hoping for important honours from him when he succeeded Augustus. This general readiness to welcome a continuance of the monarchy seemed to please Livia, but she privately announced that, in the lamentable case of the death or incapacity of Augustus, the immediate conduct of State affairs, until such time as further arrangements should be made by decrees of the Senate, must be entrusted to hands more experienced than those of Marcellus. Yet Marcellus was such a favourite of Augustus that, though Livia's private announcements usually ended as public edicts, nobody paid much attention to her on this occasion: and more and more people courted Marcellus.

The shrewd observers wondered how Livia would meet this new situation; but luck seemed to be with her. Augustus caught a slight chill which took an unexpected turn, with fevers and vomiting: Livia prepared his food with her own hands during 23 B.C. this illness, but his stomach was so delicate that he could keep nothing down. He was growing weaker and weaker and felt at last that he was on the point of death. He had often been asked to name his successor, but had not done so for fear of the political consequences, and also because the thought of his own death was extremely distasteful to him. Now he felt that it was his duty to name someone, and asked Livia to advise him. He said that sickness had robbed him of all power of judgement; he would choose whatever successor, within reason, she suggested. So she made the decision for him, and he agreed to it. She summoned to his bedside his fellow-Consul, the City magistrates, and certain representative senators and knights. He was too weak to say anything, but handed the Consul a register of the naval and military forces and a statement of the public revenues, and then beckoned to Agrippa and gave him his signet ring; which was as much as to say that Agrippa was to succeed him, though with the

34

close co-operation of the Consuls. This came as a great surprise. Everyone had expected that Marcellus would be chosen.

And from this moment Augustus began mysteriously to recover: the fever abated and his stomach accepted food. The credit for his cure went, however, not to Livia, who continued attending to him personally, but to a certain doctor called Musa, who had a harmless fad about cold lotions and cold potions. Augustus was so grateful to Musa for his supposed services that he gave him his own weight in gold pieces, which the Senate doubled. Musa was also, though a freedman, advanced to the rank of knight, which gave him the right to wear a gold ring and become a candidate for public office; and a still more extravagant decree was passed by the Senate, granting exemption from taxes to the whole medical profession.

Marcellus was plainly mortified at not being declared Augustus's heir. He was very young, only in his twentieth year. Augustus's previous favours had given him an exaggerated sense both of his talents and of his political importance. He tried to carry the matter off by being pointedly rude to Agrippa at a public banquet. Agrippa with difficulty kept his temper; but that there was no sequel to the incident encouraged Marcellus's supporters to believe that Agrippa was afraid of him. They even told each other that if Augustus did not change his mind within a year or two Marcellus would usurp the Imperial power. They grew so rowdy and boastful, Marcellus doing little to check them, that frequent clashes occurred between them and the party of Agrippa. Agrippa was most vexed by the insolence of this young puppy, as he called him – he who had borne most of the chief offices of state and fought a number of successful campaigns. But his vexation was mixed with alarm. The impression created by these incidents was that Marcellus and he were indecently wrangling as to who should wear Augustus's signet ring after he was dead.

He was ready to make almost any sacrifice to avoid seeming to play such a part. Marcellus was the offender and Agrippa wished to put the whole burden on him. He decided to withdraw from Rome. He went to Augustus and asked to be appointed Governor of Syria. When Augustus asked him the reason for his unexpected request he explained that he thought he could, in that capacity, drive a valuable bargain with the King of Parthia. He could persuade the King to return the regimental Eagles and the prisoners captured from the Romans thirty years before, in exchange for the King's son whom Augustus was holding captive at Rome. He said nothing about the quarrel with Marcellus. Augustus, who had himself been greatly disturbed by it, torn between old friendship for Agrippa and indulgent paternal love for Marcellus, did not allow himself to consider how generously Agrippa was behaving, for that would have been a confession of his own weakness, and so made no reference to the matter either. He granted Agrippa's request with alacrity, saying how important it was to get the Eagles back, and the captives – if any of them were still alive after so long – and asked how soon he would be ready to start. Agrippa was hurt, misunderstanding his manner. He thought that Augustus wanted to get rid of him, really believing that he was quarrelling with Marcellus about the succession. He thanked him for granting his request, coldly protested his loyalty and friendship, and said that he was ready to sail the following day.

He did not go to Syria. He went no farther than the island of Lesbos, sending his lieutenant ahead to administer the province for him. He knew that his stay at Lesbos would be read as a sort of banishment incurred because of Marcellus. He did not visit the province, because if he had done so it would have given the Marcellans a handle against him: they would have said that he had gone to the East in order to gather an army together to march against Rome. But he flattered himself that Augustus would need his services before long; and fully believed that Marcellus was planning to usurp the monarchy. Lesbos was conveniently near Rome. He did not forget his commission: he opened negotiations, through intermediaries, with the King of Parthia but did not expect to conclude them for a while. It takes a deal of time and patience to drive a good bargain with an Eastern monarch.

Marcellus was elected to a City magistracy, his first official appointment, and made this the occasion for a magnificent display of public Games. He not only tented in the theatres themselves, against sun and rain, and hung them with splendid tapestries, but made a gigantic multi-coloured marquee of the whole Market Place. The effect was very gorgeous, particularly from the inside when the sun shone through. In this tent-making he used a fabulous amount of red, yellow, and green cloth which when the Games were over was cut up and distributed to the citizens for clothes and bed-linen. Huge numbers of wild beasts were imported from Africa for the combats in the amphitheatre, including many lions, and there was a fight between fifty German captives and an equal number of black warriors from Morocco. Augustus himself contributed lavishly towards the expenses; and so did Octavia, as Marcellus's mother. When Octavia appeared in the ceremonial procession she was greeted with such resounding applause that Livia could hardly restrain tears of anger and jealousy. Two days later Marcellus fell sick. His symptoms were precisely the same as those of Augustus in his recent illness, so naturally Musa was sent for again. He had become excessively rich and famous, charging as much as 1,000 gold pieces for a single professional visit, and making a favour of it at that. In all cases where sickness had not taken too strong a hold on his patients his mere name was enough to bring about an immediate cure. The credit went to the cold lotions and cold potions, the secret prescriptions for which he refused to communicate to anyone. Augustus's confidence in Musa's powers was so great that he made light of Marcellus's sickness, and the Games continued. But somehow, in spite of the unremitting attention of Livia and the very coldest lotions and potions that Musa could prescribe, Marcellus died. The grief of both Octavia and Augustus was unbounded and the death was mourned as a public calamity. There were, however, a good many level-headed people who did not regret Marcellus's disappearance. There would certainly have been civil war again between him and Agrippa if Augustus had died and he had attempted to step into his place: now Agrippa was the only possible successor. But this was reckoning without Livia, whose fixed intention it was, in the event of Augustus's death – Claudius, Claudius, you said that you would not mention Livia's motives but only record her acts – whose fixed intention it was, in the event of Augustus's death, to continue ruling the Empire through my uncle Tiberius, with my father in support. She would arrange for them to be adopted as Augustus's heirs.

Marcellus's death left Julia free for Tiberius to marry, and all would have gone well with Livia's plans had there not been a dangerous outbreak of political unrest at Rome, the mob clamouring for a restoration of the Republic. When Livia tried to address them from the Palace steps they pelted her with rotten eggs and filth. Augustus happened to be away on a tour of the Eastern provinces, in company with Maecenas, and had reached Athens when the news arrived. Livia wrote shortly and in haste that the situation in the City could not be worse and that Agrippa's help must be secured at any price. Augustus at once summoned Agrippa from Lesbos and begged him, for friendship's sake, to return with him to Rome and restore public confidence. But Agrippa had been nursing his grudge too long to be grateful for this summons. He stood on his dignity. In three years Augustus had written him only three letters and those in a hard official tone; and after Marcellus's death should certainly have recalled him. Why should he help Augustus now? It was Livia, as a matter of fact, who had been responsible for this estrangement; she had miscalculated the political situation by dropping Agrippa too soon. She had even hinted to Augustus that Agrippa, though absent in Lesbos, knew more than most people about Marcellus's mysterious and fatal illness; someone, she said, had told her that Agrippa, when he heard the news, had shown no surprise and considerable complacence. Agrippa told Augustus that he had been so long away from Rome that he was out of touch with City politics and did not feel capable of undertaking what was asked of him. Augustus, fearing that Agrippa, if he went to Rome in his present mood, would be more inclined to put himself forward as a champion of popular liberties than to support the Imperial government, dismissed him with words of gracious regret and hurriedly summoned Maecenas to ask his advice. Maecenas wanted permission to talk to Agrippa freely on Augustus's behalf and undertook to find out from him exactly on what terms he would do what was wanted of him. Augustus begged Maecenas for God's sake to do so, 'as quick as boiled asparagus' (a favourite expression of his). So Maecenas took Agrippa aside and said: 'Now, old friend, what is it that you want? I realize that you think you have been badly treated, but I assure you that Augustus has a right to think himself equally injured by you. Can't you see how badly you behaved towards him, by not being frank? It was an insult both to his justice and to his friendship for you. If you had explained that Marcellus's faction put you in a very uncomfortable position and that Marcellus himself had insulted you – I swear to you that Augustus never knew about this until just the other day – he would have done all in his power to right matters. My frank opinion is that you have behaved like a sulky child – and he has treated you like a father who won't be bullied by that sort of behaviour. You say that he wrote you very cold letters? Were your own, then, written in such affectionate language? And what sort of a good-bye had you given him? I want to mediate between the two of you now, because if this breach continues it will be the ruin of us all. You both love each other dearly, as it is only right that the two greatest living Romans should. Augustus has told me that he is ready, as soon as you show your old openness to him, to renew the friendship on the same terms as before, *or even more intimate ones.*'

'He said that?'

'His very words. May I tell him how grieved you are that you offended him, and may I explain that it was a misunderstanding – that you left Rome, thinking that he was aware of Marcellus's insult to you at the banquet? And that now you are anxious, on your side, to make up for past failures in friendship and that you rely on him to meet you half-way?'

Agrippa said: 'Maecenas, you are a fine fellow and a true friend. Tell Augustus I am his to command as always.'

Maecenas said: 'I shall tell him that with the greatest pleasure. And I shall add, as my own opinion, that it would not be safe to send you back to the City now, to restore order, without some outstanding mark of personal confidence.'

Then Maecenas went to Augustus. 'I smoothed him down nicely. He'll do anything you want. But he wants to believe that you really love him, like a child jealous of his father's love for another child. I think that the only thing that would really satisfy him would be for you to let him marry Julia.'

Augustus had to think quickly. He remembered that Agrippa and his wife, who was Marcellus's sister, had been on bad terms ever since the quarrel with Marcellus, and that Agrippa was supposed to be in love with Julia. He wished Livia were present to advise him, but there was no escape from an instant decision: if he offended Agrippa now he would never recover his support. Livia had written 'at any price': so he was free to make what arrangements he pleased. He sent for Agrippa again, and Maecenas staged a dignified scene of reconciliation. Augustus said that if Agrippa would consent to marry his daughter, it would be proof to him that the friendship which he valued before any other in the world was established on a secure foundation. Agrippa wept tears of joy and asked pardon for his shortcomings. He would try to be worthy of Augustus's loving generosity.

Agrippa returned to Rome with Augustus, and immediately divorced his wife and married Julia. The marriage was so popular and his celebration so magnificently lavish that the poli-21 B.C. tical disturbances immediately subsided. Agrippa won great credit for Augustus, too, by carrying through the negotiations for the return of the Eagle standards, which were formally handed over to Tiberius as Augustus's personal representative. The Eagles were sacred objects, more truly sacred to Roman hearts than any marble statues of Gods. A few captives returned, too, but after thirty-two years of absence they were hardly worth welcoming back; most of them preferred to remain in Parthia, where they had settled down and married native women.

My grandmother Livia was far from pleased with the bargain made with Agrippa – the only cheerful side of which was the dishonour done to Octavia by the divorce of her daughter. But she concealed her feelings. It was nine years before Agrippa's 12 B.C. services could be spared. Then he died suddenly at his country house. Augustus was away in Greece at the time, so there was no inquest on the body. Agrippa left a large number of children behind him, three boys and two girls, as Augustus's heirs-in-law; it would be difficult for Livia to set their claims aside in favour of her own sons.

However, Tiberius married Julia, who had made things easy for Livia by falling in love with him and begging Augustus to use his influence with Tiberius on her behalf. Augustus consented only because Julia threatened suicide if he refused to help her. Tiberius himself hated having to marry Julia, but did not dare refuse. He was obliged to divorce his own wife, Vipsania, Agrippa's daughter by a former marriage, whom he passionately loved. Once when he met her accidentally afterwards in the street he followed her with his eyes in such a hopeless longing way that Augustus, when he heard of it, gave orders that, for decency's sake, this must not happen again. Special look-outs must be kept by the officers of both households to avoid an encounter. Vipsania married, not long afterwards, an ambitious young noble called Gallus. And before I forget it, I must mention my father's marriage to my mother, Antonia, the younger daughter of Mark Antony and Octavia. It had taken place in the year of Augustus's illness and Marcellus's death.

My uncle Tiberius was one of the bad Claudians. He was morose, reserved, and cruel, but there had been three people whose influence had checked these elements in his nature. First there was my father, one of the best Claudians, cheerful, open, and generous; next there was Augustus, a very honest, merry, kindly man who disliked Tiberius but treated him generously for his mother's sake; and lastly there was Vipsania. My father's influence was removed, or lessened, when they were both of an age to do their military service and were sent on campaign to different parts of the Empire. Then came the separation from Vipsania, and this was followed by a coolness with Augustus, who was offended by my uncle's ill-concealed distaste for Julia. With these three influences removed, he gradually went altogether to the bad.

I should at this point, I think, describe his personal appearance. He was a tall, dark-haired, fair-skinned, heavily-built man with a magnificent pair of shoulders, and hands so strong that he could crack a walnut, or bore a tough-skinned green apple through with thumb and forefinger. If he had not been so slow in his movements he would have made a champion boxer: he once killed a comrade in a friendly bout – bare-fisted, not with the usual metal boxing-gloves – with a blow on the side of the head that cracked his skull. He walked with his neck thrust slightly forward and his eyes on the ground. His face would have been handsome if it had not been disfigured by so many pimples, and if his eyes had not been so prominent, and if he had not worn an almost perpetual frown. His statues make him extremely handsome, because they leave out these defects. He spoke little, and that very slowly, so that in conversation with him one always felt tempted to finish his sentences for him and answer them in the same breath. But, when he pleased, he was an impressive public speaker. He went bald early in life except at the back of his head, where he grew his hair long, a fashion of the ancient nobility. He was never ill.

Tiberius, unpopular as he was in Roman society, was nevertheless an extremely successful general. He revived various ancient disciplinary severities, but since he did not spare himself when on campaign, seldom sleeping in a tent, eating and drinking no better than the men, and always charging at their head in battle, they preferred to serve under him than under some good-humoured, easy-going commander in whose leadership they did not have the same confidence. Tiberius never gave his men a smile or a word of praise, and often overmarched and overworked them. 'Let them hate me,' he once said, 'so long as they obey me.' He kept the colonels and regimental officers in as strict order as the men, so there were no complaints of his partiality. Service under Tiberius was not unprofitable: he usually contrived to capture and sack the enemy's camps and cities. He fought successful wars in Armenia, Parthia, Germany, Spain, Dalmatia, the Alps, and France.

My father was, as I say, one of the best Claudians. He was as strong as his brother, far better looking, quicker of speech and movement, and by no means less successful as a general. He treated all soldiers as Roman citizens and therefore as his equals, except in rank and education. He hated having to inflict punishment on them: he gave orders that as far as possible all offences against discipline should be dealt with by the offender's own comrades, whom he assumed to be jealous for the good name of their section or company. He gave it out that if they found that any offence was beyond their corrective powers – for he did not allow them to kill a culprit or incapacitate him for his daily military duties – it should be referred to the regimental colonel; but so far as possible he wished his men to be their own judges. The captains might flog, by permission of their regimental colonels, but only in cases where the offence, such as cowardice in battle or theft from a comrade, showed a baseness of character that made flogging appropriate; but he ordered that a man once flogged must never afterwards serve as a combatant; he must be degraded to the transport or clerical staff. Any soldier who considered that he had been unjustly sentenced by his comrades or his captain might appeal to him; but he thought it unlikely that such sentences would need to be revised. This system worked admirably, because my father was such a fine soldier that he inspired the troops to a virtue of which other commanders did not believe them capable. But it can be understood how dangerous it was for troops who had been handled in this way to be commanded afterwards by any ordinary general. The gift of independence once granted cannot be lightly taken away again. There was always trouble when troops who had served under my father happened to be drafted for service under my uncle. It happened the other way about too: troops who had served under my uncle reacted with scorn and suspicion to my father's disciplinary system. Their custom had been to shield each other's crimes and to pride themselves on their cunning in avoiding detection; and since under my uncle a man could be flogged, for example, for addressing an officer without being first addressed, or for speaking with too great frankness, or for behaving independently in any way, it was an honour rather than a disgrace for a soldier to be able to show the marks of the lash on his back.

My father's greatest victories were in the Alps, France, the Low Countries, but especially in Germany, where his name will, I think, never be forgotten. He was always in the thick of the fighting. His ambition was to perform a feat which had only been performed twice in Roman history, namely, as general to kill the opposing general with his own hands and strip him of his arms. He was many times very close to success, but his prey always escaped him. Either the fellow galloped off the field or surrendered instead of fighting, or some officious private soldier got the blow in first. Veterans telling me stories of my father have often chuckled admiringly: 'Oh, Sir, it used to do our hearts good to see your father on his black horse playing hide-and-seek in the battle with one of those German chieftains. He'd be forced to cut down nine or ten of the bodyguard sometimes, tough men too, before he got near the standard, and by then the wily bird would be flown.' The proudest boast of men who had served under my father was that he was the first Roman general who had marched the full length of the Rhine from Switzerland to the North Sea.

Chapter 4

MY father had never forgotten my grandfather's teaching about liberty. As quite a small boy he had fallen foul of Marcellus, five years his senior, to whom Augustus gave the title 'Leader of Cadets'. He had told Marcellus that the title had been awarded to him only for a specific occasion (a sham-fight called 'Greeks and Trojans' fought on Mars Field between two forces of mounted cadets the sons of knights and senators) and that it did not carry with it any of the general judicial powers which Marcellus had since assumed; and that, for himself, as a free-born Roman, he would not submit to such tyranny. He reminded Marcellus that the opposing side in the sham-fight had been led by Tiberius, and that Tiberius had won the honours of the engagement. He challenged Marcellus to a duel. Augustus was very much amused when he heard the story and for a long time never referred to my father except playfully as 'the free-born Roman'.

Whenever he was in Rome now my father chafed at the growing spirit of subservience to Augustus that he everywhere encountered, and always longed to be back in arms. While acting as one of the chief City magistrates during an absence of Augustus and Tiberius in France he was disgusted by the prevalence of place-hunting and political jobbery. He privately told a friend, from whom I heard it years later, that there was more of the old Roman spirit of liberty to be found in a single company of his soldiers than in the whole senatorial order. Shortly before his death he wrote Tiberius a bitter letter to this effect from a camp in the interior of Germany. He said that he wished to heaven that Augustus would follow the glorious example of the Dictator Sulla, who, when sole master of Rome after the first Civil Wars, all his enemies being either subjugated or pacified, had only paused until he had settled a few State matters to his liking before laying down his rods of office and becoming once more a private citizen. If Augustus did not do the same pretty soon – and he had always given out that this was his ultimate intention – it would be too late. The ranks of the old nobility were sadly thinned: the proscriptions and the civil wars had carried away the boldest and best, and the survivors, lost among the new nobility – nobility indeed – tended more and more to behave like family slaves to Augustus and Livia. Soon Rome would have forgotten what freedom meant and would fall at last under a tyranny as barbarous and arbitrary as those of the East. It was not to forward such a calamity that he had fought so many wearisome campaigns under Augustus's supreme command. Even his love and deep personal admiration for Augustus, who had been a second father to him, did not prevent him from expressing these feelings. He asked Tiberius's opinion: could not the two of them together persuade, even compel, Augustus to retire? 'If he consents I shall hold him in a thousand times greater love and admiration than formerly; but I am sorry to say that the secret and illegitimate pride that our mother Livia has always derived from her exercise of supreme power through Augustus will be the greatest hindrance that we are likely to encounter in this matter.'

By ill-luck the letter was delivered to Tiberius while he was in the presence of Augustus and Livia. 'A dispatch from your noble brother!' the Imperial courier called out, handing it to him. Tiberius, not suspecting that there was anything in the letter that should not be communicated to Livia and Augustus, asked permission to open and read it at once. Augustus said: 'By all means, Tiberius, but on condition that you read it aloud to us.' He motioned the servants out of the room. 'Come, let us lose no time. What are his latest victories? I am impatient to hear. His letters are always well written and interesting, much more so than yours, my dear fellow, if you'll pardon me for making the comparison.'

Tiberius read out the first few words and then grew very red. He tried to skip over the dangerous part, but found that there was little but danger throughout the letter, except just at the end, where my father complained of giddiness from a head-wound and told of his difficult march to the Elbe. Curious portents had occurred lately, he wrote. A most extraordinary display of shooting stars, night after night; sounds like the lamenting of women from the forest; and two divine youths on white horses in Greek, not German, dress, had suddenly ridden through the middle of the camp at dawn. Finally, a German woman of more than mortal size had appeared at his tent door and spoken to him in Greek, telling him to advance no further because fate ruled against it. So Tiberius read a word here and there, stumbled, said that the writing was illegible, started again, stumbled again, and finally excused himself.

'What's this?' said Augustus. 'Surely you can make out more than that.'

Tiberius pulled himself together. 'To be honest, Sir, I can, but the letter does not deserve reading. Evidently my brother was not well at the time of writing it.'

Augustus was alarmed. 'He is not seriously ill, I hope?' But my grandmother Livia, as if her mother's anxiety for once overrode good manners – though of course she guessed at once that there was something in the letter that Tiberius was afraid to read because it reflected either on Augustus or herself – snatched it from him. She read it through, frowned grimly and handed it to Augustus, saying: 'This is a matter which only concerns you. It is not my business to punish a son, however unnatural, but yours as his guardian and as the head of the State.'

Augustus was alarmed, wondering what in the world could be amiss. He read the letter, but it seemed to call for disapproval rather as something which had outraged my grandmother than as something written against himself. Indeed, except for the ugly word 'compel' he secretly approved of the sentiments expressed in the letter, even though the insult to my grandmother reflected on himself, as having been persuaded by her against his better judgement. The Senate were certainly becoming shamefully obsequious in their manners towards him and his family and staff. He disliked the situation as much as my father, and it was true that as long ago as before the defeat and death of Antony he had publicly promised to retire when no public enemy remained in the field against him; and he had several times since referred in his speeches to the happy day when his task would be done. He was weary now of perpetual State business and perpetual honours: he wanted a rest and anonymity. But my grandmother would never allow him to give up; she would always say that his task was not half accomplished yet, that nothing but civil disorder could be expected if he retired now. Yes, he worked hard, she owned, but she worked still harder and with no direct public reward. And he must not be simple-minded: once out of office and a mere private citizen he was liable to impeachment and banishment, or worse; and what of the secret grudges that the relations of men whom he had killed or dishonoured bore against him? As a private citizen he would have to give up his bodyguard as well as his armies. Let him accept another ten years of office, and at the end of them, perhaps, things might have changed for the better. So he always gave in and continued ruling. He accepted his monarchical privileges in instalments. He was voted them for five or ten years at a stretch, usually ten.

My grandmother looked hard at Augustus when he had finished reading the unlucky letter: 'Well?' she asked.

'I agree with Tiberius,' he said mildly. 'The young man must be ill. This is the derangement of overstrain. You notice the final paragraph where he mentions the results of his head-wound and seeing those visions – well, that proves it. He needs a rest. The natural generosity of his soul has been perverted by the anxieties of campaign. Those German forests are no place for a man sick in mind, are they, Tiberius? The howling of wolves gets on one's nerves the worst, I believe: the lamenting of women he talks about was surely wolves. What about recalling him now that he has given these Germans such a shaking as they'll never forget? It would do me good to see him back here at Rome again. Yes, we must certainly have him back. You'll be glad, dearest Livia, to have your boy again, won't you?'

My grandmother did not answer directly. She said, still frowning: 'And you, Tiberius?'

My uncle was more politic than Augustus. He knew his mother's nature better. He answered: 'My brother certainly seems ill, but even illness cannot excuse such unfilial behaviour and such gross folly. I agree that he should be recalled to be reminded of the heinousness of having entertained such base thoughts about his most devoted and indefatigable mother, and of the further enormity of committing them to paper and sending them by courier through unfriendly country. Besides, the argument from the case of Sulla is childish. As soon as Sulla was out of power the Civil Wars began again and his new constitution was overturned.'
So Tiberius came quite well out of the affair, but much of his severity against my father was genuine, for landing him in so embarrassing a position.

Livia was choking with rage against Augustus for allowing insults to her to go by so easily, and in her son's presence too. Her rage against my father was equally violent. She knew that when he returned he was likely to carry into execution his plan for forcing Augustus to retire. She also saw that she would never now be able to rule through Tiberius – even if she could assure the succession for him – so long as my father, a man of enormous popularity at Rome, and with all the Western regiments at his back, stood waiting to force the restoration of popular liberties. And supreme power for her had come to be more important than life or honour; she had sacrificed so much for it. Yet she was able to disguise her feelings. She pretended to take Augustus's view that my father was merely sick, and told Tiberius that she thought his censure too severe. She agreed, however, that my father should be recalled at once. She even thanked Augustus for his generous extenuation of her poor son's fault and said that she would send him out her own confidential physician with a parcel of hellebore, from Anticyra in Thessaly, which was a famous specific for cases of mental weakness.

The physician set out the next day in company with the courier

47

who took Augustus's letter. The letter was one of friendly congratulations on his victories and sympathy for his head-wound; it permitted him to return to Rome, but in language which meant that he must return whether he wished to come or not.

My father replied a few days later with thanks for Augustus's generosity. He said that he would return as soon as his health permitted, but that the letter had reached him the day after a slight accident: his horse had fallen under him at full gallop, rolled on his leg, and crushed it against a sharp stone. He thanked his mother for her solicitude, for the gift of the hellebore and for sending her physician, of whose services he had immediately availed himself. But he feared that even his well-known skill had not kept the wound from taking a serious turn. He said finally that he would have preferred to stay at his post but that Augustus's wishes were his commands; and repeated that as soon as he was well again he would return to the City. He was at present encamped near the Thuringian Saal.

On hearing this news, Tiberius, who was with Augustus and Livia at Pavia, instantly asked leave to attend his brother's sickbed. Augustus granted it, and he mounted his cob and galloped off north, with a small escort, making for the quickest pass across the Alps. A 500-mile journey lay before him, but he could count on frequent relays of horses at the posting-houses and when he was too weary for the saddle he could commandeer a gig and snatch a few hours' sleep in it without delaying his progress. The weather favoured him. He went over the Alps and descended into Switzerland, then followed the main Rhine road, not having yet stopped for as much as a hot meal, until he reached a place called Mannheim. Here he crossed the river and struck north-east by rough roads through unfriendly country. He was alone when he reached his destination on the evening of the third day, his original escort having long fallen out, and the new escort which he had picked up at Mannheim not having been able to keep up with him either. It is claimed that on the second day and night he travelled just under 200 miles between noon and noon. He was in time to greet my father but not in time to save his life; for the leg by now was gangrened up to the thigh. My father, though on the point of death, had just sufficient presence of mind to order the camp to pay my uncle Tiberius the honours due to him as an army commander. The brothers embraced and my father

9 B.C.

48

whispered, 'She read my letter?' 'Before I did myself,' groaned my uncle Tiberius. Nothing more was said except by my father, who sighed, 'Rome has a severe mother: Lucius and Gaius have a dangerous stepmother.' Those were his last words, and presently my uncle Tiberius closed his eyes.

I heard this account from Xenophon, a Greek from the island of Cos, who was quite a young man at this time. He was my father's staff-surgeon and had been most disgusted that my grandmother's physician had taken the case out of his hands. Gaius and Lucius, I should explain, were Augustus's grandchildren by Julia and Agrippa. He had adopted them as his own sons while they were still infants. There was a third boy, Postumus, so called because he was born posthumously; Augustus did not adopt him too, but left him to carry on Agrippa's name.

The camp where my father died was named 'The Accursed' and his body was carried in a marching military procession to the army's winter quarters at Mainz on the Rhine, my uncle Tiberius walking all the way as chief mourner. The army wished to bury the body there, but he brought it back for a funeral at Rome, where it was burnt on a monstrous pyre in Mars Field. Augustus himself pronounced the funeral oration, in the course of which he said, 'I pray the gods to make my sons Gaius and Lucius as noble and virtuous men as this Drusus and to vouchsafe to me as honourable a death as his.'

Livia was not sure how far she could trust Tiberius. On his return with my father's body his sympathy with her had seemed forced and insincere, and when Augustus wished himself as honourable a death as my father's she saw a brief half-smile cross his face. Tiberius, who, it appears, had long suspected that my grandfather had not died a natural death, was resolved now not to cross his mother's will in anything. Dining so often at her table he felt himself completely at her mercy. He worked hard to win her favour. Livia understood what was in his mind, and was not dissatisfied. He was the only one who suspected her of being a poisoner, and would obviously keep his suspicions to himself. She had lived down the scandal of her marriage with Augustus and was now quoted in the City as an example of virtue in its strictest and most disagreeable form. The Senate voted that four statues of her should be set up in various public places; this was by way of consoling her for her loss. They also enrolled her by a legal fiction among the 'Mothers of Three Children'. Mothers of three or more children had special privileges under Augustus's legislation, particularly as legatees – spinsters and barren women were not allowed to benefit under wills at all, and their loss was the gain of their fruitful sisters.

Claudius, you tedious old fellow, here you have come to within an inch or two of the end of the fourth roll of your autobiography and you haven't even reached your birthplace. Put it down at once or you'll never reach even the middle of your story. Write, 'My birth occurred in Lyons in France, on the first of August, a year before my father's death.' So. My parents had had six children before me, but as my mother always accompanied my father on his campaigns, a child had to be very hardy to survive. Only my brother Germanicus, five years older than myself, and my sister Livilla, a year older than myself, were living: both inherited my father's magnificent constitution. I did not. I nearly died on three occasions before my second year, and had not my father's death brought the family back to Rome it is most unlikely that this story would have been written.

Chapter 5

AT Rome we lived in the big house which had belonged to my grandfather and which he had left in his will to my grandmother. It was on the Palatine Hill, close to Augustus's palace and the temple of Apollo built by Augustus, where the library was. The Palatine Hill looked down on the Market Place. Under the steepest part of the cliff was the temple of the Twin Gods, Castor and Pollux. (This was the old temple, built of timber and sods, which sixteen years later Tiberius replaced, at his own expense, with a magnificent marble structure, the interior painted and gilded and furnished as sumptuously as a rich noblewoman's boudoir. My grandmother Livia made him do this to please Augustus, I may say. Tiberius was not religious-minded and very stingy with money.) It was healthier on that hill than down in the hollow by the river; most of the houses there belonged to senators. I was a very sickly child – 'a very battleground of diseases,' the doctors said – and perhaps only lived because the diseases could not agree as to which should have the honour of carrying me off. To begin with, I was born prematurely, at only seven months, and then my foster-nurse's milk disagreed with me, so that my skin broke out in an ugly rash, and then I had malaria, and measles, which left me slightly deaf in one ear, and erysipelas, and colitis, and finally infantile paralysis, which shortened my left leg so that I was condemned to a permanent limp. Because of one or other of these various illnesses I have all my life been so weak in the hams that to run or walk long distances has never been possible for me: a great deal of my travelling has had to be done in a sedan-chair. Then there is the appalling pain that catches me often in the pit of my stomach after eating. It has been so bad that on two or three occasions, if my friends had not intervened, I would have plunged a carving-knife (which I madly snatched up) into the place of torment. I have heard it said that this pain, which they call 'the cardiac passion', is worse than any other pain known to man except the strangury. Well, I must be thankful, I suppose, that I have never had the strangury.

It will be supposed that my mother Antonia, a beautiful and noble woman brought up to the strictest virtue by her mother Octavia, and the one passion of my father's life, would have taken the most loving care of me, her youngest child, and even made a particular favourite of me in pity for my misfortunes. But such was not the case. She did all for me that could be expected of her as a duty, but no more. She did not love me. No, she had a great aversion to me, not only because of my sickliness but also because she had had a most difficult pregnancy of me, and then a most painful delivery from which she barely escaped with her life and which left her more or less an invalid for years. My premature birth was due to a shock that she got at the feast given in honour of Augustus when he visited my father at Lyons to inaugurate the 'Altar of Rome and Augustus' there: my father was Governor of the Three Provinces of France, and Lyons was his headquarters. A crazy Sicilian slave who was acting as waiter at the feast suddenly drew a dagger and flourished it in the air behind my father's neck. Only my mother saw this happening. She caught the slave's eye and had presence of mind enough to smile at him and shake her head in deprecation, signing to him to put the dagger back. While he hesitated, two other waiters followed her glance and were in time to overpower and disarm him. Then she fainted, and immediately her pains began. It may well be because of this that I have always had a morbid fear of assassination; for they say that a pre-natal shock can be inherited. But of course there is no real reason for any pre-natal influence to be mentioned. How many of the Imperial family have died a natural death?

Since I was an affectionate child, my mother's attitude caused me much misery. I heard from my sister Livilla, a beautiful girl but cruel, vain, and ambitious – in a word a typical Claudian of the bad variety – that my mother had called me 'a human portent' and said that when I was born the Sibylline books should have been consulted. Also that Nature had begun but never finished me, throwing me aside in disgust as a hopeless start. Also that the ancients were wiser and nobler than ourselves: they exposed all weakly infants on a bare hillside for the good of the race. These may have been embroideries by Livilla on less severe remarks – for seven-months' children are very horrible objects – but I know that once when my mother grew angry on hearing that some senator had introduced a foolish motion in the House she burst out: 'That man ought to be put out of the way! He's as stupid as a donkey – what am I saying? Donkeys are sensible beings by comparison – he's as stupid as ... as ... Heavens, he's as stupid as my son Claudius!'

Germanicus was her favourite, as he was everyone's favourite, but so far from envying him for the love and admiration that he won wherever he went, I rejoiced on his behalf. Germanicus pitied me and did the most he could to make my life happier, and recommended me to my elders as a good-hearted child who would repay generous and careful treatment. Severity only frightened me, he would say, and made me more sickly than I need be. And he was right. The nervous tic of my hands, the nervous jerking of my head, my stammer, my queasy digestion, my constant dribbling at the mouth, were principally due to the terrors to which, in the name of discipline, I was subjected. When Germanicus stood up for me my mother used to laugh indulgently and say, 'Noble heart, find some better object for your overflow!' But my grandmother Livia's way of talking was: 'Don't be a fool, Germanicus. If he reacts favourably to discipline, we shall treat him with the kindness he deserves. You're putting the cart before the horse.' My grandmother seldom spoke to me, and when she did it was contemptuously and without looking at me, mostly to say

'Get out of this room, child, I want to be in it.' If she had occasion to scold me she never did so by word of mouth but sent a short, cold note. For example: 'It has come to the knowledge of the Lady Livia that the boy Claudius has been wasting his time mooning about the Apollo Library. Until he can profit from the elementary text-books provided for him by his tutors it is absurd for him to meddle with the serious works on the Library shelves. Moreover his fidgeting disturbs genuine students. This practice must cease.'

As for Augustus, though he never treated me with calculated cruelty, he disliked having me in the same room with him as much as my grandmother did. He was extraordinarily fond of little boys (remaining to the end of his life an overgrown boy himself), but only of the sort that he called 'fine manly little fellows', such as my brother Germanicus and his grandchildren, Gaius and Lucius, who were all extremely good-looking. There were a number of sons of confederate kings or chieftains, kept as hostages for their parents' good behaviour – from France, Germany, Parthia, North Africa, Syria – who were educated with his grandchildren and the sons of leading senators in the Boys' College; and he often came into the cloisters there to play at taws, or knucklebones, or tag. His chief favourites were little brown boys, the Moors and Parthians and Syrians: and those who could rattle away happily to him in boyish talk as if he were one of themselves. Only once did he try to master his repugnance to me and let me into a game of taws with his favourites: but it was so unnatural an effort that it made me more than usually nervous – and I stammered and shook like a mad thing. He never tried again. He hated dwarfs and cripples and deformities, saying that they brought bad luck and should be kept out of sight. Yet I could never find it in my heart to hate Augustus as I came to hate my grandmother, for his dislike of me was without malice and he did what he could to master it: and indeed I must have been a wretched little oddity, a disgrace to so strong and magnificent a father and so fine and stately a mother. Augustus was a fine-looking man himself, though somewhat short, with curly fair hair that went grey only very late in his life, bright eyes, merry face, and upright graceful character.

I remember once overhearing an elegiac epigram that he made about me, in Greek, for the benefit of Athenodorus, a Stoic philosopher, from Tarsus in Cilicia, whose simple serious advice he often asked. I was about seven years old, and they came upon me by the carp-pool in the garden of my mother's house. I cannot remember the epigram exactly, but the sense of it was: 'Antonia is old-fashioned: she does not buy a pet marmoset at great expense from an Eastern trader. And why? Because she breeds them herself.' Athenodorus thought for a moment and replied severely in the same metre: 'Antonia, so far from buying a pet marmoset from Eastern traders, does not even cosset and feed with sugarplums the poor child of her noble husband.' Augustus looked somewhat abashed. I should explain that neither he nor Athenodorus, to whom I had always been represented as a half-wit, guessed that I could understand what they were saying. So Athenodorus drew me towards him and said playfully in Latin: 'And what does young Tiberius Claudius think about the matter?' I was sheltered from Augustus by Athenodorus's big body and somehow forgot my stammer. I said straight out, in Greek: 'My mother Antonia does not pamper me, but she has let me learn Greek from someone who learned it directly from Apollo.' All I meant was that I understood what they were saying. The person who had taught me Greek was a woman who had been a priestess of Apollo on one of the Greek islands but had been captured by pirates and sold to a brothel-keeper in Tyre. She had managed to escape, but was not permitted to be a priestess again because she had been a prostitute. My mother Antonia, recognizing her gifts, took her into the family as a governess. This woman used to tell me that she had learned directly from Apollo, and I was merely quoting her: but as Apollo was the God of learning and poetry, my remark sounded far wittier than I intended. Augustus was startled and Athenodorus said: 'Well spoken, little Claudius: marmosets don't understand a word of Greek, do they?' I answered: 'No, and they have long tails, and steal apples from the table.' However, when Augustus began eagerly questioning me, taking me from Athenodorus's arm, I grew self-conscious and stammered as badly as ever. But from thenceforth Athenodorus was my friend.

There is a story about Athenodorus and Augustus which does great credit to both. Athenodorus told Augustus one day that he did not take nearly enough precaution about admitting visitors to his presence: one day he would get a dagger in his vitals. Augustus replied that he was talking nonsense. The next day Augustus was told that his sister, the Lady Octavia, was outside and wished to greet him on the anniversary of their father's death. He gave orders for her immediate admittance. She was an incurable invalid when this happened – it was the year she died – and was always carried about in a covered sedan. When the sedan was brought in, the curtains parted and out sprang Athenodorus with a sword, which he pointed at Augustus's heart. Augustus, so far from being angry, thanked Athenodorus and confessed that he had been very wrong to treat his warning so casually.

One extraordinary event in my childhood I must not forget to record. One summer when I was just eight years old my mother, my brother Germanicus, my sister Livilla, and I were visiting my Aunt Julia in a beautiful country-house close to the sea at Antium. It was about six o'clock in the evening and we were out taking the cool breeze in a vineyard. Julia was not with us, but Tiberius's son – that Tiberius Drusus whom we afterwards always called 'Castor' – and Postumus and Agrippina, Julia's children, were in the party. Suddenly we heard a great screeching above us. We looked up and saw a number of eagles fighting. Feathers floated down. We tried to catch them. Germanicus and Castor each caught one before it fell and stuck it in his hair. Castor had a small wing feather, but Germanicus a splendid one from the tail. Both were stained with blood. Spots of blood fell on Postumus's upturned face and on the dresses of Livilla and Agrippina. And then something dark dropped through the air. I do not know why I did so, but I put out a fold of my gown and caught it. It was a tiny wolf-cub wounded and terrified. The eagles came swooping down to retrieve it, but I had it safe hidden, and when we shouted and threw sticks they rose baffled and flew screaming off. I was embarrassed. I didn't want the cub. Livilla grabbed at it, but my mother, who looked very grave, made her give it back to me. 'It fell to Claudius,' she said. 'He must keep it.'

She asked an old nobleman, a member of the College of Augurs, who was with us, 'Tell me what this portends.'

The old man answered, 'How can I say? It may be of great significance or none.'

'Don't be afraid. Say what it seems to mean to you.'

'First send the children away,' he said.

I do not know whether he gave her the interpretation which, when you have read my story, will be forced on you as the only possible one. All I know is that while we other children kept our distance – dear Germanicus had found another tail-feather for me, sticking in a hawthorn bush, and I was putting it proudly in my hair – Livilla crept up inquisitively behind a rose-hedge and overheard something. She interrupted, laughing noisily: 'Wretched Rome, with *him* as her protector! I hope to God I'll be dead before then!'

The Augur turned on her and pointed with his finger. 'Impudent girl,' he said, 'God will no doubt grant your wish in a way that you won't like!'

'You're going to be locked up in a room with nothing to eat, child,' said my mother. Those were ominous words too, now I come to recall them. Livilla was kept in bounds for the rest of her holidays. She revenged herself on me, in a variety of ingeniously spiteful ways. But she could not tell us what the Augur had said, because she had been bound by an oath by Vesta, and our household gods, never to refer to the portent either directly or in a roundabout way in the lifetime of anyone present. We were all made to take that oath. Since I have now for many years been the only one left alive of that party – my mother and the Augur, though so much older, surviving all the rest – I am no longer bound to silence. For some time after this I often caught my mother looking curiously at me, almost respectfully, but she treated me no better than before.

I was not allowed to go to the Boys' College, because the weakness of my legs would not let me take part in the gymnastic exercises which were a chief part of the education, and my illnesses had made me very backward in lessons, and my deafness and stammer were a handicap. So I was seldom in the company of boys of my own age and class, the sons of the household slaves being called in to play with me: two of these, Callon and Pallas, both Greeks, were later to be my secretaries, entrusted with affairs of the highest importance. Callon became the father of two other secretaries of mine, Narcissus and Polybius. I also spent much of my time with my mother's women, listening to their talk as they sat spinning or carding or weaving. Many of them, such as my governess, were women of liberal education and, I confess, I found more pleasure in their society than in that of almost any society of men in which I have since been placed: they were broadminded, shrewd, modest, and kindly.

My tutor I have already mentioned, Marcus Portius Cato, who was, in his own estimation at least, a living embodiment of that ancient Roman virtue which his ancestors had one after the other shown. He was always boasting of his ancestors, as stupid people do who are aware that they have done nothing themselves to boast about. He boasted particularly of Cato the Censor, who of all characters in Roman history is to me perhaps the most hateful, as having persistently championed the cause of 'ancient virtue' and made it identical in the popular mind with churlishness, pedantry, and harshness. I was made to read Cato the Censor's self-glorifying works as text-books, and the account that he gave in one of them of his campaign in Spain, where he destroyed more towns than he had spent days in that country, rather disgusted me with his inhumanity than impressed me with his military skill or patriotism. The poet Virgil has said that the mission of the Roman is to rule: 'To spare the conquered, and with war the proud To overbear.' Cato overbore the proud, certainly, but less with actual warfare than with clever management of inter-tribal jealousies in Spain: he even employed assassins to remove redoubtable enemies. As for sparing the conquered, he put multitudes of unarmed men to the sword even when they unconditionally surrendered their cities, and he proudly records that many hundreds of Spaniards committed suicide, with all their families, rather than taste of Roman vengeance. Was it to be wondered at that the tribes rose again as soon as they could get a few arms together, and that they have been a constant thorn in our side ever since? All that Cato wanted was plunder and a triumph: a triumph was not granted unless so-and-so many corpses – I think it was 5,000 at this time – could be counted, and he was making sure that no one would challenge him, as he had himself jealously challenged rivals, for having pretended to a triumph on an inadequate harvest of dead.

Triumphs, by the way, have been a curse to Rome. How many unnecessary wars have been fought because generals wanted the glory of riding crowned through the streets of Rome with enemy captives led in chains behind them and the spoils of war heaped on carnival wagons? Augustus realized this: on Agrippa's advice, he decreed that henceforth no general, unless a member of the Imperial family, should be awarded a public triumph. This decree, published in the year that I was born, read as though Augustus were jealous of his generals, for by that time he had finished with active campaigning himself and no members of his family were old enough to win triumphs; but all it meant was that he did not wish the boundaries of the Empire enlarged any further, and that he reckoned that his generals would not provoke the frontier tribes to commit acts of war if they could not hope to be awarded triumphs by victory over them. None the less he allowed 'triumphal ornaments' – an embroidered robe, a statue, a chaplet, and so on – to be awarded to those who would otherwise have earned a triumph; this should be a sufficient incentive to any good soldier to fight a necessary war. Triumphs, besides, are very bad for military discipline. Soldiers get drunk and out of hand and usually finish the day by breaking up the wine-shops and setting fire to the oil-shops and insulting the women and generally behaving as if Rome were the city they had conquered, not some miserable log-hut encampment in Germany or sand-burrowed village in Morocco. After a triumph celebrated by a nephew of mine, whom I shall soon be telling you about, 400 soldiers and nearly 4,000 private citizens lost their lives one way and another – five big blocks of tenements in the prostitutes' quarter of the City were burned to the ground and 300 wine-shops sacked, besides any amount of other damage.

But I was on the subject of Cato the Censor. His manual of husbandry and household economy was made my spelling-book, and every time I stumbled over a word I used to get two blows; one on my left ear for my stupidity, and one on my right for insulting the noble Cato. I remember a passage in the book which summed up the mean-souled fellow very well: 'A master of a household should sell his old oxen, and all the horned cattle that are of a delicate frame; all his sheep that are not hardy, their wool, their very pelts; he should sell his old wagons and his old instruments of husbandry; he should sell such of his slaves as are old and infirm and everything else that is worn out or useless.' For myself, when I was living as a country gentleman on my little estate at Capua, I made a point of putting my worn-out beasts first to light work and then to grass until old age seemed too much of a burden to them, when I had them knocked on the head. I never demeaned myself by selling them for a trifle to a countryman who would work them cruelly to their last gasp. As for my slaves, I have always treated them generously in sickness and health, youth and old age, and expected the highest degree of devotion from them in return. I have seldom been disappointed, though when they have abused my generosity I have had no mercy on them. I have no doubt old Cato's slaves were always falling sick, with the hope of being sold to a more humane master, and I also think it likely that he got, on the whole, less honest work and service out of them than I got out of mine. It is foolish to treat slaves like cattle. They are more intelligent than cattle, capable besides of doing more damage in a week to one's property by wilful carelessness and stupidity than the entire price you have paid for them. Cato made a boast of never spending more than a few pounds on a slave: any evil-looking cross-eyed fellow that seemed to have good muscles and teeth would do. How on earth he managed to find buyers for these beauties when he had quite finished with them I cannot say. From what I know of the character of his descendant, who was supposed to resemble him closely in looks – sandy-haired, green-eyed, harsh-voiced, and heavily built – and in character, I guess that he bullied his poor neighbours into taking all his cast-off stuff at the price of new.

My dear friend Postumus, who was a little less than two years older than myself – the truest friend, except Germanicus, that I have ever had – told me that he had read in a contemporary book that old Cato was a regular crook besides being a skinflint: he was guilty of some very sharp practice in the shipping trade, but avoided public disgrace by making one of his ex-slaves the nominal trader. As Censor, in charge of public morals, he did some mighty queer things: they were allegedly in the name of public decency but really, it seems, to satisfy his personal spites. On his own showing, he expelled one man from the order of senators because he had been 'wanting in Roman gravity' – he had kissed his wife in daylight in his daughter's presence! When challenged by a friend of the expelled man, another senator, as to the justice of his decision and asked whether he himself and his wife never embraced except during the marital act, Cato replied hotly: 'Never!' 'What, *never*?' 'Well, a couple of years ago, to be frank with you, my wife happened to throw her arms around me during a thunderstorm which scared her, but fortunately nobody was about and I assure you it will be a long time before she does it again.' 'Oh,' said the senator, pretending to misunderstand him, for Cato meant, I suppose, that he had given his wife a terrible lecture for her want of gravity, 'I'm sorry about that. Some women aren't very affectionate with plain-looking husbands, however upright and virtuous they may be. But never mind, perhaps Jove will be good enough to thunder again soon.'

Cato did not forgive that senator, who was a distant relative. A year later he was going through the roll of senators, as his duty as Censor was, asking each man in turn whether he was married. There was a law, which has since lapsed, that all senators should be honourably married. The turn came for his relative to be examined, and Cato asked him in the usual formula, which enjoined the senator to answer 'in his confidence and honesty'. 'If you have a wife, in your confidence and honesty, answer!' Cato intoned in his raucous voice. The man felt a little foolish, because after joking about Cato's wife's affection for Cato, he had found that his own wife had so far lost her affection for himself that he was now forced to divorce her. So to show goodwill and turn the joke decently against himself he replied: 'Yes, indeed, I *have* a wife, but she's not in my confidence any more, and I wouldn't give much for her honesty, either.' Cato thereupon expelled him from the Order for irreverence.

And who brought the Punic Curse on Rome? That same old Cato who, whenever he was asked his opinion in the Senate on any matter whatever, would end his speech with: 'This is my opinion; and my further opinion is that Carthage should be destroyed: she is a menace to Rome.' By harping incessantly on the menace of Carthage he brought about such popular nervousness that, as I have said, the Romans eventually violated their most solemn commitments and razed Carthage to the ground.

I have written about old Cato more than I intended, but it is to the point: he is bound up in my mind both with the ruin of Rome, for which he was just as responsible as the men whose 'unmanly luxury', he said, 'enervated the State', and with the memory of my unhappy childhood under that muleteer, his great-great-great-grandson. I am already an old man and my tutor has been dead these fifty years, yet my heart still swells with indignation and hatred when I think of him.

Germanicus stood up for me against my elders in a gentle, persuasive way, but Postumus was a lion-like champion. He seemed not to care a fig for anyone. He even dared to speak out straight to my grandmother Livia herself. Augustus made a favourite of Postumus, so for a while Livia pretended to be amused at what she called his boyish impulsiveness. Postumus trusted her at first, being himself incapable of deceit. One day when I was twelve and he was fourteen he happened to be passing by the room where Cato was giving me my lessons. He heard the sound of blows and my cries for mercy and came bursting angrily in. 'Stop beating him, at once!' he shouted.

Cato looked at him in scornful surprise and fetched me another blow that knocked me off my stool.

Postumus said: 'Those that can't beat the ass, beat the saddle.' (That was a proverb at Rome.)

'Impudence, what do you mean?' roared Cato.

'I mean,' said Postumus, 'that you're revenging yourself on Claudius for what you consider a general conspiracy to keep you down. You're really too good for the job of tutoring him, eh?' Postumus was clever: he guessed that this would make Cato angry enough to forget himself. And Cato rose to the bait, shouting out with a string of old-fashioned curses that in the days of his ancestor, whose memory this stammering imp was insulting, woe betide any child who failed in reverence to his elders; for they dealt out discipline with a heavy hand in those days. Whereas in these degenerate times the leading men of Rome gave any ignorant oafish lout (this was for Postumus) or any feeble-minded decrepit-limbed little whippersnapper (this was for me) full permission – –

Postumus interrupted with a warning smile: 'So I was right. The degenerate Augustus insults the great Censor by employing you in his degenerate family. I suppose you have told the Lady Livia just how you feel about things?'

Cato could have bitten off his tongue with vexation and alarm. If Livia should hear what he had said, that would be the end of him; he had hitherto always expressed the most profound gratitude for the honour of being entrusted with the education of her grandchild, not to mention the free return of the family estates – confiscated after the Battle of Philippi, where his father had died fighting against Augustus. Cato was wise enough or cowardly enough to take the hint, and after this my daily torments were considerably abated. Three or four months later, much to my delight, he ceased to be my tutor, on his appointment to the headmastership of the Boys' College. Postumus came under his tutelage there.

Postumus was immensely strong. At the age of not quite fourteen he could bend a bar of cold iron as thick as my thumb across his knees, and I have seen him walk around the playground with two boys on his shoulders, one on his back, and one standing on each of his hands. He was not studious, but of an intellect far superior to Cato's, to say the least of it, and in his last two years at the College the boys elected him their leader. In all the school games he was 'The King' – strange how long the word 'king' has survived with schoolboys – and kept a stern discipline over his fellows. Cato had to be very civil to Postumus if he wanted the other boys to do what he wanted; for they all took their cue from Postumus.

Cato was now required by Livia to write her out half-yearly reports on his pupils: she remarked that if she felt them to be of interest to Augustus she would communicate them to him. Cato understood from this that his reports were to be non-committal unless he had a hint from her to praise or censure any particular boy. Many marriages were arranged while the boys were still at the College, and a report might be useful to Livia as an argument for or against some contemplated match. Marriages of the nobility at Rome had to be approved by Augustus as High Pontiff and were for the most part dictated by Livia. One day Livia happened to visit the College cloisters, and there was Postumus in a chair issuing decrees as the King. Cato noticed that she frowned at the sight. He was emboldened to write in his next report: 'With great unwillingness but in the interest of virtue and justice, I am compelled to report that the boy Agrippa Postumus is inclined to display a savage, domineering and intractable temper.' After this Livia behaved to him so graciously that his next report was even stronger. Livia did not show the reports to Augustus but kept them in reserve, and Postumus himself had no knowledge of them.

Under Postumus's kingship I had the happiest two years of my youth, I may say of my life. He gave orders to the other boys that I was to be freely admitted to games in the cloisters, though not a member of the College, and that he would regard any incivility or injury to me as incivility or injury to himself. So I took part in whatever sports my health allowed and it was only when Augustus or Livia happened to come along that I slipped into the background. In place of Cato I now had good old Athenodorus for my tutor. I learned more from him in six months than I had learned from Cato in six years. Athenodorus never beat me, and used the greatest patience. He used to encourage me by saying that my lameness should be a spur to my intelligence. Vulcan, the god of all clever craftsmen, was lame too. As for my stammer, Demosthenes, the noblest orator of all time, had been born with a stammer, but had corrected it by patience and concentration. Demosthenes had used the very method that he was now teaching me. For Athenodorus made me declaim with my mouth full of pebbles: in trying to overcome the obstruction of the pebbles I forgot about the stammer and then the pebbles were removed one at a time until none remained, and I found to my surprise that I could speak as well as anyone. But only in declamations. In ordinary conversation I still stammered badly. He made it a pleasant secret between himself and me that I could declaim so well. 'One day, Cercopithecion, we shall surprise Augustus,' he would say. 'But wait a little longer.' When he called me Cercopithecion ['little marmoset'], it was for affection, not scorn, and I was proud of the name. When I did badly he would shame me by rolling out, 'Tiberius Claudius Drusus Nero Germanicus, remember who you are and what you are doing.' With Postumus and Athenodorus and Germanicus as my friends I gradually began to win self-confidence.

Athenodorus told me, the very first day of his tutorship, that he proposed to teach me not facts which I could pick up anywhere for myself, but the proper presentation of facts. And this he did. One day, for example, he asked me, kindly enough, why I was so excited; I seemed unable to concentrate on my task. I A.D. 2 told him that I had just seen a huge draft of recruits parading on Mars Field under Augustus's inspection before being sent off to Germany, where war had recently broken out again. 'Well,' said Athenodorus, still in the same kindly voice, 'since this is so much on your mind that you can't appreciate the beauties of Hesiod, Hesiod can wait until to-morrow. After all, he's waited seven hundred years or more, so he won't grudge us another day. And meanwhile, suppose you were to sit down and take your tablets and write me a letter, a short account of all that you saw on Mars Field; as if I had been five years absent from Rome and you were sending me a letter across the sea, say to my home in Tarsus. That would keep your restless hands employed and be good practice too.' So I gladly scribbled away on the wax, and then we read the letter through for faults of spelling and composition. I was forced to admit that I had told both too little and too much, and had also put my facts in the wrong order. The passage describing the lamentations of the mothers and sweethearts of the young soldiers, and how the crowd rushed to the bridgehead for a final cheer of the departing column, should have come last, not first. And I need not have mentioned that the cavalry had horses: people took that for granted. And I had twice put in the incident of Augustus's charger stumbling; once was enough if the horse only stumbled once. And what Postumus had told me, as we were going home, about the religious practices of the Jews, was interesting, but did not belong here because the recruits were Italians, not Jews. Besides, at Tarsus he would probably have more opportunities of studying Jewish customs than Postumus had at Rome. On the other hand, I had not mentioned several things that he would have been interested to hear – how many recruits there were in the parade, how far advanced their military training was, to what garrison town they were being sent, whether they looked glad or sorry to go, what Augustus said to them in his speech.

Three days later Athenodorus made me write out a description of a brawl between a sailor and a clothes dealer which we had watched together that day as we were walking in the rag-market; and I did much better. He first applied this discipline to my writing, then to my declamations, and finally to my general conversation with him. He took endless pains with me, and gradually I grew less scatter-brained, for he never let any careless, irrelevant, or inexact phrase of mine pass without comment.

He had tried to interest me in speculative philosophy, but when he saw that I had no bent that way he did not force me to exceed the usual bounds of polite education in the subject. It was he who first inclined me to history. He had copies of the first twenty volumes of Livy's history of Rome, which he gave me to read as an example of lucid and agreeable writing. Livy's stories enchanted me and Athenodorus promised me that as soon as I had mastered my stammer I should meet Livy himself, who was a friend of his. He kept his word. Six months later he took me into the Apollo Library and introduced me to a bearded stooping man of about sixty with a yellowish complexion, a happy eye and a precise way of speaking, who greeted me cordially as the son of a father whom he had so much admired. Livy was at this time not quite half-way through his history, which was to be completed in one hundred and fifty volumes and to run from the earliest legendary times to the death of my father some twelve years previously. It was at this date that he had begun publishing his work, at the rate of five volumes a year, and he had now reached the date at which Julius Caesar was born. Livy congratulated me on having Athenodorus as my tutor. Athenodorus said that I well repaid the pains he spent on me; and then I told Livy what pleasure I had derived from reading his books since Athenodorus had recommended them to me as a model for writing. So everybody was pleased, especially Livy. 'What! are you to be an historian too, young man?' he asked. 'I should like to be worthy of that honourable name,' I replied, though I had indeed never seriously considered the matter. Then he suggested that I should write a life of my father, and offered to help me by referring me to the most reliable historical sources. I was much flattered and determined to start the book next day. But Livy said that writing was the historian's last task: first he had to gather his materials and sharpen his pen. Athenodorus would lend me his little sharp penknife, Livy joked.

Athenodorus was a stately old man with dark gentle eyes, a hooked nose and the most wonderful beard that surely ever grew on human chin. It spread in waves down to his waist and was as white as a swan's wing. I do not make this as an idle poetical comparison, for I am not the sort of historian who writes in pseudo-epic style. I mean that it was literally as white as a swan's wing. There were some tame swans on an artificial lake in the Gardens of Sallust, where Athenodorus and I once fed them with bread from a boat, and I remember noticing that his beard and their wings as he leaned over the side were of exactly the same colour. Athenodorus used to stroke his beard so slowly and rhythmically as he talked, and told me once that it was this that made it grow so luxuriantly. He said that invisible seeds of fire streamed off from his fingers, which were food for the hairs. This was a typical Stoic joke at the expense of Epicurean speculative philosophy.

Mention of Athenodorus's beard reminds me of Sulpicius, who, when I was thirteen years old, was appointed by Livia as my special history-tutor. Sulpicius had, I think, the most wretched-looking beard I have ever seen: it was white, but the white of snow in the streets of Rome after a thaw – a dirty greyish-white streaked with yellow, and very ragged. He used to twist it in his fingers when he was worried, and would even put the ends in his mouth and chew them. Livia chose him, I believe, because she thought him the most boring man in Rome and hoped by making him my tutor to discourage my historical ambitions; for she soon came to hear of them. Livia was right: Sulpicius had a genius for making the most interesting things seem utterly vapid and dead. But even Sulpicius's dryness could not turn me away from my work, and there was this about him, that he had a most exceptionally accurate memory for facts. If I ever wanted some out-of-the-way information, such for instance as the laws of succession to the chieftainship among one of the Alpine tribes against whom my father had fought, or the meaning and etymology of their outlandish battle-cry, Sulpicius would know what authority had treated of these points, in which book, and from which shelf of which case in which room of which library they were to be obtained. He had no critical sense and wrote miserably, the facts choking each other like flowers in a seed-bed that has not been thinned out. But he proved an invaluable assistant when later I learned to use him as such, instead of as a tutor; and he worked for me until his death at the age of eighty-seven, nearly thirty years later, his memory remaining unimpaired to the last, and his beard as discoloured and thin and disordered as ever.

Chapter 6

I MUST now go back a few years to write about my uncle Tiberius, whose fortunes are by no means irrelevant to this story. He was in an unhappy position, forced against his will to be continually in the public eye, now as general in some frontier-campaign, now as Consul at Rome, now as special commissioner to the provinces; when all he wanted was a long rest and privacy. Public honours meant little to him, if only because they were awarded him, as he once complained to my father, rather as being chief errand-boy to Augustus and Livia, than as one acting in his own right and on his own responsibility. Moreover, with the dignity of the Imperial family to maintain and Livia continually spying on him, he had to be very careful of his private morals. He had few friends, being, as I think I have said, of a suspicious, jealous, reserved, and melancholy temperament, and

6 B.C.

66

those rather hangers-on than friends, whom he treated with the cynical contempt that they deserved. And, lastly, things had gone from bad to worse between him and Julia since his marriage with her five years before. A boy had been born but he had died; and then Tiberius had refused to sleep with her ever again; for three reasons. The first was that Julia was by now getting middle-aged and losing her slender figure – Tiberius preferred immature women, the more boyish the better, and Vipsania had been a little wisp of a thing. The second was that Julia made passionate demands on him which he was unwilling to meet and that she used to become hysterical when he repulsed her. The third was that he found, after repulsing her, that she was revenging herself by finding gallants to give her what he withheld.

Unfortunately he could get no proof of Julia's infidelities apart from the evidence of slaves, for she managed things very carefully; and slave-evidence was not good enough to offer Augustus as grounds for divorcing his beloved only daughter. Rather than tell Livia about it, however, for he mistrusted her as much as he hated her, he preferred to suffer in silence. It occurred to him that, if he could once get away from Rome and Julia, the chances were that she would grow careless and Augustus would eventually find out for himself about her behaviour. His only chance of escape lay in another war breaking out somewhere on one of the frontiers important enough for him to be sent there in command. But no signs of war appeared in any quarter and, besides, he was sick of fighting. He had succeeded my father in command of the German armies (Julia had insisted on accompanying him to the Rhine) and had now only been back in Rome for a few months: but Augustus had worked him like a slave ever since his return, giving him the difficult and unpleasant task of investigating the administration of workhouses and labour conditions generally in the poorer quarters of Rome. One day, in an unguarded moment, he had burst out to Livia: 'O mother, to be free, for only a few months even, from this intolerable life.' She frightened him by making no answer and haughtily leaving the room, but later in the same day called him to her and surprised him by saying that she had decided to grant his wish and obtain temporary leave of retirement for him from Augustus. She took the decision partly because she wanted to put him under a debt of gratitude to her, and partly because she now knew about Julia's love-affairs and had the same idea as Tiberius about giving her rope and letting her hang herself with it. But her chief reason was that Postumus's elder brothers, Gaius and Lucius, were growing up and relations between them and their stepfather Tiberius were strained.

Gaius, who was not a bad fellow at bottom (and neither was Lucius), had to some extent come to fill the place in Augustus's affections that Marcellus had once held. But he spoilt them both so shamelessly, in spite of Livia's warnings, that the wonder is that they did not turn out far worse than they did. They tended to behave insolently towards their elders, particularly men towards whom they knew Augustus would secretly like them to behave so, and to live with great extravagance. When Livia saw that it was useless trying to keep Augustus's nepotism in check she changed her policy and encouraged him to make greater favourites of them than ever. By doing so, and letting them know she was doing so, she hoped to gain their confidence. She calculated, too, that if their self-importance was increased only a little more they would forget themselves and try to seize the monarchy for themselves. Her spy-system was excellent and she would get wind of any such plot in good time to have them arrested. She encouraged Augustus to have Gaius elected Consul, for four years ahead, when he was only fifteen; though the youngest age at which a man could legally become Consul had been fixed by Sulla at forty-three, before which he had to fill three different magistral offices of ascending importance. Later, Lucius was given the same honour. She also suggested that Augustus should present them to the Senate as 'Leaders of the Cadets'. The title was not, as in the case of Marcellus, given them for a specific occasion only, but put them in a position of permanent authority over all their equals in age and rank. It seemed perfectly clear now that Augustus intended Gaius as his successor; so it was not to be wondered at that the same sort of young noblemen as had boasted the untried powers of young Marcellus against the ministerial and military reputation of the veteran Agrippa now did the same for Agrippa's son Gaius against the veteran reputation of Tiberius, whom they subjected to many slights. Livia intended Tiberius to follow the example of Agrippa. If he now retired, with so many victories and public honours to his credit, to some near-by Greek island and left the political field clear for Gaius and Lucius, this would create a better impression and win him far more popular sympathy than if he stayed behind to dispute it. (The historical parallel would become still closer if Gaius and Lucius were to die during Tiberius's retirement and Augustus were to feel the need of his services again.) So she promised to prevail on Augustus to grant him indefinite leave of absence from Rome and permission to resign from all his offices; but to give him the honorary rank of Protector of the People – which would make him secure against assassination by Gaius, should Gaius think of removing him.

Livia found it extremely difficult to keep her promise, for Tiberius was Augustus's most useful minister and most successful general, and for a long time the old man refused to treat the request seriously. But Tiberius pleaded ill-health and urged that his absence would relieve Gaius and Lucius of much embarrassment: he admitted that he did not get on well with them. Still Augustus would not listen. Gaius and Lucius were mere lads, totally inexperienced as yet in war or statecraft, and would be of no service to him at all should serious disturbances break out in the City, in the provinces, or on the frontier. He realized, perhaps for the first time, that Tiberius was now his only stand-by in any such emergency. But he was irritated at having the realization forced on him. He refused Tiberius's request and said that he would listen to no arguments. Since there was no help for it, therefore, Tiberius went to Julia and told her with studied brutality that their marriage had become such a farce that he could not bear to remain in the same house with her a day longer. He suggested that she should go to Augustus and complain that she had been ill-treated by her ruffianly husband and would not be happy until she had a divorce. Augustus, he said, was for family reasons unlikely, worse luck, to consent to the divorce, but would probably banish him from Rome. He was ready even to go into exile rather than continue to live with her.

Julia decided to forget that she had ever loved Tiberius. She had suffered much from him. Not only did he treat her with the greatest contempt whenever they were alone together, but he had by now begun cautiously experimenting in those ludicrously filthy practices which later made his name so detestable to all decent-minded people; and she had found out about it. So she took him at his word and complained to Augustus in far stronger terms than Tiberius (who was vain enough to believe that she still loved him in spite of everything) could have foreseen. Augustus had always great difficulty in concealing his dislike for Tiberius as a son-in-law – which had of course encouraged the Gaius faction – and now went storming up and down his study calling Tiberius all the names that he could lay his tongue to. But he nevertheless reminded Julia that she had only herself to blame for her disappointment in a husband about whose character he had never failed to warn her. And, much as he loved and pitied her, he could not dissolve the marriage. For his daughter and stepson to separate after a union that had been given such political importance would never do, and Livia would see the matter in the same light as himself, he was sure. So Julia begged that Tiberius should at least be sent away somewhere for a year or two, because at the moment she could not abide his presence within a hundred miles of her. To this he eventually agreed, and a few days later Tiberius was on his way to the island of Rhodes, which he had, long before this, chosen as the ideal place for retirement. But Augustus, while granting him the rank of Protector, at Livia's urgent insistence, had made it plain that if he never saw his face again it would be no grief to him.

Nobody but the principals in this curious drama knew why Tiberius was leaving Rome, and Livia used Augustus's unwillingness to discuss the matter publicly, to Tiberius's advantage. She told her friends, 'in confidence', that Tiberius had decided to retire as a protest against the scandalous behaviour of the party of Gaius and Lucius. She also said that Augustus had sympathized greatly with him, and had first refused to accept his resignation, promising to silence the offenders; Tiberius had then insisted that he did not wish to make further bad blood between himself and his wife's sons, and had demonstrated the fixity of his purpose by going without food for four days. Livia kept up the farce by accompanying Tiberius to his ship at Ostia, the port of Rome, and beseeching him, in Augustus's name and her own, to reconsider his decision. She even arranged that all members of her immediate family – Tiberius's younger son Castor, and my mother, and Germanicus, Livilla, and myself – should come along with her and increase the poignancy of the occasion by adding our pleas to hers. Julia did not appear, and her absence fitted well with the impression that Livia was trying to create – that she had been siding with her sons against her husband. It was a ridiculous but well-staged scene. My mother played up well, and the three children, who had

70

been carefully coached, really spoke their parts as if they meant them. I was bewildered and dumb until Livilla gave me a good pinching, at which I burst into tears and so did better than any of them. I was four years old when all this happened, but I had turned twelve before Augustus was reluctantly compelled to recall my uncle to Rome, the political situation having by then greatly changed.

Now Julia deserves far greater sympathy than she has popularly won. She was, I believe, naturally a decent, good-hearted woman, though fond of pleasures and excitements, and the only one of my female relations who had a kindly word for me. I also believed that there were no grounds for the charges made against her many years later, of infidelity to Agrippa while she was married to him. Certainly all her boys resembled him closely. The true story is as follows. In her widowhood, as I have related, she fell in love with Tiberius and persuaded Augustus to let her marry him. Tiberius, enraged at having to divorce his own wife for her sake, treated her very coldly. She was then imprudent enough to approach Livia, whom she feared but trusted, and ask her advice. Livia gave her a love-philtre, which she was to drink, saying that within a year it would make her irresistible to her husband, but that she must take it once a month, at full moon, and make certain prayers to Venus, saying nothing about it to a living soul, or the drug would lose its virtue and do her a great deal of harm. What Livia very cruelly gave her was a distillation of the crushed bodies of certain little green flies, from Spain, which so stimulated her sexual appetite that she became like a demented woman. (I shall explain later how I came to learn all this.) For a while indeed she fired Tiberius's appetite by the abandoned wantonness to which the drug drove her, against her natural modesty; but soon she wearied him and he refused to have any further marital commerce with her. She was forced by the action of the drug, which I suppose became a habit with her, to satisfy her sexual cravings by adulterous intercourse with whatever young courtiers she could trust to behave with discretion. She did this in Rome, I mean: in Germany and France she seduced private soldiers of Tiberius's bodyguard and even German slaves, threatening, if they hesitated, to accuse them of offering her familiarities and to have them flogged to death. As she was still a fine-looking woman, they apparently did not hesitate long.

After Tiberius's banishment Julia grew careless, and all Rome soon came to know of her infidelities. Livia never said a word to Augustus, confident that in due time he would come to hear about them from some other quarter. But Augustus's blind love for Julia was a byword and nobody dared to say anything to him. After a time it was generally assumed that he could no longer be ignorant, and that his condonation of her behaviour was a further caution to silence. Julia's nocturnal orgies in the Market Place and on the Oration Platform itself had become a matter of grave public scandal, yet it was four years before so much as a rumour reached Augustus. Then he heard the whole story from none other than her sons, Gaius and Lucius, who came together into his presence and angrily asked him how long he was going to permit himself and his grandchildren to be disgraced. They understood, they said, that regard for the family's good name had made him very patient with their mother, but surely there was a limit to his long-suffering. Were they to wait until she presented them with a litter of many-fathered bastard brothers before any official notice was taken of her pranks? Augustus listened with horror and amazement and for a long time could do no more than gape and move his lips. When he found his voice it was to call in strangled tones for Livia. They repeated their story in her presence, and she pretended to sob, saying that it had been her greatest grief these three years that Augustus had deliberately shut his ears to the truth. Several times, she said, she had gathered up courage to speak to him, but it had been quite clear that he did not want to listen to a word she said. 'I was confident that you really knew all about it and that the subject was too painful for you to discuss even with me. ...' Augustus, weeping, with his head between his hands, muttered that he had never heard the slightest whisper, or entertained the faintest suspicion that his daughter was not the chastest woman at Rome. Livia asked, why then did he suppose that her son Tiberius had gone into exile. For love of exile? No, it was because he was unable to check the excesses of his wife and yet was distressed that Augustus was condoning them, for so he believed; and since he did not wish to antagonize Gaius and Lucius, her sons, by asking Augustus for leave to divorce her, there was no course open for him but to withdraw decently from the scene.

The talk about Tiberius was wasted on Augustus, who threw a

fold of his robe over his head and groped his way to the passage leading to his bedroom, where he locked himself in and was seen by nobody, not even by Livia, for four whole days, during which time he took no food or drink, nor any sleep, and what was still stronger proof – if any was required – of the violence of his grief, went all that time unshaved. Finally he pulled the string which ran through a hole in the wall and tinkled a little silver bell in Livia's room. Livia came hurrying to him with a face of loving concern, and Augustus, not yet trusting his voice, wrote down on his wax-tablet the single sentence, in Greek: 'Let her be banished for life, but do not tell me where.' He handed Livia his seal-ring so that she might write letters to the Senate by his authority, recommending the banishment. (This seal, by the way, was the great emerald cut with the helmeted head of Alexander the Great, from whose tomb it had been stolen, along with a sword and breastplate and other personal trappings of the hero. Livia insisted on his using it, in spite of his scruples – he realized how presumptuous it was – until one night he had a dream in which Alexander, frowning angrily, hacked off with his sword the finger on which he wore it. Then he had a seal of his own, a ruby from India, cut by the famous goldsmith Dioscurides, which all his successors have used as the token of their sovereignty.)

Livia wrote the recommendation for banishment in very strong terms. It was composed in Augustus's own literary style; which was easy to imitate because it always sacrificed elegance to clarity – for example, by a determined repetition of the same word, where it occurred often in a passage, instead of hunting about for a synonym or periphrasis (which is the common literary practice). And he had a tendency to over-prepositionalize his verbs. She did not show the letter to Augustus but sent it direct to the Senate, who immediately voted a decree of perpetual banishment. Livia had listed Julia's crimes in such detail and had credited Augustus with such calm expressions of detestation for them that she made it impossible for him ever afterwards to change his mind and ask the Senate to cancel their decision. She did a good piece of business on the side, too, by singling out for special mention as Julia's partners in adultery three or four men whom it was to her interest to ruin. Among them was an uncle of mine, Iulus, a son of Antony, to whom Augustus had shown great favour for Octavia's sake, raising him to the Consulship. Livia, in naming him in her letter to the Senate, strongly emphasized the ingratitude that he had shown his benefactor and hinted that he and Julia were conspiring together to seize the supreme power. Iulus committed suicide. I believe that the charge of conspiracy was groundless, but as the only surviving son of Antony, by his wife Fulvia – Augustus had put Antyllus, the eldest, to death immediately after his father's suicide, and the other two, Ptolemy and Alexander, his sons by Cleopatra, had died young – and as an ex-Consul and the husband of Marcellus's sister, whom Agrippa had divorced, he seemed dangerous. Popular discontent with Augustus often expressed itself in a wish that it had been Antony who had won the Battle of Actium. The other men whom Livia accused of adultery were banished.

A week later Augustus asked Livia whether 'a certain decree' had been duly passed – for he never mentioned Julia by name again and seldom even by a roundabout expression, though she plainly was much in his thoughts. Livia told him that 'a certain person' had been sentenced to perpetual confinement on an island and was already on her way there. At this he seemed further downcast, that Julia had not done the one honourable thing left to her to do, namely to take her own life. Livia mentioned that Phoebe, who was Julia's lady-in-waiting and chief confidant, had hanged herself as soon as the decree of banishment had been published. Augustus said: 'I wish to God I had been Phoebe's father.' He delayed his public appearance for a further fortnight. I well remember that dreadful month. We children were all, by Livia's orders, made to wear mourning and not allowed to play or make a noise or even smile. When we saw Augustus again he looked ten years older, and it was months before he had the heart to visit the playground in the Boys' College or even to resume his daily morning exercise, which consisted of a brisk walk around the Palace grounds with a run at the end over a course of low hurdles.

Tiberius had the news about Julia sent him at once by Livia. At her prompting he wrote two or three letters to Augustus, begging him to forgive Julia, as he did himself, and saying that however badly she had behaved as a wife he wished her to keep all the property that he had at any time made over to her. Augustus did not answer. He firmly believed that Tiberius's original coldness and cruelty to Julia, and the examples of immorality he had given her, were responsible for her moral degeneration. So far from recalling him from banishment he refused even to renew his Protectorate when it came to an end the following year.

There is a soldiers' marching-ballad called *The Three Griefs of Lord Augustus*, composed in the rough tragi-comic style of the camp, which was sung many years later by the regiments stationed in Germany. The theme is that Augustus grieved first for Marcellus, next for Julia, and the third time for the lost Eagles of Varus. Deeply for Marcellus's death, more deeply for Julia's disgrace, but most deeply of all for the Eagles, for with each Eagle had vanished a whole regiment of Rome's bravest men. The ballad laments in a number of verses the unhappy fate of the Seventeenth, Eighteenth, and Nineteenth Regiments which, when I was nineteen years old, were ambushed and massacred by the Germans in a remote marshy forest; and tells how, after the news of this unparalleled disaster reached him, Lord Augustus kept knocking his head against the wall:

> Lord Augustus each time bawling
>   As he fetched his head a crack,
> 'Varus, Varus, General Varus,
>   Give me my three Eagles back!'

> Lord Augustus tore his bedclothes,
>   Blankets, sheet, and counterpane.
> 'Varus, Varus, General Varus,
>   Give my Regiments back again!'

The next verses say that he never afterwards formed new regiments under the numbers of the three destroyed, but kept the gap in the Army List. He is made to swear that Marcellus's life and Julia's honour had been nothing to him by comparison with the life and honour of his soldiers, and that his spirit would have 'no more rest than a flea in an oven' until all three Eagles were recovered and safely laid in the Capitol. But though since then the Germans had been thrashed again and again in battle, nobody had been able to discover where the lost Eagles were 'roosting' – the cowards kept them so closely hidden. That was how the troops belittled Augustus's grief for Julia, but it is my opinion that for every hour he grieved for the Eagles he must have grieved a full month for her.

He did not wish to know where she had been sent, because this would have meant that his mind would be continually turning there and he would hardly be able to restrain himself from taking ship and visiting her. So it was easy for Livia to treat Julia with great revengefulness. She was not allowed wine, cosmetics, fine clothes, or luxuries of any sort, and her guard consisted of eunuchs and very old men. She was allowed no visitors and was even set to work on a daily spinning task as in her schoolgirl days. The island was off the Campanian coast. It was a very small one and Livia purposely increased her sufferings by keeping the same guards there year after year without relief; they naturally blamed her for their banishment in that confined and unhealthy spot. The one person who comes well out of this ugly story is Julia's mother, Scribonia, whom it will be recalled Augustus had divorced in order to be able to marry Livia. Now a very old woman, who had lived in retirement for a number of years, she boldly went to Augustus and asked permission to share her daughter's banishment. She told him in Livia's presence that her daughter had been stolen from her as soon as born but that she had always worshipped her from a distance and, now that the whole world was against her darling, she wished to show what *true* mother's love was. And in her opinion the poor child was not to blame: things had been made very difficult for her. Livia laughed contemptuously but must have felt pretty uncomfortable. Augustus, mastering his emotion, signed that the request was granted.

Five years later, on Julia's birthday, Augustus asked Livia suddenly: 'How big is the island?'

'Which island?' asked Livia.

'The island ... where an unlucky woman is living.'

'Oh, a few minutes' walk from end to end, I believe,' Livia said with affected carelessness.

'A few minutes' walk! Are you joking?' He had thought of her as in exile on some big island, like Cyprus or Lesbos or Corfu. After a while he asked: 'What is it called?'

'It's called Pandataria!'

'What? My God, *that* desolate place? Oh, cruel! Five years on Pandataria!'

Livia looked at him severely and said: 'I suppose you want her back here at Rome?'

Augustus then went over to the map of Italy, engraved on a thin sheet of gold studded with small jewels to mark the cities, which hung on the wall of the room in which they were. He was unable to speak, but pointed to Reggio, a pleasant Greek town on the straits of Messina.

So Julia was sent to Reggio, where she was given somewhat greater liberty, and even allowed to see visitors – but a visitor had first to apply in person to Livia for permission. He had to explain what business he had with Julia, and fill in a detailed passport for Livia's signature, giving the colour of his hair and eyes and listing distinguishing marks and scars, so that only he himself could use it. Few cared to submit to these preliminaries. Julia's daughter Agrippina asked permission to go, but Livia refused out of consideration, she said, for Agrippina's morals. Julia was still kept under severe discipline and had no friend living with her, her mother having died of fever on the island.

Once or twice when Augustus was walking in the streets of Rome there were cries from the citizens: 'Bring your daughter back! She's suffered enough! Bring your daughter back!' This was very painful to Augustus. One day he made his police-guard fetch from the crowd two men who were shouting this out most loudly, and told them gravely that Jove would surely punish their folly by letting them be deceived and disgraced by their own wives and daughters. These demonstrations expressed not so much pity for Julia as hostility to Livia, whom everyone justly blamed for the severity of Julia's exile and for so playing on Augustus's pride that he could not allow himself to relent.

As for Tiberius on *his* comfortably large island, it suited him very well for a year or two. The climate was excellent, the food was good, and he had ample leisure for resuming his literary studies. His Greek prose style was not at all bad and he wrote several elegant silly elegiac Greek poems in imitation of such poets as Euphorion and Parthenius. I have a book of them somewhere. He spent much of his time in friendly disputation with the professors at the university. The study of classical mythology amused him and he made an enormous genealogical chart, in circular form, with the stems raying out from our earliest ancestor Chaos, the father of Father Time, and spreading to a confused perimeter thickly strewn with nymphs and kings and heroes. He used to delight in puzzling the mythological experts, while building up the chart, with questions like: 'What was the name of Hector's maternal grandmother?' and 'Had the Chimaera any male issue?' and then challenging them to quote the relevant verse from the ancient poets in support of their answer. It was, by the way, from a recollection of this table, now in my possession, that many years afterwards my nephew Caligula made his famous joke against Augustus: 'Oh, yes, he was my great-uncle. He stood in precisely the same relationship to me as the Dog Cerberus did to Apollo.' As a matter of fact, now that I consider the matter, Caligula made a mistake here, did he not? Apollo's great-uncle was surely the monster Typhoeus who according to some authorities was the father, and according to others the grandfather of Cerberus. But the only genealogical tree of the Gods is so confused with incestuous alliances – son with mother, brother with sister – that it may be that Caligula could have proved his case.

As a Protector of the People Tiberius was held in great awe by the Rhodians; and provincial officials sailing out to take up their posts in the East, or returning from there, always made a point of turning aside in their course and paying him their respects. But he insisted that he was merely a private citizen and deprecated any public honours paid to him. He usually dispensed with his official escort of yeomen. Only once did he exercise the judicial powers that his Protectorship carried with it: he arrested and summarily condemned to a month in gaol a young Greek who, in a grammatical debate where he was acting as chairman, tried to defy his authority as such. He kept himself in good condition by riding and taking part in the sports at the gymnasium, and was in close touch with affairs at Rome – he had monthly news-letters from Livia. Besides his house in the island capital he owned a small villa some distance from it, built on a lofty promontory overlooking the sea. There was a secret path to it up the cliff, by which a trusted freedman of his, a man of great physical strength, used to conduct the disreputable characters – prostitutes, pathics, fortune-tellers, and magicians – with whom he customarily passed his evenings. It is said that very often these creatures, if they had displeased Tiberius, somehow missed their footing on the return journey and fell into the sea far below.

I have already mentioned that Augustus refused to renew Tiberius's Protectorship when the five years expired. It can be imagined that this put him in a very awkward position at Rhodes, where he was personally unpopular: the Rhodians, seeing him deprived of his yeoman escort, his magisterial powers, and the inviolateness of his person, began to treat him first with familiarity and then with contumely. For example, one famous Greek professor of philosophy to whom he applied for leave to join his classes told him that there was no vacancy but that he could come back in seven days' time and see whether one had occurred. Then news came from Livia that Gaius had been sent to the East as Governor of Asia Minor. But though not far away, at Chios, Gaius did not come and pay Tiberius the expected visit. Tiberius heard from a friend that Gaius believed the false reports circulating at Rome that he and Livia were plotting a military rebellion and that a member of Gaius's suite had even offered, at a public banquet at which everyone was somewhat drunk, to sail across to Rhodes and bring back the head of 'The Exile': Gaius had told the fellow that he had no fear of 'The Exile': let him keep his useless head on his useless shoulders. Tiberius swallowed his pride and sailed at once to Chios to make his peace with his stepson, whom he treated with a humility that was much commented upon. Tiberius, the most distinguished living Roman, after Augustus, paying court to a boy not yet out of his teens, and the son of his own disgraced wife! Gaius received him coldly but was much flattered. Tiberius begged him to have no fears, for the rumours that had reached him were as groundless as they were malicious. He said that he did not intend to resume the political career which he had interrupted out of regard for Gaius himself and his brother Lucius: all that he wanted now was to be allowed to spend the rest of his life in the peace and privacy which he had learned to prize before all public honours.

Gaius, flattered at the chance of being magnanimous, undertook to forward a letter to Rome asking Augustus's permission for Tiberius to return there, and to endorse it with his own personal recommendation. In this letter Tiberius said that he had left Rome only in order not to embarrass the young princes, his stepsons, but that, now they were grown up and firmly established, the obstacles to his living quietly at Rome were no longer present; he added that he was weary of Rhodes and longed to see his friends and relations again. Gaius forwarded the letter with the promised endorsement. Augustus replied, to Gaius not to Tiberius, that Tiberius had gone away, in spite of the strong pleas of his friends and relations, when the State had most need of him; he could not now make his own terms about coming back. The contents of this letter became generally known and Tiberius's anxiety increased.

He had heard that the people of Nîmes in France had overthrown the statues erected there in memory of his victories, and that Lucius too had now been given false information against him which he was inclined to believe. He removed from the city and lived in a small house in a remote part of the island, only occasionally visiting his villa on the promontory. He no longer took any care of his physical condition or even of his personal appearance, rarely shaving, and going about in dressing-gown and slippers. He finally wrote a private letter to Livia, explaining his dangerous situation. He pledged himself, if she managed to secure permission for him to return, to be solely guided by her in every thing so long as they both lived. He said that he addressed her not so much as his devoted mother but as the true, though so far unacknowledged, helmsman of the Ship of State.

This was just what Livia wanted; she had purposely refrained hitherto from persuading Augustus to recall Tiberius. She wanted him to become as weary of inaction and public contumely A.D. 2 as he had previously been of action and public honour. She sent back a brief message to say that she had his letter safe, and that it was a bargain. A few months later Lucius died mysteriously at Marseilles, on his way to Spain, and while Augustus was still stunned by the shock Livia began working on his feelings by saying how much she had missed the support of her dear son Tiberius all these years; for whose return she had not until now ventured to plead. He had certainly done wrong, but had also certainly learned his lesson by now and his private letters to her breathed the greatest devotion and loyalty to Augustus. Gaius, who had endorsed that petition for his return, would, she urged, need a trustworthy colleague now that his brother was dead.

One evening a fortune-teller called Thrasyllus, by birth an Arab, came to Tiberius at his house on the promontory. He had been two or three times before and had made a number of very encouraging predictions, but none of these had yet been fulfilled. Tiberius, growing sceptical, told his freedman that if Thrasyllus did not entirely satisfy him this time he was to lose his footing on his way down the cliff. When Thrasyllus arrived, the first thing that Tiberius said was, 'What is the aspect of my stars to-day?' Thrasyllus sat down and made very complicated astrological calculations with a piece of charcoal on the top of a stone table. At last he pronounced, 'They are in a most unusually favourable conjunction. The evil crisis of your life is now finally passing. Henceforth you are to enjoy nothing but good fortune.'

'Excellent,' said Tiberius, dryly, 'and now what about your own?'

Thrasyllus made another set of calculations, and then looked up in real or pretended terror. 'Great Heavens!' he exclaimed, 'an appalling danger threatens me from air and water.'

'Any chance of circumventing it?' asked Tiberius.

'I cannot say. If I could survive the next twelve hours, my fortune would be, in its degree, as happy even as yours; but nearly all the malevolent planets are in conjunction against me and the danger seems all but unavoidable. Only Venus can save me.'

'What was that you said just now about her? I forget.'

'That she is moving into Scorpio, which is your sign, portending a marvellously happy change in your fortunes. Let me venture a further deduction from this all-important movement: you are soon to be engrafted into the Julian house, which, I need hardly remind you, traces direct descent from Venus, the mother of Aeneas. Tiberius, my humble fate is curiously bound up with your illustrious one. If good news comes to you before dawn tomorrow, it is a sign that I have almost as many fortunate years before me as yourself.'

They were sitting out on the porch and suddenly a wren or some such small bird hopped on Thrasyllus's knee and, cocking its head on one side, began to chirp at him. Thrasyllus said to the bird, 'Thank you, sister! It came only just in time.' Then he turned to Tiberius: 'Heaven be praised! That ship has good news for you, the bird says, and I am saved. The danger is averted.'

Tiberius sprang up and embraced Thrasyllus, confessing what his intentions had been. And, sure enough, the ship carried Imperial dispatches from Augustus informing Tiberius of Lucius's death and saying that in the circumstances he was graciously permitted to return to Rome, though for the present only as a private citizen.

As for Gaius, Augustus had been anxious that he should have no task assigned to him for which he was not fitted, and that the East should remain quiet during his governorship. Unfortunately the King of Armenia revolted and the King of Parthia threatened to join forces with him; which put Augustus in a quandary. Though Gaius had shown himself an able peace-time governor, Augustus did not believe him capable of conducting so important a war as this; and he himself was too old to go campaigning and had too many affairs to attend to at Rome, besides. Yet he could not send out anybody else to take over the Eastern regiments from Gaius because Gaius was Consul and should never have been allowed to enter upon the office if he was incapable of high military command. There was nothing to be done but to let Gaius be and hope for the best.

Gaius was lucky at first. The danger from the Armenians was removed by an invasion of their Eastern border by a wandering tribe of barbarians. The King of Armenia was killed while chasing them away. The King of Parthia, hearing of this and also of the large army that Gaius was getting together, then came to terms with him: to the great relief of Augustus. But Augustus's new nominee to the throne of Armenia, a Mede, was not acceptable to the Armenian nobles, and when Gaius had sent home his extra forces as no longer necessary they declared war after all. Gaius re-assembled his army, and marched to Armenia, where a few months later he was treacherously wounded by one of the enemy generals who had invited him to a parley. It was not a serious wound. He thought little of it at the time and concluded the campaign successfully. But somehow he was given the wrong medical treatment, and his health, which from no apparent cause had been failing him for the last two years, became seriously affected: he lost all power of mental concentration. Fianlly he wrote to Augustus for permission to retire into private life. Augustus was grieved, but granted his plea. Gaius died on his way home. Thus A.D. 4 of Julia's sons only fifteen-year-old Postumus now remained, and Augustus was so far reconciled to Tiberius that, as Thrasyllus foretold, he engrafted him into the Julian house by adopting him, jointly with Postumus, as his son and heir.

The East was quiet now for a time, but when the war that had broken out in Germany again – I mentioned it in connexion with my schoolboy composition for Athenodorus – took a serious turn, Augustus made Tiberius army-commander and showed his renewed confidence in him by awarding him a ten years' Protectorship. The campaign was a severe one and Tiberius handled it with his old force and skill. Livia, however, insisted on his making frequent visits to Rome so as not to lose touch with political events there. Tiberius was keeping his part of the bargain with her and allowed himself to be led by her in everything.

Chapter 7

I WENT back in time a few years to tell of my Uncle Tiberius, but by following that history through until his adoption by Augustus, I have come out ahead of my own story. I shall try to devote these next chapters strictly to events that happened between my ninth and sixteenth years. Mostly it is a record of the betrothals and marriages of us young nobles. First Germanicus came of age – September the 30th was his fourteenth birthday, but the coming-of-age celebrations always took place in March. As the custom was, he went out garlanded from our house on the Palatine, in the early morning, wearing his purple-bordered boy's dress for the last time. Crowds of children ran ahead, singing and scattering flowers, an escort of his noble friends walked with him, and an immense throng of citizens followed behind, in their degrees. The procession went slowly down the slope of the Hill, through the Market Place, where Germanicus was greeted uproariously. He returned the greeting in a short speech. Finally the procession moved on up the slope of the Capitoline Hill. At the Capitol, Augustus and Livia were waiting to greet him, and he sacrificed a white bull in the temple there to Capitoline Jove, the Thunderer, and put on his white manly-gown for the first time. Much to my disappointment I was not allowed to come too. The walk would have been too much for me and it would have created a bad impression if I had been carried in a sedan. All I witnessed of the ceremonies was his dedication, when he returned, of his boy's dress and ornaments to the household gods; and the scattering of cakes and pence to the crowd from the steps of the house.

1 B.C.

A year later he married. Augustus did all he could by legislation to encourage marriage among men of family. The Empire was very big and needed more officials and senior army officers than the nobility and gentry were able to supply, in spite of constant recruiting to their ranks from the populace. When there were complaints from men of family about the vulgarity of these newcomers, Augustus used to answer testily that he chose the least vulgar he could find. The remedy was in their own hands, he said: every man and woman of rank should marry young and breed as large a family as possible. The steady decrease in the number of births and marriages in the governing classes became an obsession with Augustus.

On one occasion when the Noble Order of Knights, from whom the senators were chosen, complained of the severity of his laws against bachelors, he summoned the entire order into the Market Place for a lecture. When he had them assembled there he divided them up into two groups, the married and the unmarried. The unmarried were a very much larger group than the married and he addressed separate speeches to each group. He worked himself up into a great passion with the unmarried, calling them beasts and brigands and, by a queer figure of speech, murderers of their posterity. By this time Augustus was an old man with all the petulance and crankiness of an old man who has been at the head of affairs all his life. He asked them, had they an hallucination that they were Vestal Virgins? At least a Vestal Virgin slept alone, which was more than they did. Would they, pray, explain why instead of sharing their beds with decent women of their own class and begetting healthy children on them, they squandered all their virile energy on greasy slave-girls and nasty Asiatic-Greek prostitutes? And if he were to believe what he heard, the partner of their nightly bed-play was more often one of those creatures of a loathsome profession whom he would not even name, lest the admission of their existence in the City should be construed as a condonation of it. If he had his way, a man who shirked his social obligations and at the same time lived a life of sexual debauch should be subject to the same dreadful penalties as a Vestal who forgot her vows – to be buried alive.

As for us married men, for I was among them by this time, he gave us a most splendid eulogy, spreading out his arms as if to embrace us. 'There are only a very few of you, in comparison with the huge population of the City. You are far less numerous than your fellows over there, who are unwilling to perform any of their natural social duties. Yet for this very reason I praise you the more, and am doubly grateful to you for having shown yourselves obedient to my wishes and for having done your best to man the State. It is by lives so lived that the Romans of the future will become a great nation. At first we were a mere handful, you know, but when we took to marriage and begot children we came to vie with neighbouring states not only in the manliness of our citizens but in the size of our population too. We must always remember

84

this. We must console the mortal part of our nature with an endless succession of generations, like torch-bearers in a race, so that
through one another we may immortalize the one side of our
nature in which we fall short of divine happiness. It was for this
reason chiefly that the first and greatest God who created us
divided the human race in two: He made one half of it male and
the other half female and implanted in these halves mutual desire
for each other, making their intercourse fruitful so that by continual procreation He might, in a sense, make even mortality immortal. Indeed, tradition says that some of the Gods themselves
are male and others female, and that they are all interrelated by
sexual ties of kinship and parentage. So you see that even among
those beings who have really no need of such a device, marriage
and the procreation of children have been approved as a noble
custom.'

I wanted to laugh, not only because I was being praised for
what had been forced on me greatly against my will – I will soon
tell you about Urgulanilla, to whom I was married at this time –
but because the whole business was such an utter farce. What was
the use of Augustus addressing us in this way, when he was perfectly well aware that it was not the men who were shirking, as he
called it, but the women? If he had summoned the women it is just
possible that he might have accomplished something by talking
to them in the right way.

I remember once hearing two of my mother's freedwomen discussing modern marriage from the point of view of a woman of
family. What did she gain by it? they asked. Morals were so loose
now that nobody took marriage seriously any longer. Granted, a
few old-fashioned men respected it sufficiently to have a prejudice
against children being fathered on them by their friends or household servants, and a few old-fashioned women respected their
husbands' feelings sufficiently to be very careful not to become
pregnant to any but them. But as a rule any good-looking woman
nowadays could have any man to sleep with whom she chose. If
she did marry and then tired of her husband, as usually happened,
and wanted someone else to amuse herself with, there might easily
be her husband's pride or jealousy to contend with. Nor in general
was she better off financially after marriage. Her dowry passed
into the hands of her husband, or her father-in-law as master of
the household, if he happened to be alive; and a husband, or

father-in-law, was usually a more difficult person to manage than a father, or elder brother, whose foibles she had long come to understand. Being married just meant vexatious household responsibilities. As for children, who wanted them? They interfered with the lady's health and amusement for several months before birth and, though she had a foster-mother for them immediately afterwards, it took time to recover from the wretched business of childbirth, and it often happened that her figure was ruined after having more than a couple. Look how the beautiful Julia had changed by obediently gratifying Augustus's desire for descendants. And a lady's husband, if she was fond of him, could not be expected to keep off other women throughout the time of her pregnancy, and anyway he paid very little attention to the child when it was born. And then, as if all this were not enough, foster-mothers were shockingly careless nowadays and the child often died. What a blessing it was that those Greek doctors were so clever, if the thing had not gone too far – they could rid any lady of an unwanted child in two or three days, and nobody be any the worse or wiser. Of course some ladies, even very modern ladies, had an old-fashioned hankering for children, but they could always buy a child for adoption into their husband's family, from some man of decent birth who was hard pressed by his creditors. ...

Augustus gave the Noble Order of Knights permission to marry commoners, even freedwomen, but this did not improve things very much. Knights, if they married at all, married for rich dowries, not for children or for love, and a freedwoman was not much of a catch; and besides knights, especially those recently raised to the order, had strong feelings against marrying beneath them. In families of the ancient nobility the difficulty was still greater. Not only were there fewer women to choose from in the correct degree of kinship, but the marriage ceremony was stricter. The wife was more absolutely in the power of the master of the household into which she married. Every sensible woman thought twice before committing herself to this contract, from which there was no escape but divorce; and after divorce it was difficult to recover the property that she had brought him as dowry. In other than anciently noble families, however, a woman could marry a man legally and yet remain independent, with control of her own property – if she cared to stipulate that she should sleep three nights of the year outside her husband's house; for this condition would interrupt his right over her as a permanent chattel. Women liked this form of marriage for obvious reasons, the very reasons for which their husbands disliked it. The practice started among the lowest families of the City but worked upwards, and soon became the rule in all except the anciently noble families. Here there was a religious reason against it. From these families the State priests were chosen, and by religious law a priest had to be a married man, married in the strict form, and the child of a strict-form marriage too. As time went on suitable candidates for priesthood were increasingly difficult to find. Finally there were vacancies in the colleges of Priests that could not be filled and something had to be done about it, so the lawyers found a way out. Women of rank were allowed, on contracting strict-form marriages, to stipulate that the complete surrender of themselves and property was 'as touching sacred matters' and that otherwise they enjoyed all the benefits of free marriage.

But that came later. Meanwhile the best that Augustus could do, apart from his legal penalization of bachelors and childless married men, was to put pressure on masters of households to marry off their young people (with instructions to increase and multiply) while they were still too young to realize to what they were being committed or to do anything but obey implicitly. To show a good example, therefore, all we younger members of the families of Augustus and Livia were betrothed and married at the earliest possible age. It may sound strange, but Augustus was a great-grandfather at the age of fifty-four and a great-great-grandfather before he died at the age of seventy-six; while Julia, as a result of her second marriage too, had a marriageable granddaughter before she was herself beyond child bearing age. The generations somewhat overlapped in this way and the genealogical tree of the Imperial family became a rival in complexity to that of Olympus. This was not only because of the frequent adoptions and the marrying of members in closer degree of kinship than religious custom really permitted – for the Imperial family was by this time getting above the law; but because as soon as a man died his widow was made to marry again and always in the same small circle of relationship. I shall do my best now to straighten the matter out at this point, without being too long-winded.

I have mentioned Julia's children, Augustus's chief heirs since Julia herself had been banished and cut out of his will, namely, her three boys, Gaius, Lucius, and Postumus, and her two daughters, Julilla and Agrippina. The younger members of Livia's family were Tiberius's son, Castor, and his three first-cousins, namely, my brother Germanicus, my sister Livilla, and myself. But I must not forget Julia's grandchild – for Julilla had in the absence of any possible husband from Livia's family married a wealthy senator called Aemilius (her first-cousin through a previous marriage of Scribonia's) and had borne him a daughter called Aemilia. Julilla's marriage was unfortunate, for Livia grudged that any granddaughter of Augustus should marry any but a grandson of her own; but as you will soon see it did not trouble her for long, and meanwhile Germanicus married Agrippina, a handsome serious girl to whom he had as a matter of fact been long devoted. Gaius married my sister Livilla but died soon afterwards, leaving no children. Lucius, who had been betrothed to Aemilia but not yet married, was already dead.

On Lucius's death the question arose of a suitable match for Aemilia. Augustus had a shrewd notion that Livia intended Aemilia's husband to be no other than myself, but he had tender feelings for the child and could not bear the idea of her marrying a sickly creature like me. He resolved to oppose the match: for once, he promised himself, Livia should not have her way. It happened shortly after the death of Lucius that Augustus was dining with Medullinus, one of his oldest generals, who traced his descent from the dictator Camillus. Medullinus told him, smiling, when the wine cups had been filled several times, that he had a young granddaughter of whom he was very fond. She had suddenly shown a surprising advance in her literary studies and he understood that he had a young relative of his most honoured guests's to thank for this improvement.

Augustus was puzzled. 'Who on earth can that be? I have heard nothing of it. What is happening? Is it a secret love affair with a literary sauce?'

'Yes, something of the sort,' said Medullinus, grinning. 'I have spoken to the young fellow, and for all his physical misfortunes and capabilities I can't help liking him. He has a frank and noble nature, and as a young scholar he impresses me considerably.'

Augustus asked incredulously: 'What, you don't mean young Tiberius Claudius?'

'Yes, that's the one,' said Medullinus.

Augustus's face lit up with a sudden resolution and he asked rather more hastily than was decent: 'Listen, Medullinus, old friend, would you have any objection to him as your grand-daughter's husband? If you agree to the match I shall be only too glad to arrange it. Young Germanicus is now nominally master of the household, but in matters like this he takes the advice of his elders. Well, it certainly isn't every girl who could overcome her physical repugnance to such a poor deaf, stammering cripple, and Livia and myself have had a natural delicacy in betrothing him to anyone. But if your granddaughter of her own free will – –'

Medullinus said: 'The child has spoken to me about this marriage herself and weighed matters very carefully. She tells me that young Tiberius Claudius is modest and truthful and kind-hearted; and that his lameness will never allow him to go to the wars and be killed – –'

'Or to run after other women,' laughed Augustus.

'And that his deafness is only on the one side, and as for his general health – –'

'I suppose the little minx has it worked out that he is not crippled in that part of the body for which honest wives show the most solicitude? Yes, why shouldn't he be capable of begetting perfectly healthy children on her? My old lame, whistling stud-stallion Bucephalus has sired more chariot-race winners than any horse in Rome. But, joking apart, Medullinus, yours is a very honourable house and my wife's family will be proud to be connected with it by marriage. Do you seriously mean that you approve the match?'

Medullinus said that the girl could do very much worse; quite apart from the unlooked for honour to the family of being allied in marriage with the Father of the Country.

Now Medullina, the granddaughter, was my first love; and never, I swear, was there such a beautiful child seen in all the world. I met her one summer afternoon in the Gardens of Sallust, where I was taken by Sulpicius in the absence of Athenodorus, who was unwell. Sulpicius's daughter was married to Medullina's uncle, Furius Camillus, a distinguished soldier who was Consul six years later. When I first saw her it was with a shock of surprise, not only at her beauty, but at her sudden appearance, for she came up on my deaf side while I was reading a book, and when I raised my eyes, there she was standing over me laughing at my preoccupation. She was slender, with rich black hair, white skin, and very dark blue eyes, and all her movements were quick and birdlike.

'What's your name?' she asked, in a friendly voice.

'Tiberius Claudius Drusus Nero Germanicus.'

'Ye gods, all that! Mine's Medullina Camilla. How old are you?'

'Thirteen,' I said, mastering my stammer well.

'I'm only eleven, but I bet I can race you to that cedar tree and back.'

'Are you a champion runner, then?'

'I can beat any girl in Rome, and my elder brothers too.'

'Well, I'm afraid you win by default. I can't run at all, I'm lame.'

'Oh, you poor fellow. How did you come here, then? Hobble-hobbling all the way?'

'No, Camilla, in a sedan-chair, like a lazy old man.'

'Why do you call me by my last name?'

'Because it's the more appropriate one.'

'How do you make that out, clever?'

'Because among the Etruscans "Camilla" is what they call the young hunting priestesses dedicated to Diana. With a name like Camilla one is bound to be a champion runner.'

'That's nice. I never heard that. I shall make all my friends call me Camilla now.'

'And call me Claudius, will you? That's my appropriate name. It means a cripple. My family usually call me Tiberius, and that's inappropriate because the Tiber runs very fast.'

She laughed. 'Well then, Claudius, tell me what do you do all day if you can't run about with the other boys?'

'I read, mostly, and write. I have read scores of books this year already and it's only June. This one's Greek.'

'I can't read Greek yet. I only just know the alphabet. My grandfather is cross with me – I have no father, you know – he calls me lazy. Of course, I understand Greek when I hear it talked: we always have to talk Greek at meals and whenever visitors come. What's the book about?'

'It's part of Thucydides's history. This passage is about how a politician, a tanner called Cleon, began criticizing the generals who were blockading the Spartans in an island. He said that they

90

were not doing their best and that if he were general he would bring back the whole Spartan force as captives within twenty days. The Athenians were so sick of his talk that they appointed him to command the forces himself.'

'That was a funny idea. What happened?'

'He kept his promise. He chose a good staff-officer and told him to fight in any way he liked so long as he won the battle, and the man knew his job; so within twenty days Cleon brought back to Athens a hundred and twenty Spartans of the highest rank.'

Camilla said: 'I've heard my uncle Furius say that the cleverest leader is one who chooses clever people to think for him.' Then she said: 'You must be very wise by now, Claudius.'

'I am supposed to be an utter fool and the more I read the more of a fool they think me.'

'I think you're very sensible. You tell things so nicely.'

'But I stammer. My tongue's a Claudian too.'

'Perhaps that's just nervousness. You don't know many girls, do you?'

'No,' I said, 'and you're the first one I have met who hasn't laughed at me. Couldn't we see each other now and then, Camilla? You couldn't teach me to run, but I could teach you to read Greek. Would you like that?'

'Oh, I'd love it. But will you teach me from interesting books?'

'From any book you like. Do you like history?'

'I think I like poetry best; there are so many names and dates to remember in history. My eldest sister raves about the love-poetry of Parthenius. Have you read any of it?'

'Some of it, but I don't like it. It's so artificial. I like *real* books.'

'So do I. But is there any Greek love-poetry that isn't artificial?'

'There's Theocritus. I like him very much. Get your aunt to bring you here to-morrow at the same time and I'll bring Theocritus and we'll begin at once.'

'You promise he's not boring?'

'No, he's very good.'

After this we used to meet in the garden nearly every day and sit in the shade together and read Theocritus and talk. I made Sulpicius promise not to tell anybody about it, for fear Livia should hear of it and stop my going. Camilla said one day that I was the kindest boy she had ever met and that she liked me better than all her brother's friends. Then I told her how much I liked her and

91

she was very pleased and we kissed shyly. She asked whether there was any possible chance of our getting married. She said that her grandfather would do anything for her and that she would bring him along one day to the gardens and introduce us; but would my father approve? When I told her that I had no father and that it all rested with Augustus and Livia she became depressed. We had not talked much about families until then. She had never heard any good of Livia, but I said that it was possible she might consent, because she disliked me so much that I didn't think she cared very much what I did, so long as I didn't disgrace her.

Medullinus was a straight dignified old man and something of an historian, which made conversation between us easy. He had been my father's superior officer in his first campaign and was full of anecdotes of him, many of which I noted down gratefully for my biography. One day we began talking about Camilla's ancestor Camillus, and when he asked me what action of Camillus's I most admired I said: 'When the treacherous schoolmaster of Falerii decoyed the children under his charge to the walls of Rome, saying that the Falerians would offer any terms to get them back, Camillus disdained the offer. He had him stripped naked and tied his hands behind his back and gave the boys rods and scourges to whip the traitor back home. Wasn't that magnificent?' In reading this story I had pictured the schoolmaster as Cato, the boys as Postumus and myself, and so my enthusiasm for Camillus was a little mixed. But Medullinus was pleased.

When Germanicus was asked for his approval of our marriage he gave it gladly, for I had told him of my love for Camilla; and my uncle Tiberius raised no objection; and my grandmother Livia hid her anger as usual and congratulated Augustus on having been so quick to take Medullinus at his word – he must have been drunk, she said, to have approved the match, though indeed the dowry was small, and the honour of the alliance great for a man of his family. The house of Camillus had bred no men of outstanding capacity or reputation for many generations.

Germanicus told me that everything had been arranged and that the betrothal ceremony was to take place on the next lucky day – we Romans are very superstitious about days; nobody would dream, for instance, of fighting a battle or A.D. 3 marrying or buying a house on July 16, the day of the Allia disaster in Camillus's time. I could hardly believe my good fortune. I too had feared that I would be made to marry Aemilia, an ill-tempered affected little girl who copied my sister Livilla in teasing and making a fool of me whenever she came to us on a visit, which was often. The betrothal ceremony, Livia insisted, was to be as private as possible, because she could not trust me not to make a fool of myself if there was a crowd. I preferred it that way: I hated ceremonies. Only the necessary witnesses would attend, and there would be no feast, merely the usual ritual sacrifice of a ram whose entrails would then be examined to see whether the auspices were favourable. Of course they would be; Augustus, officiating as priest, in compliment to Livia, would see to that. Then a contract would be signed for the second ceremony to take place as soon as I came of age, with stipulations about the dowry. Camilla and I would join hands and kiss and then I would give her a gold ring and she would return to her grandfather's house – quietly, as she had come, without any train of singing attendants.

It hurts me even now to write about that day. I stood, very nervously, in my chaplet and clean robe waiting with Germanicus by the family altar for Camilla to appear. She was late. She was very late. The witnesses began to grow impatient and criticize the bad manners of old Medullinus in keeping them waiting on a ceremonial occasion like this. At last the porter announced Camilla's uncle Furius and he came in, ashy-white and wearing mourning garments. After a short speech of greeting and apology to Augustus and the rest of the company for his tardiness and ill-omened appearance he said: 'A great calamity has happened. My niece is dead.'

'Dead!' cried Augustus. 'What joke is this? We had a message only half an hour ago that she was already on her way here.'

'She died by poison. A crowd gathered at the door, as crowds will, when they heard that the daughter of the house was about to go to her betrothal. When my niece came out, the women all pressed admiringly around her. She gave a little cry as if someone had trod on her foot, but nobody thought anything of it, and she stepped into the sedan. We had not gone the length of the street before my wife, Sulpicia, who was with her, saw her lose colour and asked whether she felt frightened. "Oh, aunt," she said, "that woman stuck a needle into my arm and I feel faint." Those were her last words, my friends. She died a few minutes later. I hurried here as soon as I had changed my clothes. You will forgive me.'

93

I burst into tears and began to sob hysterically. My mother, furious at my disgraceful conduct, told one of the freedmen to lead me away to my room; where I remained for days, in a nervous fever, unable to eat or sleep. But for the comfort that dear Postumus gave me, I believe I should have lost my wits altogether. The murderess was never found and nobody was able to explain what motive she could have had. Livia reported to Augustus a few days later that according to reports which seemed reliable one of the women in the crowd had been a Greek girl who considered herself, no doubt groundlessly, to have been wronged by the girl's uncle and may have decided to revenge herself in this monstrous way.

When I was well again, or no iller than usual, Livia complained to Augustus that the death of young Medullina Camilla had happened most unfortunately. In spite of Augustus's pardonable sentiment against such a match, she feared that young Aemilia would, after all, now have to be betrothed to her impossible grandson: everybody, she said, had been surprised that she had not been matched with him before. So, as usual, Livia had her way. I was betrothed to Aemilia a few weeks later; and went through the ceremony without disgrace, because grief for Camilla had made me quite indifferent. But Aemilia's eyes were red when she arrived, from tears not of grief but of rage.

Now as to Postumus, poor fellow, he was in love with my sister Livilla, of whom he saw much because she had gone to live in the Palace when she married his brother Gaius, and was still there. It was generally expected that he would marry her, to renew the family connexion broken by his brother's death. Livilla was flattered by his passionate devotion. She flirted with him constantly, but had no love for him. Castor was her choice – a cruel, dissolute, handsome fellow who seemed made for her. I knew of the understanding between Livilla and Castor, which I had discovered accidentally, and this made me very unhappy on Postumus's behalf, the more so because Postumus had no suspicion of her character and I did not dare to tell him of it. Whenever Livilla and I and he were together she used to show me pretended affection, which touched Postumus as much as it angered me. I knew that as soon as he had gone she would begin her spiteful tricks again. Livia got wind of the intrigue between Livilla and Castor and kept a careful watch on them: one night she was rewarded by a message from a trusted servant that Castor had just climbed in at Livilla's window by the balcony. She put an armed guard on the balcony and then knocked at Livilla's door, calling her by name. After a minute or so Livilla opened the door, pretending to have been sound asleep; but Livia went inside and found Castor behind the curtain. She talked very plainly to them and appears to have made them understand that the matter would not be reported to Augustus, who would certainly banish them if it was, only on certain conditions; and that if these same conditions were strictly observed she would even arrange that they should marry. Not long after my betrothal to Aemilia, Livia so settled matters with Augustus that Postumus was betrothed, much to his grief, to a   A.D. 4 girl called Domitia, a first-cousin of mine on my mother's side; and Castor married Livilla. This was the year that Tiberius and Postumus were adopted as Augustus's sons.

Livia considered Julilla and her husband Aemilius as a possible obstacle to her designs. She was lucky enough to get evidence that Aemilius and Cornelius, a grandson of Pompey the Great, were plotting to remove Augustus from power and to divide up his offices between themselves and certain ex-Consuls, among them Tiberius, though Tiberius had not yet been sounded for his opinion. The plot never gathered much way, because the first ex-Consul whom Aemilius and Cornelius approached refused to have anything to do with it. Augustus did not punish either Aemilius or Cornelius by death or banishment. It had been a welcome proof of the strength of his own position that they could get so little support for their plot, and by sparing them he proved it still stronger. He merely called them to his presence and lectured them on their folly and ingratitude. Cornelius fell at his feet and thanked him abjectly for his clemency; and Augustus begged him not to make a further fool of himself. He was not a tyrant, he said, either to conspire against, or to worship for showing a tyrant's clemency: he was merely a State-official of the Roman Republic who had been temporarily granted wide powers for the better maintenance of order. Aemilius had evidently led him astray by misrepresentations. The best cure for this nonsense was for Cornelius to become Consul next year in due course and so satisfy his ambitions by attaining equal honour with himself; for there was no higher rank than Consul in Rome. (Theoretically this was true.) Aemilius was proud and remained standing; and Augustus told him that as his relative by marriage he ought to have shown more decency, and as an ex-Consul he ought to have shown more sense. He thereupon deprived him of all his honours.

An amusing feature of this case was that Livia won all the credit for Augustus's clemency by claiming to have pleaded, with a woman's tenderness, for the lives of the two conspirators; of whom, she said, Augustus had practically decided to make an example. She got his consent to the publication of a little book which she had written called *A Pillow Debate on Force and Gentleness*, full of intimate touches. Augustus is represented as restless and worried and unable to sleep. Livia begs him prettily to speak his mind and they go together over the question of the proper treatment of Aemilius and Cornelius.

Augustus explains that he does not wish to put them to death, yet he fears that he must do so, for if he lets them off it will be thought that he is afraid of them, and others will be tempted to conspire against him. 'To be always under the necessity of taking vengeance and inflicting punishments is a very painful position for any honourable man to be in, my dearest wife.'

Livia answers: 'You are quite right and I have a piece of advice to give you – that is, if you are willing to accept it and will not blame me for daring, though a woman, to suggest to you something which nobody else, even of your most intimate friends, would dare to suggest.'

Augustus says: 'Out with it, whatever it is.'

Livia answers: 'I shall tell you without hesitation, because I have an equal share in your good fortune and ill fortune and as long as you are safe I also have my part in reigning; whereas if you came to any harm, which the Gods forbid, that is the end of me too. ...' She advises forgiveness. 'Soft words turn away wrath, as harsh words excite wrath even in a gentle spirit: forgiveness will melt the most arrogant heart, as punishment will harden even the humblest. ... I do not mean by this that we must spare all criminals without distinction: for there is such a thing as an incurable and persistent depravity on which kindness is wasted. A man who offends in this way should be removed at once as a cancer in the body politic. But in the case of the rest, whose errors, committed wilfully or otherwise, are due to youth or ignorance or misapprehension, we should, I believe, merely rebuke them, or punish them in the mildest possible way. Let us make the experiment, therefore, starting with these very men.' Augustus applauds her wisdom and confesses himself persuaded. But note the reassurance to the world that on Augustus's death Livia's rule would end, and further note and remember the phrase 'incurable and persistent depravity'. My grandmother Livia was a sly one!

Livia now told Augustus that the proposed marriage between Aemilia and myself must be cancelled as a sign of Imperial displeasure with her parents; and Augustus was delighted to agree to this, because Aemilia had been complaining bitterly to him of her misfortune in having to marry me. Livia had little to fear from Julilla now, whom Augustus suspected of being an accomplice in her husband's schemes: but she would make sure of her too, before she had done. Meanwhile she had to pay a debt of honour to her friend Urgulania, a woman whom I have not yet mentioned but who is one of the most unpleasant characters in my story.

Chapter 8

URGULANIA was Livia's only confidante and bound to her by the strongest ties of interest and gratitude. She had lost her husband, a partisan of Young Pompey's, in the Civil Wars and with her infant son had been sheltered by Livia, then still married to my grandfather, from the brutality of Augustus's soldiers. Livia, on marrying Augustus, insisted that he should restore to Urgulania her husband's confiscated estates, and invite her to live with them as a member of the family. By Livia's influence – for in Augustus's name Livia could force Lepidus, the High Pontiff, to make whatever appointments she pleased – she was set in a position of spiritual authority over all the married noblewomen of Rome. I must explain that. Every year, early in December, these women had to attend an important sacrifice to the Good Goddess presided over by the Vestal Virgins, on the proper conduct of which would depend the wealth and security of Rome for the ensuing twelve months. No man was allowed to profane these mysteries on pain of death. Livia, who had put herself into the good graces of the Vestals by rebuilding their Convent, furnishing it in luxurious style, and winning them, through Augustus, many privileges from the Senate, suggested to the Chief Vestal that the chastity of some of the women who attended these sacrifices was not beyond sus-picion. She said that the troubles of Rome during the Civil Wars might well have been due to the Good Goddess's anger at the lewdness of those who attended her mysteries. She suggested further that if a solemn oath were to be given to any woman who confessed to a lapse from moral strictness that her confession would not be reported to any ear of man, and thus not involve her in public disgrace, there would be a greater chance of the Goddess being served only by the chaste, and her anger appeased.

The Chief Vestal, a religiously-minded woman, approved of the idea but asked Livia's authority for this innovation. Livia told her that she had seen the Goddess in a dream only the night before, and that she had asked that, since the Vestals themselves were not experienced in matters of sex, a widow of good family should be appointed Mother Confessor for this very purpose. The Chief Vestal asked whether the sins confessed should pass unpunished. Livia replied that she could not have expressed an opinion had not the Goddess fortunately made a pronouncement on this point in the same dream: that the Mother Confessor would be em-powered to prescribe expiatory penances and that the penances should be a matter of holy confidence between the criminal and the Mother Confessor. The Chief Vestal, she said, would be in-formed merely that such-and-such a woman was unfit to take part in the mysteries of this year; or that such-and-such had now per-formed her penance. This suited the Chief Vestal well, but she was afraid to suggest a name for fear that Livia would turn it down. Livia then said that the High Pontiff was obviously the man to make the appointment, and that if the Chief Vestal permitted her, she would explain matters to him and ask him to name a suitable person, after performing the necessary ceremonies to ensure a choice favourable to the Goddess. So Urgulania was appointed, and of course Livia did not tell Lepidus or Augustus the powers that the appointment carried. She spoke of it casually as a position of advisory assistant to the Chief Vestal in moral matters, 'the Chief Vestal, poor woman, being so unworldly'.

The sacrifice was customarily held at the house of a Consul, but now always at Augustus's palace, because he ranked above the Consuls. This was convenient for Urgulania, who made the women come into her room there (which was arranged in a way to inspire fear and truthfulness), bound them to tell the truth by the most frightful oaths, and when they had confessed, dismissed them while she considered the appropriate penance. Livia, who was in the room concealed behind a curtain, would then suggest one. The two got a great deal of amusement out of this game and Livia plenty of useful information and assistance in her plans.

As Mother Confessor in the service of the Good Goddess, Urgulania considered herself above the law. Later I shall tell how once, when summoned by a senator to whom she owed a large sum of money to appear before the magistrate in the Debtors' Court, she refused to obey the summons; and how, to avoid the scandal, Livia paid up. On another occasion she was subpoenaed as a witness in a Senatorial inquiry: having no intention of being cross-examined she excused herself from attending and a magistrate was sent to take her deposition down in writing instead. She was a dreadful old woman with a cleft chin and hair kept black with lamp-soot (the grey showing plainly at the roots), and she lived to a great age. Her son, Silvanus, had recently been Consul and was one of those whom Aemilius approached at the time of his plot. Silvanus went straight to Urgulania and told her about Aemilius's intentions. She passed the news on to Livia and Livia promised to reward them for this valuable information by marrying Silvanus's daughter Urgulanilla to me and so allying them with the Imperial family. Urgulania was in Livia's confidence and was pretty sure that my uncle Tiberius – not Postumus, though he was Augustus's nearest heir – would be the next Emperor: so this marriage was even more honourable than it seemed.

I had never seen Urgulanilla. Nobody had. We knew that she lived with an aunt at Herculaneum, a town on the slopes of Vesuvius, where old Urgulania had property, but she never came to Rome even on a visit. We concluded that she must be delicate. But when Livia wrote me one of her curt cruel notes, to the effect that it had just been decided at a family council that I should marry the daughter of Silvanus Plautius, and that this was a more appropriate match for me, considering my infirmities, than the two previously projected, I suspected that there was something much more seriously wrong with this Urgulanilla than mere ill-health. A cleft palate, perhaps, or a strawberry-mark across half her face? Something at any rate that made her quite unpresentable. Perhaps she was a cripple like myself. I wouldn't mind that. Perhaps she was a very nice girl really, but misunderstood. We might have a lot in common. Of course, it would not be like marrying Camilla, but it might at least be better than marrying Aemilia.

The day was chosen for our betrothal. I asked Germanicus about Urgulanilla, but he was as much in the dark as I was, and seemed a little ashamed of having consented to the marriage without making careful inquiries beforehand. He was very happy with Agrippina and wanted me to be happy too. Well, the day came, a 'lucky' one, and there I was again in my chaplet and clean gown again waiting at the family-altar for the bride to arrive. 'The third time's lucky,' said Germanicus. 'I am sure she's a beauty, really, and kind and sensible and just the sort for you.' But was she? Well, in my life I have had many cruel bad jokes played on me, but I think that this was the cruellest and worst. Urgulanilla was – well, in brief, she lived up to her name, which is the Latin form of Herculanilla. A young female Hercules she indeed was. Though only fifteen years old, she was over six foot three inches in height and still growing, and broad and strong in proportion, with the largest feet and hands I have ever seen on any human being in my life with the single exception of the gigantic Parthian hostage who walked in a certain triumphal procession many years later. Her features were regular but heavy and she wore an almost perpetual scowl. She stooped. She talked as slowly as my uncle Tiberius (whom, by the way, she resembled closely – there was even talk of her being really his daughter). She had no learning, wit, accomplishments, or any endearing qualities. And it is strange, but the first thoughts that struck me when I saw her were: 'This woman is capable of murder by violence' and 'I shall be very careful from the first to hide my repugnance to her, and give her no just cause to harbour resentment against me. For if once she comes to hate me, my life is not safe.' I am a pretty good actor, and though the solemnity of the ceremony was broken by smirks, whispered jokes, and repressed titters from the company, Urgulanilla had no cause to blame me for this indecorousness. After it was over the two of us were summoned into the presence of Livia and Urgulania. When the door was shut and we stood there facing them – myself nervous and fidgety, Urgulanilla massive and expressionless and clenching and unclenching her great fists – the solemnity of these two evil old grandmothers gave way, and they burst into uncontrollable laughter. I had never heard either of them laugh like that before and the effect was frightening. It was not decent healthy laughter but a hellish sobbing and screeching, like that of two old drunken prostitutes watching a torture or crucifixion. 'Oh, you two beauties!' sobbed Livia at last, wiping her eyes. 'What wouldn't I give to see you in bed together on your wedding night! It would be the funniest scene since Deucalion's Flood!'

'And what happened particularly funny on that famous occasion, my dear?' asked Urgulania.

'Why, don't you know? God destroyed the whole world with a flood, except Deucalion and his family, and a few animals that took refuge on the mountain tops. Haven't you read Aristophanes's *Flood*? It's my favourite play of his. The scene is laid on Mount Parnassus. Various animals are assembled, unfortunately only one of each kind, and each thinks himself the sole survivor of his species. So in order to replenish the earth somehow with animals they have to mate with one another in spite of moral scruples and obvious difficulties. The Camel is betrothed by Deucalion to the She-Elephant.'

'Camel and Elephant! That's a fine one!' cackled Urgulania. 'Look at Tiberius Claudius's long neck and skinny body and long silly face. And my Urgulanilla's great feet and great flapping ears, and little pig-eyes! Ha, Ha, Ha, Ha! And what was their off-spring? Giraffe? Ha, Ha, Ha, Ha!'

'The play doesn't get that far. Iris comes on the stage for the messenger speech and reports another refuge of animals on Mount Atlas Iris breaks off the nuptials just in time.'

'Was the Camel disappointed?'

'Oh, most bitterly.'

'And the Elephant?'

'The Elephant just scowled.'

'Did they kiss on parting?'

'Aristophanes does not tell. But I'm sure they did. Come on, Beasts. Kiss!'

I smiled foolishly, Urgulanilla scowled.

'Kiss, I say,' Livia insisted in a voice that meant that we had to obey.

So we kissed, and started the old women on their hysterics again. When we were outside the room again I whispered to Urgulanilla: 'I'm sorry. It's not my fault.' But she did not answer except to scowl more deeply than before.

There was still a year before we were actually to marry, for the family had decided that I should not come of age until I was fifteen and a half, and much might happen in that time. If only Iris would come!

But she didn't. Postumus had his troubles too: he had already come of age now and it was only a few months before Domitia would be of marriageable age. My poor Postumus, he was still in love with Livilla, though she was married. But before I continue with the story of Postumus I must tell of my meeting with the 'Last of the Romans'.

Chapter 9

HIS name was Pollio and I shall recall the exact circumstances of our meeting, which took place just a week after my betrothal to Urgulanilla. I was reading in the Apollo Library when along came Livy and a little brisk old man in the robe of a senator. Livy was saying: 'It seems, then, that we may as well abandon all hopes of finding it, unless perhaps ... Why, there's Sulpicius! *He'll* know if anyone does. Good morning, Sulpicius. I want you to do a favour for Asinius Pollio and myself. There's a book we want to look at, a commentary by a Greek called Polemocles on Polybius's *Military Tactics*. I seem to remember coming across it here once, but the catalogue does not mention it and the librarians here are perfectly useless.' Sulpicius gnawed his beard for a while and then said: 'You've got the name wrong. Polemocrates was the name and he wasn't a Greek, in spite of his name, but a Jew. Fifteen years ago I remember seeing it on that top shelf, the fourth from the window, right at the back, and the title tag had just "A Dissertation on Tactics" on it. Let me get it for you. I don't expect it's been moved since then.'

Then Livy saw me. 'Hullo, my friend, how goes it? Do you know the famous Asinius Pollio?'

I saluted them and Pollio said: 'What's that you're reading, boy? Trash, I'll be bound, by the shamefaced way you hide it. Young fellows nowadays read only trash.' He turned to Livy: 'I'll bet you ten gold pieces that it's some wretched "Art of Love", or Arcadian pastoral nonsense, or something of that sort.'

'I'll take the bet,' said Livy. 'Young Claudius is not that sort of young man at all. Well, Claudius, which of us wins?'

I said, stammering, to Pollio: 'I'm glad to say, sir, that you lose.'

Pollio frowned angrily at me: 'What's that you say? Glad that I *lose*, eh? Is that a proper way to speak to an old man like me, and a senator too?'

I said: 'I said it in all respect, sir. I am glad that you lose. I should not like to hear this book called trash. It's your own history of the Civil Wars and, if I may venture to praise it, a very fine book indeed.'

Pollio's face changed. He beamed and chuckled and pulled out his purse, pressing the coins on Livy. Livy, with whom he seemed on terms of friendly animosity – if you know what I mean – refused them with mock-serious insistence. 'My dear Pollio, I couldn't possibly take the money. You were quite right: these young fellows nowadays read the most wretched stuff. Not another word, please: I agree that I've lost the bet. Here are ten gold pieces of my own and I'm glad to pay them.'

Pollio appealed to me. 'Now, sir – I don't know who you are but you seem to be a lad of sense – have you read our friend Livy's work? I appeal to you, isn't that at least trashier writing than mine?'

I smiled. 'Well, at least it's easier to read.'

'Easier, eh? How's that?'

'He makes the people of Ancient Rome behave and talk as if they were alive now.'

Pollio was delighted. 'He has you there, Livy, on your weakest spot. You credit the Romans of seven centuries ago with impossibly modern motives and habits and speeches. Yes, it's readable all right, but it's not history.'

Before I record more of this conversation I must say a few words about old Pollio, perhaps the most gifted man of his day, not even excepting Augustus. He was now nearly eighty years old but in full possession of his mental powers and seemingly in better physical health than many a man of sixty. He had crossed the Rubicon with Julius Caesar and fought with him against Pompey, and served under my grandfather Antony, before his quarrel with Augustus, and had been Consul and Governor of Further Spain and of Lombardy, and had won a triumph for a victory in the

Balkans and had been a personal friend of Cicero's until he grew disgusted with him, and a patron of the poets, Virgil and Horace. Besides all this he was a distinguished orator and writer of tragedies. But he was a better historian than he was either tragedian or orator, because he had a love of literal truth, amounting to pedantry, which he could not square with the conventions of these other literary forms. With the spoils of the Balkan campaign he had founded a public library, the first public library at Rome. There were now two others: the one we were in and another called after my grandmother Octavia; but Pollio's was much better organized for reading purposes than either.

Sulpicius had now found the book, and after a word of thanks to him, they renewed their argument.

Livy said: 'The trouble with Pollio is that when he writes history he feels obliged to suppress all his finer, more poetical feelings, and make his characters behave with conscientious dullness, and when he puts a speech into their mouths he denies them the least oratorical ability.'

Pollio said: 'Yes, Poetry is Poetry, and Oratory is Oratory, and History is History, and you can't mix them.'

'Can't I? Indeed I can,' said Livy. 'Do you mean to say that I mustn't write a history with an epic theme because that's a prerogative of poetry, or put worthy eve-of-battle speeches in the mouths of my generals because to compose such speeches is the prerogative of oratory?'

'That is precisely what I do mean. History is a true record of what happened, how people lived and died, what they did and said; an epic theme merely distorts the record. As for your generals' speeches they are admirable as oratory but damnably unhistorical: not only is there no particle of evidence for any one of them, but they are inappropriate. I have heard more eve-of-battle speeches than most men and though the generals that made them, Caesar and Antony especially, were remarkably fine platform orators, they were all too good soldiers to try any platform business on the troops. They *spoke* to them in a conversational way, they did not orate. What sort of speech did Caesar make before the Battle of Pharsalia? Did he beg us to remember our wives and children and the sacred temples of Rome and the glories of our past campaigns? By God, he didn't! He climbed up on the stump of a pine-tree with one of those monster-radishes in one hand and a lump of hard soldiers' bread in the other, and joked, between mouthfuls. Not dainty jokes but the real stuff told with the straightest face: about how chaste Pompey's life was compared with his own reprobate one. The things he did with that radish would have made an ox laugh. I remember one broad anecdote about how Pompey won his surname The Great – oh, that radish! – and another still worse one about how he himself had lost his hair in the Bazaar at Alexandria. I'd tell you them both now but for this boy here, and but for your being certain to miss the point, not having been educated in Caesar's camp. Not a word about the approaching battle except just at the close: "Poor old Pompey! Up against Julius Caesar and his men! What a chance he has"!'

'You didn't put any of this in your history,' said Livy.

'Not in the public editions,' said Pollio. 'I'm not a fool. Still, if you like to borrow the private *Supplement* which I have just finished writing, you'll find it there. But perhaps you'll never bother. I'll tell you the rest: Caesar was a wonderful mimic, you know, and he gave them Pompey's dying speech, preparatory to falling on his sword (the radish again – with the end bitten off). He railed, in Pompey's name, at the Immortal Gods for always allowing vice to triumph over virtue. How they laughed! Then he bellowed: "And isn't it true, though Pompey says it? Deny it if you can, you damned fornicating dogs, you!" And he flung the half-radish at them. The roar that went up! Never were there soldiers like Caesar's. Do you remember the song they sang at his French triumph?

"Home we bring the bald whoremonger,
Romans, lock your wives away." '

Livy said: 'Pollio, my dear fellow, we were not discussing Caesar's morals, but the proper way to write history.'

Pollio said: 'Yes, that's right. Our intelligent young friend was criticizing your method, under the respectful disguise of praising your readability. Boy, have you any further charges to bring against the noble Livy?'

I said: 'Please, sir, don't make me blush. I admire Livy's work greatly.'

'The truth, boy! Have you ever caught him out in any historical inaccuracies? You seem to be a fellow who reads a good deal.'

'I would rather not venture ...'

'Out with it. There must be something.'

So I said: 'There *is* one thing that puzzles me, I confess. That is the story of Lars Porsena. According to Livy, Porsena failed to capture Rome, being first prevented by the heroic behaviour of Horatius at the bridge and then dismayed by the astounding daring of Scaevola; Livy relates that Scaevola, captured after an attempt at assassinating Porsena, thrust his hand into the flame on the altar and swore that three hundred Romans like himself had bound themselves by an oath to take Porsena's life. And so Lars Porsena made peace. But I have seen the labyrinth tomb of Lars Porsena at Clusium and there is a frieze on it of Romans emerging from the City gate and being led under a yoke. There's an Etruscan priest with a pair of shears cutting off the beards of the Fathers. And even Dionysius of Halicarnassus, who was very favourably disposed towards us, states that the Senate voted Porsena an ivory throne, a sceptre, a golden crown, and a triumphal robe; which can only mean that they paid him sovereign honours. So perhaps Lars Porsena *did* capture Rome, in spite of Horatius and Scaevola. And Aruns the priest at Capua (he's supposed to be the last man who can read Etruscan inscriptions) told me last summer that according to Etruscan records the man who expelled the Tarquins from Rome was not Brutus but Porsena, and that Brutus and Collatinus, the first two Consuls at Rome, were merely the City Stewards appointed to collect his taxes.'

Livy grew quite angry. 'I am surprised at you, Claudius. Have you no reverence for Roman tradition that you should believe the lies told by our ancient enemies to diminish our greatness?'

'I only asked,' I said humbly, 'what really happened then.'

'Come on, Livy,' said Pollio. 'Answer the young student. What really happened?'

Livy said: 'Another time. Let's keep to the matter in hand now, which is a general discussion of the proper way to write history. Claudius, my friend, you have ambitions that way. Which of us two old worthies will you choose as a model?'

'You make it very difficult for the boy, you jealous fellows,' put in Sulpicius. 'What do you expect him to answer?'

'The truth will offend neither of us,' answered Pollio.

I looked from one face to the other. At last I said, 'I think I would choose Pollio. As I am sure that I can never hope to attain

106

Livy's inspired literary elegance, I shall do my best to imitate Pollio's accuracy and diligence.'

Livy grunted and was about to walk off, but Pollio restrained him. Bottling down his glee as well as he could he said: 'Come, Livy, you won't grudge me one little disciple, will you, when you have them in regiments all over the world? Boy, did you ever hear about the old man from Cadiz? No, it's not dirty. In fact, it's rather sad. He came on foot to Rome, what to see? Not the temples or the theatres or the statues or the crowds or the shops or the Senate House. But a Man. What man? The man whose head is on the coins? No, no. A greater than he. He came to see none other than our friend Livy, whose works, it seems, he knew by heart. He saw him and saluted him and went straight back to Cadiz – where he immediately died; the disillusion and the long walk had been too much for him.'

Livy said: 'At any rate my readers are genuine readers. Boy, do you know how Pollio has built up his reputation? Well, he's rich and has a very large, beautiful house and a surprisingly good cook. He invites a great crowd of literary people to dinner, gives them a perfect meal and afterwards casually picks up the latest volume of his history. He says humbly, "Gentlemen, there are a few passages here that I am not quite sure about. I have worked very hard at them but they still need the final polish which I am counting on you to give them. By your leave. ..." Then he begins to read. Nobody listens very carefully. Everyone's belly is stuffed. "The cook's a genius," they are all thinking. "The mullet with piquant sauce, and those fat stuffed thrushes and the wild-boar with truffles – when did I eat so well last? Not since Pollio's last reading, I believe. Ah, here comes the slave with the wine again. That excellent Cyprian wine. Pollio's right: it's better than any Greek wine on the market." Meanwhile Pollio's voice – and it's a nice voice to listen to, like a priest's at evening sacrifice in summer – goes smoothly on and every now and then he asks humbly, "Is that all right, do you think?" And everyone says, thinking of the thrushes again, or perhaps of the little simnel cakes: "Admirable. Admirable, Pollio." Now and then he will pause and ask: "Now which is the right word to use here? Shall I say that the returning envoys *persuaded* or *excited* this tribe to revolt? Or shall I say that the account they gave of the situation *influenced* the tribe in its decision to revolt? Actually, I think, they gave an impartial account of what they had seen." Then a murmur goes up from the couches, "*Influenced*, Pollio. Use *influenced*!" "Thank you, friends," he says, "you are very kind. Slave, my penknife and pen! I'll change the sentence at once if you'll forgive me." Then he publishes the book and sends each of the diners a free copy. They say to their friends, chatting at the Public Baths: "Admirable book, this. Have you read it? Pollio's the greatest historian of our age; and not above asking advice in small points of style from men of taste, either. Why, this word *influenced* I gave him myself."'

Pollio said: 'That's right. My cook's too good. Next time I'll borrow yours and a few dozen bottles of your so-called Falernian wine and then I'll get really honest criticism.'

Sulpicius made a gesture of deprecation: 'Gentlemen, gentlemen, this is becoming personal.'

Livy was already going away. But Pollio grinned at the retreating back and said in a loud voice for his benefit:

'A decent fellow, Livy is, but there's one thing wrong with him. It's a disease called Paduanity.'

This made Livy stop and turn round. 'What's wrong with Padua? I won't hear a word against the place.'

Pollio explained to me. 'It's where he was born, you know. Somewhere in the Northern Provinces. There's a famous hotspring there, of extraordinary properties. You can always tell a Paduan. By bathing in the water of the spring or drinking it – and I'm told that they do both things simultaneously – Paduans are able to believe whatever they like and believe it so strongly that they can make anyone else believe it. That's how the city has got such a wonderful commercial reputation. The blankets and rugs they make there are really no better than any other sort, in fact rather inferior, because the local sheep are yellow and coarse-fleeced, but to the Paduans they are soft and white as goose-feathers. And they have persuaded the rest of the world that it's so.'

I said, playing up to him: 'Yellow sheep! That's a rarity. How do they get that colour, sir?'

'Why, by drinking the spring water. There's sulphur in it. All Paduans are yellow. Look at Livy.'

Livy came slowly towards us. 'A joke is a joke, Pollio, and I can take it in good part. But there's also a serious matter in question and that is, the proper writing of history. It may be that I have

108

made mistakes. What historian is free from them? I have not, at least, told deliberate falsehoods: you'll not accuse me of that. Any legendary episode from early historical writings which bears on my theme of the ancient greatness of Rome I gladly incorporate in the story: though it may not be true in factual detail, it is true in spirit. If I come across two versions of the same episode I choose the one nearest my theme, and you won't find me grubbing around Etruscan cemeteries in search of any third account which may flatly contradict both – what good would that do?'

'It would serve the cause of the truth,' said Pollio gently. 'Wouldn't that be something?'

'And if by serving the cause of truth we admit our revered ancestors to have been cowards, liars, and traitors? What then?'

'I'll leave this boy to answer the question. He's just starting in life. Come on, boy, answer it!'

I said at random: 'Livy begins his history by lamenting modern wickedness and promising to trace the gradual decline of ancient virtue as conquests made Rome wealthy. He says that he will most enjoy writing the early chapters because he will be able, in doing so, to close his eyes to the wickedness of modern times. But in closing his eyes to modern wickedness hasn't he sometimes closed his eyes to ancient wickedness as well?'

'Well?' asked Livy, narrowing his eyes.

'Well,' I fumbled. 'Perhaps there isn't so much difference really between their wickedness and ours. It may be just a matter of scope and opportunity.'

Pollio said: 'In fact, boy, the Paduan hasn't made you see his sulphur fleeces as snow-white?'

I was very uncomfortable. 'I have got more pleasure from reading Livy than from any other author,' I repeated.

'Oh, yes,' Pollio grinned, 'that's just what the old man of Cadiz said. But like the old man of Cadiz you feel a little disillusioned now, eh? Lars Porsena and Scaevola and Brutus and company stick in your throat?'

'It's not disillusion, sir. I see now, though I hadn't considered the matter before, that there are two different ways of writing history: one is to persuade men to virtue and the other is to compel men to truth. The first is Livy's way and the other is yours: and perhaps they are not irreconcilable.'

'Why, boy, you're an orator,' said Pollio delightedly.

Sulpicius, who had been standing on one leg with his foot held in his hand, as his habit was when excited or impatient, and twisting his beard in knots, now summed up: 'Yes, Livy will never lack readers. People love being "persuaded to ancient virtue" by a charming writer, particularly when they are told in the same breath that modern civilization has made such virtue impossible of attainment. But mere truth-tellers – "undertakers who lay out the corpse of history" (to quote poor Catullus's epigram on the noble Pollio) – people who record no more than actually occurred – such men can only hold an audience while they have a good cook and a cellar of Cyprian wine.'

This made Livy really furious. He said, 'Pollio, this talk is idle. Young Claudius here has always been considered dull-witted by his family and friends, but I didn't agree with the general verdict until to-day. You're welcome to your disciple. And Sulpicius can perfect his dullness: there's no better teacher of dullness in Rome.' Then he gave us his Parthian shot: *Et apud Apollinem istum Pollionis Pollinctorem diutissime polleat.* Which means, though the pun is lost in Greek, 'And may he flourish long at the shrine of that Undertaker Apollo of Pollio's!' Then off he went, snorting.

Pollio shouted cheerfully after him: '*Quod certe pollicitur Pollio. Pollucibiliter pollebit puer.*' ('Pollio promises you he will; the boy will flourish mightily.')

When we two were alone, Sulpicius having gone off to find a book, Pollio began questioning me.

'Who are you, boy? Claudius is your name, isn't it? You obviously come of good family, but I don't know you.'

'I am Tiberius Claudius Drusus Nero Germanicus.'

'My God! But Livy's right. You're supposed to be a half-wit.'

'Yes. My family is ashamed of me because I stammer, and I'm lame and usually ill, so I go about very little in society.'

'But dull-witted? You're one of the brightest young fellows I have met for years.'

'You are very kind, sir.'

'Not at all. By God, that was a nasty hit at old Livy about Lars Porsena. Livy has no conscience, that's the truth. I'm always catching him out. I asked him once if he always had the same trouble in finding the brass tablets he wanted among the litter of the Public Record Office. He said, "Oh, no trouble at all." And it turned out that he has never once been there to confirm a single fact! Tell me, why were you reading my history?'

'I was reading your account of the siege of Perusia. My grandfather – Livia's first husband, you know – was there. I'm interested in that period and I'm getting together materials for a life of my father. My tutor Athenodorus referred me to your book: he said it was honest. My former tutor, Marcus Porcius Cato, had once told me that it was a tissue of lies, so I was the more ready to believe Athenodorus.'

'Yes, Cato wouldn't like the book. The Catos fought on the wrong side. I helped to drive his grandfather out of Sicily. But I think you are the first youthful historian I have ever met. History is an old man's game. When are you going to win battles like your father and grandfather?'

'Perhaps in my old age.'

He laughed. 'I don't see why an historian who has made a life-study of military tactics shouldn't be invincible as a commander, given good troops and courage – –'

'And good staff-officers,' I put in, remembering Cleon.

'*And* good staff-officers, certainly – though he's never actually handled a sword or shield in his life.'

I was bold enough to ask Pollio why he was often called 'The Last of the Romans'. He looked pleased at the question and replied: 'Augustus gave me the name. It was when he invited me to join him in his war against your grandfather Antony. I asked him what sort of a man he took me for: Antony had been one of my best friends. "Asinius Pollio," he said, "I believe that you're the last of the Romans. The title is wasted on that assassin, Cassius." "And if I'm the last of the Romans," I answered, "whose fault is that? And whose fault will it be when you've destroyed Antony, that nobody but myself will ever dare hold his head up in your presence or speak out of turn?" "Not mine, Asinius," he said apologetically, "it is Antony who has declared war, not I. And as soon as Antony is beaten I shall of course restore Republican government." "If the Lady Livia does not interpose her veto," I said.'

The old man then took me by the shoulders. 'By the way, I'll tell you something, Claudius. I'm a very old man, and though I look brisk enough I have reached the end. In three days I shall be dead; and I know it. Just before one dies there comes a strange

111

lucidity. One speaks prophetically. Now listen! Do you want to live a long busy life, with honour at the end of it?'

'Yes.'

'Then exaggerate your limp, stammer deliberately, sham sickness frequently, let your wits wander, jerk your head, and twitch with your hands on all public or semi-public occasions. If you could see as much as I can see you would know that this was your only hope of safety and eventual glory.'

I said: 'Livy's story of Brutus – the first Brutus, I mean – may be unhistorical, but it's apt. Brutus pretended to be a half-wit, too, to be better able to restore popular liberty.'

'What's that? Popular liberty? You believe in that? I thought the phrase had died out among the younger generation.'

'My father and grandfather both believed in it – –'

'Yes,' Pollio interrupted sharply, 'that's why they died.'

'What do you mean?'

'I mean, that's why they were poisoned.'

'*Poisoned!* By whom?'

'Hm! Not so loud, boy. No, I'll not mention names. But I'll give you a sure token that I'm not just repeating groundless scandal. You're writing a life of your father, you say?'

'Yes.'

'Well, you'll see that you won't be allowed to get beyond a certain point in it. And the person who stops you – –'

Sulpicius came shuffling back at this point and nothing more was said of any interest except when I took my leave of Pollio and he drew me aside and muttered: 'Little Claudius, good-bye! But don't be a fool about popular liberty. That cannot come yet. Things must be far worse before they can be better.' Then he raised his voice: 'And one thing more. If, when I'm dead, you ever come across any important point in my histories that you find unhistorical I give you permission – I'll stipulate that you have the authority – to put the corrections in a supplement. Keep them up to date. Books when they grow out of date only serve as wrappings for fish.' I said that this would be an honourable duty.

Three days later Pollio died. He left me in his will a collection of early Latin histories, but they were withheld from me. My uncle Tiberius said that it was a mistake: that they were intended for him, our names being so similar. His stipulation about my having the authority to make corrections everyone treated as a joke; but I kept my promise to Pollio some twenty years later. I found that he had written very severely on the character of Cicero – a vain, vacillating, timorous fellow – and while not disagreeing with this verdict I felt it necessary to point out that he was not a traitor too, as Pollio had made him out. Pollio was relying on some correspondence of Cicero's which I was able to prove a forgery by Clodius Pulcher. Cicero had incurred Clodius's enmity by witnessing against him when he was accused of attending the sacrifice of the Good Goddess disguised as a woman-musician. This Clodius was another of the bad Claudians.

Chapter 10

WHEN I came of age, Tiberius had lately been ordered by Augustus to adopt Germanicus as his son, though he already had Castor as an heir, thus bringing him over from the Claudian into the Julian family. I now found myself head of the senior branch of the Claudians and in indisputable possession   A.D. 6 of the money and estates inherited from my father. I became my mother's guardian – for she had never married again – which she felt as a humiliation. She treated me with rather more severity than before, though all business documents had to come to me for signature and I was the family priest. My coming of age ceremony contrasted curiously with that of Germanicus. I put on my manly-gown at midnight and without any attendants or procession was carried into the Capitol in a sedan, where I sacrificed and was then carried back to bed. Germanicus and Postumus would have come, but in order to call as little attention to me as possible Livia had arranged a banquet that night at the Palace which they could not be excused from attending.

When I married Urgulanilla, the same sort of thing happened. Very few people were aware of our marriage until the day after it had been solemnized. There was nothing irregular about the ceremony. Urgulanilla's saffron-coloured shoes and flame-coloured veil, the taking of the auspices, the eating of holy cake, the two stools covered with sheepskin, the libation I poured, the anointing by her of the doorposts, the three coins, my present to her of fire and water – everything was in order, except that the torchlight procession was omitted and that the whole performance was carried through perfunctorily and hurriedly and with bad grace. In order not to stumble over her husband's threshold the first time she enters, a Roman bride is always lifted over it. The two Claudians who had to do the lifting were both elderly men and unequal to Urgulanilla's weight. One of them slipped on the marble and Urgulanilla came down with a bump, pulling them with her in a sprawling heap. There is no wedding omen worse than that. And yet it would be untrue to say that it turned out an unhappy marriage; there was not enough strain between us to justify the term unhappy. We slept together at first because that seemed expected of us, and even occasionally had sexual relations – my first experience of sex – because that too seemed part of marriage, and not from either lust or affection. I was always as considerate and courteous to her as possible and she rewarded me by indifference, which was the best that I could hope from a woman of her character. She became pregnant three months after our marriage and bore me a son called Drusillus, for whom I found it impossible to have any fatherly feeling. He took after my sister Livilla in spitefulness and after Urgulanilla's brother Plautius in the rest of his character. Soon I shall tell you about Plautius, who was my moral exemplar and paragon, appointed by Augustus.

Augustus and Livia had a methodical habit of never coming to any decision on any important matter relating to the family or the State without recording in writing both the decision and the deliberations that led up to it, usually in the form of letters exchanged between each other. From the mass of correspondence left behind them on their deaths I have made transcripts of several which illustrate Augustus's attitude to me at this time. My first extract is dated three years before my marriage.

My dear Livia,

I wish to put on record a strange thing that happened to-day. I hardly know what to make of it. I was talking to Athenodorus and happened to say to him: 'I fear that tutoring young Tiberius Claudius must be rather a weary task. He seems to me to grow daily more miserable-looking and nervous and incapable.' Athenodorus said: 'Don't judge the boy too harshly. He feels most keenly the family's disappointment in him and the slights that he everywhere meets. But he's very far from incapable and, believe it or not, I get great pleasure from his society. You never heard him declaim, did you!' 'Declaim!' I said, laughing. 'Yes, declaim,' Athenodorus repeated. 'Now let me make a suggestion. You set a subject for declamation and in half an hour's time come and hear what he makes of it. But hide behind a curtain or you'll hear nothing worth listening to.' I set for a subject 'Roman Conquests in Germany' and, listening half an hour later behind that curtain, I have never been so astonished before in my life. He had his facts at his fingers' ends, his main headings were well chosen, and his detail set in proper relation and proportion to them; more than this, his voice was under control and *he did not stammer*. God strike me dead if it wasn't positively pleasant and instructive to listen to him! But how a fellow whose daily conversation is so hopelessly foolish can make a set speech, at short notice too, in so perfectly rational and even learned a style is beyond me. I slipped away, telling Athenodorus not to mention that I had been there or how surprised I had been, but feel obliged to tell you of the matter, and even to suggest that we might henceforth occasionally allow him to dine with us at night, when there are few guests there, on the understanding that he keeps his mouth shut and his ears open. If there is, after all, as I am inclined to think, some hope that he will eventually turn out a responsible member of the family, he ought to be gradually accustomed to mix with his social equals. We can't keep him shut away with his tutors and freedmen for ever. There is, of course, great division of opinion on the question of his mental capacities. His uncle Tiberius, his mother Antonia and his sister Livilla are unanimous in regarding him as an idiot. On the other side, Athenodorus, Sulpicius, Postumus, and Germanicus swear that he's as sensible, when he wishes, as any man, but that he's easily put off his balance by nervousness. As for myself, I repeat that I cannot make up my mind on the matter yet.

To which Livia replied:

My dear Augustus,

The surprise that you had behind that curtain was no greater and no less than the surprise we once had when the Indian Ambassador took the silk cloth off the gold cage which his master the High King had sent us, and we saw the bird Parrot for the first time with his emerald feathers and ruby necklet and heard him say, 'Hail Caesar, Father of the Country!' It was not the remarkableness of the phrase, for any little lisping child can say as much, but that a *bird* spoke it astonished us. And nobody but a fool would praise Parrot for his wit in coming out with the appropriate words, for he did not know the meaning of any one of them. The credit goes to the man who trained the bird, by incredible patience, to repeat the phrase, for, as you know, on other occasions he is trained to say other things; and in general conversation he talks the most arrant nonsense and we have to keep his cage covered to silence him. So with

115

Claudius, though it is hardly complimentary to Parrot, an undeniably handsome bird, to compare my grandson to him: what you heard was without the least doubt a speech that he had happened to learn by heart. After all, 'Roman Conquests in Germany' is a very obvious subject, and Athenodorus may well have made him word-perfect in half a dozen or more model declamations of the same sort. Mind you, I don't say that I'm not pleased to hear that he is so amenable to training: I am extremely pleased. It means, for instance, that we shall be able to coach him through his marriage-ceremony. But your suggestion about his supping with us is ridiculous. I refuse ever to eat in the same room as that fellow: it would give me indigestion.

As for the testimony in favour of his mental soundness, examine it. Germanicus as a child swore to his dying father to love and protect his infant brother: you know Germanicus's nobility of soul and that rather than betray this sacred trust he would make out the best case possible for his brother's wits, hoping that they might happen one day to improve. It is equally clear why Athenodorus and Sulpicius pretend to consider him improvable: they are very well paid to improve him and their appointments give them an excuse for hanging about the Palace and giving themselves airs as privy counsellors. As for Postumus, I have been complaining now for some months past, haven't I, that I cannot understand that young man at all. I consider that Death has been extremely unkind to take off his two talented brothers and leave us only him. He delights in starting an argument with his seniors, where no argument is necessary, the facts being clearly beyond dispute, merely to exasperate us and show his own importance as your single surviving grandson. His championship of Claudius's intelligence is a case in point. He was positively insolent to me the other day when I happened to remark that Sulpicius was wasting his time in tutoring the boy: he actually said that in his opinion Claudius had more penetration than most of his immediate relatives – which I suppose was intended to include me! But Postumus is another problem. For the moment the question is about Claudius; and I cannot, I repeat, have him dining in my company – for physical reasons, which I hope you will appreciate.

Livia.

He wrote to Livia a year later, when she was away for a few days in the country:

... As for young Claudius I shall take the advantage of your absence to invite him to supper every night. I admit that his presence still embarrasses me, but I do not think it good for him always to sup alone with his Sulpicius and Athenodorus. The talk he has with them is too purely bookish and, excellent fellows though they both are, they are not

116

ideal companions for a boy of his age and station. I do sincerely wish that he would choose some young man of rank on whose bearing and dress and behaviour he might model his own. But his timidity and diffidence prevent this. He has a hero-worship for our dear Germanicus, but he feels his own shortcomings so keenly that he would no more dare to imitate him than I would go about in lion's skin and club and call myself Hercules. The poor creature is unfortunate; for in matters of importance (when his mind is not wool-gathering) the nobility of his heart is clearly shown. ....

A third letter written shortly after my marriage, when I had just been nominated as a priest of Mars, is also of interest:

My dear Livia,

As you advised me, I have discussed with our Tiberius what we are to do about young Claudius when these Games in honour of Mars are held. Now that he has come of age and been appointed to the vacancy in the College of the Priests of Mars we cannot put off our decision with regard to his future much longer: we agree about that, do we not? If he is sufficiently sound in mind and body to be eventually recognized as a reputable member of the family – as I believe he is, or I would not have adopted both Tiberius and Germanicus and left him as head of the senior branch of the Claudian house – then obviously he should be taken in hand and given the same opportunities for advancement as Germanicus. I admit that I may still be mistaken – his recent improvement has not been striking. But if we decide that, after all, the infirmities of his body are bound up with a settled infirmity of mind, we must not give malicious people a chance of making fun of him and us. I repeat, we must decide pretty quickly once and for all about the lad – if only because we would find it a continual trouble and embarrassment if we had to decide afresh on every occasion that presented itself whether or not we considered him able to undertake those duties of State for which his birth befits him.

Well, the immediate question is, what to do about him at these Games. I would have no objection to his being put in charge of the priests' mess-room, but on the strict understanding that he leaves everything to his brother-in-law, young Plautius Silvanus, and merely does what he is told. He could learn a good deal in this way and there is no reason for him to disgrace himself if he learns his lesson well. But of course it is out of the question for him to sit with me in the President's Box, along with the sacred Statue, for everybody in the theatre will constantly be looking in that direction and any oddities in his behaviour will be commented upon.

Another problem is what to do with him at the Latin Festival. Germanicus is going to the Alban Hill with the Consuls to take part in the sacrifice and Claudius wishes, I understand, to go with him. But there again I am not sure whether he can be trusted not to make a fool of himself: Germanicus will be busy with his duties and unable to look after him all the time. And if he does go people will want to know what he's doing there in any case; they will ask why we have not appointed him to act as City Warden at Rome for the duration of the festival, in the absence of the magistrates – an honour which, you will recall, we have granted in turn to Gaius, Lucius, Germanicus, young Tiberius, and Postumus, as soon as they came of age, as their first taste of office. The best way out of the difficulty is to report him sick, because, of course, the City Wardenship is out of the question for him.

If you care to show Antonia this letter I have no objection: assure her that we shall soon decide one way or the other about her son. It is an incongruous position for her to be legally under his guardianship.

Augustus.

Except that it was my first public duty there is nothing remarkable to record about my management of the priests' mess. Plautius, a vain, natty little cock-sparrow of a man, did all the work for me and did not even trouble to explain the catering system and the rules of priestly precedence; even refused to answer my questions about such matters. All he did was to drill me in certain formal gestures and phrases which I was to use on welcoming the priests and at various stages of the meal; and forbade me to say another word. This was extremely uncomfortable for me because frequently I could have taken a useful part in the conversation, and my dumbness and subservience to Plautius gave a bad impression. The games themselves I did not see.

You will have noticed Livia's disparaging remarks about Postumus. From this time on they grow more and more frequent in her letters and Augustus, though at first he tries to stand up for his grandson, gradually admits disappointment in him. I think that Livia must have told Augustus a good deal more than appears in their correspondence for Postumus to have forfeited his favour so easily; but certain definite things appear. First, Tiberius is reported by Livia as complaining of an impudent reference by Postumus to the University of Rhodes. Then Cato is reported by her as complaining of Postumus's bad influence on the younger scholars in defying his discipline; then Livia produces Cato's confidential reports, saying that she has held them back so long in hope of a change. Next come worried references to his morose-ness and sullenness – this was the time of Postumus's disappoint-ment over Livilla and his grief for the death of his brother Gaius. Then there is a recommendation, when he comes of age, that the whole of his inheritance from his father Agrippa shall not be made over to him for a few years, because that 'might give him oppor-tunities for even greater profligacy than he now indulges in!' When he is enrolled among the young men of military age he is posted to the Guards as a simple staff-lieutenant and given none of the extraordinary honours awarded to Gaius and Lucius. Au-gustus himself is of opinion that this is the safest course to take, for Postumus is ambitious: the same sort of uncomfortable situa-tion must not arise as when the young nobles supported Marcellus against Agrippa or Gaius against Tiberius. Soon we read that Postumus takes this ill, telling Augustus that he does not want the honours on their own account but that their being withheld has been misinterpreted by his friends, who believe him under a cloud at the Palace.

Then follow more serious notes. Postumus has lost his temper with Plautius – but neither of the two will tell Livia later what the circumstances of their quarrel were – and has picked him up and thrown him into a fountain, in the presence of several men of rank and their lackeys. He is then called to account by Augustus, and shows no contrition, insisting that Plautius deserved his ducking for speaking in an insulting way to me; at the same time he com-plains to Augustus that his inheritance is being unjustly withheld. Soon he is reprimanded by Livia for his changed manner and for his surliness towards her. 'What's poisoned you?' she asks. He replies, grinning, 'Maybe you've been putting something in my soup.' When she demands an explanation of this extraordinary joke he replies, grinning still more vulgarly: 'Putting things in soup is an old trick among stepmothers.' Augustus soon after this has a complaint from Postumus's general that he does not mix with the other young officers but spends all his leisure time at the sea, fishing. He has earned the nickname 'Neptune' for this.

My duties as priest of Mars were not arduous and Plautius, who was a priest of the same college, was detailed to watch me when-ever there was a ceremony. I was coming to hate Plautius. The in-sulting remark for which Postumus had thrown him into the foun-tain was one of many. He had called me a Lemur and said that it

119

was only loyalty to Augustus and Livia that prevented him from spitting at me every time I asked him foolish and superfluous questions.

Chapter 11

THE year before I came of age and married had been a bad year for Rome. There was a series of earthquakes in the south of Italy which destroyed several cities. Little rain fell in the spring and the crops looked miserable all over the country: then just before harvest time there were torrential storms which beat down and spoilt what little corn had come to ear. The down-   A.D. 5 pour was so violent that the Tiber carried away the bridge and made the lower part of the City navigable by boats for seven days. A famine seemed threatening and Augustus sent commissioners to Egypt and other parts to buy huge quantities of corn. The public granaries had been depleted because of a bad harvest the year before – though not so bad as this. The commissioners succeeded in buying a certain amount of corn, but at a high price and not really enough. There was great distress that winter, the more because Rome was overcrowded – its population had been doubled in the last twenty years; and Ostia, the port, was unsafe for shipping in the winter, so that grain-convoys from the East were unable to discharge their cargoes for weeks on end. Augustus did what he could to limit the famine. He temporarily banished all but householders and their families to country districts not nearer than 100 miles from the City, appointing a rationing-board composed of ex-Consuls, and prohibited public banquets, even on his own birthday. Much of the grain he imported at his own expense and distributed free to the needy. As usual, famine brought rioting, and rioting brought arson: whole streets of shops were set on fire at night by half-starved looters from the workers' quarters. Augustus organized a brigade of night-watchmen, in seven divisions, to prevent this sort of thing: this brigade proved so useful that it has never since been disbanded. But enormous damage had been done by the rioters. A new tax was imposed about this time to provide money for the German wars, and what with the famine, the fires, and the taxes, the commons began to

120

get restless and openly discuss revolution. Threatening manifestos were pinned at night on the doors of public buildings. A huge conspiracy was said to be on foot. The Senate offered a reward for all information which would lead to the arrest of a ringleader and many men came forward to win it, informing against their neighbours; but this only made the confusion worse. Apparently no real conspiracy existed, only hopeful talk of conspiracies. Eventually corn began to come in from Egypt, where the harvest is much earlier than ours, and the tension relaxed.

Among the people removed from Rome during the famine were the sword-fighters. They were not numerous, but Augustus thought that if there were any civil disturbances they would be likely to play a dangerous part in them. For they were a desperate crew, some of them being men of rank who had been sold as slaves for debt – to purchasers who had agreed to let them earn the price of their freedom by sword-fighting. If a young gentleman ran into debt, as sometimes happened, through no fault of his own or from youthful thoughtlessness, his distant relations would save him from slavery, or Augustus himself would intervene. So these gentlemen sword-fighters were men whom nobody had regarded as worth saving from their fate, and who, becoming the natural leaders of the Gladiatorial Guild, were just the sort to head an armed rebellion.

When things improved they were recalled and it was decided to put everybody in a good humour by exhibiting a big public sword-fight and wild-beast hunt in the names of Germanicus and myself, in memory of our father. Livia wished to remind Rome of his great exploits with a view to calling attention to Germanicus, who resembled him so closely and who would soon, it was expected, be sent to Germany to help his uncle Tiberius, another famous soldier, win fresh conquests there. My mother and Livia contributed to the expenses of the show, the main burden of which, however, fell on Germanicus and me. It was considered, however, that Germanicus in his position needed more money than I did, so my mother explained to me that it would be only right for me to contribute twice as much as he did. I was only too glad to do what I could for Germanicus. But when I found out when it was all over what had been spent I was staggered; the show was planned regardless of cost, and besides the usual expenses of a sword-fight and wild-beast hunt we threw showers of silver to the populace.

In the procession to the amphitheatre Germanicus and I rode, by special decree of the Senate, in our father's old war-chariot. We had just offered a sacrifice to his memory, at the great tomb which Augustus had built for himself when he should come to die – and where he had interred our father's ashes, alongside those of Marcellus. We went down the Appian Way and under our father's memorial arch, with the colossal equestrian figure of him on it, which had been decorated with laurel in honour of the occasion. There was a north-east wind blowing and the doctors would not allow me to come without a cloak, so with one exception I was the only person present at the sword-fight – where I sat next to Germanicus as joint-president with him – who was wearing one. The exception was Augustus himself, who was sitting on the other side of Germanicus. He felt extremes of heat and cold severely and in the winter wore no less than four coats besides a very thick gown and a long waistcoat. There were some present who saw an omen in this similarity between my dress and Augustus's, further remarking that I had been born on the first day of the month named after him, and at Lyons, too, on the very day that he had dedicated an altar there to himself. Or at any rate, that was what they said they had said, many years after. Livia was in the Box too – a peculiar honour paid her as my father's mother. Normally she sat with the Vestal Virgins. The rule was for women and men to sit apart.

It was the first sword-fight I had been permitted to attend, and to find myself in the President's Box was all the more embarrassing for me on this account. Germanicus did all the work, though pretending to consult me when a decision had to be made, and carried it through with great assurance and dignity. It was my luck that this fight was the best that had ever been exhibited at the amphitheatre. As it was my first, however, I could not appreciate its excellence, having no background of previous displays to use for purposes of comparison. But certainly I have never seen a better since, and I must have seen nearly a thousand important ones. Livia wanted Germanicus to gain popularity as his father's son and had spared no expense in hiring the best performers in Rome to fight all out. Usually professional sword-fighters were very careful about hurting themselves and each other, and spent most of their energy on feints and parries and blows which looked and sounded Homeric but which were really quite harmless, like the thwacks that slaves give each other with stage-clubs in low-comedy. It was only occasionally, when they lost their temper with each other or had an old score to settle, that they were worth watching. This time Livia had got the heads of the Gladiatorial Guild together and told them that she wanted her money's worth. Unless every bout was a real one she would have the guild broken up: there had been too many managed fights in the previous summer. So the fighters were warned by the guild-masters that this time they were not to play kiss-in-the-ring or they would be dismissed from the guild.

In the first six combats one man was killed, one so seriously wounded that he died the same day, and a third had his shield-arm lopped off close to the shoulder, which caused roars of laughter. In each of the other three combats one of the men disarmed the other, but not before he had given such a good account of himself that Germanicus and I, when appealed to, were able to confirm the approval of the audience by raising our thumbs in token that his life should be spared. One of the victors had been a rich knight a year or two before. In all these combats the rule was that the antagonists should not fight with the same sort of weapon. It was sword against spear, or sword against battle-axe, or spear against mace. The seventh combat was between a man armed with a regulation army sword and an old-fashioned round brass-bound shield and a man armed with a three-pronged trout-spear and a short net. The sword-man or 'chaser' was a soldier of the Guards who had recently been condemned to death for getting drunk and striking his captain. His sentence had been commuted to a fight against this net-and-trident man – a professional from Thessaly, very highly paid, who had killed more than twenty opponents in the previous five years, so Germanicus told me.

My sympathies were with the soldier, who came into the arena looking very white and shaky – he had been in prison for some days and the strong light bothered him. But his entire company, who it appears sympathized very much with him, for the captain was a bully and a beast, shouted in unison for him to pull himself together and defend the company's honour. He straightened up and shouted, 'I'll do my best, lads!' His camp nickname, as it happened, was 'Roach', and this was enough to put the greater part of the audience on his side, though the Guards were pretty unpopular in the City. If a roach were to kill a fisherman that would be a good joke. To have the amphitheatre on one's side is

123

half the battle to a man fighting for his life. The Thessalian, a wiry, long-armed, long-legged fellow, came swaggering in close behind him, dressed only in a leather tunic and a hard round leather cap. He was in a good humour, cracking jokes with the front-benches, for his opponent was an amateur, and Livia was paying him 1,000 gold pieces for the afternoon and 500 more if he killed his man after a good fight. They came together in front of the Box and saluted first Augustus and Livia and then Germanicus and me as joint-presidents, with the usual formula: 'Greetings, Sirs. We salute you in Death's shadow!' We returned the greetings with a formal gesture, but Germanicus said to Augustus: 'Why, sir, that chaser's one of my father's veterans. I know him well. He won a crown in Germany for being the first man over an enemy stockade.' Augustus was interested. 'Good,' he said, 'this should be a good fight, then. But in that case the net-man must be ten years younger, and years count in this game.' Then Germanicus signalled for the trumpets to sound and the fight began.

Roach stood his ground, while the Thessalian danced around him. Roach was not such a fool as to waste his strength running after his lightly armed opponent or yet to be paralysed into immobility. The Thessalian tried to make him lose his temper by taunting him, but Roach was not to be drawn. Only once when the Thessalian came almost within lunging distance did he show any readiness to take the offensive, and the quickness of his thrust drew a roar of delight from the benches. But the Thessalian was away in time. Soon the fight grew more lively; the Thessalian made stabs, high and low, with his long trident, which Roach parried easily, but with one eye on the net, weighted with small lead pellets, which the Thessalian managed with his left hand.

'Beautiful work!' I heard Livia say to Augustus. 'The best net-man in Rome. He's been playing with the soldier. Did you see that? He could have entangled him and got his stroke in then if he had wished. But he's spinning out the fight.'

'Yes,' said Augustus. 'I'm afraid the soldier is done for. He should have kept off drink.'

Augustus had hardly spoken when Roach knocked up the trident and jumped forward, ripping the Thessalian's leather tunic between arm and body. The Thessalian was away in a flash and as he ran he swung the net across Roach's face. By ill-luck a pellet struck Roach in the eye, momentarily blinding him. He checked his pace and the Thessalian, seeing his advantage, turned and knocked the sword spinning out of his hand. Roach sprang to retrieve it but the Thessalian got there first, ran with it to the barrier and tossed it across to a rich patron sitting in the front rank of the seats reserved for the Knights. Then he returned to the pleasant task of goading and dispatching an unarmed man. The net whistled round Roach's head and the trident jabbed here and there; but Roach was still undismayed, and once made a snatch at the trident and nearly got possession of it. The Thessalian had now worked him towards our Box to make a spectacular killing.

'That's enough!' said Livia in a matter-of-fact voice, 'he's done enough playing about. He ought to finish him now.' The Thessalian needed no prompting. He made a simultaneous sweep of his net round Roach's head and a stab at his belly with the trident. And then what a roar went up! Roach had caught the net with his right hand and, flinging his body back, kicked with all his strength at the shaft of the trident a foot or two from his enemy's hand. The weapon flew up and over the Thessalian's head, turned in the air and stuck quivering into the wooden barrier. The Thessalian stood astonished for a moment, then left the net in Roach's hands and dashed past him to recover the trident. Roach threw himself forward and sideways and caught him in the ribs, as he ran, with the spiked boss of his shield. The Thessalian fell, gasping, on all-fours. Roach recovered himself quickly and with a sharp downward swing of the shield caught him on the back of his neck.

'The rabbit-blow!' said Augustus. 'I've never seen that done in an arena before, have you, my dear Livia? Eh? Killed him too, I swear.'

The Thessalian was dead. I expected Livia to be greatly displeased but all she said was: 'And served him right. That's what comes of underrating one's opponent. I'm disappointed in that net-man. Still, it has saved me that five hundred in gold, so I can't complain, I suppose.'

To crown the afternoon's enjoyment there was a fight between two German hostages who happened to belong to rival clans and had voluntarily engaged each other to a death-duel. It was not pretty fighting, but savage hacking with long sword and halberd: each wore a small highly ornamented shield strapped on the left forearm. This was an unusual manner of fighting, for the ordinary

125

German soldier does all his work with the slim-shafted, narrow-headed assegai: the broad-headed halberd and the long sword are marks of high rank. One of the combatants, a yellow-headed man over six feet tall, made short work of the other, cutting him about terribly before he gave him his final smashing blow on the side of the neck. The crowd gave him a great cheer, which went to his head, for he made a speech in a mixture of German and camp-Latin, saying that he was a renowned warrior in his country and had killed six Romans in battle, including an officer, before he had been given up as hostage by his jealous uncle, the tribal chief. He now challenged any Roman of rank to meet him, sword to sword, and make the lucky seventh for him.

The first champion who sprang into the ring was a young staff-officer of an old but impoverished family, called Cassius Chaerea. He came running to the Box for permission to take up the challenge. His father, he said, had been killed in Germany under that glorious general in whose memory this display was being held: might he piously sacrifice this boastful fellow to his father's ghost? Cassius was a finer fencer. I had often watched him on Mars Field. Germanicus consulted with Augustus and then with me; when Augustus gave his consent and I mumbled mine Cassius was told to arm himself. He went to the dressing-rooms and borrowed Roach's sword, shield, and body armour, for good luck and out of compliment to Roach.

Soon there began a far grander fight than any that the professionals had shown, the German swinging his great sword and Cassius parrying with his shield and always trying to get in under the German's guard – but the fellow was as agile as he was strong and twice beat Cassius to his knees. The crowd was perfectly silent, as if it were a religious performance they were watching, and nothing was heard but the clash of steel on steel and the rattle of shields. Augustus said, 'The German's too strong for him, I'm afraid. We shouldn't have permitted this. If Cassius gets killed it will create a bad impression on the frontier when the news gets there.'

Then Cassius's foot slipped in a blood pool and he fell over on his back. The German straddled over him with a triumphant smile on his face and then ... and then there was a roaring in my ears and a blackness before my eyes and I fainted away. The emotion of seeing men killed for the first time in my life, and then the combat between Roach and the Thessalian, in which I felt so strongly for Roach, and now this fight in which it seemed that it was I myself who was desperately battling for life with the German – it was too much for me. So I did not witness Cassius's wonderful recovery as the German lifted that ugly sword to crash in his skull, the quick upward thrust with the shield-boss at the German's loins, the sideways roll, and the quick decisive stab under the arm-pit. Yes, Cassius killed his man all right. Do not forget this Cassius, for he twice and three times plays an important part in this story. As for me, nobody noticed that I had fainted for some time, and when they did I was already coming to. They propped me up again in my place until the show had formally ended. To have been carried out would have been a disgrace for everyone.

The next day the Games continued, but I was not there. It was announced that I was ill. I missed one of the most spectacular contests ever witnessed in the amphitheatre, between an Indian elephant – they are much bigger than the African breed – and a rhinoceros. Experts betted on the rhinoceros, for although it was by far the smaller animal its hide was much thicker than the elephant's and it was expected to make short work of the elephant with its long sharp horn. In Africa, they were saying, elephants had learned to avoid the haunts of the rhinoceros, which holds undisputed sway in its own territory. This Indian elephant however – as Postumus described the fight to me afterwards – showed no anxiety or fear when the rhinoceros came charging into the arena, meeting him each time with his tusks and lumbering after him with clumsy speed when he retired discomfited. But finding himself unable to penetrate the thick armour of the beast's neck as he charged, this fantastic creature had recourse to cunning. He picked up with his trunk a rough broom made of a thorn bush which a sweeper had left on the sand and darted it in his enemy's face the next time he charged: he succeeded in blinding first one eye and then the other. The rhinoceros, distracted with rage and pain, dashed here and there in pursuit of the elephant and finally ran full tilt against the wooden barrier, going right through it and shattering his horn and stunning himself on the marble barrier behind. Then up came the elephant with his mouth open as if he were laughing and, first enlarging the breach in the wooden barrier, began trampling on his fallen enemy's skull, which he crushed in. He then nodded his head as if in time to music and presently walked quietly away. His Indian driver came running out with a huge bowl full of sweetmeats, which the elephant poured into his mouth while the audience roared applause. Then the beast helped the driver up on his neck, offering his trunk as a ladder, and trotted over to Augustus; where he trumpeted the royal salute – which these elephants are taught only to utter for monarchs – and knelt in homage. But, as I say, I missed this performance.

That evening Livia wrote to Augustus:

My dear Augustus,

Claudius's unmanly behaviour yesterday in fainting at the sight of two men fighting, to say nothing of the grotesque twitching of his hands and head, which at a solemn festival in commemoration of his father's victories were all the more shameful and unfortunate, has at least had this advantage, that we can now definitely decide once and for all that except in the dignity of priest – for the vacancies in the colleges must be filled *somehow* and Plautius has managed to coach him well enough in his duties – Claudius is perfectly unfit to appear in public. We must be content to write him off as a loss, except perhaps for breeding purposes, for I hear he has now done his duty by Urgulanilla – but I shan't be sure of that until I see the child, which may well be a monster like him.

Antonia has to-day abstracted from his study what appears to be a note-book of historical material which he has been collecting for a life of his father; with it she found a painfully composed introduction to the projected work, which I send you herewith. You will observe that Claudius has singled out for praise his dear father's one intellectual foible – that wilful blindness of his to the march of time, the absurd delusion that the political forms that suited Rome when Rome was a small town at war with neighbouring small towns could be re-established after Rome had become the greatest kingdom known since the days of Alexander. Look what happened when Alexander died and nobody could be found strong enough to succeed him as supreme monarch – why, the Empire simply fell to pieces. But I should not waste my time and yours in making historical platitudes.

Athenodorus and Sulpicius, with whom I have just had a conference, say that they had not seen this introduction until I showed it them and agree on its extreme inadvisability. They swear that they have never put any subversive ideas into his head, and suggest that he must have got them from old books. Personally I think that he inherited them – his grandfather had the same curious infirmity, you remember – and it is just like Claudius to have chosen that one weakness to inherit and to have refused any legacy of physical or moral soundness! Thank God for

Tiberius and Germanicus! There's no republican nonsense about *them*, so far as I know.

Naturally I am instructing Claudius that he must desist from his biographical labours, saying that if he disgraces his father's memory by fainting at the solemn Games given in his honour, he is obviously unfit to write his life: let him find some other employment for his pen.

Livia.

Ever since Pollio had told me about the poisoning of my father and grandfather I had been greatly perplexed. I could not make up my mind whether the old man had been talking senile nonsense, or joking, or whether he really knew something. Who but Augustus himself was sufficiently interested in the monarchy to have poisoned a nobleman merely because he believed in republican government? Yet I could not believe Augustus the murderer: poison was a mean way of killing, a slave's way, and Augustus would never have stooped to it. Besides, he was not a hypocrite and when he talked about my father it was always with admiration and affection. I consulted two or three recent histories, but they told me nothing that I had not already heard from Germanicus of the circumstances of my father's death.

It was only a couple of days before the Games that I happened to be talking to our porter, who had been my father's orderly throughout his campaigns. The honest fellow had been drinking rather too much, because my father's name was on everyone's lips at the time and his veterans had come in for a good deal of reflected glory. 'Tell me what you know of my father's death,' I said boldly. 'Were there any stories current in the camp that he met his death other than by accident?' He replied: 'I wouldn't say it to anybody, sir, but yourself, but I can trust you, sir. You're the son of your father and I never knew a man who didn't trust *him*. Yes, sir, there was a rumour going about and there was more in it than in most camp rumours. Your brave and noble father, sir, was poisoned, it's my sure belief. A certain Person, whose name I won't mention because you'll know it without my saying, was jealous of your father's victories and sent him an order of recall. That's not a story, or rumour, that's history. The order came when your father had broken his leg; not much of a damage either, and it was coming along well enough until that doctor fellow arrives from Rome, at the same time as the message, with his little bag of poisons in his hand. Who sent that doctor fellow? The same person who sent the message. Two and two's four, isn't it, sir? We orderlies wanted to kill that doctor fellow but he got back safe to Rome under special escort.'

When I read my grandmother Livia's note telling me to desist from writing my father's life, my perplexity increased. Pollio could surely not have meant to point to my grandmother as the murderess of her former husband and her son? It was unthinkable. And what could have been her motive? Yet when I came to consider the matter I could more easily believe that it was Livia than that it was Augustus.

That summer Tiberius needed men for his East German war, and levies were called for from Dalmatia, a province that had lately been quiet and docile. But when the contingent assembled it happened that the tax-collector was making his annual visit to those parts and exacting from the province not more than the sum fixed by Augustus, but more than it could easily pay. There were loud protests of poverty. The tax-collector exercised his right of seizing good-looking children from the villages which could not pay and carrying them off to be sold as slaves. The fathers of some of the children thus seized were members of the contingent and naturally made a great outcry. The entire force revolted, kill-their Roman captains. A Bosnian tribe rose in sympathy and soon the whole of our frontier provinces between Macedonia and the Alps were in a blaze. Fortunately Tiberius was able to conclude a peace with the Germans, at their instance not his own – and march against the rebels. The Dalmatians would not meet him in a pitched battle but broke up into small columns and carried on a skilful guerrilla warfare. They were lightly armed and knew the country well and when winter came even dared to raid Macedonia.

Augustus at Rome could not appreciate the difficulties with which Tiberius had to contend and suspected him of purposely delaying operations for some secret private ends which he could not fathom. He decided to send out Germanicus, with an army of his own, to spur Tiberius to action.

Germanicus, who was now in his twenty-third year, had just entered, five years before the customary age, on his first City magistracy. The military appointment caused surprise: everyone expected Postumus to be chosen. Postumus had no magisterial appointment, but was busy on Mars Field training the recruits

130

for this new army: he now bore the rank of regimental commander. He was three years younger than Germanicus, but his brother
Gaius had been sent to govern Asia at the age of nineteen and had
become a Consul in the year following. Postumus was by no
means less capable than Gaius, it was agreed, and, after all, he
was Augustus's single surviving grandson.

My own feelings on hearing the news, which had not yet been
made public, were torn between joy on Germanicus's account and
sorrow on Postumus's. I went to find Postumus and arrived at his
quarters in the Palace at the same time as Germanicus. Postumus
greeted us both affectionately and congratulated Germanicus on
his command.

Germanicus said: 'It is because of this that I have come, dear
Postumus. You know well enough that I am very proud and glad
to have been chosen, but military reputation is nothing to me if I
injure you by it. You are as capable a soldier as I am and as Augustus's heir you should obviously have been chosen. With your
consent I propose to go to him now and offer to resign in your
favour. I'll point out the misconstruction that the City will be sure
to put on his preference of me to you. It is not too late yet to make
the alteration.'

Postumus answered: 'Dear Germanicus, you are very generous
and noble, and for that reason I shall speak frankly. You are right
in saying that the City will treat this as a slight on me. The fact
that your duties as a magistrate are being interrupted by the appointment, while I am perfectly free to be sent, aggravates the
matter. But, believe me, the disappointment that I feel is amply
recompensed by this further proof you have given me of your
friendship; and I wish you a speedy recovery and every possible
success.'

Then I said: 'If you will both forgive me for expressing an
opinion, I think that Augustus has considered the situation more
carefully than you give him credit for having done. From something I overheard my mother saying this morning, I gather that he
suspects my uncle Tiberius of purposely prolonging the war. If he
were to send Postumus out with the new forces, after that old history of misunderstanding between my uncle and Postumus's
brothers, my uncle might be suspicious and offended. Postumus
would seem like a spy and a rival. But Germanicus is his adopted
son and would seem to be sent out merely as a reinforcement. I

don't think that there is more to be said than that Postumus will get his chance elsewhere, no doubt, and soon enough.'

They were both very pleased with this new view of the matter, which did credit to them both, and we all parted on the most friendly terms.

That same night, or rather in the early hours of the following morning, I was working late in my room on the upper storey of our house when I heard distant shouting and presently a slight scuffling noise from the balcony outside. I went to the door and saw a head appear over the top of the balcony and then an arm. It was a man in military dress, who threw his leg over the balcony and pulled himself up. I was paralysed for the moment, and the first wild thought that came into my head was: 'It's an assassin sent by Livia.' I was just going to shout for help when he said in a low voice: 'Hush! It's all right! I'm Postumus.'

'O Postumus! What a fright you gave me. Why do you come climbing in at this time of night like a burglar? And what's wrong with you? Your face is bleeding and your cloak's torn.'

'I've come to say good-bye, Claudius.'

'I don't understand. Has Augustus changed his mind? I thought the appointment had already been made public.'

'Give me a drink, I'm thirsty. No, I'm not going to the wars. Far from it. I've been sent fishing.'

'Don't talk in riddles. Here's the wine. Drink it quick and tell me what's wrong. Where are you going fishing?'

'Oh, to some small island. I don't think they've chosen it yet.'

'You mean ...?' My heart sank and my head swam.

'Yes, I'm being banished; like my poor mother.'

'But why? What crime have you committed?'

'No crime that can be officially mentioned to the Senate. I expect the phrase will be "incurable and persistent depravity". You remember that *Pillow Debate*?'

'O Postumus! Has my grandmother ...?'

'Listen carefully, Claudius, for time is short. I am under close arrest, but just now I managed to knock down two of my escort and break away. The Palace guard has been called out and every possible way of escape is blocked. They know I am somewhere in these buildings and they'll search every room. I felt I had to see you, because I want you to know the truth and not believe the charges that they have trumped up against me. And I want you to tell Germanicus everything. Send him my most loving greeting and tell him everything, exactly as I tell it you now. I don't care what anybody else thinks of me, but I want Germanicus and you to know the truth and think well of me.'

'I'll not forget a word, Postumus. Quick, tell it me from the beginning.'

'Well, you know that I've been out of favour with Augustus lately. I couldn't make out why, at first, but soon it was obvious that Livia was poisoning his mind against me. He is extraordinarily weak where she is concerned. Imagine living with her for nearly fifty years and still believing every word she says! But Livia was not the only one in this plot. Livilla was in it too.'

'Livilla! Oh, I am so sorry!'

'Yes. You know how much I loved her and how much I have suffered on her account. You hinted once, about a year ago, that she wasn't worth my troubling about and you remember how angry I was with you. I wouldn't talk to you for days. I am sorry now that I was angry, Claudius. But you know how it is when one is hopelessly in love with someone. I didn't explain to you then that just before she married Castor she told me that Livia had forced the marriage on her and that really she loved only me. I believed her. Why shouldn't I have believed her? I hoped that one day something would happen to Castor and she and I would be free to marry. That's been in my mind day and night ever since. This afternoon, just after seeing you, I was sitting with her and Castor in the grape-arbour by the big carp-pool. He began taunting me. I realize now that the whole thing had been carefully rehearsed beforehand between them. The first thing he said was: "So Germanicus has been preferred to you, eh?" I told him that I considered it a wise appointment and that I had just congratulated Germanicus. Then he said in a jeering way: "So it has your princely approval, has it? By the way, do you still expect to succeed your grandfather as Emperor?" I kept my temper for Livilla's sake, but said that I did not think it decent to discuss the succession while Augustus was still alive and in full possession of his faculties. Then I asked him ironically whether he was offering himself as a rival candidate. He said, with an unpleasant smile: "Well, if I did, I expect I would have more chance of success than you. I usually get what I want. I use my brains. I won Livilla by

133

using my brains. It makes me laugh when I think how easily I persuaded Augustus that you weren't a suitable husband for her.
Perhaps I'll get other things I want too, that way. Who knows?"
This made me really hot. I asked him whether he meant that he
had been telling lies about me. He said, "Why not? I wanted
Livilla, and that's how I got her." Then I turned to Livilla and
asked her whether she had known about this. She pretended to be
indignant and said that she knew nothing about it at all, but that
she believed Castor capable of any crooked dealing. She forced
out a tear or two and said that Castor was rotten through and
through and that nobody could guess how much she had suffered
from him, and that she wished she were dead.'

'Yes, that's an old trick of hers. She can cry whenever it suits
her. It takes everyone in. If I'd told you all that I knew of her,
you'd have hated me perhaps for a time, but it would have saved
you all this. Then what happened?'

'This evening she sent me a verbal message by her lady-in-
waiting that Castor would probably be out all night on one of
his usual debauches and that when I saw a light at her window
shortly after midnight I was to come to her. A window would be
left open immediately underneath the light and I was to climb in
quietly. She wanted to tell me something very important. Of
course, that could only mean one thing and it set my heart pounding. I waited in the garden for hours until I saw the light appear
for a moment at her window. Then I found the window open below and climbed in. Livilla's maid was there and guided me upstairs. She showed me how to get into Livilla's room by climbing
across from one balcony to another until I reached her window;
this was to avoid the guard posted in the passage near her door.
Well, I found Livilla waiting for me in her dressing-gown, with
her hair down and looking infernally beautiful. She told me how
cruelly Castor had behaved to her. She said that she owed him
nothing as a wife, because on his own confession he had married
her by fraud, and he had behaved most brutally to her. She flung
her arms around me and I picked her up and carried her over to
the bed. I was mad with desire for her. Then suddenly she began
to scream and pummel me. I thought for the moment that she had
gone mad, and put my hand over her mouth to quiet her. She
struggled free, knocking over a little table with a lamp and a glass
jar on it. Then she screamed 'Rape! Rape!' and then the door

134

was battered down and in came the Palace guard with torches. Guess who was at their head?'

'Castor?'

'Livia. She brought us just as we were into Augustus's presence. Castor was with him, though Livilla had told me that he was dining at the other side of the City. Augustus dismissed the guard, and Livia, who had hardly said a word until then, began her attack on me. She told him that on his suggestion she had gone to my quarters to acquaint me privately with Aemilia's charges and ask me what explanation I had to offer.'

'Aemilia! Which Aemilia?'

'My niece.'

'I didn't know she had anything against you.'

'She hasn't. She was in the plot too. So Livia said that, not finding me in my quarters, she had made inquiries and had been told that the patrol had seen me sitting in the garden under a pear-tree on the south side. She sent a soldier to find me but he came back and said that I wasn't there but that he had something suspicious to report: a man climbing from one upper balcony to another just above the sundial. She knew whose rooms those were and was greatly alarmed. By good luck she arrived just in time. She had heard Livilla's screams for help: I had broken into her bedroom by way of the balcony and was on the point of raping her. The guards had burst down the door and pulled me away from "the terrified and half-naked young woman". She had brought me here at once, and Livilla as a witness. While Livia was telling her story that whore Livilla was sobbing and hiding her face. Her dressing-gown was ripped across – she must have torn it herself deliberately. Augustus called me a beast and a satyr and asked me whether I had gone mad. Of course, I couldn't deny that I had been in her bedroom or even that I had been making love to her. I said that I had come by invitation, and tried to explain things from the beginning, but Livilla began screaming, "It's a lie. It's a lie. I was asleep and he came in by the window and tried to rape me." Then Livia said, "And I suppose your niece Aemilia invited you to assault her too? You seem very popular with the young women." That was clever of Livia. I had to justify myself about Aemilia and leave the Livilla story. I told Augustus that I had dined with my sister Julilla the night before and that Aemilia was there, but that this was the first time I had seen the girl for six

135

months. I asked on what occasion I was supposed to have assaulted her and Augustus said that I knew very well when it was – after dinner in the temporary absence of her parents, who were called away by an alarm of thieves – and that I had only been prevented by the return of her parents. The story was so ridiculous that, furious as I was, I could not help laughing; but this increased Augustus's rage. He was about to rise from his ivory chair and strike me.'

I said: 'I don't understand? Was there really an alarm of thieves?'

'Yes, and Aemilia and I were left alone for a few minutes, but the conversation was most blameless and her governess was there! We were discussing fruit-trees and garden-pests until Julilla and Aemilius came back and said that it was a false alarm. Julilla and Aemilius aren't in Livia's pay, you may be sure – they hate her – so Aemilia must have arranged it. I began to think quickly what spite she held against me, but I could remember nothing. Suddenly the explanation occurred to me. Julilla had told me as a secret that Aemilia was at last getting what she wanted: she was to marry Appius Silanus. You know that young dandy, don't you?'

'Yes. But I don't follow.'

'It's quite simple. I said to Livia: "Aemilia's reward for this lie is to be marriage to Silanus, isn't it? And what does Livilla get? Did you promise to poison her present husband and provide her with a handsomer one?" Once I had mentioned poison I knew that I was doomed. So I decided to say as much as I could while I had the opportunity. I asked Livia just how she had arranged the poisoning of my father and brothers and whether she favoured slow poisons or quick ones. Claudius, do you think that she killed them? I'm sure of it.'

'You dared ask her that? It's very probable. I think she poisoned my father and my grandfather, too,' I said, 'and I don't suppose they were her only victims. But I have no proof.'

'Neither have I, but I enjoyed accusing her of it. I shouted at the top of my voice so that half the Palace must have heard. Livia hurried from the room and called the guard. I saw Livilla smiling. I made a grab at her throat but Castor got between us and she escaped. Then I grappled with Castor and broke his arm and knocked out two of his front teeth on the marble floor. But I did

136

not struggle with the soldiers. It would have been undignified. Besides, they were armed. Two of them held each of my arms as Augustus thundered abuse and threats at me. He said that I am to be banished for life to the most desolate island in his dominions and that only his unnatural daughter could have borne him so unnatural a grandson. I told him that in name he was Emperor of the Romans but that in fact he was less free than the girl slave of a drunken bawdmaster, and that one day his eyes would be opened to the unnatural crimes and deceits of his abominable wife. But meanwhile, I said, my love and loyalty to him remained unchanged.'

The hue and cry was now sounding through the lower storey of our house. Postumus said: 'I don't want to compromise you, dear Claudius. I must not be found in your room. If I had a sword now I'd use it. Better to die fighting than to rot away on an island.'

'Patience, Postumus. Yield now and your chance will come later. I promise you it will come. When Germanicus knows the truth he'll not rest until you're free again, and neither will I. If you get yourself killed it will only be a cheap triumph for Livia.'

'You and Germanicus can't explain away all that evidence against me. You'd only get yourself into trouble if you tried.'

'The opportunity will come, I say. Livia has had things her own way too long and she'll grow careless. She's bound to make a slip soon. She wouldn't be human if she didn't.'

'I don't think she *is* human,' Postumus said.

'And when Augustus suddenly realizes how he has been deceived, don't you think he'll be as merciless towards her as he was towards your mother?'

'She'll poison him first.'

'Germanicus and I will see that she doesn't. We'll warn him. Don't despair, Postumus. Everything will be all right in the end. I'll write you letters as often as I can, and send you books to read. I'm not afraid of Livia. If you don't get my letters you'll know that they are being held back. Look carefully at the seventh page of any sewn-sheet book that reaches you from me. If I have a private message for you I'll write in milk there. It's a trick that the Egyptians use. The writing is invisible until you warm it in front of a fire. Oh, listen to those doors banging. You must go now. They're at the end of the next corridor.'

Tears were in his eyes. He embraced me tenderly without another word and walked quickly to the balcony. He climbed over the edge, waved his hand in farewell, and slid down the old vine up which he had climbed. I heard him running away through the garden and a moment later cries and shouts from the guard.

* * *

I have no recollection at all of anything that happened for the next month or more. I was ill again: so ill that they talked of me as already dead. By the time that I began to recover, Germanicus was already at the wars and Postumus had been disinherited and banished for life. The island chosen for him was Planasia. It lay about twelve miles from Elba in the direction of Corsica and had not been inhabited within human memory. But there were some prehistoric stone huts on it which were converted into living quarters for Postumus and a barracks for the guard. Planasia was roughly triangular in shape, the longest side being about five miles long. It was treeless and rocky and only visited by the Elba boatmen in the summer when they·came to bait lobster-pots. By Augustus's orders this practice was discontinued, for fear Postumus might bribe someone and escape.

A.D. 7

Tiberius was now Augustus's sole heir, with Germanicus and Castor to carry on the line after him – Livia's line.

Chapter 12

IF I were to confine my account of the events of the next twenty-five years or more merely to my own performances it would not cost me much in paper and make very dull reading; but the later part of this autobiography, in which I figure more prominently, will only be intelligible if I continue here with the personal histories of Livia, Tiberius, Germanicus, Postumus, Castor, Livilla, and the rest, which are far from dull, I promise you.

Postumus was in exile, and Germanicus was at the wars, and only Athenodorus remained of my true friends. Soon he left me too, returning to his native Tarsus. I did not grudge his going because he went at the urgent appeal of two of his nephews there who begged him to help them free the city from the tyranny of its governor. They wrote that this governor had insinuated himself so cleverly into their God Augustus's good graces that it would need the testimony of a man like Athenodorus, in whose integrity their God Augustus had complete confidence, to persuade their God Augustus that the fellow's expulsion was justified. Athenodorus succeeded in ridding the city of this blood-sucker, but afterwards found it impossible to return to Rome as he had intended. He was needed by his nephews to help them rebuild the city administration on a firm foundation. Augustus, to whom he wrote a detailed report of his actions, showed his gratitude and confidence by granting Tarsus, as a personal favour to him, a five years' remission from the Imperial tribute. I corresponded regularly with the good old man until his death two years later at the age of eighty-two. Tarsus honoured his memory with an annual festival and sacrifice; at which the leading citizens took turns to read his *Short History of Tarsus* through from beginning to end, starting at sunrise and finishing after sunset.

Germanicus wrote to me occasionally but his letters were as brief as they were affectionate: a really good commander has no time for writing letters home to his family, his entire time between campaigns being spent in getting to know his men and officers, in studying their comfort, in increasing their military efficiency, and in gathering information about the disposition and plans of his enemy. Germanicus was one of the most conscientious commanders who ever served in the Roman army – and more beloved even than our father. I was very proud when he wrote asking me to make for him, as quickly and thoroughly as I could, a digest of all reliable reports that I could find in the libraries on the domestic customs of the various Balkan tribes against whom he was fighting, the strength and geographical situation of their cities, and their traditional military tactics and ruses, particularly in guerrilla warfare. He said that he could not get enough reliable information locally: Tiberius had been most uncommunicative. With Sulpicius's help and a small group of professional research-men and copyists working night and day I managed to get together exactly what he wanted and sent off a copy to him within a month of his asking for it. I was prouder than ever when he wrote to me not long afterwards for an edition of twenty copies of the book for circulation among his senior officers, for it had already proved of the greatest service to him. He said that every paragraph was clear

139

and relevant, the most useful sections being those giving particulars of the secret extra-tribal military brotherhood against which, rather than against the tribes themselves, the war was being fought; and of the various sacred trees and bushes – a different sort was reverenced by each tribe – under whose protective shade the tribesmen were accustomed to bury their stores of corn, money, and weapons when they had to abandon their villages in a hurry. He promised to tell Tiberius and Augustus of my valuable services.

No public mention of this book was made, perhaps because if the enemy had heard of its existence they would have modified their tactics and dispositions. As it was, they believed that they were being constantly betrayed by informers. Augustus rewarded me unofficially by appointing me to a vacancy in the Augurs' College, but it was clear that he gave all the credit for the compilation to Sulpicius, though Sulpicius did not write a word – he merely found me some of the books. One of my chief authorities was Pollio, whose Dalmatian campaign had been a model of military thoroughness combined with brilliant intelligence-work. Though his account of local customs and conditions seemed nearly fifty years out of date, Germanicus found my extracts from it more helpful than any more recent campaign-history. I wished Pollio had been alive to hear that. I told Livy instead, who said rather crossly that he had never denied Pollio credit for writing competent military text-books; he had merely denied him the title of historian in the higher sense.

I must add to this, that if I had been more tactful I am pretty sure that Augustus would have commended me in his speech to the Senate at the conclusion of the war. But my references to his own Balkan campaigns had been fewer than they might have been had he written a detailed account of it, as Pollio did of his; or if the official historians had been less concerned with flattering their Emperor, and more with recording his successes and reverses in an unprejudiced, technical way. I could extract little or no useful matter from these eulogies, and Augustus in reading my book must have felt himself slighted. He identified himself so closely with the success of the war that during the last two campaigning seasons he moved from Rome to a town on the North-East frontier of Italy, to be as near as he could to the fighting; and as Commander-in-Chief of the Roman Armies he was continually sending Tiberius not very helpful military advice.

I was now working on an account of my grandfather's part in the Civil Wars: but I had not gone very far before I was once more stopped by Livia. I had only managed to complete two volumes. She told me that I was no more capable of writing a life of my grandfather than a life of my father and that I had behaved dishonestly in starting it behind her back. If I wanted a useful employment for my pen, I had better choose a subject that did not allow of so much misrepresentation. She offered me one: the reorganization of religion by Augustus since the Pacification. It was not an exciting subject, but had not been treated before in any detail and I was quite willing to undertake it. Augustus's religious reforms had been almost without exception excellent: he had revived several ancient societies of priests, built and endowed eighty-two new temples in Rome and its environs, re-edified numerous old ones that were falling into decay, introduced foreign cults for the benefit of visiting provincials, and reinstituted a number of interesting old public festivals that had been allowed to lapse one after the other during the civil disturbances of the previous half-century. I went into the subject very closely and completed my survey within a few days of the death of Augustus six years later. It was in forty-one volumes, averaging five thousand words apiece, but a great deal of this consisted of transcripts of religious decrees, nominal lists of priests, catalogues of gifts made to temple treasuries, and so on. The most valuable volume was the introductory one dealing with primitive ritual at Rome. Here I found myself in difficulties, because Augustus's ritualistic reforms were based on the findings of a religious commission which had not done its work properly. There had apparently been no antiquarian expert among the commissioners, so that a number of gross misunderstandings of ancient religious formulas had been embodied in the new official liturgies. Nobody who has not made a study of the Etruscan and Sabine languages is capable of interpreting the more ancient of our religious incantations; and I devoted a great deal of time to mastering the rudiments of both. At this time there were a few countrymen who still talked nothing but Sabine in the home and I persuaded two of them to come to Rome and provide Pallas, who was now acting as my secretary, with material for a short Sabine dictionary. I paid them well for this. Callon, the best of my other secretaries, I sent to Capua to collect material for a similar dictionary of the Etruscan language from

141

Aruns, the priest who had given me the information about Lars Porsena which had so pleased Pollio and so disgusted Livy. These two dictionaries, which later I enlarged and published, enabled me to clear up, to my own satisfaction, a number of outstanding problems of ancient religious worships; but I had learned to be careful and nothing that I wrote reflected on Augustus's scholarship or judgement.

I shall not spend any time on an account of the Balkan War, beyond saying that in spite of the wise generalship of my uncle Tiberius, the able assistance given him by my father-in-law Silvanus, and the dashing exploits of Germanicus it dragged on for three years. In the end the whole country was reduced, and practically made into a desert, because these tribes, men and women, fought with extraordinary desperation and only acknowledged defeat when fire, famine, and plague had more than halved the population. When the rebel leaders came to Tiberius to treat for peace he questioned them closely. He wanted to know why they had taken it into their heads to revolt in the first instance and then to offer so desperate a resistance. The chief rebel, a man called Bato, answered: 'You yourselves are to blame. You send as guardians of your flocks neither shepherds nor watch-dogs, but wolves.'

This was not exactly true. Augustus chose the governors of his frontier provinces himself and paid them a substantial salary and saw to it that they did not divert any of the Imperial revenues into their own pockets. Taxes were paid directly to them, no longer farmed out to unprincipled tax-collecting companies. Augustus's governors were never wolves, as had been most of the Republican governors, whose only interest in their provinces was how much they could squeeze out of them. Many of them were good watch-dogs and some were even honest shepherds. But it often happened that Augustus would unintentionally put the tax at too high a rate, discounting the distress caused by a bad harvest or a cattle plague or an earthquake; and rather than complain to him that the assessment was too high the governors would collect it to the last penny, even at the risk of revolt. Few of them took any personal interest in the people they were supposed to govern. A governor would settle in the Romanized capital town, where there were fine houses and theatres and temples and public baths and markets, and never think of visiting the outlying districts of his province. The real governing was done by deputies and by deputies of deputies, and there must have been a great deal of petty jack-in-office oppression by the smaller men: perhaps it was these whom Bato called wolves, though 'fleas' would have been a better word. There can be no doubt that under Augustus the provinces were infinitely more prosperous than under the Republic, and further that the home-provinces, which were governed by nominees of the Senate, were not nearly so well off as the frontier-provinces governed by Augustus's nominees. This comparison provided one of the few plausible arguments that I ever heard advanced against republican government; though based on the untenable hypothesis that the standard of personal morality among the leading men of an average republic is likely to be lower than the personal morality of an average absolute monarch and his chosen subordinates; and on the fallacy that the question of how the provinces are governed is more important than the question of what happens in the City. To recommend a monarchy on account of the prosperity it gives the provinces seems to me like recommending that a man should have liberty to treat his children as slaves, if at the same time he treats his slaves with reasonable consideration.

For this costly and wasteful war a great triumph was decreed by the Senate for Augustus and Tiberius. It will be recalled that now only Augustus himself or members of his family were to be permitted a proper triumph, other generals being awarded what were called 'triumphal ornaments'. Germanicus, though a Caesar, was granted only these ornaments, on technical   A.D. 9 grounds. Augustus might have stretched the point, but he was so grateful to Tiberius for his successful conduct of the war that he did not wish to antagonize him by giving Germanicus equal honours with him. Germanicus was also raised a degree in magisterial rank, and allowed to become Consul several years before the customary age. Castor, though he had taken no part in the war, was granted the privilege of attending meetings of the Senate before becoming a member of it, and was also advanced a degree in magisterial rank.

At Rome the populace was looking forward with excitement to the triumph, which would mean largesse in corn and money and all sorts of good things: but a great disappointment was in store for them. A month before the date fixed for the triumph a terrible omen was observed – in Mars Field the temple of the War God was struck by lightning and nearly destroyed – and a few days later news came through from Germany of the heaviest military reverse suffered by Roman arms since Carrhae, I might even say since The Allia, not quite 400 years before. Three regiments had been massacred and all the conquests east of the Rhine had been lost at a stroke; it seemed that there was nothing to prevent the Germans crossing the river and laying waste the three settled and prosperous provinces of France.

I have already told of the crushing effect that this news had on Augustus. He felt it so strongly because he was not only officially responsible for the disaster, as the man charged by the Roman Senate and people with the security of all frontiers, but morally responsible as well. The disaster had been due to his imprudence in trying to force civilization on the barbarians too rapidly. The Germans conquered by my father had been gradually adapting themselves to Roman ways, learning the use of coinage, holding regular markets, building and furnishing houses in civilized style, and even meeting in assemblies that did not end, as their former assemblies had always ended, in armed battles. They were allies in name and if they had been allowed to forget their old barbarous ways gradually and to rely on the Roman garrison to protect them from their still uncivilized neighbours while they enjoyed the luxuries of provincial peace, they might perhaps in a couple of generations or less have grown as peaceful and docile as the French of Provence. But Varus, a connexion of mine, whom Augustus appointed Governor of Germany Across the Rhine, began treating them not as allies but as a subject race: he was a vicious man and showed little regard for the extraordinarily strong feelings that Germans have about the chastity of their womenfolk. Then Augustus needed money for the military treasury which the Balkan War had emptied. He imposed a number of new taxes from which the Across-Rhine Germans were not exempted. Varus advised him as to the paying capacity of the province and in his zeal assessed it too high.

There were in Varus's camp two German chieftains, Hermann and Siegmyrgth, who spoke Latin fluently and appeared to be completely Romanized. Hermann had commanded German auxiliaries in the previous war and his loyalty was unquestioned. He had spent some time in Rome and had actually been enrolled among the noble knights. These two often ate at Varus's table and were on terms of the most intimate friendship with him. They encouraged him to suppose that their compatriots were no less loyal and grateful to Rome for the benefits of civilization than they themselves were. But they were in constant secret communication with malcontent fellow-chieftains whom they persuaded for the time being to make no armed resistance to the Roman power and to pay their taxes with the greatest possible show of willingness. Soon they would be given the signal for mass-revolt. Hermann, whose name means 'warrior', and Siegmyrgth – or let us call him Segimerus – whose name means 'joyful victory', were too clever for Varus. Members of his staff were constantly warning him that the Germans were unnaturally well-behaved of recent months and that they were trying to disarm his suspicions before making a sudden rising; but he laughed at the suggestion. He said that the Germans were a very stupid race and incapable either of thinking out any such plan or of executing it without giving the secret away long before the time was ripe. Their docility was mere cowardice; the harder you hit a German the more he respected you: he was arrogant in prosperity and independence, but once defeated came crawling to your feet like a dog and kept to heel ever afterwards. He refused even to heed warnings given him by another German chieftain who had a grudge against Hermann and saw far into his designs. Instead of keeping his forces concentrated as he should have done in an only partially subdued country, he broke them up.

On the secret instructions of Hermann and Segimerus, outlying communities sent Varus requests for military protection against bandits and for escorts to convoys of merchandise from France. Next came an armed uprising at the Eastern extremity of the province. A tax-collector and his staff were murdered. When Varus gathered his available forces for a punitive expedition, Hermann and Segimerus escorted him for part of his journey and then excused themselves from further attendance, promising to assemble their auxiliary forces and come to his help, if needed, as soon as he sent for them. These auxiliaries were already under arms and in ambush a few days' journey ahead of Varus on his line of march. The two chieftains now sent word to the outlying communities to fall upon the Roman detachments sent for their protection and not to let a man escape.

No news came to Varus about this massacre because there were no survivors, and he was, in any case, out of touch with his headquarters. The road he was following was a mere forest track. But he did not take the precaution of putting out an advance guard of skirmishers or flank-guards, but let the whole force – which contained a large number of non-combatants – string out in a disorderly column with as little precaution as if he had been within fifty miles of Rome. The march was very slow because he had constantly to be felling trees and bridging streams to enable the commissariat carts to get across; and this gave time for huge numbers of tribesmen to join the ambushing forces. The weather suddenly broke, a downpour of rain lasting for twenty-four hours or more soaked the men's leather shields, making them too heavy for fighting, and putting the archers' bows out of commission. The clay track became so slippery that it was difficult to keep one's footing and the carts were constantly getting stuck. The distance between the head and the tail of the column increased. Then a smoke signal went up from a neighbouring hill and the Germans suddenly attacked from front, rear, and both flanks.

The Germans were no match for the Romans in fair fight and Varus had not much exaggerated their cowardice. At first they only dared to attack stragglers and transport drivers, avoiding hand-to-hand fighting but flinging volleys of assegais and darts from behind cover, and running back into the forest if a Roman so much as shook a sword and shouted. But they caused many casualties by these tactics. Parties led by Hermann, Segimerus, and other chieftains made blocks on the road by wheeling captured carts together, breaking their wheels, and felling trees across the wreckage. They made several of these blocks and left tribesmen behind them to harass the soldiers when they tried to clear them away. This so delayed the men at the tail of the column that, afraid of losing touch, they abandoned all the carts which were still in their possession and hurried forward, hoping that the Germans would be so busy plundering that they would not return to the attack for some time.

The leading regiment had reached a hill where there were not many trees because of a recent forest fire and here they formed up in safety and waited for the other two. They still had their transport and had only lost a few hundred men. The other two regiments were suffering much more heavily. Men got separated from their companies, and new units were formed of from fifty to 200 men apiece, each with a rear-guard, an advance-guard, and flank guards. The flank guards could only go forward very slowly because of the denseness and marshiness of the forest and frequently lost touch with their little units; the advance-guards lost heavily at the barricades and the rear-guards were constantly being assegaied from behind. When the roll was called that night Varus found that nearly a third of his force was killed or missing. The next day he fought his way into open country, but he had been obliged to abandon the remainder of his transport. Food was scarce and on the third day he had to plunge into the forest again. The casualties on the second day had not been severe, for a large number of the enemy were occupied plundering the wagons and carrying the loot away with them, but when the roll was called on the evening of the third day only a quarter of the original force was present to answer their names. On the fourth day Varus was still advancing, for he was too wrong-headed to admit defeat and abandon his original objective, but the weather, which had improved somewhat, now became worse than ever, and the Germans, who were accustomed to heavy rain, grew bolder and bolder as they saw resistance weakening. They came to closer quarters.

About noon Varus saw that all was over and killed himself rather than fall alive into the hands of the enemy. Most of the senior officers surviving followed his example, and many of the men. Only one officer kept his head – the same Cassius Chaerea who fought that day in the amphitheatre. He was commanding the rear-guard, composed of mountaineers from Savoy, who were more at home in a forest than most; and when news came by a fugitive that Varus was dead, the Eagles captured, and not 300 men of the main body left on their feet, he determined to save what he could from the slaughter. He turned his force about and broke through the enemy with a sudden charge. Cassius's great courage, something of which he managed to convey to his men, awed the Germans. They left this small resolute body of men alone and ran forward to make easier conquests. It stands as perhaps the finest soldiering feat of modern times that of the 120 men whom Cassius had with him when he turned about he managed after eight days' march through hostile country to bring eighty safely back, under the company banner, to the fortress from which he had set out twenty days previously.

It is difficult to convey an impression of the panic that reigned at Rome when the rumours of the disaster were confirmed. People started packing up their belongings and loading them on carts as if the Germans were already at the City gates. And indeed there was good reason for anxiety. The losses in the Balkan War had been so heavy that nearly all the available reserves of fighting men in Italy had been used up. Augustus was at his wits' end to find an army to send out under Tiberius to secure the Rhine bridge-heads, which apparently the Germans had not yet seized. Of Roman citizens who were liable for service few came forward willingly on the publication of the order calling them up; to march against the Germans seemed like going to certain death. Augustus then issued a second order that of those who did not offer themselves within three days every fifth man would be disenfranchised and deprived of all his property. Many hung back even after this, so he executed a few as an example and forced the remainder into the ranks, where some of them, as a matter of fact, made quite good soldiers. He also called up a class of men over thirty-five years of age and re-enlisted a number of veterans who had completed their sixteen years with the colours. With these and a regiment or two composed of freedmen, who were not normally liable for service (though Germanicus's reinforcements in the Balkan War had consisted largely of such), he built up quite an imposing force and sent each company off North on its own as soon as it was armed and equipped.

It was the greatest shame and grief to me that in this hour of Rome's supreme need I was incapable of serving as a soldier in her defence. I went to Augustus and begged to be sent out in some capacity where my bodily weakness would not be a disability: I suggested going as intelligence-officer to Tiberius and undertaking such useful tasks as collecting and collating reports on enemy movements, questioning prisoners, making maps, and giving special instructions to spies. Failing this appointment (for which I considered myself qualified because I had made a close study of the campaigns in Germany and I had learned to think in an orderly way and to direct clerks) I volunteered to act as Tiberius's Quartermaster-General: I would indent to Rome for necessary military supplies, and check and distribute them on their arrival at the base. Augustus seemed pleased that I had come forward so willingly and said that he would speak to Tiberius about my offer.

But nothing came of it. Perhaps Tiberius believed me incapable of any useful service; perhaps he was merely annoyed at my coming forward with this request when his son Castor had hung back and had persuaded Augustus to send him to raise and train troops in the South of Italy. However, Germanicus was in the same case as myself, which was some comfort. He had volunteered for service in Germany, but Augustus needed him at Rome, where he was very popular, to help him quell the civil disturbances which he feared might break out as soon as the troops had left the City.

Meanwhile the Germans hunted down all the fugitives from Varus's army and sacrificed scores of them to their forest-gods, burning them alive in wicker cages. The remainder they held as captives. (Some of them were later ransomed by their relatives at an extravagantly high price, but Augustus forbade them ever to enter Italy again.) The Germans also enjoyed a long succession of tremendous drinking-bouts on the captured wine, and quarrelled bloodily over the glory and plunder. It was a long time before they became active again and realized how little opposition they would meet if they marched to the Rhine. But as soon as the wine began to give out they attacked the weakly-held frontier-fortresses and one by one captured and sacked them. Only a single fortress put up a decent resistance: it was the one held by Cassius. The Germans would have occupied this as easily as the rest because the garrison was small, but Hermann and Segimerus were elsewhere and none of the rest understood the Roman art of siege-warfare with catapults, mangonels, the tortoise, and sapping. Cassius had a big supply of bows and arrows in his fortress and taught everyone, even the women and slaves, to use them. He successfully beat off several wild attacks on the gates and had great pots of boiling water always ready to pour on any Germans who attempted to scale the walls with ladders. The Germans were so busy trying to capture this place, where they expected to find rich plunder, that they did not push on to the Rhine bridge-heads which were held by inadequate guards.

News came of Tiberius's rapid approach at the head of his new army. Hermann at once rallied his forces, determined to capture the bridges before Tiberius could reach them. A detachment was left to invest the fortress, which was known to be badly supplied with provisions. Cassius, who got wind of Hermann's plans, decided to get away while there was still time. One stormy night he slipped out with the whole garrison, and managed to get past the first two enemy outposts before the crying of some of the children who were with him gave the alarm. At the third outpost there was hand-to-hand fighting and if the Germans had not been so anxious to get into the town to plunder it Cassius's party would have had no chance of survival. But he got clear somehow and half an hour later told his trumpeters to sound the 'advance at the double' to make the Germans believe that a relief force was coming up; so there was no pursuit. The troops at the nearest bridge heard the distant sound of Roman trumpets, for the wind was blowing from the east, and guessing what was happening sent out a detachment to escort the garrison back to safety. Cassius two days later successfully held the bridge against a mass-attack of Segimerus's men; after which Tiberius's vanguard came up and the situation was saved.

The close of the year was marked by the banishment of Julilla, on the charge of promiscuous adultery – just like her mother Julia – to Tremerus, a small island off the coast of Apulia. The real reason for her banishment was that she was just about to bear another child, which if it were a boy would be a great-grandson of Augustus, and unrelated to Livia; Livia was taking no risks now. Julilla had one son already, but he was a delicate, timorous, slack-twisted fellow and could be disregarded. Aemilius himself provided Livia with grounds for the accusation. He had quarrelled with Julilla and now charged her in the presence of their daughter Aemilia with trying to father another man's child on him. He named Decimus, a nobleman of the Silanus family, as the adulterer. Aemilia, who was clever enough to realize that her own life and safety depended on keeping in Livia's good books, went straight to her and told what she had heard. Livia made her repeat the story in Augustus's presence. Augustus then summoned Aemilius and asked him whether it was true that he was not the father of Julia's child. It did not occur to Aemilius that Aemilia could have betrayed her mother and himself, so he assumed that the intimacy which he suspected between Julilla and Decimus was a matter of common scandal. He therefore held by his accusation, though it was founded rather on jealousy than on knowledge. Augustus took the child as soon as it was born and had it exposed on the mountain-side. Decimus went into voluntary exile and several other men accused of having been Julilla's lovers at one time or another followed him: among them was the poet Ovid whom Augustus, curiously enough, made the principal scapegoat as having also written (many years before) *The Art of Love*. It was this poem, Augustus said, that had debauched his granddaughter's mind. He ordered all copies of it found to be burned.

Chapter 13

AUGUSTUS was over seventy years of age. Until recently nobody had thought of him as an old man. But these new public and private calamities made a great change in him. His temper grew uncertain and he found it increasingly difficult to welcome chance visitors with his usual affability or to keep his patience at public banquets. He was even inclined to be short-tempered with Livia. Nevertheless he continued his work conscientiously as ever and even accepted another ten years' instalment of the monarchy. Tiberius and Germanicus when they were in the City undertook many tasks for him that normally he would have undertaken himself, and Livia worked harder than ever. During the Balkan War she had remained at Rome while Augustus was away and, armed with a duplicate seal of his and in close touch with him by dispatch-riders, had managed everything herself. Augustus was becoming more or less reconciled to the prospect of Tiberius's succeeding him. He judged him capable of ruling reasonably well, with Livia's help, and of carrying on his own policies, but he also flattered himself that everyone would miss the Father of the Country when he was dead and would speak of the Augustan Age as they spoke of the Golden Age of King Numa. In spite of his signal services to Rome, Tiberius was personally unpopular and would surely not gain in popularity when he was Emperor. It was a satisfaction to Augustus that Germanicus, being older than Castor, his brother by adoption, was Tiberius's natural successor, and tha. Germanicus's infant sons, Nero and Drusus, were his own great-grandsons. Though Fate had decreed against his grandsons succeeding him he would surely one day reign again, as it were, in the persons of his great-grandchildren. For by this time Augustus had forgotten about the Republic, as almost everybody else had, and accepted the view that his forty years of hard and anxious service on Rome's behalf had earned him the right of appointing his Imperial successors, to the third generation, even, if it so pleased him.

When Germanicus was in Dalmatia I did not write to him about Postumus for fear of some agent of Livia's intercepting my letter, but I told him everything as soon as he returned from the war. He was greatly troubled and said that he did not know what to believe. I should explain that Germanicus's way was always to refuse to think evil of any person until positive proof of such evil should be forced on him, and, on the contrary, to credit everyone with the highest motives. This extreme simplicity was generally of service to him. Most people with whom he came in contact were flattered by his high estimate of their moral character and tended in their dealings with him to live up to it. If he were ever to find himself at the mercy of a downright wicked character, this generosity of heart would of course be his undoing; but on the other hand if any man had any good in him Germanicus always seemed to bring it out. So now he told me that he would not willingly believe either Livilla or Aemilia capable of such criminal baseness, though lately, he owned, he had been disappointed in Livilla. He also said that I had not made their possible motives clear except by dragging our grandmother Livia into it, which was plainly ridiculous. Who in his senses, he asked, suddenly indignant, could suspect Livia of inciting them to such evil? One might as easily suspect the Good Goddess of poisoning the City wells. But when I asked in reply whether he really believed Postumus guilty of two attempted rapes on successive nights, both excessively imprudent, or capable of lying to Augustus and us about them even if he had been guilty, he was silent. He had always loved and trusted Postumus. I pursued my advantage and made him swear by the ghost of our dead father that if ever he found the least piece of evidence to show that Postumus had been unjustly sentenced he would tell Augustus all that he knew about the case and force him to bring Postumus back and punish the liars as they deserved.

In Germany nothing much was happening. Tiberius held the bridges but did not attempt to cross the Rhine, not having confidence yet in his troops, whom he was busy knocking into shape. The Germans did not attempt to cross either. Augustus grew impatient again with Tiberius, and urged him to avenge Varus without further delay and win back the lost Eagles. Tiberius answered

152

that nothing was nearer to his own heart but that his troops were not yet fit to attempt the task. Augustus sent out Germanicus when he had finished his term of magistracy, and Tiberius then had to show some activity; he was not really lazy, or a coward, only extremely cautious. He crossed the Rhine and over-ran parts of the lost province, but the Germans avoided a A.D. 11 pitched battle; and Tiberius and Germanicus, both very careful not to fall into any ambush, did not do much more than burn a few enemy encampments near the Rhine and parade their military strength. There were a few skirmishes in which they came off well – some hundreds of prisoners were taken. They remained in this region until the autumn, when they recrossed the Rhine; and in the next spring the long-delayed triumph over the Dalmatians was celebrated at Rome, to which was added another for this German expedition, just to restore confidence. I must not fail here to award Tiberius credit for a generous action, to which Germanicus persuaded him: after displaying Bato, the captured Dalmatian rebel, in his triumph, he gave him his freedom and a large present of money and settled him comfortably at Ravenna. Bato deserved it: he had once chivalrously allowed Tiberius to escape from a valley where he was trapped with most of his army.

Germanicus was Consul now and Augustus wrote a special letter commending him to the Senate and the Senate to Tiberius. (By thus commending the Senate to Tiberius, instead of the other way about, Augustus showed both that he intended Tiberius as his Imperial successor, in authority over the Senate, and that he did not wish to utter any eulogy on him as he did on Germanicus.) Agrippina always accompanied Germanicus when he went to the wars, as my mother had accompanied my father. She did this chiefly for love of him but also because she did not want to stay alone in Rome and perhaps be summoned before Augustus on a trumped-up charge of adultery. She could not be sure how she stood with Livia. She was the typical Roman matron of ancient legend – strong, courageous, modest, witty, pious, fertile, and chaste. She already had borne four children to Germanicus and was to bear him five more.

Germanicus, though Livia's rule against my presence at her table still held, and though my mother showed no change of heart towards me either, brought me into the company of his noble friends whenever occasion offered. For his sake I was treated with a certain respect; but the family opinion of my capacities was known and Tiberius was understood to share it, so nobody took the trouble to cultivate my acquaintance. On Germanicus's advice I advertised that I would give a reading of my recent historical work and invited a number of prominent literary people to attend it. The book I had chosen to read was one at which I had worked very hard, and one which should have been very interesting to my audience – an account of the formulas used during ritual washing by the Etruscan priests, with a Latin translation in each case which threw light on many of our own lustral rites, the exact significance of which had been obscured by time. Germanicus read it through beforehand and showed it to my mother and Livia, who approved it, and then was generous enough to sit with me through a rehearsal of my reading. He congratulated me both on the work and on my delivery and I think must have spoken about it widely, for the room in which I was to give the reading was packed. Livia was not there, nor Augustus, but my mother attended, and Germanicus himself and Livilla.

I was in high spirits and not nervous at all. Germanicus had suggested that I should fortify myself with a cup of wine beforehand and I thought this good advice. There was a chair put for Augustus in case he should arrive and one for Livia, both very splendid ones – the chairs which were always reserved for them when they visited our house. When everyone had arrived and sat down the doors were shut and I began reading. I was getting along splendidly, conscious that I was not reading too fast or too slow or too loud or too soft, but just right, and that the audience, which had not expected much of me, was interested in spite of itself, when a most unlucky thing happened. A loud knock came at the door and then, when nobody opened it, another. Then there was a great rattle of the handle and in walked the fattest man I had ever seen in my life, dressed in a knight's robe, and carrying in his hand a large embroidered cushion. I stopped reading because I had come to a difficult and important passage and nobody was listening – all eyes were fixed on the knight. He recognized Livy and greeted him in a sing-song accent, which I learned later was that of Padua, and then made a general salutation to the rest of the company; which caused a lot of titters. He paid no especial attention to Germanicus as Consul or to my mother and myself as hosts. Then he looked round for a seat and saw Augustus's, but it seemed rather too narrow for him, so he took possession of Livia's. He put his cushion on it, gathered his gown about his knees and sat down with a grunt. And of course the chair, which was an ancient one from Egypt, part of the spoil of Cleopatra's palace, and of very delicate workmanship, collapsed with a crash.

Everyone except Germanicus and Livy and my mother and the graver members of the audience laughed very loudly; but when the knight had picked himself up and groaned and sworn and rubbed himself and had been escorted from the room by a freedman, there was an attentive silence and I tried to go on again. But I was almost hysterical with laughter. Perhaps it was the wine I had drunk, or perhaps it was because I had seen the expression on the fellow's face when the chair was giving under him, which nobody else had, because he was in the front row and I was the only person facing him; but at any rate I found concentration on the lustral rites of the Etruscans impossible. At first the audience sympathized with my amusement and even laughed with me, but when, struggling through another paragraph, very badly, I happened with the corner of my eye to see the chair which the knight had broken propped up insecurely on its splintered legs, I broke down again and the audience began to get impatient. To make matters still worse, when I had just fought hard with myself and got into my stride again, to the evident relief of Germanicus, the doors were thrown open and who should come in but Augustus and Livia! They walked grandly between the rows of chairs and Augustus sat down. Livia was about to do the same when she saw that something was amiss. She asked in a loud ringing voice: 'Who's been sitting in *my* chair?' Germanicus did his best to explain matters but she decided that she was being insulted. She went out. Augustus, looking uncomfortable, followed. Can anyone blame me for making a mull of the rest of my reading? The cruel god Momus must have been in that chair, for five minutes later the legs slid apart and once more the thing collapsed, a little gold lion's head breaking off from one arm, skidding across the floor and sliding under my right foot, which was slightly raised. I broke down again, choking and wheezing and guffawing.

Germanicus came over to me and implored me to control myself, but I could only pick up the lion's head and point helplessly at the chair. If I ever saw Germanicus annoyed with me it was then. It upset me very much to see him annoyed and sobered me instantly. But I had lost all self-confidence and began to stammer so badly that the reading came to a dismal end. Germanicus did his best by moving a vote of thanks for my interesting paper – regretting that an untoward accident had disturbed me half-way through and that in consequence of the same accident the Father of the country and the Lady Livia his wife had withdrawn their presences, and hoping that on a more auspicious day in the near future I might give a further reading. There was never so considerate a brother as Germanicus, or so noble a man. But I have not given a single public reading of my works since.

Germanicus came to me one day looking very grave. It was a long time before he could make up his mind to speak, but at last he said: 'I was talking to Aemilius this morning and the subject of poor Postumus happened to come up. He introduced it first by asking me what the precise charges against Postumus had been; and said, apparently quite ingenuously, that he understood that Postumus had attempted to violate two noblewomen, but that nobody seemed to know who they were. I looked hard at him when he said this, but could see that he was speaking the truth. So I offered to exchange my knowledge with his, but only if he promised to keep what I told him to himself. When I said that it was his own daughter who had charged Postumus with trying to outrage her, and in his own house, he was astonished and refused to believe it. He got very angry. He said Aemilia's governess had surely been with them all the time. He wanted to go to Aemilia and ask her if the story was true and if so, why this was the first he had heard of it; but I restrained him, reminding him of his promise. I mistrusted Aemilia. Instead I suggested that we should question the governess, but not so as to alarm her. So he sent for her and asked what conversation Aemilia and Postumus had had, during that alarm of thieves, on the last occasion he had dined with them. She looked blank at first, but when I asked "Wasn't it about fruit-trees?" she said "Yes, of course, about pests on fruit-trees." Aemilius then wanted to know whether any other conversation had taken place during his absence and she said that she believed not. She recalled that Postumus had been explaining new Greek methods for dealing with the pest called "blacka-moor" and that she had been extremely interested because she knew about gardens. No, she said, she had not left the room for a moment. So next I went to Castor and casually introduced the subject of Postumus. You remember that Postumus's estate was confiscated and sold while I was away in Dalmatia and that the proceeds were devoted to the military treasury? Well, I asked him what had happened to certain pieces of plate of mine that Postumus had borrowed from me for a banquet; and he told me how to recover them. Then we discussed his banishment. Castor talked quite freely and I am glad to say that I am now quite satisfied in my mind that he was not in the plot.'

'You admit now that it was a plot?' I asked eagerly.

'I'm afraid, after all, that is the only explanation. But Castor himself was innocent, I am convinced. He told me, without being prompted, that on Livilla's suggestion he had teased Postumus in the garden, as Postumus told you he had. He explained that it was only because Postumus had been making sheep's eyes at Livilla and as her husband he did not like it. But he said that he did not regret having done so – though it was perhaps not a joke in the best of taste – because Postumus's attempt to outrage Livilla and his own serious injuries at that madman's hands made any regrets foolish.'

'He believed that Postumus tried to outrage Livilla?'

'Yes. I did not undeceive him. I did not want Livilla to know what you and I suspect. Because, if she did, Livia would hear of it.'

'Germanicus, you believe now that Livia arranged the whole thing?'

He did not answer.

'You will go to Augustus?'

'I gave you my word. I always keep my word.'

'When are you going to him?'

'Now.'

What happened at the interview I do not know and shall never know. But Germanicus seemed much happier that evening at dinner and the manner in which he later evaded my questions suggested that Augustus had believed him and had sworn him to secrecy for the present. It was a long time before I learned as much of the sequel as I can tell now. Augustus wrote to the Corsicans, who had been complaining for some years A.D. 13 of pirate raids on their coasts, that he would soon come in person to investigate the matter; he would stop on his way to Marseilles where he intended to dedicate a temple. Shortly afterwards he set sail, but broke his journey at Elba for two days. On

the first day he ordered Postumus's guards at Planasia to be relieved at once by an entirely new set. This was done. The same
night he sailed secretly across to the island in a small fishing-boat,
accompanied only by Fabius Maximus, a close friend, and one
Clement, who had once been a slave of Postumus's and bore a
remarkably close resemblance to his former master. I have heard
that Clement was a natural son of Agrippa's. They were lucky
enough to meet Postumus as soon as they landed. He had been
setting night-lines for fish and had seen the sail of the boat from
some distance away in the light of a strong moon; he was alone.
Augustus revealed himself, and stretched out his hand crying,
'Forgive me, my son!' Postumus took the hand and kissed it.
Then the two went apart while Fabius and Clement kept watch.
What was said between them nobody knows; but Augustus was
weeping when they came back together. Then Postumus and
Clement changed clothes and names, Postumus sailing back to
Elba with Augustus and Fabius, and Clement taking Postumus's
place at Planasia until the word should come for his release, which
Augustus said would not be long delayed. Clement was promised
his freedom and a large sum of money if he played his part well.
He was to feign sick for the next few days and grow his hair and
beard long, so that nobody would notice the imposture, especially
since that afternoon he had not been seen by the new guard for
more than a few minutes.

Livia suspected that Augustus was doing something behind her
back. She knew his dislike of the sea and that he never went by
ship when he could go by land, even if it meant losing valuable
time. It is true that he could not have gone to Corsica except by
sea, but the pirates were not a serious menace and he could easily
have sent Castor or any one of several other subordinates to investigate the matter on his behalf. So she began to make inquiries
and eventually heard that when Augustus stopped at Elba he had
ordered Postumus's guards to be changed, and that he and Fabius
had gone out catching cuttle-fish the same night in a small boat,
accompanied only by a slave.

Fabius had a wife called Marcia who shared all his secrets, and
Livia, who had paid little attention to her, now began to cultivate
her acquaintance. Marcia was a simple woman and easily deceived. When Livia was sure that she was completely in Marcia's
confidence she took her aside one day and asked: 'Come, my dear,

tell me, was Augustus very much affected when he met Postumus again after all those years? He's much more tender-hearted than he makes out.' Now Fabius had told Marcia that the story of the voyage to Planasia was a secret which she must not reveal to anyone in the world, or the consequences might be fatal to him. So she would not answer at first. Livia laughed and said, 'Oh, you *are* cautious. You're like that sentry of Tiberius's in Dalmatia who wouldn't let Tiberius himself into the camp one evening when he came back from a ride because he couldn't give the watchword. "Orders are orders, General," the idiot said. My dear Marcia, Augustus has no secrets from me, nor I from Augustus. But I commend your prudence.' So Marcia apologized and said: 'Fabius said he wept and wept.' Livia said, 'Of course he did. But, Marcia, perhaps it would be wiser not to let Fabius know that we've talked about it – Augustus doesn't like people to know how much he confides in me. I suppose Fabius told you about the slave?'

This was a shot in the dark. The slave may have been of no importance, but it was a question worth asking. Marcia said: 'Yes. Fabius said that he was extraordinarily like Postumus, only a little shorter.'

'You don't think the guards will notice the difference?'

'Fabius said he thought they wouldn't. Clement was one of Postumus's household staff, so if he's careful he won't betray himself by ignorance and, as you know, the guard was changed.'

So Livia now only had to find out the whereabouts of Postumus, whom she assumed to be hidden somewhere under the name of Clement. She thought that Augustus was planning to restore him to favour and might even pass over Tiberius and appoint him his immediate successor in the monarchy, by way of making amends. She now took Tiberius into her confidence, more or less, and warned him of her suspicions. Trouble had started again in the Balkans and Augustus was proposing to send Tiberius to suppress it before it took a serious turn. Germanicus was in France collecting tribute. Augustus spoke of sending Castor away too, to Germany; and he had been having frequent conversations with Fabius, who Livia concluded was acting as his go-between with Postumus. As soon as the coast was clear Augustus would no doubt suddenly introduce Postumus into the Senate, get the decree against him reversed and have him appointed his colleague in place of Tiberius. With Postumus restored her own life would not be safe: Postumus had accused her of poisoning his father and brothers and Augustus would not be taking him back into favour unless he believed that these accusations were well grounded. She set her most trusted agents to spy on Fabius's movements with a view to tracing a slave called Clement; but they could discover nothing. She decided at any rate to lose no time in removing Fabius. He was waylaid in the street one night on his way to the Palace and stabbed in twelve places: his masked assailants escaped. At the funeral a scandalous thing happened. Marcia threw herself on her husband's corpse and begged his pardon, saying that she alone had been responsible for his death by her thoughtlessness and disobedience. However, nobody understood what she meant and it was thought that grief had crazed her.

Livia told Tiberius to keep in constant communication with her on his way to the Balkans and to travel as slowly as possible: he might be sent for at any moment. Augustus, who had accompanied him as far as Naples, cruising easily along the coast, now fell sick: his stomach was disordered. Livia prepared to nurse him but he thanked her and told her that it was A.D. 14 nothing; he could cure himself. He went to his own medicine-cabinet and chose a strong purge, then fasted for a day. He positively forbade her to worry about his health; she had enough cares without that. He laughingly refused to eat anything but bread from the common table and water from the pitcher which she used herself and green figs which he picked from the tree with his own hands. Nothing in his manner to Livia seemed altered, nor was hers altered towards him, but each read the other's mind.

In spite of all precautions his stomach grew worse again. He had to break his journey at Nola; from there Livia sent a message recalling Tiberius. When he arrived Augustus was reported to be sinking and to be earnestly calling for him. He had already taken his farewell of certain ex-Consuls who had hurried from Rome at the news of his illness. He had asked them with a smile whether they thought he had acted well in the farce; which is the question that actors in comedies put to the audience at the conclusion of the piece. And smiling back, though many of them had tears in their eyes, they answered: 'No man better, Augustus.' 'Then send me off with a good clap,' he said. Tiberius went to his bedside, where he remained for some three hours, and then emerged to announce in sorrowful tones that the Father of the Country had just passed away, in Livia's arms, with a final loving salutation to himself, to the Senate, and to the people of Rome. He thanked the Gods that he had returned in time to close the eyes of his father and benefactor. As a matter of fact, Augustus had been dead a whole day, but Livia had concealed this, giving out reassuring or discouraging bulletins every few hours. By a strange coincidence he died in the very room in which his father had died, seventy-five years before. I remember well how the news came to me. It was on the 20th of August. I was sleeping late after working nearly all night on my history; I found it easier in the summer to work by night and sleep by day. I was awakened by the arrival of two old knights who excused themselves for disturbing me but said that the matter was urgent. Augustus was dead and the Noble Order of Knights had met hurriedly and elected me their representative to go to the Senate. I was to ask that they might be honoured by the permission to bring Augustus's dead body back to the City on their shoulders. I was still half-asleep and did not think what I was saying. I shouted, 'Poison is Queen, Poison is Queen!' They glanced anxiously and uncomfortably at each other and I recalled myself and apologized, saying that I had been dreaming a fearful dream and was repeating words that I heard in it. I asked them to repeat their message and when they did so thanked them for the honour and undertook to do what was asked of me. It was not altogether an honour, of course, to be singled out as a distinguished knight. Everyone was a knight who was free-born, and had not disgraced himself in any way, and owned property above a certain value; and, with my family connexions, if I had shown even average ability I should by now have been an honoured member of the Senate like my contemporary Castor. I was chosen in fact as being the only member of the Imperial family who still belonged to the lower order, and to avoid jealousy among the other knights. This was the first time that I had ever visited the Senate during a session. I made the plea without stammering or forgetting my words or otherwise disgracing myself.

Chapter 14

ALTHOUGH it had been clear that Augustus's powers were failing and that he had not many more years to live, Rome could not accustom itself to the idea of his death. It is not an idle comparison to say that the City felt much as a boy feels when he loses his father. Whether the father has been a brave man or a coward, just or unjust, generous or mean, signifies little: he has been that boy's father, and no uncle or elder brother can ever take his place. For Augustus's rule had been a very long one and a man had to be already past middle age to remember back behind it. It was therefore not altogether unnatural that the Senate met to deliberate whether the divine honours which had, even in his lifetime, been paid him by the provinces should now be voted him in the City itself.

Pollio's son, Gallus – hated by Tiberius because he had married Vipsania (Tiberius's first wife, you will recall, whom he had been forced to divorce on Julia's account), and because he had never given a public denial of the rumour which made him the real father of Castor, and because he had a witty tongue – this Gallus was the only senator who had dared to question the propriety of the motion. He rose to ask what divine portent had occurred to suggest that Augustus would be welcomed in the Heavenly Mansions – merely at the recommendation of his mortal friends and admirers?

There followed an uncomfortable silence, but at last Tiberius rose slowly and said: 'One hundred days ago, it will be recalled, the pediment of my father Augustus's statue was struck by lightning. The first letter of his name was blotted out, which left the words AESAR AUGUSTUS. What is the meaning of the letter C? It is the sign for one hundred. What does AESAR mean? I shall tell you. It means God, in the Etruscan tongue. Clearly, in a hundred days from that lightning stroke Augustus is to become a God in Rome. What clearer portent than this can you require?' Though Tiberius took the sole credit for this interpretation it was I who had first given meaning to AESAR (the queer word had been much discussed), being the only person at Rome who was acquainted with the Etruscan language. I told my mother about it and she

162

called me a fanciful fool; but she must have been sufficiently impressed to repeat what I said to Tiberius, for I told nobody but her.

Gallus asked why Jove should give his messages in Etruscan rather than in Greek or Latin? Could nobody swear to having observed any other more conclusive omen? It was all very well to decree new gods to ignorant Asiatic provincials, but the honourable House ought to pause before ordering educated citizens to worship one of their own number, however distinguished. It is possible that Gallus would have succeeded in blocking the decree by this appeal to Roman pride and sanity had it not been for a man called Atticus, a senior magistrate. He solemnly rose to say that when Augustus's corpse had been burned on Mars Field he had seen a cloud descending from heaven and the dead man's spirit then ascending on it, precisely in the way in which tradition relates that the spirits of Romulus and Hercules ascended. He would swear by all the Gods that he was testifying the truth.

This speech was greeted with resounding applause and Tiberius triumphantly asked whether Gallus had any further remarks to make. Gallus said that he had. He recalled, he said, another early tradition about the sudden death and disappearance of Romulus, which appeared in the works of even the gravest historians as an alternative to the one quoted by his honourable and veracious friend Atticus: namely, that Romulus was so hated for his tyranny over a free people that one day, taking advantage of a sudden fog, the Senate murdered him, cut him up, and carried the pieces away under their robes.

'But what about Hercules?' someone hurriedly asked.

Gallus said: 'Tiberius himself in his eloquent oration at the funeral repudiated the comparison between Augustus and Hercules. His words were: "Hercules in his childhood dealt only with serpents, and even when a man only with a stag or two, and a wild boar which he killed, and a lion; and even this he did reluctantly and at somebody's command; whereas Augustus fought not with beasts but with men and of his own free will" – and so forth and so forth. But *my* reason for repudiating the comparison lies in the circumstances of Hercules's death.' Then he sat down. The reference was perfectly clear to anybody who considered the matter; for the legend was that Hercules died of poison administered by his wife.

163

But the motion for Augustus's deification was carried. Shrines were built to him in Rome and the neighbouring cities. An order of priests was formed for administering his rites and Livia, who had at the same time been granted the titles of Julia and Augusta, was made his High Priestess. Atticus was rewarded by Livia with a gift of ten thousand gold pieces, and was appointed one of the new priests of Augustus, being even excused the heavy initiation fee. I was also appointed a priest, but had to pay a higher initiation fee than anyone, because I was Livia's grandson. Nobody dared ask why this vision of Augustus's ascent had only been seen by Atticus. And the joke was that on the night before the funeral Livia had concealed an eagle in a cage at the top of the pyre, which was to be opened as soon as the pyre was lit by someone secretly pulling a string from below. The eagle would then fly up and was intended to be taken for Augustus's spirit. Unfortunately the miracle had not come off. The cage door refused to open. Instead of saying nothing and letting the eagle burn, the officer who was in charge clambered up the pyre and opened the cage door with his hands. Livia had to say that the eagle had been thus released at her orders, as a symbolic act.

I shall not write more about Augustus's funeral, though a more magnificent one has never been seen at Rome, for I must now begin to omit all things in my story except those of the first importance: I have already filled more than thirteen rolls of the best paper – from the new paper-making factory I have recently equipped – and not reached a third of the way through it. But I must not fail to tell about the contents of Augustus's will, the reading of which was awaited with general interest and impatience. Nobody was more anxious to know what it contained than I was, and I shall explain why.

A month before his death Augustus had suddenly appeared at the door of my study – he had been visiting my mother who was just convalescent after a long illness – and after dismissing his attendants had begun to talk to me in a rambling way, not looking directly at me, but behaving as shyly as though he were Claudius and I were Augustus. He picked up a book of his history and read a passage. 'Excellent writing!' he said. 'And how soon will the work be finished?'

I told him, 'In a month or less', and he congratulated me and said that he would then give orders to have a public reading of it at his own expense, inviting his friends to attend. I was perfectly astonished at this, but he went on in a friendly way to ask if I would not prefer a professional reciter to do justice to it rather than read myself: he said that public reading of one's own work must be very embarrassing – even tough old Pollio had confessed that he was always nervous on such occasions. I thanked him most sincerely and heartily and said that a professional would obviously be more suitable, if my work indeed deserved such an honour.

Then he suddenly held out his hand to me: 'Claudius, do you bear me any ill-will?'

What could I say to that? Tears came to my eyes and I muttered that I reverenced him and that he had never done anything to deserve my ill-will. He said with a sigh: 'No, but on the other hand little to earn your love. Wait a few months longer, Claudius, and I hope to be able to earn both your love and your gratitude. Germanicus has told me about you. He says that you are loyal to three things – to your friends, to Rome, and to the truth. I should be very proud if Germanicus thought the same of me.'

'Germanicus's love for you falls only a little short of outright worship,' I said. 'He has often told me so.'

His face brightened. 'You swear it? I am very happy. So now, Claudius, there's a strong bond between us – the good opinion of Germanicus. And what I came to tell you was this: I have treated you very badly all these years and I'm sincerely sorry and from now on you'll see that things will change.' He quoted in Greek: 'Who wounded thee, shall make thee whole,' and with that he embraced me. As he turned to go he said over his shoulder: 'I have just paid a visit to the Vestal Virgins and made some important alterations in a document of mine in their charge: and since you yourself are partly responsible for these I have given your name greater prominence there than it had before. But not a word!'

'You can trust me,' I said.

He could only have meant one thing by this: that he had believed Postumus's story as I had reported it to Germanicus and was now restoring him in his will (which was in charge of the Vestals) as his heir; and that I was to benefit too as a reward for my loyalty to him. I did not then, of course, know of Augustus's visit to Planasia but confidently expected that Postumus would be

165

brought back and treated with honour. Well, I was disappointed. Since Augustus had been so secretive about the new will, which had been witnessed by Fabius Maximus and a few decrepit old priests, it was easy to suppress it in favour of one which had been made six years before at the time of the disinheriting of Postumus. The opening sentence was: 'Forasmuch as a sinister fate has bereft me of Gaius and Lucius, my sons, it is now my will that Tiberius Claudius Nero Caesar become heir, in the first range, of two-thirds of my estate; and of the remaining third, in the first range also, it is now my will that my beloved wife Livia shall become my heir, if so be that the Senate will graciously permit her to inherit this much (for it is in excess of the statutory allowance for a widow's legacy), making an exception in her case as having deserved so well of the State.' In the second range – that is, in the event of the first-mentioned legatees dying or becoming otherwise incapable to inherit – he put such of his grandchildren and great-grandchildren as were members of the Julian house and had incurred no public disgrace; but Postumus had been disinherited, so this meant Germanicus, as Tiberius's adopted son and Agrippina's husband, and Agrippina herself and her children, and Castor, Livilla, and their children. In this second range Castor was to inherit a third, and Germanicus and his family two-thirds of the estate. In the third range the will named various senators and distant connexions; but as a mark of favour rather than as likely to benefit. Augustus cannot have expected to outlive so many heirs of the first and second ranges. The third range heirs were grouped in three categories: the most favoured ten were set down to be joint-heirs of half the estate, the next most favoured fifty were set down to share a third of the estate, and the third class contained the names of fifty more who were to inherit the remaining sixth. The last name in this last list of the last range was Tiberius Claudius Drusus Nero Germanicus, which meant Clau-Clau-Claudius, or Claudius the Idiot, or as Germanicus's little boys were already learning to call him: 'Poor Uncle Claudius' – in fact, myself. There was no mention of Julia or Julilla except a clause forbidding their ashes to be interred in the mausoleum beside his own when they came to die.

Now, although Augustus had in the previous twenty years benefited under the wills of the old friends he had outlived, to the extent of no less than 140 million gold pieces, and had lived a most parsimonious life, he had spent so much on temples and public works, on doles and entertainments for the populace, on frontier wars (when there was no money left in the military treasury), and on similar State expenses, that of those 140 millions and a great mass of private treasure besides, accumulated from various sources, a mere fifteen million remained for bequest, much of this not easily realizable in cash. This did not, however, include certain important sums of money, not reckoned in the estate and ready tied up in sacks in the vaults of the Capitol, which had been set aside as particular bequests to confederate kings, to senators and knights, to his soldiers, and to the citizens of Rome. These amounted to two million more. There was also a sum set aside for the expenses of his funeral. Everyone was surprised at the smallness of the estate, and all sorts of ugly rumours went round until Augustus's accounts were produced and it was clear that there was no fraud on the part of the executors. The citizens were most discontented with their meagre bequests, and when a memorial play was exhibited in Augustus's honour at the public expense there was a riot in the theatre: the Senate had so stinted the grant that one of the actors in the play refused to appear for the fee offered him. Of the discontent in the Army I shall tell shortly. But first about Tiberius.

Augustus had made Tiberius his colleague and his heir but could not bequeath him the monarchy, or not in so many words. He could only recommend him to the Senate to whom all the powers he had exercised now reverted. The Senate did not like Tiberius or wish him to be Emperor, but Germanicus, whom they would have chosen if they had been given the chance, was away. And Tiberius's claims could not be disregarded.

So nobody dared to mention any name but that of Tiberius, and there were no dissentients from the motion, introduced by the Consuls, inviting him to take over Augustus's task where he had laid it down. He gave an evasive answer, emphasizing the immense responsibility that they were trying to put on him and his own unaspiring disposition. He said that the God Augustus alone had been capable of this mighty charge, and that in his opinion it would be best to divide up Augustus's offices into three parts and so divide the responsibility.

Senators anxious to curry favour with him pleaded that the triumvirate, or three-man rule, had been tried more than once in the preceding century and that a monarchy had been found the only remedy for the resulting civil wars. A disgraceful scene followed. Senators pretended to weep and lament, and embraced Tiberius's knees, imploring him to do as they asked. Tiberius, to cut this business short, said that he did not wish to shirk any charge laid upon him, but held by his assertion that he was not equal to the whole burden. He was no longer a young man: he was fifty-six years old, and his eyesight was not good. But he would undertake any particular part entrusted to him. All this was done so that nobody would be able to accuse him of seizing power too eagerly: and especially so that Germanicus and Postumus (wherever he happened to be) might be impressed by the strength of his position in the City. For he was afraid of Germanicus, whose popularity with the Army was infinitely greater than his own. He did not believe Germanicus capable of seizing the power for his own selfish ends but thought that if he knew of the suppressed will he might try to restore Postumus to his rightful inheritance and even to make him the third – Tiberius, Germanicus, and Postumus – in the new triumvirate. Agrippina was devoted to Postumus, and Germanicus took her advice as consistently as Augustus had taken Livia's. If Germanicus marched on Rome the Senate would go out in a body to welcome him: Tiberius knew that. And, at the worst, by behaving modestly now he would be able to escape with his life and live in honourable retirement.

The Senate realized that Tiberius really wanted what he was so modestly refusing and were about to renew their pleas when Gallus interposed in a practical voice: 'Very well, then, Tiberius, which part of the government do you want to be entrusted to you?'

Tiberius was confounded by this awkward and unforeseen question. He was silent for some time and at last said: 'The same man cannot both make the division and choose; and even if this were possible it would be immodest for me to choose or reject any particular branch of the administration when, as I have explained, I really want to be excused the whole of it.'

Gallus pressed his advantage: 'The only possible division of the Empire would be: first, Rome and all Italy; second, the armies; and third, the provinces. Which of these would you choose?'

When Tiberius was silent Gallus continued: 'Good. I know there's no answer. That's why I asked the question. I wanted you to admit by your silence that it was nonsense to speak of splitting into three an administrative system that has been built up and centrally co-ordinated by a single individual. Either we must return to the republican form of government or we must continue with the monarchy. It is wasting the time of the House, which appears to have decided in favour of the monarchy, to go on talking about triumvirates. You have been offered the monarchy. Take it or leave it.'

Another senator, a friend of Gallus's, said: 'As Protector of the People you have the power of vetoing the motion of the Consuls offering you the monarchy. If you really don't want it you should have used your veto half an hour ago.'

So Tiberius was forced to beg the Senate's pardon and to say that the suddenness and unexpectedness of the honour had overcome him: he begged leave to consider his answer a little longer.

The Senate then adjourned, and in succeeding sessions Tiberius gradually allowed himself to be voted, one by one, all Augustus's offices. But he never used the name Augustus, which had been bequeathed him, except when writing letters to foreign kings; and was careful to discourage any tendency to pay him divine honours. There was another explanation of this cautious behaviour of his, namely that Livia had boasted in public that he was receiving the monarchy as a gift from her hands. She made the boast not only to strengthen her position as Augustus's widow but to warn Tiberius that if her crimes ever came to light he would be regarded as her accomplice, being the person who principally benefited from them. Naturally he wished to appear under no obligation to her but as having had the monarchy forced on him against his will by the Senate.

The Senate were profuse in their flattery of Livia and wanted to confer many unheard-of honours on her. But Livia as a woman could not attend the debates in the Senate and was legally now under Tiberius's guardianship – he had become head of the Julian house. So having himself refused the title 'Father of the Country', he had refused, on her behalf, the title 'Mother of the Country' which had been offered her, on the ground that modesty would not allow her to accept it. Nevertheless, he was greatly afraid of Livia and at first wholly dependent on her for learning the inner secrets of the Imperial system. It was not merely a matter of understanding the routine. The criminal dossiers of every man of importance in the two Orders and of most of the important women, secret service reports of various sorts, Augustus's private correspondence with confederate kings and their relatives, copies of treasonable letters intercepted but duly forwarded – all these were in Livia's keeping and written in cipher, and Tiberius could not read them without her help. But he also knew that she was extremely dependent on him. There was an understanding between them of guarded co-operation. She even thanked him for refusing the title offered her, saying that he had been right to do so; and in return he promised to have her voted whatever titles she wished as soon as their position seemed secure. As proof of his good faith he put her own name alongside his own in all letters of State. As a proof of hers she gave him the key of the common cipher, though not that of the cipher extraordinary, the secret of which, she pretended, had died with Augustus. It was in the cipher extraordinary that the dossiers were written.

Now about Germanicus. When, at Lyons, he heard of Augustus's death and of the terms of his will, and of Tiberius's succession, he felt it his duty to stand loyally by the new régime. He was Tiberius's nephew and adopted son, and though there was no true affection between the two they had been able to work together without friction both at home and on campaign. He did not suspect Tiberius of complicity in the plot that had brought about Postumus's banishment; and he knew nothing of the suppressed will, and further, he still believed Postumus to be on Planasia – for Augustus had told nobody but Fabius either of the visit or of the substitution. He decided, however, to return to Rome as soon as he could and frankly discuss the case of Postumus with Tiberius. He would explain that Augustus had told him privately that he intended to restore Postumus to favour as soon as he had evidence of his innocence to offer the Senate; and that though death had prevented him from putting his intentions into execution, they should be respected. He would insist on Postumus's immediate recall, the restoration of his confiscated estates and his elevation to honourable office; and lastly on Livia's compulsory retirement from State affairs as having unjustly engineered his banishment. But before he could do anything in the matter news came from Mainz of an army mutiny on the Rhine, and then, as he was hurrying to put it down, news of Postumus's death. Postumus, it was reported, had been killed by the captain of the guard, who was under orders from Augustus not to let his grandson survive him. Germanicus was shocked and grieved that Postumus had been executed but had no leisure for the moment to think of anything but the mutiny. You may be sure, though, that it caused poor Claudius the greatest possible grief, for poor Claudius at this time never wanted for leisure. On the contrary poor Claudius was hard put to it often to find occupation for his mind. Nobody can write history for more than five or six hours a day, especially when there is little hope of anyone ever reading it. So I gave myself up to my misery. How was I to know that it was Clement who had been killed, and that not only was the murder not ordered by Augustus but that Livia and Tiberius were also innocent of it?

For the man really responsible for Clement's murder was an old knight called Crispus, the owner of the Gardens of Sallust and a close friend of Augustus. At Rome, as soon as he heard of Augustus's death, he had not waited to consult Livia and Tiberius at Nola but immediately dispatched the warrant for Postumus's execution to the captain of the guard at Planasia, attaching Tiberius's seal to it. Tiberius had entrusted him with this duplicate seal for the signing of some business papers which he had not been able to deal with before being sent to the Balkans. Crispus knew that Tiberius would be angry or pretend to be angry, but explained to Livia, whose protection he at once claimed, that he had put Postumus out of the way on learning of a plot among some of the Guards officers to send a ship to rescue Julia and Postumus and carry them off to the regiments at Cologne; there Germanicus and Agrippina could hardly fail to welcome and shelter them and the officers would then force Germanicus and Postumus to march on Rome. Tiberius was furious that his name had been used in this way, but Livia made the best of things and pretended that it really *was* Postumus who had been killed. Crispus was not prosecuted and the Senate was unofficially informed that Postumus had died by the orders of his deified grandfather who had wisely foreseen that the savage-tempered young man would attempt to usurp supreme power as soon as news came of his grandfather's death; as indeed he had done. Crispus's motive in having Postumus murdered was not a wish to curry favour with Tiberius and Livia or to prevent civil war. He was revenging an insult. For Crispus, who was as lazy as he was rich, had once boasted that he had never stood for office, content to be a simple Roman knight. Postumus

171

had replied: 'A simple Roman knight, Crispus? Then you had better take a few simple Roman riding-lessons.'

Tiberius had not yet heard of the mutiny. He wrote Germanicus a friendly letter condoling with him on the loss of Augustus and saying that Rome now looked to him and his adoptive brother Castor for the defence of the frontiers, himself being now too old for foreign service and required by the Senate to manage affairs at Rome. Writing of Postumus's death, he said that he deplored its violence but could not question the wisdom of Augustus in the matter. He did not mention Crispus. Germanicus could only conclude that Augustus had once more changed his mind about Postumus on the strength of some information of which he himself knew nothing; and was content for awhile to let the matter rest there.

Chapter 15

THE Rhine mutiny had broken out in sympathy with a mutiny among the Balkan forces. The soldiers' disappointment with their bequests under Augustus's will – a mere four months' bounty of pay, three gold pieces a man – aggravated certain long-standing grievances; and they reckoned that the insecurity of Tiberius's position would force him to meet any reasonable demands they made, in order to win their favour. These demands included a rise in pay, service limited to sixteen years, and a relaxation of camp discipline. The pay was certainly insufficient: the soldiers had to arm and equip themselves out of it, and prices had risen. And certainly the exhaustion of military reserves had kept thousands of soldiers with the Colours who should have been discharged years before, and veterans had been recalled to the Colours who were quite unfit for service. And, certainly too, the detachments formed from recently liberated slaves were such poor fighting material that Tiberius had considered it necessary to tighten up discipline, choosing martinets for his captains, and giving them instructions to keep the men constantly employed on fatigue duty and to keep the vine-branch saplings – their badges of rank – constantly employed on the men's backs.

When the news of Augustus's death reached the Balkan forces, three regiments were together in a summer camp, and the General gave them a few days' holiday from parades and fatigues. This experience of ease and idleness unsettled them and they refused to obey their captains when called out on parade again. They formulated certain demands. The General told them that he had no authority to grant these demands and warned them of the danger of a mutinous attitude. They offered him no violence but refused to be awed into obedience and finally obliged him to send his son to Rome to convey their demands to Tiberius. After the son had left the camp on this mission the disorder increased. The less-disciplined men began plundering the camp and the neighbouring villages, and when the General arrested the ringleaders, the rest broke open the guard-room and released them, finally murdering a captain who tried to oppose them. This captain was nicknamed 'Old Give-me-Another' because after breaking one sapling over a man's back, he would call for a second and a third. When the General's son arrived at Rome, Tiberius sent Castor to the General's support at the head of two battalions of Guards, a squadron of Guards cavalry, and most of the Household Battalion, who were Germans; a staff-officer called Sejanus, the son of the Commander of the Guards and one of Tiberius's few intimates, went with Castor as his lieutenant. Of this Sejanus I shall later have more to write. Castor on arrival addressed the mob of soldiers in a dignified and fearless way and read them a letter from his father, promising to take care of the invincible regiments with whom he had shared the hardships of so many wars, and to negotiate with the Senate about their demands as soon as he had recovered from his grief for Augustus's death. Meanwhile, he wrote, his son had come to them to make whatever immediate concessions might be practicable – the rest must be reserved for the Senate.

The mutineers made one of their captains act as their spokesman and present their demands, for no soldier would risk doing so for fear of being singled out later as a ringleader. Castor said that he was very sorry, but that the sixteen-year limit of service, the discharge of veterans, and the increase of pay to a full silver piece a day were demands which he had no authority to grant. Only his father and the Senate could make such concessions.

This put the men into an ugly temper. They asked why in Hell's name had he come then if he had no power to do anything for them. His father Tiberius, they said, used always to play the same trick on them when they presented their grievances: he used to shelter behind Augustus and the Senate. What was the Senate, anyhow? A pack of rich good-for-nothing lazybones, most of whom would die of fear if they ever caught sight of an enemy shield or saw a sword drawn in anger! They began throwing stones at Castor's staff and the situation became dangerous. But it was saved that night by a fortunate chance. The moon was eclipsed, which affected the army – all soldiers are superstitious – in a surprising way. They took the eclipse for a sign that Heaven was angry with them for their murder of Old Give-me-Another and for their defiance of authority. There were a number of secret loyalists among the mutineers, and one of these came to Castor suggesting that he should get hold of others like himself and send them around the tents in parties of two or three to try to bring the disaffected men to their senses. This was done. By morning there was a very different atmosphere in the camp and Castor, though he consented to send the General's son again to Tiberius with the same demands endorsed by himself, arrested the two men who appeared to have started the mutiny and publicly executed them. The rest made no protest and even voluntarily handed over the five murderers of the captain as a proof of their own fidelity. But there was still a firm refusal to attend parades, or do any but the most necessary fatigues until an answer came from Rome. The weather broke and incessant rain flooded the camp and made it impossible for the men to keep communication between tent and tent. This was taken as a fresh warning from Heaven, and before the messenger had time to return the mutiny was at an end, the regiments marching obediently back to winter quarters under their officers.

But the mutiny on the Rhine was a far more serious affair. Roman Germany was now bounded on the east by the Rhine and divided into two provinces, the Upper and the Lower. The capital of the Upper Province, which extended up into Switzerland, was Mainz, and that of the Lower, which reached north to the Scheldt and Sambre, was Cologne. An army of four regiments manned each of the provinces and Germanicus was Commander-in-Chief. Disorders broke out in a summer camp of the Lower Army. The grievances were the same here as in the Balkan army, but the conduct of the mutineers was more violent because of the greater proportion of newly-recruited City freedmen in the ranks. These freedmen were still slaves by nature and accustomed to a far more idle and luxurious life than the freeborn citizens, mostly poor peasants, who formed the backbone of the army. They made thoroughly bad soldiers and their badness went unchecked by any regimental *esprit-de-corps*. For these were not the regiments which had been under the command of Germanicus in the recent campaign; they were Tiberius's men.

The General lost his head and was unable to check the insolence of the mutineers who came crowding round him with complaints and threats. His nervousness encouraged them to fall on their most hated captains, about twenty of whom they beat to death with their own vine-saplings, throwing their bodies into the Rhine. The remainder they jeered at and insulted and drove from the camp. Cassius Chaerea was the only senior officer who made any attempt to oppose this monstrous and unheard-of behaviour. He was set upon by a large party, but instead of running away or begging for mercy rushed straight into the thick of them with his sword drawn, stabbing right and left, and broke through to the sacred tribunal-platform where he knew that no soldier would dare to touch him.

Germanicus had no battalions of Guards to support him but rode at once to the mutinous camp with only a small staff behind him. He did not yet know of the massacre. The men surged about him in a mob, as they had done about their General, but Germanicus calmly refused to say anything to them until they had formed up decently in companies and battalions under their proper banners so that he should know whom he was addressing. It seemed a small concession to authority; and they wanted to hear what he had to tell them. Once they were back in military formation a certain sense of discipline returned, and though by the murder of their officers they had put themselves beyond hope of his trust or forgiveness, their hearts suddenly went out to him as a brave and humane and honourable man. One old veteran – there were many there who had been serving in Germany twenty-five and thirty years before this – called out: 'How like he is to his father!' And another: 'He's got to be cursed good to be as cursed good as him.' Germanicus began in a voice of ordinary conversational pitch, to command more attention. He first spoke of the death of Augustus and the great grief it had inspired, but assured

175

them that Augustus had left behind him an indestructible work and a successor capable of carrying on the government and commanding the armies in the way that he himself would have wished. 'Of my father's glorious victories in Germany you are not unaware. Many of you have shared in them.'

'Never was there a better general or a better man,' shouted a veteran. 'Hurrah for Germanicus, father and son!'

It is a comment on my brother's extreme simplicity that he did not realize the effect his words were having. By his father, he meant Tiberius (who also was often styled Germanicus), but the veterans thought he meant his real father; and by Augustus's successor he meant Tiberius again, but the veterans thought that he meant himself. Unaware of these cross-purposes he went on to speak of the harmony that prevailed in Italy and of the fidelity of the French, from whose territory he had just come, and said that he could not understand the sudden feeling of pessimism that had overcome them. What ailed them? What had they done with their captains and their colonels and their generals? Why weren't these officers on parade? Had they really been expelled from the camp, as he had heard?

'A few of us are still alive and about, Caesar,' someone said, and Cassius came limping through the ranks and saluted Germanicus. 'Not many! They pulled me off the tribunal and have kept me tied up in the guardroom without food for the last four days. An old soldier has just been good enough to release me.'

'*You*, Cassius! They did that to *you*! The man who brought back the eighty from the Teutoburger Forest? The man who saved the Rhine bridge?'

'Well, at least they spared my life,' said Cassius.

Germanicus asked with horror in his voice: 'Men, is this true?'

'They brought it on themselves,' someone shouted, and then a fearful hubbub arose. Men stripped themselves to the skin to show the clean silver scars of honourable wounds on their breasts and the ragged discoloured marks of flogging on their backs. One decrepit old man broke from the ranks, and running forward pulled his mouth open with his fingers to show his bare gums. Then he shouted, 'I can't eat hard tack without teeth, General, and I can't march and fight on slops. I served under your father in his first campaign in the Alps and I'd done six years' service even then. I've two grandsons serving in the same company as myself. Give

176

me my discharge, General. I dandled you on my knees when you were a baby! And look, General, I've got a rupture and they expect me to march twenty miles with a hundred pounds' weight on my back.'

'Back to the ranks, Pomponius,' ordered Germanicus, who recognized the old man and was shocked to find him still under arms. 'You forget yourself. I'll look into your case later. For Heaven's sake show a good example to the young soldiers!'

Pomponius saluted and returned to the ranks. Germanicus held up his hand for silence, but the men went on shouting about their pay and the unecessary fatigues put on them so that they hardly had a moment to themselves from reveille to lights out, and that the only discharge a man got from the Army now was to drop dead from old age. Germanicus made no attempt to speak until he had complete quiet again. Then he said: 'In the name of my father Tiberius I promise you justice. He has your welfare at heart as deeply as I have and whatever can be done for you without danger to the Empire he will do. I'll answer for that.'

'Oh, to hell with Tiberius!' someone shouted, and the cry was picked up on all sides with groans and catcalls. And then suddenly they all began to shout: 'Up, Germanicus! You're the Emperor for us. Chuck Tiberius into the Tiber! Up, Germanicus! Germanicus for Emperor! To hell with Tiberius! To hell with that bitch Livia! Up, Germanicus! March on Rome! We're your men! Up, Germanicus, son of Germanicus! Germanicus for Emperor!'

Germanicus was thunderstruck. He shouted: 'You're mad, men, to talk like that. What do you think I am? A traitor?'

A veteran shouted: 'None of that, General! You said just now that you'd take on Augustus's job. Don't back out!'

Germanicus then realized his mistake, and when the cheers of 'Up, Germanicus' continued he jumped off the tribunal and hurried to where his horse was standing tied to a post, intending to mount and gallop wildly away from this accursed camp. But the men drew their swords and barred his way.

Germanicus, beside himself, cried: 'Let me pass, or by God, I'll kill myself.'

'You're the Emperor for us,' they answered.

Germanicus drew his sword, but someone caught at his arm. It was clear to any decent man that Germanicus was in earnest, but a good many of the ex-slaves thought that he was just making a hypocritical gesture of modesty and virtue. One of them laughed and called out: 'Here, take my sword. It's sharper!' Old Pomponius, who was standing next to this fellow, flared up and struck him on the mouth. Germanicus was hurried away by his friends to the General's tent. The General was lying in bed half-dead with dismay, hiding his head under a coverlet. It was a long time before he could get up and pay his respects to Germanicus. His life and that of his staff had been saved by his bodyguard, mercenaries from the Swiss border.

A hurried council was held. Cassius told Germanicus that from a conversation which he had overheard while lying in the guardroom the mutineers were about to send a deputation to the regiments in the Upper Province, to secure their co-operation in a general military revolt. There was talk of leaving the Rhine unguarded and marching into France, sacking cities, carrying off the women, and setting up an independent military kingdom in the south-west, protected in the rear by the Pyrenees. Rome would be paralysed by this move and they would remain undisturbed long enough to be able to make their kingdom impregnable.

Germanicus decided to go at once to the Upper Province and make the regiments there swear allegiance to Tiberius. These were the troops who had recently served directly under his command and he believed that they would remain loyal if he reached them before the deputation of mutineers. They had the same grievance about pay and service, he was aware, but their captains were a better set of men, chosen by himself for their patience and soldierly qualities rather than for their reputation. But first something had to be done to quiet the mutinous regiments here. There was only one course to take. He committed the first and only crime in his life: he forged a letter purporting to come from Tiberius and had it delivered to him at his tent door the next morning. The courier had been secretly sent out at night with instructions to steal a horse from the horse-lines, ride twenty miles south-west and then gallop back at top speed by another route.

The letter was to the effect that Tiberius had heard that the regiments in Germany had voiced certain legitimate grievances, and was anxious to remove them at once. He would see that Augustus's legacy was promptly paid to them and as a mark of his confidence in their loyalty would double it from his own purse. He would negotiate with the Senate about the rise in pay. He would give an immediate and unqualified discharge to all men of twenty years' service and a qualified discharge to all who had completed sixteen years – these would be called on for no military duty whatsoever except garrison duty.

Germanicus was not as clever a liar as his uncle Tiberius or his grandmother Livia or his sister Livilla. The courier's horse was recognized by its owner and so was the courier, one of Germanicus's own grooms. Word went round that the letter was a forgery. But the veterans were in favour of treating it as authentic and asking for the promised discharge and the legacy at once. They did so, and Germanicus replied that the Emperor was a man of his word and that the discharges could be granted that very day. But he asked them to have patience about the legacy, which could only be paid in full when they marched back to their winter quarters. There was not sufficient coin in the camp, he said, for every man to have his six gold pieces, but he would see that the General would hand over as much as there was. This quieted them, though opinion had somewhat turned against Germanicus as not being the man they had taken him to be: he was afraid of Tiberius, they said, and not above committing forgery. They sent parties out to look for their captains and undertook to obey orders from their General again. Germanicus had told the General that he would have him impeached before the Senate for cowardice if he did not immediately take himself in hand.

So having seen that the discharges were made in due form and all the available money distributed, Germanicus rode off to the Upper Province. He found the regiments standing by waiting for news of what was happening in the Lower Province; but not yet in open mutiny, for Silius, their General, was a strong-minded man. Germanicus read them the same forged letter and made them swear allegiance to Tiberius; which they did at once.

There was great emotion at Rome when news arrived of the Rhine mutiny. Tiberius, who had been strongly criticized for sending Castor out to the Balkan mutiny – which had not yet been put down – instead of going there himself, was now booed in the streets and asked why it was that the troops who mutinied were the ones whom he had personally commanded, while the others remained loyal. (For the regiments that Germanicus had commanded in Dalmatia had not mutinied either.) He was called on to go to Germany at once and do his own dirty work on the Rhine instead of leaving it to Germanicus. He therefore told the Senate that he would go to Germany, and began slowly to make preparations, choosing his staff and fitting out a small fleet. But by the time he was ready the approach of winter made navigation dangerous and the news from Germany was more hopeful. So he did not go. He had not intended to go.

Meanwhile, I had had a hasty letter from Germanicus, begging me to raise 200,000 gold pieces at once from his estate, but with the greatest secrecy; they were needed for the safety of Rome. He said no more but sent me a signed warrant which enabled me to act for him. I went to his chief steward, who said that he could only raise half that amount without selling property, and that to sell property would make talk, which was what Germanicus evidently wanted to avoid. So I had to find the rest myself – 50,000 from my strong-box, which left me with only 10,000 after I had paid my initiation fee to the new priesthood – and another 50,000 from the sale of some City property which had been left me by my father – luckily I had already had an offer for it – and such of my slaves as I could spare, but only men and women whom I considered not particularly devoted to my service. I sent the money out within two days of getting the letter asking for it. My mother was extremely angry when she heard that the property had been sold, but I was pledged not to tell her why the money was needed, so I said that I had been playing dice for too high stakes lately and in trying to recoup my heavy losses had lost twice as much again. She believed me, and 'gambler' was another stick to beat me with. But the thought that I had not failed Germanicus or Rome was ample compensation for her taunts.

I was gambling a good deal at this time, I must say, but never either lost or gained much. I used to play as a relaxation from my work. After finishing my history of Augustus's religious reforms I wrote a short humorous book about Dice, dedicated to the divinity of Augustus; which was to tease my mother. I quoted a letter that Augustus, who had been very fond of dice, had once written to my father: in which he said how much he had enjoyed their game on the previous night, for my father was the best loser he had ever met. My father, he wrote, always made a great laughing outcry against fate whenever he threw the Dog, but if a fellow-gambler threw Venus he seemed as pleased as if he had thrown her himself. 'It is, indeed, a pleasure to win from you, my dear fellow, and to say this is the highest praise I can bestow on a man, for usually I hate winning because of the insight it gives me into the hearts of my supposedly most devoted friends. All but the very best grudge losing to me, because I am the Emperor and, they think, of infinite wealth, and obviously the Gods should not give more to a man who already has too much. It is my policy therefore – perhaps you have noticed it – always to make a mistake in the reckoning after a round of throws. Either I claim less than I have won, as if by mistake, or I pay more than I owe, and hardly anyone but yourself, I find, is honest enough to put me right.' (I should have liked to quote a further passage in which there was a reference to Tiberius's bad sportsmanship, but of course I could not.)

In this book I began with a mock-serious inquiry into the antiquity of dice, quoting a number of non-existent authors, and describing various fanciful ways of shaking the dice-cup. But the main subject was, naturally, that of winning and losing, and the title was *How to Win at Dice*. Augustus had written in another letter that the more he tried to lose, the more he seemed to win, and even by cheating himself in the reckoning it was seldom that he rose from the table poorer than he sat down. I quoted an opposite statement attributed by Pollio to my grandfather Antony to the effect that the more he tried to win at dice-play the more he seemed to lose. Putting these statements together I deduced that the fundamental law of dice was that the Gods, unless they had a grudge against him on another score, always let the man win who cared least about winning. The only way to win at dice therefore was to cultivate a genuine desire to lose. Written in a heavy style, parodying that of my bugbear Cato, it was, I flatter myself, a very funny book, the argument being so perfectly paradoxical. I quoted the old proverb which promises a man 1,000 gold pieces every time he meets a stranger riding on a piebald mule, but only on condition that he does not think of the mule's tail until he gets the money. I had hoped that this squib would please people who found my histories indigestible. It did not. It was not read as a humorous work at all. I should have realized that old-fashioned readers who had been brought up on the works of Cato were hardly the sort to enjoy a parody of their hero and that the younger generation, who had not been brought up on Cato, would not recognize it as a parody. The book was therefore dismissed as a

fantastically dull and stupid production written in painful seriousness and proving my rumoured mental incapacity beyond further
dispute.

But this has been a very ill-judged digression, leaving Germanicus, as it were, waiting anxiously for his money while I write a
book about dice. Old Athenodorus would criticize me pretty
severely, I think, if he were alive now.

Chapter 16

GERMANICUS was met at Bonn by a deputation of senators sent
by Tiberius. They really came to see whether Germanicus had
been either exaggerating or minimizing the seriousness of the
mutiny. They also brought a private letter from Tiberius approving the promises made to the men on his behalf with the exception
of the doubled bequest, which would now have to be promised to
the entire Army, not merely the regiments in Germany. Tiberius
congratulated Germanicus on the apparent success of the ruse but
deplored the necessity of forgery. He added that whether he fulfilled the promises depended on the behaviour of the men. (By this
he did not mean, as Germanicus supposed, that if the men returned to obedience he would fulfil the promises, but exactly the
reverse.) Germanicus wrote back at once apologizing for the expense involved in the doubling of the bequest, but explained that
the money was being paid from his own purse and the men would
not know that it was not Tiberius who was their benefactor: and
that in the forged letter he had made it plain that only the German
regiments were to benefit, making the payment a reward for their
recent successful campaign across the Rhine. As for the other
specific promises, the veterans of twenty years' service had already
been discharged and were only remaining with the Colours until
the bounty-money arrived for them.

Germanicus could ill afford this heavy charge on his estate and
wrote asking me not to press him for repayment of my 50,000 for
awhile. I answered that it had not been a loan but a gift, which I
was proud to have been able to make. But to return to the order
of events. Two of the regiments were in their winter quarters at
Bonn when the deputation arrived. Their march back under their

General had been a disgraceful display: the bags which had contained the money were tied to long poles and carried mouth downwards, between the standards. The other two regiments had refused to leave the summer camp until the whole bequest was paid them. The Bonn regiments, the First and Twentieth, suspected that the deputation had been sent to cancel the concessions and began to riot again. Some of them were for marching to their new kingdom at once and at midnight a party broke into Germanicus's quarters where the Eagle of the Twentieth Regiment was kept in a locked shrine and, pulling him out of bed, tore the key of the shrine from the thin gold chain which he wore round his neck, unlocked the shrine, and seized the Eagle. As they marched shouting down the streets, calling on their comrades to 'follow the Eagle', they met the senators of the deputation, who had heard the noise and came running for protection to Germanicus. The soldiers cursed and drew their swords. The senators changed their direction and darted into the headquarters of the First Regiment, where they took sanctuary with its Eagle. But their pursuers were mad with rage and drink, and if the Eagle-bearer had not been a man of courage, and a good swordsman too, the leader of the deputation would have had his skull split open – a crime which would have outlawed the regiment beyond pardon and been the signal for civil war throughout the country.

The disorders continued all night, but fortunately without bloodshed except as the result of drunken brawls between rival companies of soldiers. When dawn came Germanicus told the trumpeter to blow the Assembly, and stepped on the tribunal, putting the leader of the senatorial deputation beside him. The men were in a nervous, guilty, irritable mood, but Germanicus's courage fascinated them. He stood up, commanded silence, and then gave a great yawn. He covered his mouth with his hand and apologized, saying that he had not slept well because of the scuffling mice in his quarters. The men liked that joke and laughed. He did not laugh with them. 'Heaven be praised that dawn is here. Never have I known such an evil night. At one moment I dreamed that the Eagle of the Twentieth flew away. What a delight to see it on parade this morning! There were destructive spirits hovering in the camp, sent beyond doubt by some God whom we have offended. You all felt the madness and it was only by a miracle that you were prevented from committing a crime unparalleled in

183

the history of Rome – the unprovoked murder of an ambassador of your own City who had taken sanctuary from your swords with your own regimental Deities!' He then explained that the deputation had come merely to confirm Tiberius's original promises on behalf of the Senate and to report whether they were being faithfully executed by himself.

'Well, what about it, then? Where's the rest of the bounty?' someone shouted, and the cry was taken up. 'We want our bounty.' But by a lucky chance the money-wagons were sighted at that moment, driving into camp under convoy of a troop of auxiliary horse. Germanicus took advantage of the situation to send the senators hurriedly back to Rome under escort of these same auxiliaries; then he supervised the distribution of the coin, having difficulty in restraining some of the men from plundering the money intended for the other regiments.

The disorder increased that afternoon; so much gold in the men's purses meant heavy drinking and reckless gambling. Germanicus decided that it was not safe for Agrippina, who was now with him, to remain in the camp. She was pregnant again; and though her young sons, my nephews Nero and Drusus, were here at Rome staying with my mother and myself, she had little Gaius there with her. This pretty child had become the army mascot and someone had made him a miniature soldier-suit, complete with tin breastplate and sword and helmet and shield. Everyone spoilt him. When his mother put on his ordinary clothes and sandals he used to cry and plead for his sword and his little boots to go visiting the tents. So he was nicknamed Caligula, or Little Boot.

Germanicus insisted on Agrippina's going away, though she swore that she was afraid of nothing and would far rather die with him there than have news from safety of his murder by the mutineers. But he asked her whether she thought that Livia would make a good mother for their orphaned children, and this decided her to do as he wished. With her went several officers' wives, with their children, all weeping and wearing mourning clothes. They passed on foot slowly through the camp, without their usual attendants, like fugitives from a doomed city. A single rough cart, drawn by a mule, was all their transport. Cassius Chaerea went with them as guide and sole protector. Caligula rode on Cassius's back as if on a charger, shouting and making the regulation sword-cuts and parries in the air with his sword, as the cavalrymen had taught him. They left the camp very early in the morning, and hardly anyone saw them go; for there was no guard at the gate and nobody now took the trouble to blow the reveille, most of the men sleeping like pigs till ten or eleven o'clock. A few old soldiers who woke early from long habit were outside the camp gathering firewood for their breakfasts and called to ask where the ladies were off to. 'To Treves,' shouted Cassius. 'The Commander-in-Chief is sending his wife and child away to the protection of the uncivilized but loyal French allies of Treves rather than risk their murder by the famous First Regiment. Tell your comrades that.'

The old soldiers hurried back to the camp and one of them, the old man Pomponius, got hold of a trumpet and blew the alarm. The men came tumbling out of their tents half-asleep with their swords in their hands. 'What's wrong? What's happened?'

'He's been sent away from us. That's the end of our luck and we'll never see him again.'

'Who's that? Who's been sent away?'

'Our boy has. Little Boot. His father says he can't trust the First Regiment with him, so he's sent him away to the damned French allies. God knows what will happen to him there. You know what the French are. His mother's been sent off too. Seven months gone with her latest, and walking on foot, like a slave woman, poor lady. O lads! Germanicus's wife and the daughter of old Agrippa whom we used to call the Soldier's Friend! And our Little Boot.'

Soldiers really are an extraordinary race of men, as tough as shield-leather, as superstitious as Egyptians, and as sentimental as Sabine grandmothers. Ten minutes later there were about 2,000 men besieging Germanicus's tent in a drunken ecstasy of sorrow and repentance and imploring him to let his lady come back with their darling little boy.

Germanicus came out to them with a pale angry face and told them to trouble him no more. They had disgraced themselves and him and the name of Rome and he could never trust them so long as he lived; they had done him no kindness in wresting his sword from him when he was on the point of plunging it into his breast.

'Tell us what to do, General! We'll do anything you say. We swear we'll never mutiny again. Forgive us. We'll follow you to the world's end. But give us back our little playfellow.'

185

Germanicus said: 'These are my conditions. Swear allegiance to my father Tiberius, and sort out from among yourselves the men responsible for the death of your captains, the insult to the deputation, and the stealing of the Eagle. If you do this you will so far have my forgiveness that I shall let you have your play-fellow back. My wife, however, must not be brought to bed in this camp until it has been purged of guilt. Her time is near now and I want no evil influence to cloud the life of the child. But I can send her to Cologne instead of Treves if you do not wish it said that I confided her to the protection of barbarians. My full pardon will only be given when you have wiped out the memory of your bloody crimes by a bloodier victory over your country's enemies, the Germans.'

They swore to abide by his conditions. So he sent a messenger to overtake Agrippina and Cassius; he was to explain matters and fetch Caligula back. The men ran to the tents and called on every loyal comrade to join them and arrest the ringleaders of the mutiny. About 100 men were seized and frog-marched to the tribunal, about which the remainder of the two regiments formed a hollow square with drawn swords. A colonel made each prisoner in turn mount a rough scaffold which had been put up beside the tribunal, and if the men of his company judged him guilty he was thrown down and beheaded by them. Germanicus said nothing throughout the two hours of this informal trial, sitting with folded arms and an impassive face. All but a few of the prisoners were found guilty.

When the last head had fallen and the bodies had been taken out of camp to be burned, Germanicus called up every captain in turn to the tribunal and asked him to give particulars of his service. If he had a good record and had evidently not been appointed by favouritism, Germanicus appealed to the company veterans for their opinion of him. If they gave him a good name and the battalion colonel had nothing against him the man was confirmed in his rank. But if his record was bad or if there were complaints from his company he was degraded, and Germanicus called on the company to choose the best man they had among them to succeed him. Germanicus then thanked the men for their co-operation and called on them to take the oath of allegiance to Tiberius. They took it solemnly; and a moment later a great cheer went up. They saw Germanicus's messenger galloping back; and there was Caligula on the crupper in front of him shouting in his shrill voice and waving his toy sword.

Germanicus embraced the child and said that he had one more thing to add. Fifteen hundred time-expired veterans had been discharged from the two regiments in accordance with instructions from Tiberius. But if any of them, he said, wanted his full pardon, which their fellows were soon going to earn by crossing the Rhine and avenging Varus's defeat, they could still win it. He would permit the more active men to re-enlist in their old companies; while those who were only fit for garrison duty could enlist in a special force for service in the Tyrol, where dangerous raids from Germany had lately been reported. Would you believe it? – every man stepped forward and more than half volunteered for active service across the Rhine. Among these active volunteers was Pomponius, who protested that he was as fit as any man in the army, in spite of his bare gums and his rupture. Germanicus made him his tent-orderly and put his grandsons into the bodyguard. So everything was all right again at Bonn, and Caligula was told by the men that he had put down the mutiny single-handed and that one day he'd be a great emperor and win wonderful victories; which was very bad for the child, who was already, as I say, disgracefully spoilt.

But there remained the two other regiments who were at a place called Xanten to bring to their senses. They had continued to behave mutinously even after the payment of their bounty and their General could do nothing with them. When news came of the change of heart in the Bonn regiments the chief mutineers became seriously alarmed for their own safety and stirred up their comrades to fresh acts of violence and depredation. Germanicus sent their General word that he was coming down the Rhine at once at the head of a powerful force and that if such loyal men as remained under his command did not quickly follow the example of the Bonn regiments and execute the troublemakers he would put the whole lot to the sword indiscriminately. The General read the letter privately to the standard-bearers, non-commissioned officers, and a few trustworthy old soldiers and told them that there was little time for delay; for Germanicus might be on them any moment. They promised him to do what they could and, letting a few more loyalists into the secret, which was well kept, they rushed into the tents at midnight on a given signal and began to massacre the mutineers. These defended themselves as best they could and killed a number of the loyalists, but they were soon overpowered. Five hundred men were killed or wounded that night. The rest, leaving only sentries in the camp, marched out to meet Germanicus, begging him to lead them at once across the Rhine against the enemy.

Although the campaigning season was nearly at an end, the fine weather still held and Germanicus promised to do what they asked. He threw a pontoon bridge over the river and marched across at the head of 12,000 Roman infantry, twenty-six battalions of allies, and eight squadrons of cavalry. From his agents in enemy territory he knew of a large concentration of the enemy in the villages of Münster, where an annual autumn festival in honour of the German Hercules was being held. News of the mutiny had reached the Germans – the mutineers had actually been in treaty with Hermann and had exchanged presents with him – and they were only waiting for the regiments to march away to their new kingdom in the south-west before crossing the Rhine and marching direct for Italy. Germanicus followed a rarely used forest-route and surprised the Germans completely, catching them at their beer-drinking. (Beer is a fermented drink made from steeped grain and they drink it to extraordinary excess at their feasts.) He divided his forces into four columns and wasted the country on a fifty-mile frontage, burning the villages and slaughtering the inhabitants without respect for age or sex. On his return he found detachments of various neighbouring tribes posted to dispute his passage through the forest; but he advanced in skirmishing order and was pressing the enemy back well when there was a sudden alarm from the Twentieth Regiment, which was acting as rearguard, and Germanicus found that a huge force of Germans under the personal command of Hermann was upon him. Fortunately the trees at this point were not dense and allowed room for manoeuvre. Germanicus rode back to the position of most danger and cried out 'Break their line, Twentieth, and everything will be forgiven and forgotten'. The Twentieth fought like madmen and threw the Germans back with huge slaughter, pursuing them far into the open country at the back of the wood. Germanicus caught sight of Hermann and challenged him to combat, but Hermann's men were running away: it would have been death for him to have accepted the challenge. He galloped off. Germanicus was as unlucky as our father had been in his pursuit of enemy chieftains; but he won his victories in the same style, and the name 'Germanicus' which he had inherited he bore now in his own right. He marched the exultant army back to safety in their camps across the Rhine.

Tiberius never understood Germanicus, nor Germanicus Tiberius. Tiberius, as I have said, was one of the bad Claudians. Yet he was, at times, easily tempted to virtue, and in a noble age might well have passed for a noble character: for he was a man of no mean capacity. But the age was not a noble one and his heart had been hardened, and for that hardening Livia must, you will agree, bear the chief blame. Germanicus, on the other hand, was wholly inclined to virtue and, however evil the age into which he had been born, could never have behaved any differently from the way he did. So it was that when he refused the monarchy offered him by the German regiments, and made them swear allegiance to Tiberius, Tiberius could not make out why he should have done so. He decided that he must be even more subtle than himself and playing some very deep game indeed. The simple explanation, that Germanicus put honour above all other considerations and that he was bound to Tiberius by military allegiance and by having been adopted as his son, never occurred to him. But Germanicus, since he did not suspect Tiberius of complicity in Livia's designs and since Tiberius never offered him any slights or injuries, but on the contrary praised him greatly for his handling of the mutiny and decreed him a full triumph for his campaign in Münster, believed him to be as honourably-intentioned as himself, only a little simple-minded not to have seen through Livia's designs yet. He determined to have a frank talk with Tiberius as soon as he went home for the triumph. But Varus's death was not yet avenged; it was three years before Germanicus came back. The tone of the letters exchanged between Germanicus and Tiberius during this period was set by Germanicus, who wrote with dutiful affection. Tiberius replied in the same friendly strain because he thought that by so doing he was beating Germanicus at his own clever game. He undertook to repay him the amount of the doubled bequest and to extend the bounty to the Balkan regiments too. As a matter of policy he did pay the Balkan regiments this extra three gold pieces a man – there were threats of another mutiny – but excused himself from repaying Germanicus for a few months on the grounds of financial embarrassment. Naturally

Germanicus did not press him for the money and naturally Tiberius never gave it him. Germanicus wrote again to ask me whether he might wait to repay me until Tiberius repaid him, and I wrote back that I really meant the money as a gift.

Shortly after Tiberius's accession I wrote to him and said that I had been studying law and administration – as was the case – for some time, in the hope that I would at last be given an opportunity of serving my country in some responsible capacity. He wrote back to say that it certainly was an anomaly for a man who was the brother of Germanicus and his own nephew to go about as a mere knight, and that since I was now being made a priest of Augustus I must certainly be allowed to wear the dress of a senator: in fact, if I could undertake not to make a fool of myself in it he should ask permission for me to adopt the brocaded gown now worn by Consuls and ex-Consuls. I wrote back at once to say that I would even prefer office without dress to dress without office; but his only answer to this was to send me a present of forty golden pieces 'to buy toys with next All Fools' Day'. The Senate did vote me the brocaded gown, and as a mark of honour to Germanicus, who was now in the middle of a new successful campaign in Germany, proposed to decree me a seat in the House among the ex-Consuls. But Tiberius here interposed his veto, telling them that I was in his opinion incapable of delivering a speech on matters of State which would not be a trial of his fellow-members' patience.

There was another decree proposed at the same time, which he also vetoed. The circumstances were as follows: Agrippina had been delivered of her child, a girl called Agrippinilla, at Cologne; and I must say at once that this Agrippinilla turned out one of the very worst of the Claudians – in fact, I may say that she shows signs of outdoing all her ancestors and ancestresses in arrogance and vice. Agrippina was ill for some months after her delivery, and unable to keep Caligula in hand properly, so he was sent away on a visit to Rome as soon as Germanicus began his spring campaign. The child became a sort of national hero. Whenever he went out for a walk with his brothers he was cheered and stared at and made much of. Not yet three years old but marvellously precocious, he was a most difficult case, only pleasant when flattered and only docile when treated firmly. He came to stay with his great-grandmother Livia, but she had no time to look after him properly, and because he was always getting into mischief and quarrelling with his elder brothers, he came from her to live with my mother and me. My mother never flattered him, but neither did she treat him with enough firmness, until one day he spat at her in a fit of temper and she gave him a good spanking. 'You horrid old German woman,' he said, 'I'll burn your German house down!' He used 'German' as the worst insult he knew. And that afternoon he sneaked away into a lumber-room, which was next to the slaves' attic and full of old furniture and rubbish, and there set fire to a heap of worn-out straw mattresses. The fire soon swept the whole upper storey, and since it was an old house with dry-rot in the beams and draught-holes in the flooring there was no putting it out even with an endless bucket-chain to the carp pool. I managed to save all my papers and valuables and some of the furniture, and no lives were lost except two old slaves who were lying sick in bed, but nothing was left of the house except the bare walls and the cellars. Caligula was not punished, because the fire had given him such a great fright. He nearly got caught in it himself, hiding guiltily under his bed until the smoke drove him screaming out.

Well, the Senate wanted to decree that my house should be re-built at the expense of the State, on the ground that it had been the home of so many distinguished members of my family: but Tiberius would not allow this. He said that the outbreak of fire had been due to my negligence and that the damage could easily have been confined to the attics if I had acted in a responsible way; and rather than that the State should pay he undertook to rebuild and refurnish the house himself. Loud applause from the House. This was most unjust and dishonest, particularly as he had no intention of keeping his undertaking. I was forced to sell my last important piece of property in Rome, a block of houses near the Cattle Market and a large building site adjoining, to rebuild the house at my own expense. I never told Germanicus that Caligula had been the incendiary, because he would have felt obliged to make good the damage himself; and I suppose it was, in a way, an accident, because one couldn't hold so young a child responsible.

When Germanicus's men went out to fight the Germans again they had a new addition to that ballad of Augustus's Three Griefs, of which I recall two or three verses and odd lines of others, most of them ridiculous:

> Six gold bits a man he left us
>   For to buy us pork and beans,
> For to buy us cheese and cracknels
>   In the German dry canteens.

and

> God Augustus walks in Heaven,
>   Ghost Marcellus swims in Styx,
> Julia's dead and gone to join him –
>   That's the end of Julia's tricks.
>
> But our Eagles still are straying
>   And by shame and sorrow stirred
> To the tomb of God Augustus
>   We'll bring back each wandering bird.

There was another which began:

> German Hermann lost his sweetheart
>   And his little pot of beer,

but I can't remember the finish, and the verse is not important except as reminding me to tell of Hermann's 'sweetheart'. She was the daughter of a chieftain called, in German, Siegstoss or something of the sort; but his Roman name was Segestes. He had been to Rome, like Hermann, and enrolled among the Knights, and unlike Hermann had felt morally bound by the oath of friendship he had sworn to Augustus. It was this Segestes who had warned Varus about Hermann and Segimerus and suggested that Varus should arrest them at the banquet to which he had invited them just before his unfortunate expedition started. Segestes had a favourite daughter whom Hermann had carried off and married and Segestes never forgave him for this injury. He could not, however, come out openly on the side of the Romans against Hermann, who was a national hero; all that he had been able to do as yet was to maintain a secret correspondence with Germanicus, giving him intelligence of military movements and constantly assuring him that he had never wavered in his loyalty to Rome and was only waiting for an opportunity to make proof of it. But now he wrote to Germanicus that he was being besieged in his stockaded village by Hermann, who had sworn to give no quarter; and that he could not hold out much longer. Germanicus made a forced march, defeated the besieging force, which was not numerous – Hermann himself was away, wounded – and rescued

192

Segestes: when he found that he had a valuable prize awaiting him – Hermann's wife, who had been visiting her father when the quarrel broke out between them and her husband, and who was far gone in pregnancy. Germanicus treated Segestes and his household very kindly, giving them an estate on the western side of the Rhine. Hermann, who was enraged at his wife's capture, feared that Germanicus's clemency might induce other German chieftains to make overtures of peace. He built up a strong new confederation of tribes, including some which had always hitherto been friendly to Rome. Germanicus was undaunted. The more Germans he had in the field openly against him, the better he was pleased. He had never trusted them as allies.

And before the summer was out he had beaten them in a series of battles, forced Segimerus to surrender, and won back the first of the three lost Eagles, that of the Nineteenth Regiment. He also visited the scene of Varus's defeat and gave the bones of his comrades-in-arms a decent burial, laying the first sod of their tomb with his own hands. The General who had behaved so supinely in the mutiny fought bravely at the head of his corps, and on one occasion turned what had seemed a hopeless defeat into a creditable victory. Premature news that this battle was lost and that the conquering Germans were marching towards the Rhine caused such consternation at the nearest bridge that the captain of the guard gave his men orders to retreat across it and then break it down: which would have meant abandoning everyone on the other side to their fate. But Agrippina was there and countermanded the order. She told the men that she was captain of the guard now and would remain so until her husband returned to relieve her of her command. When eventually the victorious troops came marching back she was at her post to welcome them. Her popularity now almost equalled that of her husband. She had organized a hospital for the wounded as Germanicus sent them back after each battle and had given them the best available medical treatment. Ordinarily, wounded soldiers remained with their units until they either died or recovered. The hospital she paid for out of her own purse.

But I mentioned the death of Julia. When Tiberius became Emperor, Julia's daily supply of food at Reggio was reduced to four ounces of bread a day and one ounce of cheese. She was already in a consumption from the unhealthiness of her quarters and this starvation diet soon carried her off. But there was still no news of Postumus, and Livia, until she was certain of his death, could not be easy in her mind.

Chapter 17

TIBERIUS continued to rule with moderation and consulted the Senate before taking any step of the least political importance. But the Senate had been voting according to direction for so long that they seemed to have lost the power of independent decision; and Tiberius never made it plain which way he wanted them to vote even when he was very anxious for them to vote one way or another. He wanted to avoid all appearance of tyranny and yet to keep his position at the head of affairs. The Senate soon found that if he spoke with studied elegance in favour of a motion he meant that he wanted it voted against, and that if he spoke with studied elegance against it this meant that he wanted it passed; and that on the very few occasions when he spoke briefly and without any rhetoric he meant to be taken literally. Gallus and an old wag called Haterius used to delight in making speeches in warm agreement with Tiberius, enlarging his arguments to a point only just short of absurdity and then voting the way he really wanted them to vote; thus showing that they understood his tricks perfectly. This Haterius in the debate about Tiberius's accession had cried out: 'O Tiberius, how long will you allow unhappy Rome to remain without a head?' – which had offended him because he knew that Haterius saw through his intentions. The next day Haterius pursued the joke by falling at Tiberius's feet and pleading for pardon for not having been warm enough. Tiberius started back in disgust, but Haterius grabbed at his knees and Tiberius went over, catching the back of his head a bang on the marble floor. Tiberius's German bodyguard did not understand what was happening and sprang forward to slaughter their master's assailant; Tiberius only just stopped them in time.

Haterius excelled in parody. He had an enormous voice, a comic face, and great fertility of invention. Whenever Tiberius in his speeches introduced any painfully far-fetched or archaic phrase Haterius would pick it up and make it the key-word of his reply.

(Augustus had always said that the wheels of Haterius's eloquence needed a drag-chain even when he was driving uphill.) The slow-witted Tiberius was no match for Haterius. Gallus's gift was for mock zeal. Tiberius was extremely careful not to appear a candidate for any divine honours and refused to allow himself to be spoken about as if he had any superhuman attributes: he did not even allow the provincials to build him temples. Gallus was therefore fond of referring, as if accidentally, to Tiberius as 'His Sacred Majesty'. When Haterius, who was always ready to carry on the gag, rose to rebuke him for this incorrect way of speaking he would apologize profusely and say that nothing was farther from his mind than to do anything in disobedience of the orders of His Sacred ... oh, dear, it was so easy to fall into that mistaken way of speaking, a thousand apologies once more ... he meant, contrary to the wishes of his honoured friend and fellow-senator Tiberius Nero Caesar Augustus.

'*Not* Augustus, fool,' Haterius would say in a stage whisper. 'He's refused that title a dozen times. He only uses it *when he writes letters to other monarchs*.'

They had one trick which annoyed Tiberius more than any other. If he made a show of modesty when thanked by the Senate for performing some national service – such as undertaking to complete the temples which Augustus had left unfinished – they would praise his honesty in not taking credit for his mother's work, and congratulate Livia on having so dutiful a son. When they saw that there was nothing that Tiberius hated so much as hearing Livia praised they kept it up. Haterius even suggested that just as the Greeks were called by their father's names, so Tiberius should be named after his mother and that it should be a crime to call him other than Tiberius Liviades – or perhaps Livigena would be the more correct Latin form. Gallus found another weak spot in Tiberius's armour, and that was his hatred of any mention of his stay at Rhodes. The most daring thing he did was to praise Tiberius one day for his clemency – it was the very day that news reached the city of Julia's death – and to tell the story of the teacher of rhetoric at Rhodes who had refused Tiberius's modest application to join his classes, on the ground that there was no vacancy at present, saying that he must come back in seven days. Gallus added, 'And what do you think His Sacred ... I beg your pardon, I should say, what do you think my honoured friend and fellow-senator Tiberius Nero Caesar did on his recent accession to the monarchy, when the same impertinent fellow arrived to pay his respects to the new divinity? Did he cut off that impudent head and give it as a football to his German bodyguard? Not at all: with a wit only equalled by his clemency he told him that he had no vacancies at present in his corps of flatterers and that he must come back in seven years.' This was an invention, I think, but the Senate had no reason to disbelieve it and applauded so heartily that Tiberius had to let it go by as the truth.

Tiberius at last silenced Haterius by saying very slowly one day: 'You will please forgive me, Haterius, if I speak rather more frankly than it is usual for one senator to speak to another, but I must say that I think you are a dreadful bore and not in the least witty.' Then he turned to the House: 'You will forgive me, my lords, but I have always said and will say again that since you have been good enough to entrust such absolute power to me I ought not to be ashamed to use it for the common good. If I use it now to silence buffoons who insult you as well as myself by their silly performances, I trust that I will earn your approval. You have always been kind and patient with me.' Without Haterius, Gallus had to play a lone game.

Though Tiberius hated his mother more than ever, he continued to let her rule him. All the appointments which he made to Consulships or provincial governorships were really hers: and they were very sensible ones, the men being chosen for merit, not for family influence or because they had flattered her or done her some private service. For I must make it plain, if I have not already done so, that however criminal the means used by Livia to win the direction of affairs for herself, first through Augustus and then through Tiberius, she was an exceptionally able and just ruler; and it was only when she ceased to direct the system that she had built up that it went wrong.

I have spoken of Sejanus, the son of the Commander of the Guards. He now succeeded to his father's command and was one of the only three men to whom Tiberius in any way opened his mind. Thrasyllus was another; he had come to Rome with Tiberius and never lost his hold on him. The third was a senator called Nerva. Thrasyllus never discussed State policy with Tiberius and never asked for any official position; and when Tiberius gave him large sums of money he accepted them casually, as if money were something of little importance to him. He had a big observatory in a dome-shaped room in the Palace which had windows of glass so clear and transparent that you hardly knew they were there. Tiberius used to spend a great deal of his time here with Thrasyllus, who taught him the rudiments of astrology and many other magic arts, including that of interpreting dreams in the Chaldean style. Sejanus and Nerva Tiberius seems to have chosen for their totally opposite characters. Nerva never made an enemy and never lost a friend. His one fault, if you may call it so, was that he kept silent in the presence of evil when speech would not remedy it. He was sweet-tempered, generous, courageous, utterly truthful, and was never known to stoop to the least fraud, even if good promised to come from so doing. If he had been in Germanicus's position, for instance, he would never have forged that letter, though his own safety and that of the Empire had hung upon it. Tiberius made Nerva superintendent of the City aqueducts and kept him constantly by him; I suppose by way of providing himself with a handy yardstick of virtue – as Sejanus certainly served as a handy yardstick of wickedness. Sejanus had as a young man been a friend of Gaius, on whose staff he had served in the East, and had been clever enough to foresee Tiberius's return to favour: he had contributed to it by reassuring Gaius that Tiberius meant what he said when he disclaimed any ambition to rule, and by urging him to write that letter of recommendation to Augustus. He let Tiberius know at the time that he had done this and Tiberius wrote him a letter, still in his possession, promising never to forget his services. Sejanus was a liar but so fine a general of lies that he knew how to marshal them into an alert and disciplined formation – this was a clever remark of Gallus's, it is not mine – which would come off best in any skirmish with suspicions or any general engagement with truth. Tiberius envied him this talent as he envied Nerva his honesty: for though he had progressed far in the direction of evil, he still felt hampered by unaccountable impulses towards the good.

It was Sejanus who first began poisoning his mind against Germanicus, telling him that a man who could forge a letter from his father in whatever circumstances was not to be trusted; and that Germanicus was really aiming at the monarchy but was acting with caution – first winning the men's affection by bribery and then making sure of their fighting capacities and his own leader-

197

ship by this unnecessary campaign across the Rhine. As for Agrippina, Sejanus said, she was a dangerously ambitious woman: look how she had behaved – styled herself captain of the bridge and welcomed the regiments on their return as if she were Heaven knows who! That the bridge was in danger of being destroyed was probably an invention of her own. Sejanus also said that he knew from a freedman of his who had once been a slave in Germanicus's household that Agrippina somehow believed Livia and Tiberius responsible for the death of her three brothers and the banishment of her sister, and had sworn to be revenged. Sejanus also began discovering all kinds of plots against Tiberius and kept him in constant fear of assassination while assuring him that he need not have the least anxiety with himself on guard. He encouraged Tiberius to cross Livia in trifling ways, to show her that she over-estimated the strength of her position. It was he who, a few years later, organized the Guards into a disciplined body. Hitherto the three battalions stationed at Rome had been billeted by sections in various parts of the City, in inns and such-like places, and were difficult to fetch out on parade in a hurry and slovenly in their dress and movements. He suggested to Tiberius that if he built a single permanent camp for them outside the City it would give them a strong corporate sense, prevent them from being influenced by the rumours and waves of political feeling which were always running through the City, and attach them more closely to his person as their Emperor. Tiberius improved on his advice by recalling the remaining six battalions from their stations in other parts of Italy and making the new camp big enough to house them all – 9,000 infantry and 2,000 cavalry. Apart from the four City battalions, one of which he now sent to Lyons, and various colonies of discharged veterans, these were the only soldiers in Italy. The German bodyguard did not count as soldiers, being technically slaves. But they were picked men and more fanatically loyal to their Emperor than any true-born Roman. There was not a man of them who really wanted to return to his cold, rude, barbarous land, though they were always singing sad choruses about it; they had too good a time here.

As for the criminal dossiers, to which Tiberius, because of his fear of plots against his life, was most anxious now to have access, Livia still pretended that the key to the cipher was lost. Tiberius, at Sejanus's suggestion, told her that since they were of no use to anyone he would burn them. She said that he could do so if he liked, but surely it would be better to keep them, just in case the key turned up? Perhaps she might even suddenly remember the key. 'Very well, mother,' he answered, 'I'll take charge of them until you do; and meanwhile I'll spend my evenings trying to work the cipher out myself.' So he took them off to his own room and locked them in a cupboard. He tried his hardest to find the key to that cipher but it beat him. The common cipher was simply writing Latin E for Greek Alpha, Latin F for Greek Beta, G for Gamma, H for Delta, and so on. The key of the high cipher was next to impossible to discover. It was provided by the first hundred lines of the first book of the *Iliad*, which had to be read concurrently with the writing of the cipher, each letter in the writing being represented by the number of letters of the alphabet intervening between it and the corresponding letter in Homer. Thus the first letter of the first word of the first line of the first book of the *Iliad* is Mu. Suppose the first letter of the first word of an entry in the dossier to be Upsilon. There are seven letters in the Greek alphabet intervening between Mu and Upsilon, so Upsilon would be written as 7. In this plan the alphabet would be thought of as circular, Omega, the last letter, following Alpha, the first, so that the distance between Upsilon and Alpha would be 4, but the distance between Alpha and Upsilon would be 18. It was Augustus's invention and must have taken rather a long time to write and decode, but I suppose by practice they came to know the distance between any two letters in the alphabet without having to count up, which saved a lot of time. And how do I know about all this? Because many many years later when the dossiers came into my possession I worked the cipher out myself. I happened to find a roll of the first book of Homer, written on sheepskin, filed among the other rolls. It was clear that the first hundred lines only had been studied; because the sheepskin was badly soiled and inked at the beginning and quite clear at the end. When I looked closer and saw tiny figures – 6, 23, 12 – faintly scratched under the letters of the first line, it was not difficult to connect them with the cipher. I was surprised that Tiberius had overlooked this clue.

Speaking of the alphabet, I was interested at this time in a simple plan for making Latin truly phonetic. It seemed to me that three letters were missing. These three were consonantal u to distinguish it from u the vowel; a letter to correspond to the Greek

Upsilon (which is a vowel between Latin I and U) for use in Greek words which have become Latinized; and a letter to denote the double consonant which we now write in Latin as BS but pronounce like the Greek Psi. It was important, I wrote, for provincials learning Latin to learn it correctly; if the letters did not correspond to the sound how could they avoid mistakes in pronunciation? So I suggested, for consonantal U, the upside-down F (which is used for that purpose in Etruscan): thus LAꟼINIA instead of LAUINIA; and a broken H for Greek Upsilon: thus BⱵBLIOTHECA instead of BIBLIOTHECA; and an upside-down C for BS: thus AↃQUE for ABSQUE. The last letter was not so important, but the other two seemed to me essential. I suggested the broken H and the upside-down F and C because these would cause the least trouble to the men who use letter-punches for metal or clay: they would not have to make any new punches. I published the book and one or two people said that my suggestions were sensible; but of course it had absolutely no result. My mother told me that there were three impossible things in the world: that shops should stretch across the bay from Baiae to Puteoli, that I should subdue the island of Britain, and that any one of these absurd new letters would ever appear on public inscriptions in Rome. I have always remembered this remark of hers, for it had a sequel.

My mother was extremely short-tempered with me these days because our house took such a long time to rebuild and the new furniture I bought was not equal to the old, and because her income was greatly reduced by the share she took in these expenses – I could not have found all the money myself. We lived for two years in quarters at the Palace (not very good ones) and she vented her irritation on me so constantly that in the end I could not bear it any longer and moved out of Rome to my villa near Capua, only visiting the City when my priestly functions demanded it, which was not often. You will ask about Urgulanilla. She never came to Capua; in Rome we had little to do with each other. She scarcely greeted me when we met and took no notice of me except, for appearances sake, when guests were present; and we always slept apart. She seemed fond enough of our boy, Drusillus, but did little for him in any practical way. His bringing-up was left to my mother, who managed the household, and never called on Urgulanilla for any help. My mother treated Drusillus as if he were her own child, and somehow contrived to forget who his parents were. I never learned to like Drusillus myself; he was a surly, stolid, insolent child, and my mother scolded me so often in his presence that he learned to have no respect for me.

I don't know how Urgulanilla got through her days. But she never seemed bored and ate enormously and, so far as I know, entertained no secret lovers. This strange creature had one passion, though – Numantina, the wife of my brother-in-law Silvanus, a little fair-haired elf-like creature who had once done or said something (I don't know what) which had penetrated through that thick hide and muscular bulging body and touched what served Urgulanilla for a heart. Urgulanilla had a life-size portrait of Numantina in her boudoir: she used, I believe, to sit gazing at it for hours whenever there was no opportunity for gazing at Numantina herself. When I moved to Capua, Urgulanilla stayed at Rome with my mother and Drusillus.

The only inconvenience of Capua as a home for me was the absence of a good library. However, I began a book for which a library was not needed – a history of Etruria. I had by now made some progress in Etruscan, and Aruns, with whom I spent a few hours every day, was most helpful in giving me access to the archives of his half-ruined temple. He told me that he had been born on the day that the comet appeared which had announced the beginning of the tenth and last cycle of the Etruscan race. A cycle is a period reckoned by the longest life: that is to say, a cycle does not close until the death of everyone who was alive at the festival celebrating the close of the previous cycle. The Etruscans reckoned it at 110 years. This was the last cycle and it would end with the total disappearance of Etruscan as a spoken language. The prophecy was already as good as fulfilled because he had no successors in his priestly office, and the country-people now talked Latin even in the home; so he was glad to help me to write my history, he said, as a mausoleum for the traditions of a once great race. I started it in the second year of Tiberius's reign and I finished it twenty-one years later. I consider it my best work: certainly I worked hardest at it. So far as I know, there is no other book on the subject of the Etruscans at all and they were a very interesting race indeed; so I think that historians of the future will be grateful to me.

I had Callon and Pallas with me and lived a quiet orderly life. I took an interest in the farm attached to my villa and enjoyed occasional visits from friends in Rome who came out for a holiday. There was a woman permanently living with me, called Actë, a professional prostitute and a very decent woman. I never had any trouble with her in the fifteen years she was with me. Our relationship was a purely business one. She had deliberately chosen prostitution as her profession; I paid her well; there was no nonsense about her. We were quite fond of each other in a way. At last she told me that she wanted to retire on her earnings. She would marry a decent man, an old soldier for choice, and settle down in one of the colonies and have children before it was too late. She had always wanted to have a houseful of children. So I kissed her and said good-bye and gave her enough dowry-money to make things very easy for her. She did not go away, though, until she had found me a successor whom she could trust to treat me properly. She found me Calpurnia, who was so like her that I have often thought she must have been her daughter. Actë did once mention having had a daughter whom she had put out to nurse because one couldn't be a prostitute and a mother at the same time. Well, so Actë married an ex-Guardsman who treated her quite well and had five children by her. I have always kept an eye on that family. I mention her only because my readers will wonder what sort of sexual life I led when living apart from Urgulanilla. I do not think it is natural for an ordinary man to live long without a woman, and since Urgulanilla was impossible as a wife I do not think that I can be blamed for living with Actë. Actë and I had an understanding that while we were together we would neither of us have to do with anyone else. This was not sentiment but a medical precaution: there was so much venereal disease now in Rome – another fatal legacy, by the way, of the Punic War.

Here I wish to put it on record that I have never at any time of my life practised homosexuality. I do not use Augustus's argument against it, that it prevents men having children to support the State, but I have always thought it at once pitiful and disgusting to see a full-grown man, a magistrate, perhaps, with a family of his own, slobbering luxuriously over a plump little boy with a painted face and bangles; or an ancient senator playing Queen Venus to some tall young Adonis of the Guards cavalry who tolerates the old fool only because he has money.

When I had to go up to Rome I stayed there for as short a time as possible. I felt something uncomfortable in the atmosphere on the Palatine Hill, which may well have been the growing tension between Tiberius and Livia. He had begun building a huge palace for himself on the north-west of the hill, and now moved into the lower rooms, before the upper ones were finished, leaving her in sole possession of Augustus's palace. Livia, as if to show that Tiberius's new building, though three times the size, would never have the prestige of the old one, put a magnificent gold statue of Augustus in her hall and proposed, as High-Priestess of his cult, to invite all the senators and their wives to the dedicatory banquet. But Tiberius pointed out that he must first ask the Senate to vote on the matter: it was a State occasion, not a private entertainment. He so managed the debate that the banquet was held in two parts simultaneously: the senators in the hall with himself as host, and their wives in a big room leading off it with Livia as hostess. She swallowed the insult by not treating it as such, only as a sensible arrangement more in keeping with what Augustus would have wished himself; but gave orders to the Palace cooks that the women were to be served first with the best joints and sweetmeats and wine. She also appropriated the most costly dishes and drinking-vessels for her feast. She got the better of him on that occasion and the senators' wives all had a good laugh at the expense of Tiberius and their husbands.

Another uncomfortable thing about coming to Rome was that I never seemed to be able to avoid meeting Sejanus. I disliked having anything to do with him, though he was always studiously polite to me and never did me any direct injury. I was astonished that a man with a face and manner like his and not well-born or a famous fighter, or even particularly rich, could have made such a huge success in the City: he was now the next most important man after Tiberius, and extremely popular with the Guards. It was a completely untrustworthy face – sly, cruel, and irregular-featured – and the one thing that held it together was a certain animal hardiness and resolution. What was stranger still to me, several women of good family were said to be rivals in love for him. He and Castor got on badly together, which was only natural, for there were rumours that Livilla and Sejanus had some sort of understanding. But Tiberius seemed to have complete confidence in him.

I have mentioned Briseis, my mother's old freedwoman. When I told her that I was leaving Rome and settling at Capua she said how much she would miss me, but that I was wise to go. 'I had a funny dream about you last night, Master Claudius, if you'll forgive me. You were a little lame boy; and thieves broke into his father's house and murdered his father and a whole lot of relations and friends; but he squeezed through the pantry-window and went hobbling into the neighbouring wood. He climbed up a tree and waited. The thieves came out of the house and sat down under the tree where he was hiding, to divide the plunder. Soon they began to quarrel about who should have what, and one of the thieves got killed, and then two more, and then the rest began drinking wine and pretended to be great friends; but the wine had been poisoned by one of the murdered thieves, so they all died in agony. The lame boy climbed down the tree and collected the valuables and found a lot of gold and jewels among them that had been stolen from other families: but he took it all home with him and became quite rich.'

I smiled. 'That's a funny dream, Briseis. But he was still as lame as ever and all that wealth could not buy his father and family back to life again, could it?'

'No, my dear, but perhaps he married and had a family of his own. So choose a good tree, Master Claudius, and don't come down till the last of the thieves are dead. That's what my dream said.'

'I'll not come down even then, if I can help it, Briseis. I don't want to be the receiver of stolen goods.'

'You can always give them back, Master Claudius.'

This was all very remarkable in the light of what happened later. I have no great faith in dreams. Athenodorus once dreamed that there was treasure in a badger's den in a wood near Rome. He found his way to the exact spot, which he had never visited before, and there in a bank was the hole leading to the den. He fetched a couple of countrymen to dig away the bank until they came to the den at the end of the hole – where they found a rotten old purse containing six mouldy coppers and a bad shilling, which was not enough to pay the countrymen for their work. And one of my tenants, a shopkeeper, dreamed once that a flight of eagles wheeled round his head and one settled on his shoulder. He took it for a sign that he would one day be Emperor, but all that happened was that a piquet of Guards visited him the next morning (they had eagles on their shields) and the corporal arrested him for some offence that brought him under military jursidiction.

Chapter 18

ONE summer afternoon at Capua I was sitting on a stone bench behind the stables of my villa, thinking out some problem of Etruscan history and idly shooting dice, left hand against right, on the rough plank table in front of me. A raggedly-dressed man came up and asked whether I was Tiberius A.D. 16 Claudius Drusus Nero Germanicus: he had been directed here from Rome, he said.

'I have a message for you, sir. I don't know whether it's worth delivering, but I'm an old soldier on the tramp – one of your father's veterans, sir – and you know what it is, I'm glad of having an excuse for taking one road rather than another.'

'Who gave you the message?'

'A fellow I met in the woods near Cape Cosa. Curious sort of fellow. He was dressed like a slave, but he spoke like a Caesar. A big thick-set fellow and looked half starved.'

'What name did he give?'

'No name at all. He said you'd know who he was by the message, and be surprised to hear from him. He made me repeat the message twice to make sure I had it right. I was to say that he was still fishing, but that a man couldn't live wholly on fish, and that you were to pass the word to his brother-in-law, and that if the milk was sent it never reached him, and that he wanted a little book to read, at least seven pages long. And that you were not to do anything until you heard from him again. Does that make sense, sir, or was the fellow cracked?'

When he said that, I could not believe my ears. Postumus! But Postumus was dead. 'Has he a big jaw, blue eyes, and a way of tilting his head on one side when he asks you a question?'

'That's the man, sir.'

I poured him out a drink with a hand so shaky that I spilt as much as I poured. Then, signing that he was to wait there for me, I went into the house. I found two good plain gowns and some underclothes and sandals and a pair of razors and some soap. Then I took the first sewn-sheet book that came to hand – it happened to be a copy of some recent speeches of Tiberius to the Senate – and on the seventh page I wrote in milk: *What joy ! I shall write to G. at once. Be careful. Send for whatever you need. Where can I see you? My dearest love to you. Here are twenty gold pieces, all I have at the moment, but quick gifts are double gifts, I hope.*

I waited for the page to dry and then gave the man the book and clothes wrapped in a bundle, and a purse. I said: 'Take these thirty gold pieces. Ten are for yourself. Twenty are for the man in the woods. Bring back a message from him and you shall have ten more. But keep your mouth shut and be back soon.'

'Good enough, sir,' he said. 'I'll not fail you. But what's to prevent me from going off with this bundle and all the money?'

I said: 'If you were a dishonest man you wouldn't ask that question. So let us have another drink together and off you go.'

To cut a long story short, he went away with the bundle and money and a few days later brought me back a verbal answer from Postumus, which was thanks for the money and clothes and that I was not to seek him out, but that the Crocodile's mother would know where he was and that his name was now Pantherus and would I forward him his brother-in-law's answer as soon as possible. I paid the old soldier the ten pieces I had promised him and ten more for his faithfulness. I understood whom Postumus meant by the Crocodile's mother. The Crocodile was an old freedman of Agrippa's whom we called that because of his torpidity and greed and his enormous jaws. He had a mother living at Perusia, where she kept an inn. I knew the place well. I sent off a letter to Germanicus at once to tell him the news; I sent it by Pallas to Rome telling him to send it off with the next post to Germany. In the letter I merely said that Postumus was alive and in hiding – I did not say where – and begged Germanicus to acknowledge the receipt of the letter at once. Then I waited and waited for an answer, but none came. I wrote again, rather more fully; but still no answer. I sent a message to the Crocodile's mother by a country-carrier that no message had yet arrived for Pantherus from his brother-in-law.

I did not hear again from Postumus. He did not wish to compromise me further, and now that he had money and was able to move about without being arrested on suspicion as a runaway slave he was not dependent on my help. Somebody at the inn recognized him and he had to move from there for safety's sake. Very soon the rumour that he was alive was all over Italy. Everyone was talking about it at Rome. A dozen people, including three senators, came out to me from the City to ask me privately if it were true. I told them that I had not seen him but that I had met someone who had, and that there was no doubt that it was Postumus. In return I asked them what they intended to do if he came to Rome and won the support of the populace. But the directness of my question embarrassed and hurt them, and I got no answer.

Postumus was reported to have visited various country towns in the neighbourhood of Rome, but apparently he took the precaution of not entering them before nightfall and always going away, in disguise, before dawn. He was never seen publicly but would lodge at some inn and leave behind a message of thanks for the kindness shown him – signed with his real name. At last one day he landed at Ostia from a small coasting vessel. The port knew, a few hours beforehand, that he was coming, and he had a tremendous ovation at the quay as he stepped ashore. He chose to land at Ostia because it was the summer headquarters of the Fleet, of which his father Agrippa had been Admiral. His vessel flew a green pennant which Augustus had given Agrippa the right to fly whenever he was at sea (and his sons after him) in memory of his sea victory off Actium. Agrippa's memory was honoured at Ostia almost beyond that of Augustus.

Postumus was in great danger of his life, being still under sentence of banishment and therefore outlawed by his public reappearance in Italy. He made a short speech of thanks to the crowd for their welcome. He said that if Fortune was kind to him and if he won back the esteem of the Roman Senate and people which he had forfeited because of certain lying accusations brought against him by his enemies – accusations which his grandfather, the God Augustus, had realized too late were untrue – he would reward the loyalty of the men and women of Ostia in no niggardly fashion. A company of Guards was there with orders to arrest him, for Livia and Tiberius had got the news too, somehow. But the men would have had no chance against that crowd of sailors. The captain wisely made no attempt to carry out his commission; he ordered two men to change into sailors' slops and not lose sight of Postumus. But by the time they had changed he had disappeared and they could find no trace of him.

The next day Rome was full of sailors who picketed the principal streets: whenever they met a knight or senator or public official they asked him the pass-word. The pass-word was 'Neptune', and if he did not already know it he was given it and made to repeat it three times unless he wanted a beating. Nobody wanted a beating, and popular feeling now ran so strongly in sympathy with Postumus and against Tiberius and Livia that if a single favourable word had come from Germanicus the whole City, including the Guards and the City battalions, would have come over to him at once. But without Germanicus's support any rising in favour of Postumus would have meant civil war; and nobody had much confidence in Postumus's chances if it came to a struggle with Germanicus.

In this crisis the same Crispus who had antagonized Tiberius two years before by sending Clement to his death on the island (but had been forgiven) came forward and offered to redeem his fault by this time making sure of Postumus. Tiberius gave him a free hand. He found out somehow where Postumus's headquarters were and, going to him with a large sum of money which he said was for the payment of his sailors, who had already lost two working-days by this picketing work, he undertook to bring over the German bodyguard to Postumus's side as soon as he gave the signal. He had, he said, already given them enormous bribes. Postumus believed him. They arranged a meeting for two hours after midnight at a certain street corner where Postumus's sailors were also to assemble in force. They would march to Tiberius's Palace. Crispus would order the bodyguard to admit Postumus. Tiberius, Castor, and Livia would be arrested, and Crispus said that Sejanus, while not active in the plot, had undertaken to bring the Guards over in support of the new régime as soon as the first blow had been successfully struck: on condition that he retained his command.

The sailors were punctual at the rendezvous but Postumus did not arrive. At that hour no citizens were in the street; so when a combined force of Germans from the bodyguard and picked men of Sejanus's suddenly fell on the sailors – who were mostly drunk and not in any regular formation – the pass-word 'Neptune' lost its power. Many of them were killed on the spot, many more as they broke and ran, and the rest never once slowed down, it is said, before they reached Ostia again. Crispus and two soldiers had waylaid Postumus in a narrow alley between his headquarters and the rendezvous, stunned him with a sandbag, gagged and bound him, put him into a covered sedan, and carried him off to the Palace. The next day Tiberius made a statement to the Senate. A certain slave of Postumus Agrippa's called Clement, he said, had caused a deal of unnecessary alarm in the City by impersonating his dead former master. This bold fellow had run away from the provincial knight who had bought him when Postumus's estate was sold and had hidden in a wood on the coast of Tuscany until his beard grew long enough to hide his receding chin – the chief point of dissimilarity between himself and Postumus. Some rowdy sailors at Ostia had pretended to believe in him, but only as an excuse for marching to Rome and creating a disturbance there. They had assembled in the suburbs a little before dawn that morning under his leadership with the object of marching to the centre of the City and plundering shops and private houses. When challenged by a force of Watchmen they had dispersed and deserted their leader, who had since been put to death: so the House need have no further anxiety about the matter.

I heard later that Tiberius pretended not to recognize Postumus when he was brought before him at the Palace and asked him, mockingly: 'How did you happen to become one of the Caesars?' To which Postumus answered: 'In the same way and on the same day as you did. Have you forgotten?' Tiberius told a slave to strike Postumus on the mouth for his insolence, and he was then put on the rack and asked to reveal his fellow-conspirators. But he would only tell scandalous anecdotes of the private life of Tiberius, which were so disgusting and so circumstantial that Tiberius lost his temper and battered his face in with his great bony fists. The soldiers finished the bloody work by beheading him and hacking him into pieces in the cellar of the Palace.

What greater sorrow can there be than to mourn a beloved friend as murdered – at the close of a long and undeserved exile, too – and then, after the brief joy and astonishment of hearing that he has somehow cheated his executioners, to have to mourn him a second time – this time without hope of error and without even seeing him in the interval – as treacherously recaptured and shamefully tortured and killed? My one consolation was that when Germanicus heard what had happened – and I would at once write him the whole story so far as I knew it – he would leave his campaigns in Germany and march back to Rome at the head of as many regiments as could be spared from the Rhine and avenge Postumus's death on Livia and Tiberius. I wrote, but he did not answer; I wrote again, and still no answer. But eventually a long affectionate letter came in which there was a wondering reference to the success which Clement had had in impersonating Postumus – how in the world had he managed to do it? From this sentence it was quite clear that none of my important letters had arrived: the only one to arrive had been sent off by the same post as the second. In this I had merely given him particulars of a business matter which he had asked me to look into for him: he now thanked me for the information, which he said was exactly what he wanted. I realized with a sudden feeling of dread that Livia or Tiberius must have intercepted all the rest.

My digestion had always been bad and fear of poison in every dish did not improve it. My stammer returned and I had attacks of aphasia – sudden blanks in the mind which brought me into great ridicule: if they caught me in the middle of a sentence I would finish it anyhow. The most unfortunate result of this weakness was that I made a mess of my duties as priest of Augustus, which hitherto I had carried out without cause for complaint from anyone. There is an old custom at Rome that if any mistake is made in the ritual of a sacrifice or other service the whole thing has to be gone over again from the beginning. It now often happened when I was officiating that I would lose my way in a prayer and perhaps go on repeating the same sequence of sentences two or three times before I realized what I was doing, or that I would take up the flint knife for cutting the victim's throat before sprinkling its head with the ritual flour and salt – and this sort of thing meant going back to the beginning again. It was tedious to make three or four attempts at a service before I could get through it perfectly, and the congregation used to get very restless. At last I wrote to Tiberius as High Pontiff and asked to be relieved from all my religious duties for a year on the ground of ill-health. He granted the request without comment.

Chapter 19

GERMANICUS'S third year of war against the Germans was more successful even than the first two. He had worked out a new plan of campaign, by which he would take the Germans by surprise

and save his men a lot of dangerous and weary marching.
This was to build on the Rhine a fleet of nearly a thousand A.D. 16
transports, embark with most of his forces, and sail down
the river and, by way of the canal that our father had once cut,
through the Dutch lakes and by sea to the mouth of the Ems.
Here he would anchor his transports on the near bank, except for
a few which would serve for making a pontoon bridge. He would
then attack the tribes across the Weser, a river, fordable in places,
which runs parallel to the Ems about fifty miles beyond. The plan
worked well in every detail.

When the advance-guard reached the Weser they found Hermann and some allied chieftains waiting on the further bank.
Hermann shouted across to ask whether Germanicus was in command. When they answered yes, he asked whether they would
take him a message? The message was: 'Hermann's courteous
greetings to Germanicus, and might he be permitted speech with
his brother?' This was a brother of Hermann's called, in German,
something like Goldkopf, or at any rate a name so barbarous that
it was impossible to transliterate it into Latin – as 'Hermann' had
been made into 'Arminius', or as 'Siegmyrgth' into 'Segimerus',
so it was translated as Flavius, meaning the golden-headed.
Flavius had been in the Roman Army for years, and being at
Lyons at the time of the disaster of Varus had there made a de-
claration of his continued loyalty to Rome, repudiating all the
family ties which bound him to his treacherous brother Hermann.
In the next year's campaign of Tiberius and Germanicus he had
fought bravely and lost an eye.

Germanicus asked Flavius whether he wished to address his
brother. Flavius said he didn't much want to but that it might be
an offer to surrender. So the two brothers started shouting at each
other across the river. Hermann began talking German, but
Flavius said that unless he talked Latin the conversation was at an
end. Hermann did not want to talk Latin, which the other chiefs
did not understand, for fear of being thought a traitor, and Flavius did not want to be thought a traitor by the Romans, who did
not understand German. On the other hand, Hermann wanted to
make an impression on the Romans, and Flavius on the Germans.
Hermann tried to keep to German, and Flavius to Latin, but as
they grew more and more heated they fell into such a dreadful
mixture of both languages that, as Germanicus wrote to me, it

was as good as a comedy to hear them. I quote from Germanicus's account of the dialogue.

Hermann: Hullo, brother. What's happened to your face? That scar's an awful deformity. Lost an eye?

Flavius: Yes, brother. Did you happen to pick one up? I lost it that day you galloped away out of the wood with mud smeared on your shield so that Germanicus wouldn't recognize you.

Hermann: You're wrong, brother. That wasn't me. You must have been drinking again. You were always like that before a battle: a bit nervous unless you had drunk at least a gallon of beer, and had to be strapped to the saddle by the time the war-horns sounded.

Flavius: That's a lie, of course, but it reminds me what a barbarous gut-rotting drink your German beer is. I never drink it now even when there's a great consignment come into the camp from one of your captured villages. The men only drink it when they have to: they say that it's better than swamp water spoilt by German corpses.

Hermann: Yes, I like Roman wine myself. I have a few hundred jars left of what I captured from Varus. This summer I'll be getting in another good supply, if Germanicus doesn't look out. By the way, what reward did you get for losing your eye?

Flavius (with great dignity): The personal thanks of the Commander-in-Chief, and three decorations, including the Crown and the Chain.

Hermann: Ho, ho! The Chain! Do you wear it round your ankles, you Roman slave?

Flavius: I'd rather any day be a slave to the Romans than a traitor to them. By the way, your dear Thrusnelda's very well and so's your boy. When are you coming to Rome to visit them?

Hermann: At the end of this campaign, brother. Ho, ho!

Flavius: You mean when you walk behind Germanicus's car in the triumph and the crowd pelts you with rotten eggs? How I'll laugh!

Hermann: You had better do all your laughing in advance, because if you still have any throat left to laugh through in three days from now my name's not Hermann. But enough of this. I have a message to you from your mother.

Flavius (suddenly serious and fetching a deep sigh): Ah, my dear,

212

dear mother! What message does my mother send me? Have I her sacred blessing still, brother?

Hermann: Brother, you have wounded our wise and noble and prolific mother to the soul. She says that she will turn her blessing into a curse if you continue to be a traitor to your family and tribe and race, and do not instantly come over to us again and act as joint-General with me.

Flavius (*in German, bursting into tears of rage*): Oh, she never said that, Hermann. She couldn't have said that. It's a lie you made up yourself just to make me unhappy. Confess it's a lie, Hermann!

Hermann: She gave you two days to make up your mind.

Flavius (*to his groom*): Hi, you ugly-faced pig, give me my horse and arms! I'm going over the stream to fight my brother. Hermann, you foul thing, I'm coming to fight you!

Hermann: Come on then, you one-eyed bean-eating slave, you!

Flavius jumped on his horse and was about to swim it across the river when a Roman colonel caught at his leg and pulled him off the saddle: he knew German and he knew the absurd veneration that Germans have for their wives and mothers. Suppose Flavius really meant to desert? So he told him not to bother about Hermann or believe his lies. But Flavius couldn't resist having the last word. He dried his eyes and shouted across: 'I saw your father-in-law last week. He'd got a nice place near Lyons. He told me that Thrusnelda came to him because she couldn't bear the disgrace of being married to a man who broke his solemn oath as an ally of Rome and betrayed a friend at whose table he had eaten. She said that the only way you can ever win back her esteem is by not using the arms which she gave you on your wedding-day against your sworn friends. She has not been unfaithful to you yet, but that won't last long if you don't instantly come to your senses.'

Then it was Hermann's turn to weep and storm and accuse Flavius of telling lies. Germanicus privately detailed a captain to watch Flavius very carefully during the next battle and at the least sign of treachery to run him through.

Germanicus wrote seldom, but when he did they were long letters and he put into them, he said, all the interesting and amusing things that did not seem quite suitable for his official dispatches to Tiberius: I lived for those letters. I was never anxious about

Germanicus's safety when he was fighting the Germans: he had the same sort of confidence with them as an experienced bee-keeper has with bees, who can go boldly to a hive and remove the honey, and the bees somehow never sting him as they would you or me if we tried to do the same thing. Two days after fording the Weser he fought a decisive battle with Hermann. I have always been interested in speeches made before a battle: there is nothing that throws such light on the character of a general. Germanicus neither harangued his men in an oratorical way nor joked obscenely with them like Julius Caesar. He was always very serious, very precise, and very practical. His speech on this occasion was about what he really thought of the Germans. He said that they were not soldiers. They had a certain bravado and fought well in a mob, as wild cattle fight, and they had a certain animal cunning too which made it unwise to neglect ordinary precautions in fighting them. But they soon tired after their first furious charge and they had no discipline in any true military sense, only a spirit of mutual rivalry. Their chiefs could never count on them to do what was wanted: either they did too much or not enough. 'The Germans,' he said, 'are the most insolent and boastful nation in the world when things go well with them, but once they are defeated they are the most cowardly and abject. Never trust a German out of your sight, but never be afraid of him when you have him face to face. And that's all that need be said except this: most of the fighting to-morrow will be in among those woods, where from all accounts the enemy will be so tightly packed that they will have no room for manoeuvre. Go straight at them, never mind their assegais, and get to close quarters at once. Stab at their faces: that is what they hate most.'

Hermann had chosen his battle-ground carefully: a narrowing plain lying between the Weser and a range of wooded hills. He would fight at the narrow end of this plain with a big oak and birch forest at his back, the river on his right and the hills on his left. The Germans were in three detachments. The first of these, young assegai-men of local tribes, were to advance into the plain against the leading Roman regiments, who would probably be French auxiliaries, and drive them back. Then when the Roman supports came up they were to break off the fight and pretend to fly in panic. The Romans would press on towards the wood and at this point the second detachment, consisting of Hermann's own

214

tribe, would charge down from an ambush on the hill and take them in the flank. This would cause great confusion and the first detachment would then return, closely supported by the third – the experienced elder men of the local tribes – and drive the Romans into the river. The German cavalry by this time would have come round from behind the hill and taken the Romans in the rear.

It would have been a good plan if Hermann had been in command of disciplined troops, But it went ludicrously wrong. Germanicus's order of battle was as follows: first, two regiments of French heavy infantry on the river flank, and two of the auxiliary Germans on the mountain flank, then the foot archers, then four regular regiments, then Germanicus with two Guards battalions and the regular cavalry, then four more regular regiments, then the French mounted archers, then the French light infantry. As the German auxiliaries advanced along the spurs of the mountain, Hermann, who was watching events from the top of a pine tree, called out excitedly to his nephew who was standing by for orders below: 'There goes my traitor brother! He must never leave this battle alive.' The stupid nephew sprang forward shouting, 'Hermann's orders are to charge at once!' He rushed down into the plain with about half the tribe. Hermann with difficulty managed to restrain the rest. Germanicus sent the regular cavalry out at once to charge the fools in the flank before they could reach Flavius's men, and the French mounted archers to cut off their retreat.

The German skirmishing detachment had meanwhile advanced from the wood, but the Roman cavalry charge sent the men under Hermann's nephew rushing back on top of them and they caught the panic and ran back too. The German third detachment, the main body, then came out of the wood, expecting the skirmishers to halt and turn back with them as arranged. But the skirmishers' only thought was to get away from the cavalry: they ran back through the main body. At this moment there came a most cheering omen for the Romans – eight eagles, who had been frightened from the hill by the sortie and were wheeling about the plain, uttering loud shrieks, now flew all together towards the wood. Germanicus called out: 'Follow the Eagles! Follow the Roman Eagles!' The whole army took up the cry: 'Follow the Eagles!' Meanwhile Hermann had charged with the rest

215

of his men and taken the foot-archers by surprise, killing a number of them; but the rear regiment of French heavy infantry wheeled round to the archers' assistance. Hermann's force, which consisted of some 15,000 men, might still have saved the battle by crushing the French infantry and thus driving a formidable wedge between the Roman advance guard and the main body. But the sun flashed in their faces from the weapons and breast-plates and shields and helmets of the long ranks of advancing regular infantry, and the Germans lost courage. Most of them rushed back to the hill. Hermann rallied a thousand or two, but not enough, and by this time two squadrons of regular cavalry had come charging back among the fugitives, and cut off his retreat to the hill. How he got away is a mystery, but it is generally believed that he spurred his horse towards the wood and overtook the German auxiliaries who were advancing to attack it. Then he shouted: 'Make way, cattle! I'm Hermann!' Nobody dared to kill him because he was Flavius's brother and Flavius would feel bound in family honour to avenge his death.

It was no longer a battle but a slaughter. The German main body was outflanked and forced towards the river, which many managed to swim, but not all. Germanicus pushed his second line of regular infantry into the wood and routed the skirmishers who were waiting there in the vague hope of the battle suddenly turning in their favour. (The archers had good sport shooting down Germans who had climbed trees and were hiding in the foliage at the top.) All resistance was now over. From nine o'clock in the morning until seven o'clock in the evening, when it began to get dark, the killing went on. For ten miles beyond the battlefield the woods and plains were scattered with German corpses. Among the captives was the mother of Hermann and Flavius. She begged for life, saying that she had always tried to persuade Hermann to abandon his futile resistance to the Roman conquerors. So Flavius's loyalty was now assured.

A month later another battle was fought, in thick forest-land on the banks of the Elbe. Hermann had chosen an ambush and made dispositions which might have been most effective if Germanicus had not heard all about them a few hours beforehand from deserters. As it was, instead of the Romans being driven into the river, the Germans were forced back through the wood, in which they were packed too closely for their usual strike-and-run tactics

– back into a quaking bog which surrounded it, where thousands slowly sank out of sight, yelling with rage and despair. Hermann, who had been disabled by an arrow wound in the previous battle, was not much to the fore this time. But he carried on the fight in the wood as stubbornly as he could and, meeting by chance with his brother Flavius, thrust him through with an assegai. He escaped across the bog, jumping from tussock to tussock with extraordinary nimbleness and good luck.

Germanicus raised a huge trophy-heap of German weapons and put on it the following inscription: 'The Forces of Tiberius Caesar having subdued the tribes between Rhine and Elbe consecrate these memorials of their victory to Jove, to Mars, and to Augustus.' No mention of himself. His total casualties in these two battles were not above 2,500 men killed and seriously wounded. The Germans must have lost at least 25,000.

Germanicus considered that he had done enough this year and sent some of his men back to the Rhine by land and embarked the rest on transports. But then came misfortune: a sudden storm from the south-west caught the fleet soon after it weighed anchor and scattered it in all directions. Many vessels went to the bottom and only Germanicus's own ship managed to reach the mouth of the Weser, where he reproached himself as a second Varus with the loss of a whole Roman army. He was with difficulty prevented by his friends from leaping into the sea to join the dead. However, a few days later the wind veered round to the north and one by one the scattered ships came back, almost all oarless and some with cloaks spread instead of sails, the less disabled taking turns to tow the ones that could barely keep afloat.

Germanicus hurried set to work repairing the damaged hulls and sent off as many of the fit vessels as he could to search the desolate neighbouring islands for survivors. Many were found there, but in a half-starved state, kept alive only by shell-fish and the carcases of horses thrown up on the beach. Many more came in from points further up the coast; they had been respectfully treated by the inhabitants, who had lately been forced to swear alliance with Rome. About twenty ship-loads returned from as far away as Britain, which had been paying a nominal tribute since its conquest seventy years before by Julius Caesar, sent back by the petty kings of Kent and Sussex. In the end not more than a quarter of the lost men were unaccounted for, and nearly 200 of these were found, years later, in Central Britain. They were rescued from the lead-mines, where they had been put to forced labour.

The inland Germans, when they first heard of this disaster, thought that their gods had avenged them. They overthrew the battlefield trophy and even began talking of a march to the Rhine. But Germanicus suddenly struck again, sending an expedition of sixty infantry battalions and 100 cavalry squadrons against the tribes of the upper Weser, while he himself marched with eighty more infantry battalions and another 100 cavalry squadrons against the tribes between the lower Rhine and the Ems. Both expeditions were completely successful and, what was better than the killing of many thousand Germans, the Eagle of the Eighteenth Regiment was found in an underground temple in a wood and triumphantly borne away. Only the Eagle of the Seventeenth now remained unredeemed, and Germanicus promised his men that next year, if he was still in command, they would rescue that too. Meanwhile he marched them back to winter quarters.

Then Tiberius wrote pressing him to come home for the triumph which had been decreed him, for he had surely done enough. Germanicus wrote back that he would not be content until he had altogether broken the power of the Germans, for which not many more battles were now needed, and recovered the third Eagle. Tiberius wrote again that Rome could not afford such high casualties even at the reward of such splendid victories: he was not criticizing Germanicus's skill as a general, for his battles had been most economical in men, but between battle casualties and the sea-disaster he had lost the equivalent of two whole regiments, which was more than Rome could afford. He reminded Germanicus that he had himself been sent nine times into Germany by Augustus and so was not talking without experience. His opinion was that it was not worth the life of a single Roman to kill even as many as ten Germans. Germany was like a Hydra: the more heads you lopped off the more it grew. The best way of managing Germans was to play on their inter-tribal jealousies and foment war between neighbouring chieftains: encouraging them to kill each other without outside help. Germanicus wrote back begging for one year more in which to complete his work of subjugation. But Tiberius told him that he was wanted at Rome as Consul again, and touched him on his most tender spot by saying that he should remember his brother Castor. Germany was the only country now where any important war was being fought and if he insisted on finishing it himself, Castor would have no opportunity of winning a triumph or the title of field-marshal. Germanicus persisted no longer but said that Tiberius's wishes were his law and that he would return as soon as relieved.

He came back in the early spring and celebrated his triumph. The whole population of Rome streamed out to welcome him twenty miles from the City. A great arch to com- A.D. 17 memorate the recovery of the Eagles was dedicated near the temple of Saturn. The triumphal procession passed under it. There were cars heaped with the spoil of German temples, and with enemy shields and weapons; others carried tableaux representing battles or German river-gods and mountain-gods dominated by Roman soldiers. Thrusnelda and her child were on one car, with halters about their necks, followed by an enormous train of manacled German prisoners. Germanicus rode, crowned, in his chariot with Agrippina seated beside him and his five children – Nero, Drusus, Caligula, Agrippinilla, and Drusilla – seated behind. He won more applause than any other triumphant general had won since Augustus's triumph after Actium.

But I was not there. Of all places in the world I was in Carthage! Only a month before Germanicus's return I had been sent a note by Livia instructing me to prepare for a journey to Africa. A representative of the Imperial family was needed to dedicate a new temple to Augustus at Carthage, and I was the only one who could be spared for the task. I would be given ample advice on how to conduct myself and how to perform the ceremony, and it was to be hoped I would not once more make a fool of myself, even before African provincials. I guessed at once why I was being sent. There was no reason for anyone to go yet, because the temple would not be completed for at least another three months. I was being got out of the way. While Germanicus was in the City I would not be allowed to return, and all my letters home would be opened. So I never had an opportunity of telling Germanicus what I had been saving up for him so long. On the other hand, Germanicus had his talk with Tiberius. He told him that he knew that Postumus's banishment had been due to a cruel plot on Livia's part – he had positive proof of it. Livia certainly ought to be removed from public affairs. Her actions could not be justified by any

219

subsequent misbehaviour of Postumus's. It was only natural for him to try to escape from undeserved confinement. Tiberius professed to be shocked by Germanicus's revelations; but said that he could not create a public scandal by suddenly dishonouring his mother: he would charge her privately with the crime and gradually take away her powers.

What he really did was to go to Livia and tell her exactly what Germanicus had said to him, adding that Germanicus was a credulous fool, but seemed to be in earnest and was so popular at Rome and in the Army that perhaps it would be advisable for Livia to convince him that she was not guilty of what he charged her, unless she thought this beneath her dignity. He added that he would send Germanicus away somewhere as soon as possible, probably to the East, and would raise the question again in the Senate of her being called Mother of the Country, a title which she had well deserved. He had taken exactly the right line with her. She was pleased that he still feared her sufficiently to tell her so much, and called him a dutiful son. She swore that she had not arranged false charges against Postumus: this story was probably invented by Agrippina, whom Germanicus followed blindly and who was trying to persuade him to usurp the monarchy. Agrippina's plan, she said, was no doubt to make trouble between Tiberius and his loving mother. Tiberius, embracing her, said that though little disagreements might occasionally occur nothing could break the ties that bound them. Livia then sighed, she was getting to be an old woman now – she was well on in her seventies – and was beginning to find her work too much for her: perhaps he would anyhow relieve her of the more tedious part and only consult her on important questions of appointments and decrees? She would not even be offended if he discontinued his practice of putting her name above his on all official documents: she did not want it said that he was under her tutelage. But, she said, the sooner he persuaded the Senate to give her that title the more pleased she would be. So there was a show of reconciliation: but neither trusted the other.

Tiberius now named Germanicus as his colleague in the Consulship and told him that he had persuaded Livia to retire from public business, though as a matter of form he would still pretend to consult her. This seemed to satisfy Germanicus. But Tiberius did not feel at all comfortable. Agrippina would hardly speak to him, and knowing that Germanicus and she had only one soul between them, he could not believe in their continued loyalty. Besides, things were going on at Rome which a man of Germanicus's character would naturally detest. First of all, the informers. Since Livia would not give him access to the criminal dossiers or let him share the control of her very efficient spy-system – she had a paid agent in almost every important household or institution – he had to adopt another method. He made a decree that if anyone was found guilty of plotting against the State or blaspheming the God Augustus his confiscated estates would be divided among his loyal accusers. Plots against the State were less easy to prove than blasphemies against Augustus. The first case of blasphemy against Augustus was that of a wag, a young shopkeeper, who happened to be standing near Tiberius in the Market Place as a funeral passed. He sprang forward and whispered something in the ear of the corpse. Tiberius was curious to know what it was. The man explained that he was asking the dead man to tell Augustus when he met him down below that his legacies to the people of Rome had not yet been paid. Tiberius had the man arrested and executed for speaking of Augustus as if he were a mere ghost, not an immortal God, and said that he was sending him down below to convince him of his mistake. A month or two later, by the way, he did pay the legacies in full. In a case like this Tiberius had some justification, but later the most harmless abuses of Augustus's name were enough to put a man on trial for his life.

A class of professional informers sprang up who could be counted on to make out a case against any man who was indicated to them as having incurred Tiberius's displeasure. Thus criminal dossiers based on a record of real delinquency were superfluous. Sejanus was Tiberius's go-between with these scoundrels. In the year before Germanicus's return Tiberius had put the informers to work on a young man called Libo who was a A.D. 16 great-grandson of Pompey and a cousin of Agrippina's through their grandmother Scribonia. Sejanus had warned Tiberius that Libo was dangerous and had been making disrespectful remarks about him: but Tiberius was careful at this stage not to make disrespect to himself an indictable offence, so he had to invent other charges. Now, Tiberius, to cover his own association with Thrasyllus, had expelled from Rome all astrologers, magicians, fortune-tellers, and interpreters of dreams, and forbidden anyone to consult such of them as secretly stayed on. A few stayed with Tiberius's connivance, on condition that they gave séances only with an Imperial agent concealed in the room. Libo was persuaded by a senator who had turned professional informer to visit one of these decoys and have his fortune told. His questions were noted down by the hidden agent. In themselves they were not treasonable, only foolish: he wanted to know how rich he would become and whether he would ever be the leading man at Rome, and so on. But a forged document was produced at his trial which was said to have been discovered by slaves in his bedroom – a list, in what appeared to be his handwriting, of names of all the members of the Imperial family and of the leading senators, with curious Chaldean and Egyptian characters written against each name in the margin. The penalty for consulting a magician was banishment, but the penalty for practising magic oneself was death. Libo denied authorship of the document, and the evidence of slaves, even under torture, would not be sufficient to condemn him: slave-evidence was accepted only when the accusation was that of incest. There was no freedman evidence, because Libo's freedman could not be persuaded to testify against him nor might a freedman be put to torture to force a confession from him. On Sejanus's advice, however, Tiberius made a new legal ruling that when a man was charged with a capital crime his slaves could be bought at a fair valuation by the Public Steward and thus enabled to give evidence under torture. Libo, who had not been able to get a lawyer brave enough to defend him, saw that he was caught and asked for an adjournment of the trial until the next day. When this was granted he went home and killed himself. The charge against him was nevertheless gone through with in the Senate with the same formality as if he had been alive, and he was found guilty on all charges. Tiberius said that it was unfortunate that the foolish young man had killed himself, because he would have interceded for his life. Libo's estate was divided among his accusers, among whom were four senators. Such a disgraceful farce could never have been played when Augustus was Emperor, but under Tiberius it was played, with variations, over and over again. Only one man made a public protest, and that was a certain Calpurnius Piso, who rose in the Senate to say that he was so disgusted with the atmosphere of political intrigue in the City, the corruption of justice, and the disgraceful spectacle of his fellow-senators acting as paid informers, that he was leaving Rome for good and retiring to some village in a remote part of Italy. Having said this he walked out. The speech made a powerful impression on the House. Tiberius sent someone to call Calpurnius back, and when he was once more in his seat told him that if there were miscarriages of justice any senator was at liberty to call attention to them at question-time. He said, too, that a certain amount of political intrigue was inevitable in the capital city of the greatest Empire the world had ever known. Did Calpurnius suggest that the senators would not have come forward with their accusations if they had had no hopes of reward? He said that he admired Calpurnius's earnestness and independence and envied his talents; but would it not be better to employ these noble qualities for the improvement of social and political morality at Rome than to bury them in some wretched hamlet of the Apennines, among shepherds and bandits? So Calpurnius had to stay. But soon after he showed his earnestness and independence by summoning old Urgulania to appear in court for non-payment of a large sum of money which she owed him for some pictures and statuary: Calpurnius's sister had died and there had been a sale. When Urgulania read the summons, which was for her immediate attendance at the Debtor's Court, she told her chair-men to take her straight to Livia's Palace. Calpurnius followed her and was met in the hall by Livia, who told him to be off. Calpurnius courteously but firmly excused himself, saying that Urgulania must obey the summons without fail unless too ill to attend, which clearly she was not. Even Vestal Virgins were not exempt from attendance at court when subpoenaed. Livia said that his behaviour was personally insulting to her and that her son, the Emperor, would know how to avenge her. Tiberius was sent for and tried to smooth things over, telling Calpurnius that Urgulania surely meant to come as soon as she had composed herself after the sudden shock of the summons, and telling Livia that it was no doubt a mistake, that Calpurnius certainly meant no disrespect, and that he himself would attend the trial and see that Urgulania had a capable counsel and a fair trial. He left the Palace, walking beside Calpurnius towards the courts and talking with him of this and that. Calpurnius's friends tried to persuade him to drop the charge, but he replied that he was old-fashioned: he liked being paid money that was owed him. The trial never came off. Livia sent a mounted messenger after them with the whole amount of the debt in gold in his saddle-bags: he overtook Calpurnius and Tiberius before they arrived at the door of the Court.

But I am writing about informers and the demoralizing effect they had on life at Rome, and about judicial corruption. I was about to record that while Germanicus was at Rome there was not a single charge heard in the courts of blaspheming Augustus or of plotting against the State, and the informers were warned to keep absolutely quiet. Tiberius was on his best behaviour and his speeches in the Senate were models of frankness. Sejanus retired into the background, Thrasyllus was removed from Rome to the shelter of Tiberius's village on the island of Capri, and Tiberius appeared to have no intimate friend but the honest Nerva, whose advice he was always asking.

Castor I never could learn to like. He was a foul-mouthed, bloody-minded, violent-tempered, dissolute fellow. His character showed up most clearly at a sword-fight, where he took more delight in seeing blood spurting from a wound than in any act of skill or courage on the part of the combatants. But I must say that he behaved very finely towards Germanicus and seemed to undergo a real change of heart in his company. City factions tried to force the two into the wretched position of rivals for succession to the monarchy, but they never on any occasion encouraged this view. Castor treated Germanicus with the same brotherly consideration that Germanicus gave him. Castor was not exactly a coward, but he was a politician rather than a soldier. When he was sent across the Danube in answer to an appeal for help by the tribes of East Germany who were fighting a defensive and bloody war against Hermann's Western confederacy, he managed by clever intrigue to bring into the war the tribes of Bohemia, and of Bavaria too. He was carrying out Tiberius's policy of encouraging the Germans to exterminate each other. Maroboduus ('He who walks on the lake bottom'), the priest-king of the East Germans, fled for protection to Castor's camp. Maroboduus was given a safe retreat in Italy; and since the East Germans had sworn an oath of perpetual allegiance he remained for eighteen years a hostage for their good behaviour. These East Germans were a fiercer and more powerful race than the West Germans and Germanicus was lucky not to have had them at war with him too. But Hermann had become a national hero by his defeat of Varus, and

Maroboduus was jealous of his success. Rather than that Hermann should become High King of all the German nations, which was his ambition, Maroboduus had refused to give him any help in his campaign against Germanicus, even by making a diversion on another frontier.

I have often thought about Hermann. He was a remarkable man in his way, and though it is difficult to forget his treachery to Varus, Varus had done much to provoke the revolt and Hermann and his men were certainly fighting for liberty. They had a genuine contempt for the Romans. They could not understand in what sense the extremely severe discipline in the Roman army under Varus, Tiberius, and almost every other general but my father and my brother, differed from downright slavery. They were shocked at the disciplinary floggings and regarded the system of paying soldiers at so much a day, instead of engaging them by promises of glory and plunder, as most base. The Germans have always been very chaste in their morals, and Roman officers openly practised vices which in Germany, if they ever came to light – but this was seldom – were punished by smothering both culprits in mud under a hurdle. As for German cowardice, all barbarous people are cowards. If Germans ever become civilized it will then be time to judge whether they are cowards or not. They seem, however, to be an exceptionally nervous and quarrelsome people, and I cannot make up my mind whether there is any immediate chance of their becoming really civilized. Germanicus thought that there was none. Whether his policy of extermination was justified or not (certainly it was not the usual Roman policy with frontier tribes) depends on the answer to the first question. Of course, the captured Eagles had to be won back, and Hermann had shown no mercy, after the defeat of Varus, when he overran the province, and Germanicus, who was a most gentle and humane man, disliked general massacre so much that he must have had very good reasons for ordering it.

Hermann did not die in battle. When Maroboduus was forced to fly from the country, Hermann thought that his way was now clear to a monarchy over all the nations of Germany. But he was mistaken: he was not even able to make himself monarch of his own tribe, which was a free tribe, the chieftain having no power to command, only to lead and advise and persuade. One day, a year or two later, he tried to issue orders like a king. His family, which had hitherto been greatly devoted to him, were so scandalized that, without even first discussing the matter together, they all rushed at him with their weapons and hacked him to pieces. He was thirty-seven when he died, having been born the year before my brother Germanicus, his greatest enemy.

Chapter 20

I WAS nearly a year in Carthage. (It was the year that Livy died, at Padua, where his heart had always been.) Old Carthage had been razed to the ground and this was a new city, built by Augustus on the south-east of the peninsula and destined to A.D. 18 become the first city of Africa. It was the first time I had been out of Italy since my babyhood. I found the climate very trying, the African natives savage, diseased, and over-worked; the resident Romans dull, quarrelsome, mercenary, and behind the times; the swarms of unfamiliar creeping and flying insects most horrible. What I missed most was the absence of any wild wooded countryside. In Tripoli there is nothing to mediate between the regularly planted land – fig and olive orchards, or cornfields – and the bare, stony, thorny desert. I stayed at the house of the Governor, who was that Furius Camillus, my dear Camilla's uncle, of whom I have already written; he was very kind to me. Almost the first thing he told me was how useful my *Balkan Summary* had been to him in that campaign and that I should certainly have been publicly rewarded for compiling it so well. He did everything he could to make my dedication ceremony a success and to exact from the provincials the respect due to my rank. He was also most assiduous in showing me the sights. The town did a flourishing trade with Rome, exporting not only vast quantities of grain and oil, but slaves, purple dye, sponges, gold, ivory, ebony, and wild beasts for the Games. But I had little occupation here and Furius suggested that it would be a good thing for me, while I was here, to collect materials for a complete history of Carthage. There was no such book to be found in the libraries at Rome. The archives of the old town had recently come into his hands, discovered by natives quarrying in the ruins for hidden treasure, and if I cared to use them they were mine. I told him that I had no

226

knowledge of the Phoenician language; but he undertook, if I was sufficiently interested, to set one of his freedmen the task of translating the more important manuscripts into Greek.

The idea of writing the history pleased me very much: I felt that historical justice had never been done to the Carthaginians. I spent my leisure time in making a study of the ruins of the Old City, with the help of a contemporary survey, and familiarizing myself with the geography of the country in general. I also learned the rudiments of the language well enough to be able to read simple inscriptions and understand the few Phoenician words used by authors who have written about the Punic Wars from the Roman side. When I returned to Italy I began to write the book concurrently with my Etruscan history. I like having two tasks going at the same time: when I tire of one I turn to the other. But I am perhaps too careful a writer. I am not satisfied merely with copying from ancient authorities while there is any possible means of checking their statements by consulting other sources of information on the same subject, particularly accounts by writers of rival political parties. So these two histories, each of which I could have written in a year or two if I had been less conscientious, kept me busy between them for some twenty-five years. For every word I wrote I must have read many hundreds; and in the end I became a very good scholar both of Etruscan and Phoenician, and had a working knowledge of several other languages and dialects too, such as Numidian, Egyptian, Oscan, and Faliscan. I finished the *History of Carthage* first.

Shortly after my dedication of the temple, which went off without a hitch, Furius had suddenly to take the field against Tacfarinas with the only forces available in the province – a single regular regiment, the Third, together with a few battalions of auxiliaries and two cavalry squadrons. Tacfarinas was a Numidian chief, originally a deserter from the ranks of the Roman auxiliaries, and a remarkably successful bandit. He had recently built up a sort of army on the Roman model in the interior of his own country and had allied himself with the Moors for an invasion of the province from the West. The two armies together outnumbered Furius's force by at least five to one. They met in open country about fifty miles from the City and Furius had to decide whether to attack Tacfarinas's two semi-disciplined regiments which were in the centre of the undisciplined Moorish forces on the flank. He sent the cavalry and auxiliaries, mostly archers, to keep the Moors in play and with his regular regiment marched straight at Tacfarinas's Numidians. I was watching the battle from a hill some 500 paces away – I had ridden out on a mule – and never before or since, I think, have I been so proud of being a Roman. The Third kept perfect formation: it might have been a ceremonial parade on Mars Field. They advanced in three lines at fifty paces' distance. Each line consisted of 150 files, eight men deep. The Numidians halted in a defensive posture. They were in six lines, with a frontage the same as ours. The Third did not halt but marched straight at them without pausing a moment, and it was only when they were ten paces off that the leading line discharged their javelins in a shining shower. Then they drew their swords and charged, shield to shield. They rolled the enemy's first line, who were pike-men, back on the second. The new line they broke with a fresh discharge of javelins – every soldier carried a pair. Then the Roman support-line passed through them, to give them a chance to reorganize. Soon I saw still another shower of javelins, simultaneously thrown, fly shining at the Numidians' third line. The Moors on the flanks, who were greatly bothered by the arrows of the auxiliaries, saw the Romans cutting their way deep into the centre. They began howling, as if the battle was lost, and scattered in all directions. Tacfarinas had to fight a costly rear-guard action back to his camp. The only unpleasant memory I have of this victory was the banquet with which it was celebrated: in the course of which Furius's son, who was called Scribonianus, made satiric references to the moral support I had given the troops. He did this chiefly to call attention to his own gallantry, which he thought had not been sufficiently praised. Furius afterwards made him beg my pardon. Furius was voted triumphal ornaments by the Senate – the first member of his family to win military distinction since his ancestor Camillus saved Rome more than 400 years previously.

When I was finally recalled to Rome, Germanicus had already gone to the East, where the Senate had voted him supreme command of all the provinces. With him went Agrippina, and Caligula, who was now aged eight. The elder children remained at Rome with my mother. Though Germanicus was greatly disappointed at having to leave the German War unfinished, he decided to make the most of things and improve his education by visiting places famous in history or literature. He visited the Bay of Actium, and there saw the memorial chapel dedicated to Apollo by Augustus, and the camp of Antony.

As Antony's grandson the place had a melancholy fascination for him. He was explaining the plan of the battle to young Caligula, when the child interrupted with a silly laugh: 'Yes, father, my grandfather Agrippa and my great-grandfather Augustus gave your grandfather Antony a pretty good beating. I wonder you're not ashamed to tell me the story.' This was only one of many recent occasions on which Caligula had spoken insolently to Germanicus, and Germanicus now decided that it was no use treating him in the gentle, friendly way he treated other children – that the only course with Caligula was strict discipline and severe punishments.

He visited Boeotian Thebes, to see Pindar's birth-chamber, and the island of Lesbos, to see Sappho's tomb. Here another of my nieces was born, who was given the unlucky name of Julia. We always called her Lesbia, though. Then he visited Byzantium, Troy, and the famous Greek cities of Asia Minor. From Miletus he wrote me a long letter describing his journey in terms of such delighted interest that it was clear that he no longer greatly regretted his recall from Germany.

Meanwhile affairs at Rome relapsed into the condition in which they had been before Germanicus's Consulship; and Sejanus revived Tiberius's old fears about Germanicus. He reported a remark of Germanicus's made at a private dinner-party at which one of his agents had been present, to the effect that the Eastern regiments probably needed the same sort of overhauling as he had given the ones on the Rhine. This remark had actually been made, but meant no more than that these troops were probably being mishandled by the inferior officers in much the same way as the others had been: and that he would review all appointments at the first opportunity. Sejanus made Tiberius understand the remark as meaning that the reason why Germanicus had delayed his usurpation of power so long was that he could not count on the affection of the Eastern regiments: which he was now going to win by letting the men choose their own captains, and giving them presents and relaxing the severity of their discipline – just as he had done on the Rhine.

Tiberius was alarmed and thought it wise to consult Livia: he counted on her to work with him. She knew what to do at once.

They appointed a man called Gnaeus Piso to the governorship of the province of Syria – an appointment which would give him command, under Germanicus, of the greater part of the Eastern regiments – and told him in private that he could count on their support if Germanicus tried to interfere with any of his political or military arrangements. It was a clever choice. Gnaeus Piso, an uncle of that Lucius Piso who had offended Livia, was a haughty old man who twenty-five years before had earned the bitter hatred of the Spanish, when sent to them by Augustus as Governor, for his cruelty and avarice. He was deeply in debt and the hint that he could behave how he liked in Syria, so long as he provoked Germanicus, seemed an invitation to make another fortune to replace the one he had made in Spain and had long since run through. He disliked Germanicus for his seriousness and piety and used to call him a superstitious old woman; and he was also extremely jealous of him.

Germanicus, when he had visited Athens, had shown his respect for her ancient glories by appearing at the city gates with only a single yeoman as escort. He had also made a long and earnest speech in eulogy of Athenian poets, soldiers, and philosophers, at a festival which was organized in his honour. Now Piso came through Athens on his way to Syria and, since it was not part of his province and he did not take any pains to be civil to them as Germanicus had done, the Athenians did not take any pains to be civil to him. A man called Theophilus, the brother of one of Piso's creditors, had just been condemned for forgery by a vote of the City Assembly. Piso asked as a personal favour that the man should be pardoned, but his request was refused, which made Piso very angry: if Theophilus had been pardoned, the brother would have certainly cancelled the debt. He made a violent speech in which he said that the latter-day Athenians had no right to identify themselves with the great Athenians of the days of Pericles, Demosthenes, Aeschylus, Plato. The ancient Athenians had been extirpated by repeated wars and massacres and these were mere mongrels, degenerates, and the descendants of slaves. He said that any Roman who flattered them as if they were the legitimate heirs of those ancient heroes was lowering the dignity of the Roman name; and that for his part he could not forget that in the last Civil War they had declared against the great Augustus and supported that cowardly traitor Antony.

230

Piso then left Athens and sailed for Rhodes on his way to Syria. Germanicus was at Rhodes too, visiting the University, and news of the speech, which was plainly directed at himself, reached him just before Piso's ships were sighted. A sudden squall rose and Piso's ships were seen to be in difficulties. Two smaller vessels went down before Germanicus's eyes, and the third, which was Piso's, was dismasted and was being driven on the rocks of the northern headland. Who but Germanicus would not have abandoned Piso to his fate? But Germanicus sent out a couple of well-manned galleys which succeeded by desperate rowing in reaching the wreck just before it struck and towing it safely to port. Or who but a man as depraved as Piso would not have rewarded his rescuer with lifelong gratitude and devotion? But Piso actually complained that Germanicus had delayed the rescue until the last moment, in the hope that it would come too late; and without stopping a day at Rhodes, he sailed away again while the sea was still rough in order to reach Syria before Germanicus.

As soon as he arrived at Antioch he began to overhaul the regiments in just the opposite sense to that intended by Germanicus. Instead of removing slack, bullying captains, he reduced to the ranks every officer who had a good record and appointed scoundrelly favourites of his own in their places – with the understanding that a commission of half whatever they succeeded in making out of their appointments should be paid to him, and no questions asked. So a bad year began for the Syrians. Shopkeepers in the towns and farmers in the country had to pay secret 'protection-money' to the local captains; if they refused to pay there would be a raid at night by masked men, their houses would be burned down, and their families murdered. At first there were many appeals made to Piso against this terrorism by city guilds, farmers' associations, and so forth. He always promised an immediate inquiry but never made one; and the complainers were usually found beaten to death on the road home. A delegation was sent to Rome to enquire privately from Sejanus whether Tiberius was aware of what was going on and, if so, whether he countenanced it. Sejanus told the provincials that Tiberius knew nothing officially; and though he would, no doubt, promise an inquiry, Piso had done as much for them as that, had he not? Perhaps the best course for them to take, he said, would be to pay whatever protection-money was demanded with as little fuss as possible.

Meanwhile the standard of camp-discipline in the Syrian regiments had sunk so low that Tacfarinas's bandit-army would by comparison have seemed a model of efficiency and devotion to duty.

Delegates also came to Germanicus at Rhodes, and he was disgusted and amazed at their revelations. In his recent progress through Asia Minor he had made it his task to enquire personally into all complaints of maladministration and to remove all magistrates who had acted in an illegal or oppressive way. He now wrote to Tiberius telling him of the reports that had reached him of Piso's behaviour, saying that he was setting out for Syria at once; and asking for permission to remove Piso and put a better man in his place if even a few of the complaints were justified. Tiberius wrote back that he had also heard certain complaints, but they appeared to be unfounded and malicious; he had confidence in Piso as a capable and just Governor. Germanicus did not suspect Tiberius of dishonesty and was confirmed in the opinion he had already had of him as simple-minded and easily imposed upon. He regretted having written for permission to do what he should have done at once on his own responsibility. He now heard another serious charge against Piso, namely, that he was plotting with Vonones, the deposed king of Armenia, who was in refuge in Syria, to restore him to his throne. Vonones was immensely wealthy, having fled to Syria with most of the contents of the Armenian treasury, so Piso hoped to do well out of the business. Germanicus went at once to Armenia, called a conference of nobles and, with his own hands, but in Tiberius's name, put the diadem on the head of the man they had chosen for king. He then ordered Piso to visit Armenia at the head of two regiments to pay his neighbourly respects to the new monarch: or, if he was held by more important business, to send his son. Piso neither sent his son nor went himself. Germanicus, having visited other outlying provinces and allied kingdoms and settled affairs there to his satisfaction, came down into Syria and met Piso at the winter quarters of the Tenth Regiment.

There were several officers present as witnesses of this meeting, because Germanicus did not wish Tiberius to be misinformed as to what was said. He began, in as gentle a voice as he could command, by asking Piso to explain disobedience of orders. He said that if there was no explanation of it but the same personal animosity and discourtesy which he had shown in his speech at Athens, in his ungrateful remarks at Rhodes, and on several occasions since, a strong report would have to be forwarded to the Emperor. He went on to complain that, for troops living under peace-time conditions in a healthy and popular station, he found the Tenth Regiment in a most shockingly undisciplined and dirty condition.

Piso said, grinning: 'Yes, they *are* a dirty lot, aren't they? What would the people of Armenia have thought if I had sent them there as representatives of the power and majesty of Rome?' ('The power and majesty of Rome' was a favourite phrase of my brother's.)

Germanicus, keeping his temper with difficulty, said that the deterioration seemed to date only from Piso's arrival in the province, and that he would write to Tiberius to that effect.

Piso made an ironical plea for forgiveness, coupled with an insulting remark about the high ideals of youth which often have to yield, in this hard world, to less exalted but more practical policies.

Germanicus interrupted with flashing eyes: 'Often, Piso, but not always. To-morrow, for instance, I shall sit with you on the appeal tribunal and we shall see whether the high ideals of youth are controlled by any obstacle at all: and whether justice to the provincials can be denied them by any incompetent, avaricious, bloody-minded sexagenarian debauchee.'

This ended the interview. Piso at once wrote to Tiberius and Livia, telling what had happened. He quoted Germanicus's last sentence in such a way that Tiberius believed that the 'incompetent, avaricious, bloody-minded sexagenarian debauchee' was himself. Tiberius replied that he had the fullest confidence in Piso, and that if a certain influential person continued to speak and act in this disloyal way, any steps, however daring, taken by a subordinate to check this disloyalty would doubtless be pleasing to the Senate and people of Rome. Meanwhile Germanicus sat on the tribunal and heard appeals from the provincials against unjust sentences in the courts. Piso did his best at first to embarrass him by legal obstructionism, but when Germanicus kept his patience and continued the hearing of the cases without any respite for meals or siestas, he gave up that policy and excused himself from attendance altogether on the grounds of ill-health.

Piso's wife, Plancina, was jealous of Agrippina because, as

Germanicus's wife, she took precedence over her at all official functions. She thought out various petty insults to annoy her, chiefly discourtesies by subordinates which could be explained away as due to accident or ignorance. When Agrippina retaliated by snubbing her in public, she went still further. One morning in the absence of both Piso and Germanicus she appeared on parade with the cavalry and put them through a burlesque series of movements in front of Germanicus's headquarters. She wheeled them through a cornfield, charged a line of empty tents, which were slashed to ribbons, had every possible call sounded from 'Lights Out!' to the fire-alarm, and arranged collisions between squadrons. She finally galloped the whole force round and round in a gradually dwindling circle, and then, when she had narrowed the centre space to only a few paces across, gave the order, 'Right about wheel,' as if to reverse the movement. Many horses went down, throwing their riders. There never was such a mess-up seen in the whole history of cavalry manoeuvre. The rowdier men increased it by sticking daggers into their neighbours' horses to make them buck, or wrestling from the saddle. Several men were badly kicked, or had legs broken, their horses falling on them. One man was picked up dead. Agrippina sent a young staff-officer to request Plancina to stop making a fool of herself and the Army. Plancina sent back the answer, in parody of Agrippina's own brave words at the Rhine bridge: 'Until my husband returns *I* am in command of the cavalry. I am preparing them for the expected Parthian invasion.' Some Parthian ambassadors had, as a matter of fact, just arrived in camp, and were watching this display in astonishment and contempt.

Now Vonones, before he had been king of Armenia, had been king of Parthia, from which he had been quickly expelled. His successor had sent these ambassadors to Germanicus to propose that the alliance between Rome and Parthia should be renewed and to say that in honour of Germanicus he would come to the River Euphrates (the boundary between Syria and Parthia) to greet him. In the meantime he requested that Vonones might not be allowed to remain in Syria, where it was easy for him to carry on a treasonable correspondence with certain Parthian nobles. Germanicus replied that as representative of his father, the Emperor, he would be pleased to meet the king, and renew the alliance, and that he would remove Vonones to some other province. So Vonones was sent to Cilicia, and Piso's hope of a fortune vanished. Plancina was as angry as her husband; Vonones had been giving her almost daily presents of beautiful jewels.

Early the next year news reached Germanicus of great scarcity in Egypt. The last harvest had not been good, but there was plenty of corn from two years before, stored in granaries. The big corn-brokers kept up the price by putting only very small supplies on the market. Germanicus sailed at once to Alexandria and forced the brokers to sell at a reasonable price all the A.D. 19 corn that was needed. He was glad of this excuse for visiting Egypt, which interested him even more than Greece. Alexandria was then, as it is now, the true cultural centre of the world, as Rome was, and is, the political centre, and he showed his respect for its traditions by entering the city in simple Greek costume, with bare feet and no bodyguard. From Alexandria he sailed up the Nile, visiting the pyramids and the Sphinx and the gigantic ruins of Egyptian Thebes, a former capital, and the great stone statue of Memnon, the breast of which is hollow, and which shortly after the sun rises begins to sing, because the air in the hollow becomes warm and rises in a current through the pipe-shaped throat. He went as far as the ruins of Elephantis, keeping a careful diary of his travels. At Memphis he visited the pleasure-ground of the great God Apis, incarnate as a bull with peculiar markings; but Apis gave him no encouraging sign, walking away from him the moment that they met and entering the 'malevolent stall'. Agrippina was with him but Caligula had been left behind at Antioch in the charge of a tutor, as a punishment for his continued disobedience.

Germanicus could do nothing now that did not encourage Tiberius's suspicions of him; but going to Egypt was the worst mistake he had yet made. I shall explain why. Augustus, realizing early in his reign that Rome was now chiefly dependent on Egypt for her corn supply and that Egypt, if it fell into the hands of an adventurer, could be successfully defended by a quite small army, had laid it down as a precept of government that no Roman knight or senator should henceforth be allowed to visit the province without express permission from himself. It was generally understood that the same rule held under Tiberius. But Germanicus, alarmed by reports of the corn famine in Egypt, had not wasted time by waiting to get permission to go there. Tiberius was certain now that Germanicus was about to strike the blow that he had withheld so long; he had certainly gone to Egypt to bring the garrison there over to his side; the sight-seeing up the Nile was merely an excuse for visiting the frontier-guards; it had been a great mistake to send him to the East at all. He made a public complaint in the Senate against so daring a breach of Augustus's strict injunctions.

When Germanicus returned to Syria, feeling much hurt by Tiberius's reprimand, he found that all his orders to the regiments and to the cities had either been neglected or superseded by contradictory ones from Piso. He re-issued them and now for the first time gave public notice of his displeasure by issuing a proclamation that all orders issued by Piso during his own absence in Egypt were hereby declared cancelled and that, until further notice, no order signed by Piso would be valid in the province unless endorsed by himself. He had hardly signed this proclamation when he fell ill. His stomach was so disordered that he could keep nothing down. He suspected that his food was being poisoned and took every possible precaution against this. Agrippina prepared all his meals herself and none of the household staff had any opportunity of handling the food either before or after she cooked it. But it was some time before he was sufficiently recovered to leave his bed and sit propped in a chair. Hunger made his sense of smell abnormally acute and he said that there was a stench of death in the house. Nobody else smelt it and Agrippina at first dismissed the complaint as a sick fancy. But he persisted in it. He said that the stench grew daily worse. At last Agrippina herself became aware of it. It seemed to be in every room. She burned incense to cleanse the air but the smell persisted. The household grew alarmed and whispered that witches were at work.

Germanicus had always been extremely superstitious, like every member of our family but myself: I am only somewhat superstitious. Germanicus not only believed in the luckiness or unluckiness of certain days or omens, but had found himself in a whole network of superstitions of his own. The number seventeen and the midnight crowing of cocks were the two things which distressed him most. He took it as a most unlucky sign that, having been able to recover the lost Eagles of the Eighteenth and Nineteenth Regiments, he had been recalled from Germany before he could recover that of the Seventeenth. And he was terrified of

236

black magic of the sort that Thessalian witches use, and always slept with a talisman under his pillow which was proof against them: a green jasper figure of the Goddess Hecate (who alone has power over witches and phantoms) represented with a torch in one hand and the keys of the Underworld in another.

Suspecting that Plancina was practising witchcraft against him – for she had the reputation of being a witch – he made a propitiatory sacrifice of nine black puppies to Hecate; which was the proper course to take when so victimized. The next day a slave reported with a face of terror that as he had been washing the floor in the hall he had noticed a loose tile and, lifting it up, had found underneath what appeared to be the naked and decaying corpse of a baby, the belly painted red and horns tied to the forehead. An immediate search was made in every room and a dozen equally gruesome finds were made under the tiles or in niches scooped in the walls behind hangings. They included the corpse of a cat with rudimentary wings growing from its back, and the head of a negro with a child's hand protruding from its mouth. With each of these dreadful relics was a lead tablet in which was Germanicus's name. The house was ritually cleansed and Germanicus began to be more cheerful, though his stomach continued troublesome.

Soon after this hauntings began in the house. Cocks' feathers smeared in blood were found among the cushions and unlucky signs were scrawled on the walls in charcoal, sometimes low down, as if a dwarf had written them, sometimes high up, as if written by a giant – a man hanging, the word Rome upside down, a weasel; and, though only Agrippina knew of his private superstition about the number seventeen, this number was constantly recurring. Then appeared the name Germanicus, upside down, every day shortened by a letter. It would have been possible for Plancina to hide charms in his house during his absence in Egypt, but for this continued haunting there was no explanation. The servants were not suspected, because the words and signs were written in rooms to which they had no access, and in one locked room, with a window too small for a man to squeeze through, they covered the walls from floor to ceiling. Germanicus's one consolation was the courage with which Agrippina and little Caligula behaved. Agrippina did her best to make light of the hauntings, and Caligula said that *he* felt safe because a great-grandson of the God Augustus couldn't be hurt by witches, and that if he met a witch he would run her through with his sword. But Germanicus had to take to his bed again. In the middle of the night following the day when only three letters remained of his name, Germanicus was awakened by the noise of crowing. Weak as he was, he leaped out of bed, snatched up his sword and rushed into the adjoining room where Caligula and the baby Lesbia slept. There he saw a cock, a big black one with a gold ring around its neck, crowing as if to wake the dead. He tried to strike off its head but it flew out of the window. He fell down in a faint. Agrippina somehow got him back to his bed again, but when he recovered consciousness he told her that he was doomed. 'Not while you have your Hecate with you,' she said. He felt under his pillow for the charm and his courage returned.

When morning came he wrote a letter to Piso, in the old Roman manner, declaring private war between them; ordering him to leave the Province, and defying him to do his worst. Piso had, however, already sailed and was now at Chios waiting for news of Germanicus's death and ready to return to govern the Province as soon as it reached him. My poor brother was growing hourly weaker. The next day while Agrippina was out of the room and he was lying half insensible he felt a movement under his pillow. He turned on his side and fumbled in terror for the charm. It was gone; and there was nobody in the room.

The next day he called his friends together and told them that he was dying and that Piso and Plancina were his murderers. He charged them to tell Tiberius and Castor what had been done to him and implored them to avenge his cruel death. 'And tell the people of Rome,' he said, 'that I entrust my dear wife and my six children to their charge, and that they must not believe Piso and Plancina if they pretend to have had instructions to kill me; or, if they do believe it, that they must not on that account pardon them.' He died on the ninth of October, the day that the single letter G appeared on the wall of his room facing his bed, and on the seventeenth day of his illness. His wasted body was laid out in the market-place of Antioch so that everyone could see the red rash on his belly and the blueness of his nails. His slaves were put to torture. His freedmen, too, were cross-examined in turn, each for twenty-four hours on end and always by fresh questioners, and they were so broken in spirit at the end of this that if they had known anything they would certainly have revealed it, only to be left in peace. The most that could be discovered, however, either from freedmen or slaves, was that a notable witch, one Martina, had been frequently seen in Plancina's company and that she had actually been in the house one day with Plancina when nobody was there but Caligula. And that one afternoon, just before Germanicus's return, the house had been left unattended except by a single deaf old janitor, all the remaining staff having gone out to see a sword-fight exhibited by Piso in the local amphitheatre. No natural explanations could, however, be offered for the cock, or for the writing on the wall, or for the disappearance of the talisman.

There was a meeting of regimental commanders and all the other Romans of rank in the Province, to appoint a temporary Governor. The Commander of the Sixth Regiment was chosen. He immediately arrested Martina and had her sent under escort to Rome. If Piso came up for trial she would be one of the most important witnesses.

When he heard that Germanicus was dead, Piso, so far from concealing his joy, offered up sacrifices of thanksgiving in the temples. Plancina, who had recently lost a sister, actually threw off her mourning and put on her gayest clothes again. Piso wrote to Tiberius saying that he had only been dismissed from his governorship, to which he had been personally appointed by Tiberius, because of his bold opposition to Germanicus's treasonable designs against the State; he was now returning to Syria to resume his command. He also referred to Germanicus's 'luxury and insolence'. He did try to return to Syria and even got some troops to support him, but the new Governor besieged the castle in Cilicia which he had made his stronghold, forced him to surrender, and sent him to Rome to answer the charges that would surely be brought against him there.

Meanwhile Agrippina had sailed for Italy with the two children and the ashes of her husband in an urn. At Rome the news of his death had brought such grief that it was as though every single household in the City had lost its most beloved member. Three whole days, though there was no decree of the Senate or order of the magistrates for it, were consecrated to public sorrow: shops shut, law-courts were deserted, no business of any sort was transacted, everyone wore mourning. I heard a man in the street say that it was as though the sun had set, and would never rise again. Of my own sorrow I cannot trust myself to write.

Chapter 21

LIVIA and Tiberius shut themselves in their palaces and pretended to be so grief-stricken that they could not show their faces abroad. Agrippina should have come by the overland route, because the winter had already begun and the sailing season was over. But she put to sea in spite of storms and a few days later reached Corfu, from where it is only a day's sail, with a good breeze, to the port of Brindisi. Here she rested for a while, sending messengers ahead to say that she was coming to throw herself on the protection of the people of Italy. Castor, who was now back at Rome, her four other children and myself went out from Rome to meet her. Tiberius had immediately sent two Guards battalions forward to the port with directions that the magistrates of the country districts through which the ashes passed should pay his dead son the last offices of respect. When Agrippina disembarked, greeted with respectful silence by an enormous crowd, the urn was put in a catafalque and carried towards Rome on the shoulders of the Guards' officers. The battalion standards were undecorated, as a sign of public calamity, and the axes and rods were borne reversed. As the procession, many thousands strong, passed through Calabria, Apulia, and Campania, everyone came flocking, the country people dressed in black, the knights in purple robes, with tears and loud lamentations, and burned offerings of perfumes for their dead hero's ghost.

We met the procession at Terracina, about sixty miles southeast of Rome, where Agrippina, who had walked dry-eyed and marble-faced, without a word to anyone all the way from Brindisi, let her grief break out afresh at the sight of her four fatherless children. She cried to Castor: 'By the love you had for my dear husband swear that you will defend the lives of his children with your own, and avenge his death! It was his last charge to you.' Castor, weeping, for the first time perhaps since his childhood, swore that he would accept the charge.

If you ask why Livilla did not come with us, the answer is that she had just been delivered of twin boys: of which, by the way, Sejanus seems to have been the father. If you ask why my mother did not come, the answer is that Tiberius and Livia did not allow her even to attend the funeral. If overwhelming grief prevented their own attendance, as grandmother and adoptive father of the dead man, it was clearly quite impossible for her, as his mother, to attend. And they were wise not to show themselves. If they had done so, even with a pretence of grief, they would certainly have been assaulted by the populace; and I think that the Guards would have stood by and not raised a finger to protect them. Tiberius had neglected to make even such preparations as were customary at the funeral of far less distinguished persons: the family masks of the Claudians and Julians did not appear nor the usual effigy of the dead man himself, laid on a bed; no funeral speech was made from the Oration Platform; no funeral hymns sung. Tiberius's excuse was that the funeral had already been cele-brated in Syria and that the Gods would be offended if the rites were repeated. But never was such unanimous and sincere grief shown in Rome as on that night. Mars Field was ablaze with torches, and the crowd about Augustus's tomb, in which the urn was reverently placed by Castor, was so dense that many people were crushed to death. Everywhere people were saying that Rome was lost, and that no hope remained: for Germanicus had been their last bulwark against oppression, and Germanicus was now foully murdered. And everywhere Agrippina was praised and pitied, and prayers were offered for the safety of her children.

Tiberius published a proclamation a few days later saying that though many illustrious Romans had died for the common-wealth, none had been so universally and vehemently regretted as his dear son. But it was now time for the people to compose their minds and return to their daily business: princes were mortal, but the commonwealth eternal. In spite of this, All Fools' Festival at the end of December passed without any of the usual jokes and jollity, and it was not until the Festival of the Great Mother in April that mourning ended and normal public business was re-sumed. Tiberius's suspicions were now concentrated on Agrip-pina. She visited him at the Palace on the morning after the funeral and fearlessly told him that she would hold him respon-sible for her husband's death until he had proved his innocence and taken vengeance on Piso and Plancina. He cut short the inter-view at once by quoting at her the Greek lines:

> And if you are not queen, my dear,
> Think you that you are wronged?

Piso did not return to Rome for some time. He sent his son ahead to intercede for him with Tiberius while he himself went to visit Castor, who was now back with the legions on the Danube. He expected Castor to be grateful to him for his removal of a rival heir to the monarchy and willing to believe the story of Germanicus's treason. Castor refused to receive him and publicly told Piso's messenger that, if current rumours were true, it was on Piso that he would have to inflict the vengeance that he had sworn for his dear brother's death, and that Piso would be advised to keep away until he had plainly established his innocence. Tiberius received Piso's son without either particular graciousness or particular disfavour, as if to show that he would remain unprejudiced until a public enquiry had been made into Germanicus's death.

Eventually Piso appeared at Rome with Plancina. They came sailing down the Tiber and disembarked with a number of retainers at the tomb of Augustus, where they nearly created a riot by strutting with broad smiles through the hostile crowd which soon gathered, and stepping into a decorated carriage drawn by a pair of well-matched white French cobs which was waiting for them on the Flaminian road. Piso had a house overlooking the Market Place and this was decorated too. He invited all his friends and relations to a banquet celebrating his return and made a great deal of disturbance: merely to show the people of Rome that he was not afraid of them and that he counted on the support of Tiberius and Livia. Tiberius had planned for Piso to be prosecuted in the ordinary Criminal Court by a certain senator who could be trusted to do it so clumsily, contradicting himself and neglecting to produce proper evidence in support of his charges, that the proceedings could only end in an acquittal. But Germanicus's friends, especially the three senators who had been on his staff in Syria and had returned with Agrippina, opposed Tiberius's choice. Tiberius was forced in the end to judge the case himself, and in the Senate too, where Germanicus's friends could count on all the support they needed. The Senate had voted a number of exceptional honours to Germanicus's memory – cenotaphs, memorial arches, semi-divine rites – which Tiberius had not dared to veto.

Castor now returned once more from the Danube and, though an ovation (or lesser triumph) had been decreed him for his management of the Maroboduus affair, he entered the City on foot as a private citizen instead of on horseback with a chaplet on his head. After visiting his father he went straight to Agrippina and swore to her that she could count on him to see that justice was done.

Piso asked four senators to defend him; three of them excused themselves on the ground of sickness or incapacity; the fourth, Gallus, said that he never defended anyone on a murder charge of which he seemed guilty unless there was at least a chance of pleasing the Imperial family. Calpurnius Piso, though he had not attended his uncle's banquet, volunteered to defend him for the honour of the family, and three others afterwards joined him because they were sure that Tiberius would acquit Piso, whatever the evidence, and that they would later be rewarded for their part in the trial. Piso was pleased to be judged by Tiberius himself, because Sejanus had assured him that it would be all properly managed, that Tiberius would pretend to be very severe but finally adjourn the court *sine die* for fresh evidence. Martina, the principal witness, had already been put out of the way – smothered by Sejanus's agents – and the prosecutors now had a poor case.

Two days only were allowed for the prosecution, and the man who had been originally commissioned to bungle it for Piso's benefit came forward and did his best to talk the time out by bringing stale charges against him of misgovernment and corruption in Spain under Augustus. Tiberius let him continue with this irrelevant matter for some hours, until the Senate, by scuffling feet, coughing and clattering writing-tablets together, warned him that the principal witnesses must be heard or there would be trouble. Germanicus's four friends had their case well prepared and each in turn rose and testified to Piso's corruption of military discipline in Syria, his insulting behaviour to Germanicus and themselves, his disobedience of orders, his intrigues with Vonones, his oppression of the provincials. They accused him of murdering Germanicus by poison and witchcraft, of offering thanksgiving sacrifices at his death, and finally of having made an armed attack on the Province with private forces illegally raised.

Piso did not deny the charges of corrupting military discipline, of insulting and disobeying Germanicus, or of oppressing the provincials; he merely said that they were exaggerated. But he indignantly denied the charge of poison and witchcraft. The accusers did not mention the supernatural events at Antioch for fear of encouraging sceptical laughter, nor could they accuse Piso of interfering with Germanicus's household servants and slaves, because it had already been shown that they had nothing to do with the murder. So Piso was accused of poisoning Germanicus's food while he sat next to him at a banquet in Germanicus's own house. Piso ridiculed this charge: how could he possibly have done such a thing without someone noticing it, when the whole table, not to mention the waiters, were watching every movement he made? By magic perhaps?

He had a bundle of letters in his hand which everyone knew, by the size and colour and the way they were tied, were from Tiberius. Germanicus's friends moved that any instructions that Piso had had sent from Rome should be read. Piso refused to read the letters on the ground that they were sealed as with the Sphinx seal (originally Augustus's), which made them 'secret and confidential': it would be treasonable to read them. Tiberius ruled against the motion, saying that it would be a waste of time to read the letters, which contained nothing of importance. The Senate could not press the point. Piso handed the letters to Tiberius as a sign that he trusted him to save his life.

Angry noises were now heard from the crowd outside, which was being kept informed of the progress of the trial, and a man with a huge raucous voice shouted through a window: 'He may escape you, my Lords, but he won't escape us!' A messenger came to tell Tiberius that some statues of Piso had been seized by the crowd and were being dragged to the Wailing Stairs to be broken up. The Wailing Stairs were a flight of steps at the foot of the Capitoline Hill where the corpses of criminals were customarily exposed before being dragged by a hook in the throat to the Tiber and thrown in. Tiberius ordered the statues to be rescued and replaced on their pedestals. But he complained that he could not continue to judge a case under such conditions and adjourned it until the evening. Piso was conveyed away under escort.

Plancina, who had hitherto boasted that she would share her husband's fate whatever it might be, and if necessary die with him, now grew alarmed. She decided to make a separate defence and counted on Livia, with whom she had been on intimate terms, to get her off. Piso knew nothing of this treachery. When the trial was resumed Tiberius gave him no sign of sympathy, and though he told the accusers that they should have provided more conclusive evidence of poisoning, he warned Piso that his armed attempt to win back his province could never be forgiven. At home that evening Piso shut himself in his room and was found the next morning stabbed to death with his sword beside him. It was not, as a matter of fact, suicide.

For Piso had retained the most incriminating letter of all, one written to him by Livia but in the names of Tiberius and herself, and not stamped with the Sphinx seal (which Tiberius reserved for his own use). He told Plancina to bargain for their lives with it. Plancina went to Livia. Livia told her to wait while she consulted Tiberius. Livia and Tiberius then had their first open quarrel. Tiberius was furious with Livia for having written the letter, and Livia said that it was his own fault for not allowing her to use the Sphinx seal and complained that he had been behaving very insolently to her lately. Tiberius asked, who was Emperor, he or she? Livia said that if he was, it was by her connivance and that it was foolish of him to be rude to her, because as she had found means to make him, she could find means to break him. She took a letter from her purse and began reading it: it was an old letter written to her by Augustus during Tiberius's absence in Rhodes, accusing him of treachery, cruelty, and bestiality, and saying that if he were not her son he would not live another day. 'This is only a copy,' she said. 'But I have the original in safe keeping. It's only one of many letters in the same strain. You wouldn't like them handed about the Senate, would you?'

Tiberius controlled himself and apologized for his bad temper: he said that it was clear that he and she were each able to ruin the other and that therefore it was absurd for them to quarrel. But how could be spare Piso's life, especially after having said that, if the charge of raising private forces and trying to win back Syria with them was proved, this would mean the death penalty, beyond hope of pardon?

'Plancina didn't raise any forces, though, did she?'

'I don't see what that has to do with it. I can't get the letter back from Piso merely by promising to spare Plancina.'

'If you promise to spare Plancina, I'll get the letter from Piso: leave that to me. If Piso's killed that will satisfy public opinion. And if you are afraid of sparing Plancina on your own responsibility you can say that it was I who pleaded for her. That's fair enough, because I admit that it is a letter I wrote that all the trouble is about.'

So Livia went to Plancina and told her that Tiberius refused to listen to reason, and that he would rather sacrifice his own mother to popular hatred than risk his own skin in standing by his friends. All that she had been able to get from him, she said, was a grudging promise of pardon for her if the letter were given up. So Plancina went to Piso with a letter in Tiberius's name, forged by Livia, and said that she had arranged everything so beautifully and here was the promise of acquittal. As Piso handed her the letter in exchange she suddenly stabbed him in the throat with a dagger. As he lay dying she dipped the point of his sword in blood, clasped his sword-hand around the pommel and left him. She took the letter, and the forged promise, back to Livia as arranged.

In the Senate next day Tiberius read a statement which he said that Piso had made before his suicide, pleading complete innocence of the crimes charged against him, protesting his loyalty to Livia and himself, and imploring their protection for his sons as having taken no part in the events which had been made the subject of his impeachment. Plancina's trial then began. She was proved to have been seen in the society of Martina, and Martina's reputation as a poisoner was sworn to, and it came out that when Martina's corpse was prepared for burial a phial of poison was found knotted in her hair. Old Pomponius, Germanicus's orderly, testified to the horrible putrid relics planted in the house and to Plancina's visit there with Martina in Germanicus's absence; and when questioned by Tiberius he gave detailed evidence of the hauntings. Nobody came forward to defend Plancina. She protested her innocence with tears and oaths and said that she knew nothing of Martina's reputation as a poisoner and that her only business with her had been to buy perfumes. She said that the woman who had come with her to the house was not Martina but the wife of one of the colonels. And that surely it was an innocent thing to go calling and find nobody at home but a little boy. As for her insults to Agrippina, she was heartily sorry for them and begged Agrippina's pardon most humbly; but she had been obeying her husband's orders, as a wife was bound to do, and moreover her husband had told her that Agrippina was plotting with Germanicus against the Senate, so she had the more willingly done what was expected of her.

Tiberius summed up. He said that there seemed to be a certain doubt as to Plancina's guilt. Her connexion with Martina seemed proved, and so did Martina's reputation as a poisoner. But that it was a guilty connexion remained open to question. The prosecution had not even produced in court the phial found in Martina's hair nor any evidence that the contents were poisonous: it might well have been a sleeping draught or aphrodisiac. His mother Livia had a high opinion of Plancina's character and wished the Senate to give her the benefit of the doubt if the evidence of guilt was not conclusive; for the ghost of her beloved grandson had appeared to her in a dream and begged her not to allow the innocent to suffer for the crimes of a husband or father.

So Plancina was acquitted, and of Piso's two sons, one was allowed to inherit his father's estate and the other, who had taken part in the fighting in Cilicia, was merely banished for a few years. A senator proposed that public thanks be paid to the dead hero's family – to Tiberius, Livia, my mother Antonia, Agrippina, and Castor – for having avenged his death. This motion was just about to be voted upon when a friend of mine, an ex-Consul who had been Governor of Africa before Furius, rose to make an amendment. The motion was, he objected, not in order: one important name had been omitted, that of the dead hero's brother Claudius, who had done more than anyone to prepare the case for the prosecution and to protect the witnesses from molestation. Tiberius shrugged his shoulders and said that he was surprised to hear that I had been called upon for any assistance and that perhaps if I had not been, the charges against Piso would have been more clearly presented. (It was quite true that I had presided at the meeting of my brother's friends and decided what evidence each witness was to bring; and I had, as a matter of fact, advised them against accusing Piso of administering poison at the banquet with his own hands, but they had overruled me. And I had kept Pomponius and his grandsons and three of my brother's freedmen safely hidden in a farmhouse near my villa at Capua until the day of the trial. I had also tried to hide Martina away at the house of a merchant I knew at Brindisi, but Sejanus traced her.) Well, Tiberius let my name be included in the vote of thanks; but that meant little to me compared with the thanks that Agrippina gave me: she said that she understood now what Germanicus had meant when he told her, just before his death, that the truest friend he had ever had was his poor brother Claudius.

Feeling against Livia was so strong that Tiberius made it an excuse for her again not asking the Senate to vote her the title that he had so often promised. Everyone was wanting to know what it meant when a grandmother gave gracious interviews to the murderess of her grandson and rescued her from the vengeance of the Senate. The answer could only be that the grandmother had instigated the murder herself and was so utterly ashamed of herself that the wife and children of the victim would not survive him long.

Chapter 22

GERMANICUS was dead, but Tiberius did not feel much more secure than before. Sejanus came to him with stories of what this or that prominent man had whispered against him during Piso's trial. Instead of saying, as he had once said of his soldiers, 'let them fear me, so long as they obey me,' he now told Sejanus, 'Let them hate me, so long as they fear me.' Three knights and two senators who had been most outspoken in their recent criticism of him he put to death on the absurd charge of having expressed pleasure on hearing of the death of Germanicus. The informers divided up their estates between them.

About this time Germanicus's eldest boy Nero * came of age, and though he showed little promise of being as capable a soldier or as talented an administrator as his father, he had much of his father's good looks and sweetness of character and the City hoped much from him. There was great popular rejoicing when he married the daughter of Castor and Livilla, whom at first we called Helen because of her surprising beauty (her real name was Julia), but afterwards Heluo, which means Glutton, because she spoilt her beauty by over-eating. Nero was Agrippina's favourite. The family was divided, being of Claudian stock, into good and bad; or, in the words of the ballad, 'crabs and apples'. The crabs outnumbered the apples. Of the nine children whom Agrippina bore Germanicus three died young – two girls and a boy – and from what I saw of them this boy and the elder girl were the best of the nine. The boy, who died on his eighth birthday, had been such a favourite with Augustus that the old man kept a picture of him,

* This Nero is not to be confused with the Nero who became Emperor. – R. G.

dressed in Cupid's costume, in his bedroom and used to kiss it every morning as soon as he got out of bed. But of the surviving children only Nero had a wholly good character. Drusus was morose and nervous and easily inclined to evil. Drusilla was like him. Caligula, Agrippinilla, and the youngest, whom we called Lesbia, were wholly bad, as the younger of the girls who died seemed also to be. But the City judged the whole family by Nero because, so far, he was the only one old enough to make a strong public impression. Caligula was still only nine years old.

Agrippina visited me in great distress one day when I was in Rome and asked my advice. She said that wherever she went she felt that she was being followed and spied on, and it was making her ill. Did I know anyone beside Sejanus who had any influence over Tiberius? She was sure that he had decided to kill or banish her if he could get the slightest handle against her. I said that I only knew two people who had any influence for good over Tiberius. One was Cocceius Nerva, and the other was Vipsania. Tiberius had never been able to root his love for Vipsania out of his heart. When a granddaughter was born to her and Gallus, who at the age of fifteen exactly resembled Vipsania as she had been when Tiberius's wife, Tiberius could not bear the thought of anyone marrying her but himself; and was only prevented from doing so by her being Castor's niece, which would have made the marriage technically incestuous. So he appointed her the Chief Vestal in succession to old Occia who had just died. I told Agrippina that if she made friends with Cocceius and Vipsania (who as Castor's mother would do all in her power to help her) she was safe, and so were her children. She took my advice. Vipsania and Gallus, who were very sorry for her, made her free of their house and their three country villas and took a great deal of trouble with the children. Gallus, for instance, choose new tutors for the boys because Agrippina suspected the old ones of being agents of Sejanus. Nerva was not so much help. He was a jurist and the greatest living authority on the laws of contract, about which he had written several books: but in all other respects he was so absent-minded and unobservant as to be almost a simpleton. He was kind to her, as he was to everyone, but did not realise what she expected from him.

Unfortunately Vipsania died soon afterwards and the effect on Tiberius was apparent at once. He no longer made any serious attempt to conceal his sexual depravity, the rumours of which everyone had shrunk from taking literally. For some of his perversities were so preposterous and horrible that nobody could seriously reconcile them with the dignity of an Emperor of Rome, Augustus's chosen successor. No women or boys were safe in his presence now, even the wives and children of senators; and if they valued their own lives or those of their husbands and fathers they willingly did what he expected of them. But one woman, a Consul's wife, committed suicide afterwards in the presence of her friends, telling them that she had been forced to save her young daughter from Tiberius's lust by consenting to prostitute herself to him, which was shameful enough; but then the Old He-Goat had taken advantage of her complaisance by forcing her to such abominable acts of filthiness with him that she preferred to die rather than to live on with the memory of them.

There was a popular song circulated about this time which began with the words: 'Why, oh, why, did the Old He-Goat ...?' I should be ashamed to quote more of it, but it was as witty as it was obscene and was supposed to have been written by Livia herself. Livia was the author of a number of similar satires against Tiberius which she circulated anonymously through Urgulania. She knew that they would reach him sooner or later and that he was extremely sensitive to satires, and thought that while he felt his position insecure because of them, he would not dare to break with her. She also now went out of her way to be pleasant to Agrippina, and even told her in confidence that Tiberius alone had given Piso the instructions about baiting Germanicus. Agrippina did not trust her, but it was clear that Livia and Tiberius were at enmity, and she felt, she told me, that if she had to choose between the protection of one or the other she would prefer to be under Livia's. I was inclined to agree with Agrippina. I had observed that no favourite of Livia had yet been made the victim of Tiberius's informers. But I had forebodings of what might happen when Livia died.

What had begun to impress me as particularly ominous, though I could not altogether account for my feelings, was the strong bond between Livia and Caligula. Caligula had in general only two ways of behaving: he was either insolent or servile. To Agrippina and my mother and myself and his brothers and Castor, for instance, he was insolent. To Sejanus and Tiberius and Livilla he

250

was servile. But to Livia he was something else, difficult to express. He was almost like her lover. It was not the usual tender tie that binds little boys to indulgent grandmothers or great-grand-mothers, though it is true that he once took great pains over a copy of affectionate verses for her seventy-fifth birthday and that she was always giving him presents. I mean that there was a strong impression of some unpleasant secret between them – but I don't mean to suggest that there was any indecent relationship between them. Agrippina felt this too, she told me, but could find out nothing definite about it.

One day I began to understand why Sejanus had been so polite to me. He suggested the betrothal of his daughter to my son Drusillus. My personal feelings against the marriage were that the girl, who seemed a nice little thing, was unlucky to be matched to Drusillus, who seemed more of a lubber every time I saw him. But I could not say so. Still less could I say that I loathed the thought of being even remotely related in marriage with a scoundrel like Sejanus. He noticed my hesitation in answering and wanted to know whether I considered the match beneath the dignity of my family. I stammered and said no, certainly I did not: his branch of the Aelian family was a very honourable one. For Sejanus, though the son of a mere country knight, had been adopted in early man-hood by a rich senator of the Aelian family, a Consul, who had left him all his money; there was a scandal connected with this adoption, but the fact remained that Sejanus was an Aelian. He anxiously pressed me to explain my hesitation and said that if I had any feeling against the marriage, he was sorry he had men-tioned it, but of course he had only done so on Tiberius's sugges-tion. So I told him that if Tiberius proposed the match I would be glad to give my consent: that my chief feeling had been that four years old was rather young for a girl to be betrothed to a boy of thirteen, who would be twenty-one before he could legally con-summate the marriage and by that time might have formed other entanglements. Sejanus smiled and said that he trusted me to keep the lad out of serious mischief.

There was great alarm in the City when it was known that Sejanus was to become related with the Imperial family, but every-one hastened to congratulate him, and me too. A few days later Drusillus was dead. He was found lying behind a A.D. 23 bush in the garden of a house at Pompeii where he had

251

been invited, from Herculaneum, by some friends of Urgula-nilla's. A small pear was found stuck in his throat. It was said at the inquest that he had been seen throwing fruit up in the air and trying to catch it in his mouth: his death was unquestionably due to an accident. But nobody believed this. It was clear that Livia, not having been consulted about the marriage of one of her own great-grandchildren, had arranged for the child to be strangled and the pear crammed down his throat afterwards. As was the custom in such cases, the pear tree was charged with murder and sentenced to be uprooted and burned.

Tiberius asked the Senate to decree Castor Protector of the People, which was as much as pointing him out as heir to the monarchy. This request caused general relief. It was taken as a sign that Tiberius was aware of Sejanus's ambitions and intended to check them. When the decree was passed someone proposed that it should be printed on the walls of the House in letters of gold. Nobody realized that it was at Sejanus's own suggestion that Castor was so honoured; he had hinted to Tiberius that Castor, Agrippina, Livia, and Gallus were in league together and pro-posed this as the best way to see who else belonged to their party. It was a friend of his own who had made the proposal about the gold inscription, and the names of senators who supported this extravagant motion were carefully noted. Castor was more popu-lar now among the better citizens than he had been. He had given up his drunken habits – the death of Germanicus seemed to have sobered him – and though he still had an inordinate love of blood-shed at sword-fights and dressed extravagantly and betted enor-mous sums on the chariot races, he was a conscientious magistrate and a loyal friend. I had little to do with him, but when we met he treated me with far greater consideration than before Germani-cus's death.

The bitter hatred between him and Sejanus always threatened to blaze up into a quarrel, but Sejanus was careful not to provoke Castor until the quarrel could be turned to account. The time had now come. Sejanus went to the Palace to congratulate Castor on his protectorship and found him in his study with Livilla. There were no slaves or freedmen present, so Sejanus could say what he pleased. By this time Livilla was so much in love with him that he could count on her to betray Castor as she had once betrayed Pos-tumus – somehow he knew that story – and there had even been talk between them in which they had regretted that they were not Emperor and Empress, to do as they pleased. Sejanus said, 'Well, Castor, I've worked it for you all right! Congratulations?'

Castor scowled. He was only 'Castor' to a few intimates. He had won the name, as I think I have explained, because of his resemblance to a well-known sword-fighter, but it had stuck because one day he had lost his temper in an argument with a knight. The knight had told him bluntly at a banquet that he was drunk and incapable, and Castor, shouting 'Drunk and incapable, am I? I'll show you if I'm drunk and incapable,' staggered from his couch and hit the knight such a terrific blow in the belly that he vomited up the whole meal. Castor now said to Sejanus: 'I don't allow anyone to address me by a nickname except a friend or an equal, and you're neither. To you I'm Tiberius Drusus Caesar. And I don't know what you claim to have "worked" for me. And I don't want your congratulations on it, whatever it is. So get out.'

Livilla said: 'If you ask *me*, I call it pretty cowardly of you to insult Sejanus like this, not to mention the ingratitude of kicking him out like a dog when he comes to congratulate you on your protectorship. You know that your father would never have given it you except on Sejanus's recommendation.'

Castor said: 'You're talking nonsense, Livilla. This filthy spy has had no more to do with the appointment than my eunuch Lygdus. He's just pretending to be important. And tell me, Sejanus, what's this about cowardice?'

Sejanus said: 'Your wife is quite right. You're a coward. You wouldn't have dared to talk to me like this before I got you appointed Protector and so made your person sacrosanct. You know perfectly well that I'd have thrashed you.'

'And serve you right,' said Livilla.

Castor looked from one face to the other and said slowly: 'So there's something between you two, is there?'

Livilla smiled scornfully: 'And suppose there is? Who's the better man?'

Castor shouted: 'All right, my girl, we'll see. Just forget for a moment that I'm a Protector of the People, Sejanus, and put your fists up.'

Sejanus folded his arms.

'Put them up, I say, you coward.'

Sejanus said nothing, so Castor struck him hard across the face with his open palm. 'Now get out!'

Sejanus went out with an ironical obeisance and Livilla followed him.

This blow settled Castor's fate. The account that Tiberius heard from Sejanus, who came to him with the mark of Castor's slap still red on his cheek, was that Castor had been drunk when Sejanus had congratulated him on his protectorship and had struck him across the face saying: 'Yes, it's good to feel that I can do this now without fear of being hit back. And you can tell my father that I'll do the same to every other dirty spy of his.' Livilla confirmed this the next day when she came to complain that Castor had beaten her; she said that he had beaten her because she told him how disgusted she was with him for striking a man who could not strike back and for insulting his father. Tiberius believed them. He said nothing to Castor but put up a bronze statue of Sejanus in the theatre of Pompey, an extraordinary honour to be paid to any man in his lifetime. This was understood to mean that Castor was out of favour with Tiberius in spite of his protectorship (for Sejanus and Livilla had circulated their version of the quarrel) and that Sejanus was now the one person whose favour was worth courting. Many replicas of the statue were therefore made, which his partisans put in a place of honour in their halls on the right hand of Tiberius's statue: but statues of Castor were rarely seen. Castor's face showed his resentment so clearly now whenever he met his father that Sejanus's task was made easy. He told Tiberius that Castor was sounding various senators as to their willingness to support him if he usurped the monarchy and that some of them had already promised their help. The ones who seemed most dangerous to Tiberius were therefore arrested on the familiar charge of blaspheming against Augustus. One man was condemned to death for having gone into a privy with a gold coin of Augustus's in his hand. Another was accused of having included a statue of Augustus in a list of furniture for sale in a country villa. He would have been condemned to death if the Consul who was judging the case had not asked Tiberius to give his vote first. Tiberius was ashamed to vote for the death-penalty, so the man was acquitted, but condemned soon after on another charge.

Castor became alarmed and asked Livia for her help against Sejanus. Livia told him not to be afraid: she would soon bring

Tiberius to his senses. But she had no confidence in Castor as an ally. She went to Tiberius and told him that Castor had accused Sejanus of debauching Livilla, of abusing his position of confidence by levying blackmail on rich men in Tiberius's name, and of aiming at the monarchy; that he had said that unless Tiberius dismissed the rascal soon he would take the matter into his own hands; and that he had then asked for her co-operation. By putting the case like this to Tiberius she hoped to make him as mistrustful of Sejanus as he was of Castor and thus to cause him to fall back into his old habit of dependence on her. For a time at least she succeeded. But then an accident suddenly convinced Tiberius that Sejanus was as loyally devoted as he pretended to be and as all his actions had hitherto shown him. They were picnicking together one day with three or four friends in a natural cave by the sea-shore, when there was a sudden rattle and roar and part of the roof fell in, killing some of the attendants and burying others, and blocking up the entrance. Sejanus crouched with arched back over Tiberius – they were both unhurt – to shield him from a further fall. When the soldiers dug them out an hour later he was found still in the same position. Thrasyllus, too, by the way, increased his reputation on this occasion: he had told Tiberius that there would be an hour of darkness about noon that day. Tiberius had Thrasyllus's assurance that he would outlive Sejanus by a great many years, and that Sejanus was not dangerous to him. I think that Sejanus had arranged this with Thrasyllus, but I have no proof: Thrasyllus was not altogether incorruptible, but when he made prophecies to suit his clients' wishes they seemed to come off just as well as his ordinary ones. Tiberius did outlive Sejanus, as it happens, by a number of years.

Tiberius gave a further public sign that Castor was out of favour by censuring him in the Senate for a letter he had written. Castor had excused himself from attending the sacrifice when the House opened after the summer recess, explaining that he was prevented by other public business from returning to the City in time. Tiberius said scornfully that anyone would think that the young fellow was on campaign in Germany or on a diplomatic visit to Armenia: when all the 'public business' that kept him was boating and bathing at Terracina. He said that he himself, now in the decline of life, might be excused for an occasional absence from the City: he might plead that his energies had been exhausted by prolonged public service with the sword and the pen. But what except insolence could detain his son? This was most unjust: Castor had been commissioned to make a report on coastal defence during the recess and had not been able to collect all the evidence in time: rather than waste time by a journey to Rome and then back again to Terracina he was finishing his task.

When Castor returned he almost immediately fell ill. The symptoms were those of rapid consumption. He lost colour and weight and began coughing blood. He wrote to his father and asked him to come and visit him in his room – he lived at the other end of the Palace – because he believed that he was dying, and to forgive him if he had in any way offended. Sejanus advised Tiberius against the visit: the illness might be real, but on the other hand it might easily be a trick for assassinating him. So Tiberius did not visit him and a few days later Castor died.

There was not much sorrow at the death of Castor. The violence of his temper and his reputation for cruelty had made the City apprehensive of what would happen if he succeeded his father. Few believed in his recent reformation. Most people A.D. 23 thought it had merely been a trick to win popular affection, and that he would have been just as bad as his father as soon as he found himself in his father's place. And now Germanicus's three sons were growing up – Drusus, too, had just come of age – and were unquestionably Tiberius's heirs. But the Senate, out of respect for Tiberius, mourned for Castor as noisily as it could and voted the same honours in his memory as it had voted Germanicus. Tiberius made no pretence of sorrow on this occasion but pronounced the panegyric he had prepared for Castor in a firm resonant voice. When he saw tears rolling down the faces of several senators he remarked in an audible aside to Sejanus at his elbow: 'Faugh! The place smells of onions!' Gallus afterwards rose to compliment Tiberius on his mastery over his grief. He recalled that even the God Augustus, during his presence among them in mortal shape, had so far given way to his feelings at the death of Marcellus, his adopted son (not even his real son), that when he was thanking the House for its sympathy he had to break off in the middle, unable to go on for emotion. Whereas the speech they had just heard was a masterpiece of restraint. (I may mention here that when four or five months later deputies arrived from Troy to condole with Tiberius on the death of his only son,

Tiberius thanked them: 'And I condole with you, gentlemen, on the death of Hector.' Tiberius then sent for Nero and Drusus, and when they arrived at the House he took them by the hand and introduced them: 'My Lords, three years ago I committed these fatherless children to their uncle, my dear son whom today we are all so bitterly mourning, desiring him to adopt them as his sons, though he already had sons of his own, and bring them up as worthy inheritors of the family tradition. (Hear, hear! from Gallus, and general applause.) But now that he has been snatched from us by cruel fate (groans and lamentations) I make the same request of *you*. In the presence of the Gods, in the face of your beloved Country, I beseech you, receive into your protection, take under your tuition, these noble great-grandchildren of Augustus, descended from ancestors whose names resound in Roman history: see that your duty and mine is honourably fulfilled towards them. Grandsons, these senators are now in the place of fathers to you, and your birth is such that whatever good or evil may befall you will spell the good or evil of the entire State.' (Resounding applause, tears, benedictions, shouts of loyalty.)

But instead of leaving off there he spoilt the whole effect by ending on a familiar note with his old stale phrases about presently retiring and restoring the Republic – when 'the Consuls or someone else' would 'take the burden of government off' his 'aged shoulders'. If he did not intend Nero and Drusus (or one or other of them) as his Imperial successors, what did he mean by identifying their fortune so closely with that of the State?

Castor's funeral was less impressive than Germanicus's, being marked by very few genuine expressions of grief, but on the other hand far more magnificent. Every one of the family masks of the Caesars and Claudians was worn in the procession, beginning with those of Aeneas, the founder of the Julian family, and Romulus, the founder of Rome, and ending with those of Gaius, Lucius, and Germanicus. Julius Caesar's mask appeared because, like Romulus, he was only a demi-god, but Augustus's did not appear, because he was a major Deity.

Sejanus and Livilla had now to consider how to achieve their ambition of becoming Emperor and Empress. Nero, Drusus, and Caligula stood in the way and would have to be removed. Three seemed rather many to get rid of safely, but, as Livilla pointed out, her grandmother had apparently managed to get rid of

257

Gaius, Lucius, and Postumus when she wanted to put Tiberius into power. And Sejanus was clearly in a much better position than Livia had been for carrying their plans through. To show Livilla that he really intended to marry her, as he had promised, Sejanus divorced his wife Apicata, by whom he had three children. He charged her with adultery and said that she was about to become the mother of a child which was not his own. He did not publicly name her lover but told Tiberius in private that he suspected Nero. Nero, he said, was getting a bad reputation for his affairs with the wives of prominent men and seemed to think that, as heir-presumptive to the monarchy, he could behave how he liked. Livilla meanwhile did her best to detach Agrippina from Livia's protection, by warning Agrippina that Livia was only using her as a weapon in her conflict with Tiberius — which happened to be true – and by warning Livia, through one of her ladies-in-waiting, that Agrippina was only using *her* as a weapon in her conflict with Tiberius – which was also true. She made each believe that the other had sworn to kill her as soon as her usefulness ended.

The twelve pontiffs now began to include Nero and Drusus in the customary prayers they offered for the health and prosperity of the Emperor, and the other priests followed their example. Tiberius as High Pontiff sent a letter of complaint to them, saying that they had made no difference between these boys and himself, a man who had honourably held most of the highest offices of the State twenty years before they were born, and all the rest since: it was not decent. He called them into his presence and there asked them whether Agrippina had merely coaxed them to make this addition to the prayer or whether she had frightened them into making it by using threats. They denied, of course, that she had done either, but he was not convinced; four of the twelve, including Gallus, were in some way connected with her by marriage and five others were on very friendly terms with her and her sons. He reprimanded them severely. In his next speech he warned the Senate to 'award no further premature distinctions that might encourage the giddy minds of young men to indulge in presumptuous aspirations'.

Agrippina found an unexpected ally in Calpurnius Piso. He told her that he had defended his uncle Gnaeus Piso merely out of regard for family honours and that he must not be thought of as her enemy; he would do all that he could to protect her and her children. But Calpurnius did not live long after this. He was charged in the Senate with 'treasonable words spoken in private', and of keeping poison in his house, and of coming into the Senate armed with a dagger. These two last articles were so absurd that they were dropped, but a day was fixed for his trial on the 'treasonable words' charge. He killed himself before the trial came off.

Tiberius believed Sejanus's story that there was a secret party, called the Leek Green party, now being formed by Agrippina, the sign of which was an extravagant partisanship of the Leek Green faction in the chariot-races in the Circus. In these races there were four colours – scarlet, white, sea blue, and leek green. The Leek Green faction happened to be most in favour at this time and the Scarlet the most unpopular. So now when Tiberius went to watch the races on public holidays, as he was bound to do in his official position – though he had not hitherto been at all interested in them and discouraged idle racing-talk at the Palace or at banquets to which he was invited – and began for the first time to notice what sort of support the different colours were being given he was greatly disturbed to hear the Leek Green so cried up. He had been also told by Sejanus that Scarlet was the secret symbol used by Leek Greens when they wished to refer to his own supporters, and he noticed that whenever a Scarlet chariot won, which was seldom, it came in for loud groans and hisses. Sejanus was clever: he knew that Germanicus had always backed the Leek Green and that Agrippina, Nero, and Drusus, for sentimental reasons, continued to favour the colour.

There was a nobleman called Silius who had been for many years a corps-commander on the Rhine. I think I have mentioned him as the General of the four regiments in the Upper Province of Germany which did not take part in the great mutiny. He had been my brother's most capable lieutenant and had been granted triumphal ornaments for his successes against Hermann. Recently, at the head of the combined forces of the Upper and Lower Provinces he had put down a dangerous revolt of the French tribes in the neighbourhood of my birthplace, Lyons. He was not a modest man but not particularly boastful and if he had really said in public, as was reported, that but for his tactful handling of those four regiments in the mutiny they would have joined the other mutineers, and that therefore, but for him, Tiberius would not have had any Empire at all to rule over – well, that was not far from the truth. But naturally Tiberius did not like it, if only because the mutinous regiments were, as I explained, the ones with which he himself had most to do. Silius's wife Sosia was Agrippina's best woman friend. It so happened that Silius at the great Roman Games, which were held early in September, was betting very heavily on the Leek Green. Sejanus shouted across to him: 'I'll take you up to any amount. My money's on Scarlet.' Silius shouted back: 'You're backing the wrong colour, my friend. The Scarlet charioteer hasn't the least idea of managing his reins. He tries to do it all with the whip. I'll bet you an even thousand that Leek Green wins. Young Nero here says he'll make it fifteen hundred; he's an enthusiastic Leek Greener' Sejanus looked significantly at Tiberius, who had heard the whole exchange and was astonished at Silius's boldness. He took it as a good omen when the leader of the Leek Green chariot fell in rounding the mark on the last lap but one, and Scarlet came in an easy winner.

Ten days later Silius was impeached before the Senate. The charge was high treason. He was accused of having connived at the French revolt during its earlier stages and having taken a third part of the plunder as payment for non-intervention, of making his victory the excuse for further plunder of loyal provincials, and of afterwards imposing excessive emergency taxes on the province for the expenses of the campaign. Sosia was accused of complicity in the same offences. Silius had been unpopular at the Palace ever since the French rebellion. Tiberius had come in for a good deal of criticism for not having taken the field against the rebels, and for having shown more interest in the treason trials that were going on at the time than in the campaign. He had excused himself to the Senate on the ground of age – and Castor had been engaged in important business – and explained that he had been keeping in touch with Silius's headquarters all along, giving him valuable advice. Tiberius was very sensitive about the whole French revolt. When the French were beaten he had been made ridiculous by the motion of a waggish senator, an imitator of Gallus's tricks, that he should be awarded a triumph for being the man really responsible for victory. He was so displeased by this, taking the line that in any case the victory was not worth talking about, that nobody dared to vote Silius the triumphal ornaments which he thoroughly well deserved. Silius had been disappointed and what he had said about the Rhine mutiny had been said in resentment of Tiberius's ingratitude.

Silius disdained to reply to the charges of treason. He was not guilty of any understanding with the rebels and if the soldiers under his command had in some cases failed to distinguish between the property of rebels and the property of loyalists that was only to be expected: many pretended loyalists were secretly financing the rebellion. As for the taxation, the fact was that Tiberius had promised him a special grant from the Treasury to cover the expenses of the campaign and to indemnify Roman citizens for their loss of houses, crops, and cattle. In anticipation of the payment of this grant Silius had imposed a tax on certain Northern tribes, promising to refund the money when it was paid him by Tiberius: which it never was. Silius was a poorer man by 20,000 gold pieces after the revolt than before it, because he had raised a troop of volunteer horse which he armed and paid at his own expense. His chief accuser, who was one of the Consuls of the year, pressed the charges of extortion with great malice. He was a friend of Sejanus and was also the son of the military governor of the Lower Province who had wished to take supreme command of the Roman forces against the French and had been forced to stand aside in Silius's favour. Silius could not even produce evidence of Tiberius's promised grant, because the letter in which it was contained was sealed with the Sphinx. And the charges of extortion were in any case irrelevant, because the trial was for treason, not for extortion.

He finally burst out: 'My Lords, I could say much in my defence but shall say nothing, because this trial is not being conducted in a constitutional manner and the verdict has been long ago decided. I understand that my real crime is having said that, but for my handling of them, the regiments in Upper Germany would have mutinied. I shall now put my culpability in this matter beyond question. I shall say that, but for Tiberius's previous handling of them, the troops in Lower Germany would *not* have mutinied. My Lords, I am the victim of an avaricious, jealous, bloodthirsty, tyrannical ...' The rest of his speech was drowned in a roar of horrified protest from the House. Silius saluted Tiberius and walked out with his head high in the air. When he arrived at his house he embraced Sosia and his children, gave an affectionate message of farewell to Agrippina, Nero, Gallus, and his other friends, and going to his bedroom drove his sword into his throat.

His guilt was held to be proved by his insults to Tiberius. His entire estate was confiscated, with a promise that the provincials should have the unjust tax repaid them out of it, and that his accusers should be given the fourth part of what remained, as the law required, and that the money which had been left him under Augustus's will as an earnest of loyalty should return to the Treasury as paid him under a misapprehension. The provincials did not dare to press for the tax to be refunded, so Tiberius kept three-quarters of the estate: for there was no longer any real distinction between the Military Treasury, the Public Treasury, and the Privy Purse. This was the first time that he had benefited directly from the confiscation of an estate or that he had let a spoken insult to himself be construed as a proof of treason.

Sosia had property of her own and, to save her life and keep the children from becoming paupers, Gallus moved that she should be banished and that half of her effects should be forfeited to her accusers, half left to the children. But a cousin by marriage of Agrippina's, who was a confederate of Gallus, proposed that the accusers should only be paid one-fourth, which was the legal minimum, saying that Gallus was more loyal to the Emperor than just to Sosia; for Sosia was known, at least, to have reproved her husband, as he lay dying, for his treasonable and ungrateful utterances. So Sosia was only banished – she went to live in Marseilles; and since Silius as soon as he knew that he would be tried for his life had secretly given Gallus and certain other friends most of his money in cash to hold in trust for the children, the family came off quite well. His eldest son lived to cause me much distress.

From now onward Tiberius, who had hitherto made his accusations of treason hang on supposed blasphemies of Augustus, enforced more and more strongly the edict which had been passed in the first year of his monarchy, making it treason for anyone to assail his own honour and reputation in any way. He accused a senator, whom he suspected to be of Agrippina's party, of having recited a scurrilous epigram aimed against him. The fact was that the senator's wife one morning noticed a sheet of paper posted high up on the gate of the house. She asked her husband to read out what was on it – he was taller. He slowly spelt out,

He is no drunkard now of wine
As he was drunkard then:
He warms him up with a richer cup –
The blood of murdered men.

She asked innocently what the verse meant and he said, 'It's
unsafe to explain in public, my dear.' A professional informer was
hanging about the gate on the chance that when the senator read
the epigram, which was Livia's work, he would say something
worth reporting. He went straight to Sejanus. Tiberius himself
cross-examined the senator, asking what he meant by 'unsafe',
and to whom, in his opinion, the epigram referred. The senator
shuffled and would not give direct answers. Tiberius then said that
many libels had been current when he was a younger man, all accusing him of being a drunkard, and that in recent years he had
been ordered by his doctors to abstain from wine because of a
tendency to gout, and that several libels had lately been published
accusing him of bloodthirstiness. He asked the accused whether
he was not aware of these facts, and whether he thought that the
epigram could refer to anyone but his Emperor. The wretched
man agreed that he had heard the libels on Tiberius's drunkenness
but he knew them to have no foundation in truth and had not
made any connexion in his mind between them and the one on his
gate. He was then asked why he had not reported the former libels
to the Senate as it was his duty to do. He answered that when he
had heard them it was not yet a punishable offence to utter or repeat any epigram, however scurrilous, written against anyone,
however virtuous; nor treason to utter or repeat scurrilities
directed even against Augustus so long as one did not publish them
in writing. Tiberius asked to what time he referred, for Augustus
had late in life made an edict against spoken scurrilities too. The
senator answered: 'It was during your third year at Rhodes.'
Tiberius cried out, 'My Lords, how can you permit this fellow to
insult me so?' So the Senate actually condemned him to be thrown
down the Tarpeian cliff, a punishment ordinarily reserved for the
worst traitors – generals who sold battles to the enemy, and such-like.

Another man, a knight, was put to death for writing a tragedy
about King Agamemnon in which Agamemnon's queen, who
murdered him in his bath, cried as she swung the axe:

Know, bloody tyrant, 'tis no crime
T' avenge my wrongs like this.

Tiberius said that he was intended by the character Agamemnon and that the line quoted was an incitement to assassinate him. So the tragedy, which everyone had laughed at because it was so lamely and wretchedly composed, won a sort of dignity by having all its copies called in and burned and its author executed.

This prosecution was followed two years later – but I put it down here because the Agamemnon story reminds me of A.D. 25 it – by that of Cremutius Cordus, an old man who had come into collision with Sejanus some time before over a trifle. Sejanus entering the House one wet day had hung his cloak on the peg which had always been Cremutius's, and Cremutius, when he came in, not knowing that it was Sejanus's cloak, had moved it to another peg to make room for his own. Sejanus's cloak had fallen down from this new peg and somebody with muddy sandals had trampled on it. Sejanus retaliated in a variety of malicious ways, and Cremutius came so to loathe the sight of his face and the sound of his name that when he heard that Sejanus's statue had been set up on the Theatre of Pompey he exclaimed: 'That just about ruins the Theatre.' So now he was named to Tiberius as one of Agrippina's principal adherents. But as he was a venerable, mild old man who had no enemy in the world but Sejanus and never a spoke a word more than necessary, it was difficult to support any accusation against him with evidence that even a brow-beaten Senate could decently accept. In the end Cremutius was charged with having written in praise of Brutus and Cassius, the murderers of Julius Caesar. The evidence produced was an historical work which he had written thirty years before and which Augustus himself, Julius's adopted son, was known to have included in his private library and occasionally consulted.

Cremutius made a spirited defence against this absurd charge, saying that Brutus and Cassius had been dead so long and had been so frequently praised for their deed by subsequent historians that he could not believe that the trial was not a hoax – such a hoax as a young traveller recently suffered in the city of Larissa. This young man was publicly accused of having murdered three men, though they were no more than wineskins, hanging outside a shop, which he had slashed at in the dark, mistaking them for robbers. But this Larissan trial had taken place on the annual festival of Laughter, which gave some point to the proceedings, and the young man was a drunkard and much too ready with his sword and perhaps deserved a lesson. But he, Cremutius Cordus, was too old and too sober to be made a fool of in this way, and this was no festival of Laughter but, on the contrary, the four hundred and seventy-sixth anniversary of the solemn promulgation of the Laws of the Twelve Tables, that glorious monument to the legislative genius and the moral rectitude of our forefathers. He went home and starved himself to death. All copies of his book were called in and burned except for two or three which his daughter hid away somewhere and republished them many years later when Tiberius was dead. It was not very good writing; it got more fame than it really deserved.

I had been all this time saying to myself, 'Claudius, you're a poor fellow and not much use in this world, and you have led a pretty miserable life with one thing and another, but at least your life is safe.' So when old Cremutius whom I knew very well – we had often met and chatted in the Library – lost his life on a charge like this it was a great shock to me. I felt like a man living on the slopes of a volcano when it suddenly throws up a warning shower of ash and red-hot stones. I had written far more treasonable things in my time than Cremutius. My history of Augustus's religious reforms contained several phrases that could easily be made the subject of an accusation. And though my estate was so small that it would hardly be worth an accuser's while to impeach me for the sake of a fourth share, I realized well enough that all the recent victims of treason-trials were friends of Agrippina, whom I continued to visit whenever I went to Rome. I was not at all sure how far my being a brother-in-law of Sejanus would be sufficient protection to me.

Yes, I had lately become Sejanus's brother-in-law, and now I shall tell how it came about.

Chapter 23

ONE day Sejanus had told me that I ought to marry again, as I did not seem to get on well with my wife. I said that Urgulanilla had been the choice of my grandmother Livia and that I could not divorce her without Livia's permission.

'Oh, no, of course not,' he said. 'I quite understand that, but it must be very unhappy for you without a wife.'

'Thank you,' I said, 'I manage all right.'

He pretended to find this a good joke and laughed loudly, calling me a very wise man, but afterwards said that if by any chance I found it possible to divorce my wife I was to come to him. He had just the woman for me in mind – well-born, young, and intelligent. I thanked him but felt uncomfortable. As I was going away he said: 'My friend Claudius, I have a word of advice to you. Back Scarlet to-morrow in every race and don't mind losing a bit of money at first: you'll not lose in the long run. And *don't back Green Leek*: it's an unlucky colour these days. And don't tell anyone that I gave you the tip.' I felt much relieved that Sejanus thought me still worth cultivating, but I couldn't make sense of what he told me. However, at the chariot-race next day – it was the festival of Augustus – Tiberius saw me take my seat in the Circus and, being in an affable mood, sent for me and asked, 'What are you doing these days, nephew?'

I stammered that I was writing a history of the ancient Etruscans, if it pleased him.

He said: 'Oh, really? That does credit to your judgement. There's no ancient Etruscan left to protest and no modern Etruscan who cares: so you can write as you please. What else are you doing?'

'Wr-r-riting a history of the ancient C-C-C-C-C-Carthaginians, if you please.'

'Splendid! And what else? Hurry up with that stammer. I'm a busy man.'

'At the m-m-moment I'm b-b-b-b – –'

'Beginning a history of C-C-C-Cloud C-C-C-Cuckoo Land?'

'N-no, sir, b-b-b-backing Scarlet.'

He looked at me very shrewdly and said: 'I see, nephew, that you are not altogether a fool. What makes you back Scarlet?'

I was in difficulties, because I couldn't say that Sejanus had given me the tip. So I said: 'I dreamed that Leek Green was d-disqualified for using his whip on his c-c-c-competitors and Scarlet c-c-came in first with Sea-b-b-blue and White nowhere.'

He gave me a purse of money and muttered in my ear: 'Tell nobody that I'm staking you, but put this on Scarlet and let's see what happens.'

It proved to be Scarlet's day, and by betting with young Nero on every race I won close on 2,000 gold pieces. That evening I thought it wise to visit Tiberius at the Palace and to say: 'Here's the lucky purse, sir, with a family of little purses which it littered during the day.'

'All mine?' he exclaimed. 'Well, I *am* in luck. Scarlet's the colour, eh?'

This was just like my uncle Tiberius. He hadn't made it clear who was to keep the winnings and I had supposed that I was. But if I had lost all the money he would have said something to make me feel in his debt to that amount. He might at least have given me a commission.

The next time I came up to Rome I found my mother in such a distracted state that I did not dare at first utter a word in her presence for fear of her flying into a temper and boxing my ears. I gathered that her trouble was connected with Caligula, then aged twelve, and Drusilla, then aged thirteen, who were staying with her. Drusilla was confined to her room without food and Caligula was at liberty but looking thoroughly frightened. He visited me that evening and said: 'Uncle Claudius. Beg your mother not to tell the Emperor. We were doing no wrong, I swear. It was just a game. You can't believe it of us. Say you can't.'

When he explained what he did not want told to the Emperor, and swore by his father's honour that he and Drusilla were entirely innocent, I felt bound to do what I could for the children. I went to my mother and said: 'Caligula swears you are mistaken. He swears by his father's honour, and if there is the least possible doubt in your mind about his guilt you ought to respect that oath. For my part, I can't believe that a boy of twelve – –'

'Caligula's a monster and Drusilla's a she-monster, and you're a blockhead, and I believe my eyes more than their oaths or your nonsense. I shall go to Tiberius the first thing to-morrow.'

'But, Mother, if you tell the Emperor, it will not be only those two who will suffer. For once let's talk frankly, and be damned to informers! I may be a blockhead, but you know as well as I do that Tiberius suspects Agrippina of having poisoned Castor to get her elder boys made heirs to the monarchy, and that he lives in terror of a sudden rising in their favour. If you, as their grandmother, accuse these children of incest, do you suppose that he won't find a way of involving the elder members of the family in the charge?'

'You're a blockhead, I say. I can't bear the way your head twitches and your Adam's apple goes up and down.' But I could see that I had made an impression on her, and decided that if I kept out of her sight for the rest of my visit to Rome, so that my presence was not a reminder to her of my advice, it was likely that Tiberius would hear nothing from her about the matter. I packed up a few things and went to my brother-in-law Plautius's house, to ask him to put me up. (By now Plautius was well advanced in his career and in four years he would be Consul.) Supper was long over by the time I called and he was reading legal documents in his study. His wife had gone to bed, he said. I asked, 'How is she? She looked rather worried when I saw her last.'

He laughed. 'Why, you rustic fellow, haven't you heard? I divorced Numantina a month ago or more. When I said "my wife" I meant my new one, Apronia, daughter of the man who gave Tacfarinas such a beating recently!'

I apologized and said that I supposed I ought to offer my congratulations. 'But why did you divorce Numantina? I thought you two got on very well together.'

'Not badly at all. But, to tell the truth, I've been in rather a fix lately with debts. I had bad luck some years ago as a junior magistrate. You know how much one is expected to spend out of one's own pocket on Games. Well, to begin with, I spent more than I could afford and had extremely bad luck besides, you may remember. Twice there was a mistake made in procedure half-way through the Games and I had to start all over again the next day. The first time it was my own fault: I used a form of prayer which had been altered by statute two years previously. The next time a trumpeter who was blowing a long call had not taken a deep enough breath: he broke off short and that was enough to end things a second time. So I had to pay the sword-fighters and charioteers three times over. I have never been out of debt since. I had to do something about it at last, because my creditors were getting nasty. Numantina's dowry was spent long ago, but I managed to arrange matters with her uncle. He has taken her back without it on condition that I let him adopt our younger son. He wants an heir and has taken a fancy to the boy. And Apronia's very rich, so now I'm all right. Of course, Numantina didn't like leaving me at all. I had to tell her that I was only doing this because I had a hint from a Certain Friend of a Certain Personage that if I didn't marry Apronia, who has been in love with me and has interest at Court, I'd be charged with blasphemy against Augustus. You see, the other day one of my slaves tripped and dropped an alabaster bowl full of wine in the middle of the hall. I had a riding whip with me and when I heard the crash I rushed at the fellow and fairly laced into him. I was blind with fury. He said, "Steady on, Master, look where we are!" And the brute had one foot within that holy white square of marble around Augustus's statue. I dropped my whip at once but half a dozen freedmen must have seen me. I am confident that I can trust them not to inform against me, but Numantina was worried by the incident, so I used it to reconcile her to the divorce. By the way, this is entirely confidential. I trust you not to pass it on to Urgulanilla. I don't mind telling you she's rather annoyed about the Numantina business.'

'I never see her now.'

'Well, if you see her, you won't tell her what I've told you? Swear you won't.'

'I swear by Augustus's Godhead.'

'That's good enough. You know the bedroom that you used last time you were here?'

'Yes, thanks. If you're busy, I'll go to bed now. I've had a long journey from the country to-day and worries at home too. My mother practically threw me out of the house.'

So we said good night and I went upstairs. A freedman gave me a lamp, with rather a queer look, and I went into the bedroom which was on the corridor nearly opposite Plautius's, and after shutting myself in began undressing. The bed was behind a curtain. I took off my clothes and washed my hands and feet in the little washplace at the other end of the room. Suddenly there was a heavy step behind me and my lamp was blown out. I told myself: 'You're done for now, Claudius. Here's someone with a dagger.' But I said aloud as calmly as I could: 'Please light the lamp, whoever you may be, and see if we can't talk things over quietly. And if you decide to kill me you'll be able to see better with the lamp lit.'

A deep voice answered: 'Stay where you are.'

There was shuffling and grunting and the sound of someone dressing and then of flint and steel struck together and at last the lamp was lit. It was Urgulanilla. I had not seen her since Drusillus's funeral and she had not grown any prettier in those five years. She was stouter than ever, colossally stout, and bloated faced: there was enough strength in this female Hercules to have overpowered a thousand Claudiuses. I am pretty strong in the arms; but she had only to throw herself on me and she would have crushed me to death.

She came towards me and said slowly: 'What are you doing in my bedroom?'

I explained myself as well as I could, and said that it was a bad joke of Plautius's, sending me into her room without telling me that she was there. I had the greatest respect for her, I said, and apologized sincerely for my intrusion and would leave her at once and sleep on a couch in the Baths.

'No, my dear, now you're here you stay! It isn't often that I have the pleasure of my husband's company. Please understand that once you're here you can't escape. Get into bed and go to sleep and I'll join you later. I'm going to read a book until I feel sleepy. I've not been able to sleep properly for nights.'

'I am very sorry indeed if I woke you up just now. ...'

'Get into bed.'

'I am very sorry indeed about Numantina's divorce. I knew nothing about it until the freedman told me a moment ago.'

'Get into bed and stop talking.'

'Good night, Urgulanilla. I really am very ...'

'Shut up.' She came over and drew the curtain.

Although I was dead tired and could hardly keep my eyes open I did my best to stay awake. I was convinced that Urgulanilla would wait until I went to sleep and then strangle me. Meanwhile she was reading to herself very slowly from a very dull book, a Greek love-story of the most idiotic sort, rustling the pages and spelling out each syllable slowly to herself in a hoarse whisper:

'*O schol-ar*,' she said, '*you have tast-ed now both hon-ey and gall. Be care-ful that the sweet-ness of your pleas-ure does not turn to-morr-ow in-to the bit-ter-ness of re-pen-tance!*' '*Pshaw*,' I re-turned. '*My sweet-heart, I am read-y, if you give me an-oth-er kiss like that last one, to be roast-ed up-on a slow fire like a-ny chick-en or duck-ling.*'

She chuckled at this and then said aloud, 'Go to sleep, husband. I'm waiting until I hear you snore.'

I protested, 'Then you shouldn't read such exciting stories.'

I heard Plautius go to bed after a time. 'O Heavens,' I thought. 'He'll be asleep in a few minutes and with two doors between us he won't hear my cries when Urgulanilla throttles me.' Urgulanilla stopped reading and I had no muttering and crackling of paper to help me fight against my sleepiness. I felt myself falling asleep. I was asleep. I knew that I was asleep and I simply must wake up. I struggled frantically to be awake. At last I was awake. There was a thud and a rustle of paper. The book had blown off the table on to the floor. The lamp had gone out; I was aware of a strong draught in the room. The door must be open. I listened attentively for about three minutes. Urgulanilla was certainly not in the room.

As I was trying to make up my mind what to do I heard the most dreadful shriek ring out – from quite close it seemed. A woman screamed, 'Spare me! Spare me! This is Numantina's doing! O! O!' Then came the bump of a heavy metal object falling, then the crash of splintering glass, another shriek, a distant thud, then hurried footsteps across the corridor. Somebody was in my room again. The door was softly closed and barred. I recognized Urgulanilla's panting breath. I heard her clothes being taken off and laid on a chair, and soon she was lying beside me. I pretended to be asleep. She groped for my throat in the dark. I said, as if half-waking: 'Don't do that, darling. It tickles. And I've got to go to Rome to-morrow to buy some cosmetics for you.' Then in a more wakeful voice: 'O Urgulanilla! Is that you? What's all the noise? What's the time? Have we been asleep long?'

She said, 'I don't know. I must have been asleep about three hours. It's just before dawn. It sounds as though something dreadful has happened. Let's go and see.'

So we got up and put on our clothes in a hurry and unlocked the door. Plautius, naked except for a coverlet hastily wrapped round him, stood in the middle of an excited crowd armed with torches. He was quite distracted and kept saying, 'I didn't do it. I was asleep. I felt her torn from my arms and heard her borne through the air screaming for help, and then a crash of something falling and another crash as she went through the window. It was pitch dark. She called out: "Spare me! It's Numantina's doing."'

'Tell that to the judges,' said Apronia's brother, striding up,

271

'and see whether they'll believe you. You've killed her all right. Her skull's smashed in.'

'I didn't do it,' said Plautius. 'How could I have done? I was asleep. It was witchcraft. Numantina's a witch.'

At dawn he was taken before the Emperor by Apronia's father. Tiberius cross-examined him severely. He said now that while he was sound asleep she had torn herself from his arms and leaped across the room, shrieking, and crashed through the window into the courtyard below. Tiberius made Plautius accompany him at once to the scene of the murder. The first thing he noticed in the bedroom was his own wedding-gift to Plautius, a beautiful Egyptian bronze-and-gold candelabra taken from the tomb of a queen, now lying broken on the ground. He glanced up and saw that it had been wrenched from the ceiling. He said: 'She clung to it and it came down. She was being carried towards the window on somebody's shoulders. And look how high up in the window the hole is! She was pitched through, she did not jump through.'

'It was witchcraft,' said Plautius. 'She was carried through the air by an unseen power. She shrieked and blamed my former wife Numantina.'

Tiberius scoffed. Plautius's friends realized that he would be convicted of murder and executed, and his property confiscated. His grandmother Urgulania therefore sent him a dagger, telling him to think of his heirs, who would be allowed to keep the property if he anticipated the verdict by immediate suicide. He was a coward and could not bring himself to drive the dagger home. Eventually he got into a hot bath and ordered a surgeon to open his veins for him; he slowly and painlessly bled to death. I felt very badly about his death. I had not accused Urgulanilla of the murder at once because I would have been asked why when I heard the first shrieks I had not jumped up and rescued Apronia. I had decided to wait until the trial and only come forward if Plautius seemed likely to be condemned. I knew nothing about the dagger until it was too late. I comforted myself by the thought that he had treated Numantina very cruelly and had been a bad friend to me, besides. To clear Plautius's memory his brother brought a charge against Numantina of having disordered Plautius's wits by witchcraft. But Tiberius intervened and said that he was satisfied that Plautius had been in full possession of his faculties at the time. Numantina was discharged.

There was not another word spoken between Urgulanilla and myself. But a month later Sejanus paid me a surprise visit as he was passing through Capua. He was in Tiberius's company, on the way to Capri, an island near Naples, where Tiberius had twelve villas and frequently went for amusement. Sejanus said: 'You'll be able to divorce Urgulanilla now. She's due to have a child in about five months' time, so my agents inform me. You have me to thank for this. I knew Urgulanilla's obsession about Numantina. I happened to see a young slave, a Greek, who might have been Numantina's male twin. I made her a present of him and she fell in love with him at once. His name's Boter.'

What could I do but thank him? Then I said, 'And who's my new wife to be?'

'So you remember our conversation? Well, the lady I have in mind is my sister by adoption – Aelia. You know her, of course?'

I did, but I hid my disappointment, and merely asked whether anyone so young, beautiful, and intelligent would be content to marry an old, lame, sick, stammering fool like myself.

'Oh,' he answered brutally, 'she won't mind in the least. She'll be marrying Tiberius's nephew and Nero's uncle, that's all she thinks about. Don't imagine that she's in love with you. She might bring herself to have a child by you for the sake of its ancestry, but as for any sentiment – –'

'In fact, apart from the honour of becoming your brother-in-law, I might just as well not divorce Urgulanilla for all the improvement it will make to my life?'

'Oh, you'll manage,' he laughed. 'You don't live too lonely a life here, by the look of this room. There's a nice woman about somewhere, I can see. Gloves, a hand-mirror, an embroidery frame, that box of sweets, flowers carefully arranged. And Aelia won't be jealous. She has her own men friends, probably, though I don't pry into her affairs.'

'All right,' I said. 'I'll do it.'

'You don't sound very grateful.'

'It's not ingratitude. You have taken great trouble on my account, and I don't know how to thank you properly. I was only feeling rather nervous. From what I know of Aelia she's rather critical, if you understand what I mean.'

He burst out laughing. 'She has a tongue like a sacking-needle. But surely by now you're hardened against mere scolding?

Your mother has given you a good enough training, hasn't she?'

'I am still a little thin-skinned,' I said, 'in places.'

'Well, I mustn't stay here any longer, my dear Claudius. Tiberius will be wondering where I've gone. So it's a bargain?'

'Yes, and I thank you very much.'

'Oh, by the way, it *was* Urgulanilla, wasn't it, who killed poor Apronia? I rather expected a tragedy. Urgulanilla had a letter from Numantina begging her to avenge her. Numantina didn't really write it, you understand.'

'I know nothing. I was sound asleep at the time.'

'Like Plautius?'

'Sounder even than Plautius.'

'Sensible fellow! Well, good-bye, Claudius.'

'Good-bye, Aelius Sejanus.' He rode off.

I divorced Urgulanilla, after first writing to my grandmother for permission. Livia wrote that the child should be exposed as soon as born; this was her wish and the wish of Urgulania.

I sent a reliable freedman to Urgulanilla at Herculaneum to tell her the orders I had been given, warning her that if she wanted the child to live she must exchange it, as soon as born, for a dead baby; I had to have a baby of sorts to expose, and so long as it wasn't too long dead, any dead baby would serve the purpose. So the child was saved that way and later Urgulanilla took it back from its foster parents, from whom she had got the dead baby. I don't know what happened to Boter, but the child, who was a girl, grew up the living image of Numantina, they say. Urgulanilla has been dead many years now. When she died they had to break down a wall to get her enormous body out of the house – and it was all honest bulk, not dropsy. In her will she paid a curious tribute to me: 'I don't care what people say, but Claudius is no fool.' She left me a collection of Greek gems, some Persian embroideries, and her portrait of Numantina.

Chapter 24

TIBERIUS and Livia never met now. Livia had offended Tiberius by dedicating a statue to Augustus in their joint names and putting her name first. He retaliated by doing the one thing that she could not even pretend to forgive – when ambassadors came to A.D. 25 him from Spain asking that they might erect a temple to him and his mother he refused on behalf of both. He told the Senate that he had, perhaps in a moment of weakness, allowed the dedication of a temple in Asia to the Senate and its leader (namely, himself) – together symbolizing the paternal government of Rome. His mother's name also occurred in the dedicatory inscription as High-Priestess of the cult of Augustus. But to assent to the deification of himself and his mother would be carrying indulgence too far.

'For myself, my lords, that I am a mortal man, that I am bound by the trammels of human nature, and that I fill the principal place among you to your satisfaction – if I do – I solemnly assure you is quite enough for me: this is how I prefer to be remembered by posterity. If posterity believes me to have been worthy of my ancestors, watchful of your interest, unmoved in dangers, and, in defence of the commonwealth, fearless of private enmities, I shall be sufficiently remembered. The loving gratitude of the Senate and the people of Rome and of our allies is the fairest temple I would raise – a temple not of marble but more enduring than marble, a temple of the heart. Marble temples, when the hallowed beings to whom they are raised fall into disrepute, are despised as mere sepulchres. I therefore invoke Heaven to grant me until the end of my life an untroubled spirit and the power of clear discernment in all duties human and sacred: and therefore too I implore our citizens and allies that whenever dissolution comes to this mortal body of mine, they will celebrate my life and deeds (if they are so worthy) with inward thankfulness and praise rather than with outward pomp and temple-building and annual sacrifice. The true love that Rome felt for my father Augustus when he was among us as a man is already obscured both by the awe which his Godhead excites in the religious-minded and by the indiscriminate use of his name as a market-place oath. And while we are on the subject, my Lords, I propose that we henceforth make it a criminal offence to use the sacred name of Augustus for any but the most solemn occasions and that we enforce this law vigorously.' No mention of Livia's feelings in the matter. And the day before he had refused to appoint one of her nominees to a vacant judgeship, unless he were permitted to qualify the appointment with: 'This person is the choice of my mother, Livia Augusta, to whose importunities in his interest I have been forced to give way, against my better knowledge of his character and capacities.'

Soon after this Livia invited all the noblewomen of Rome to an all-day entertainment. There were jugglers and acrobats and recitations from the poets and marvellous cakes and sweetmeats and liqueurs and a beautiful jewel for each guest as a memento of the occasion. To conclude the proceedings Livia gave a reading of Augustus's letters. She was now eighty-three years old and her voice was weak and she whistled a good deal on her s's, but for an hour and a half she held her audience spellbound. The first letters she read contained pronouncements on public policy, all of which seemed especially written as warnings against the present state of affairs at Rome. There were some very apposite remarks about treason trials, including the following paragraph:

Though I have been bound to protect myself legally against all sorts of libel I shall exert myself to the utmost, my dear Livia, to avoid staging so unpleasant a spectacle as a trial for treason for any foolish historian, caricaturist, or epigram-maker who has made me a target of his wit or eloquence. My father Julius Caesar forgave the poet Catullus the most filthy lampoons imaginable: he wrote to Catullus that if he were trying to show that he was no servile flatterer like most of his fellow-poets, he had now fully proved his case and could return to other more poetical subjects than the sexual abnormalities of a middle-aged statesman: and would he come to dinner the next day and bring any friend he liked? Catullus came and thenceforward the two were fast friends. To use the majesty of the law for revenging any petty act of private spite is to make a public confession of weakness, cowardice, and an ignoble spirit.

There was a notable paragraph about informers:

Except where I am convinced that an informer does not expect to benefit directly or indirectly by his accusations, but brings them from a sense of true patriotism and public decency, I not only discount their importance as evidence but I put a black mark against that informer's name and never afterwards employ him in any position of trust. ...

276

And, to finish up, she read a series of very illuminating letters. Livia had tens of thousands of Augustus's letters, written over a stretch of fifty-two years, carefully sewn into book-form and indexed. She chose from these thousands the fifteen most damaging ones she could find. The series began with complaints against Tiberius's disgusting behaviour as a little boy, his unpopularity with his schoolfellows as a big boy, his close-fistedness and haughtiness as a young man, and so on, with signs of growing irritation and the phrase, often repeated, 'and if it were not that he was your son, my dearest Livia, I should say – –' Then came complaints of his brutal severity with the troops under his command – 'almost an encouragement to mutiny' – and his dilatoriness in pressing his attacks on the enemy, with unfavourable comparisons between his methods and my father's. Then an angry refusal to consider him as a son-in-law, and a detailed list of his moral shortcomings. Then more letters relating to the painful Julia story, written for the most part in terms of almost insane loathing and disgust for Tiberius. She read one important letter written on the occasion of Tiberius's recall from Rhodes:

Dearest Livia:

I take advantage of this forty-second anniversary of our marriage to thank you with all my heart for the extraordinary services you have rendered the State ever since we joined forces. If I am styled the Father of the Country it seems absurd to me that you should not be styled the Mother of the Country: I swear you have done twice as much as I have in our great work of public reconstruction. Why do you ask me to wait another few years before asking the Senate to vote you this honour? The only way that I can show my absolute confidence in your disinterested loyalty and profound judgement is to give way at last to your repeated pleas for the recall of Tiberius, a man to whose character I confess I continue to feel the greatest repugnance, and I pray to Heaven that by giving way to you now I do not inflict lasting damage on the commonwealth.

Livia's last choice was a letter written about a year before Augustus's death:

I had a sudden feeling of profoundest regret and despair, my dearest wife, when discussing State policy with Tiberius yesterday, that the people of Rome should be fated to be glared at by those protruding eyes of his and pounded by that bony fist of his and chewed by those dreadfully slow jaws of his and stamped on by those huge feet of his. But I was for the moment reckoning without yourself and our dear Germanicus. If I did not believe that when I am dead he will both be guided by you in all matters of State and shamed by Germanicus's example into at least a semblance of decent living, I would even now, I swear, disinherit him and ask the Senate to revoke all his titles of honour. The man's a beast and needs keepers.

When she had finished she rose and said: 'Perhaps, ladies, it would be best to say nothing to your husbands about these peculiar letters. I did not realize, in fact, when I began to read, how – how peculiar they were. I am not asking you this on my own account but for the sake of the Empire.'

Tiberius heard the whole story from Sejanus just as he was about to take his seat in the Senate, and he was overcome with shame and rage and alarm. It so happened that his business that afternoon was to hear a charge of treason brought against Lentulus, one of the pontiffs who had incurred his suspicion in the matter of the prayer for Nero and Drusus, and also because he had voted for the mitigation of Sosia's sentence. When Lentulus, a simple old man, distinguished equally for his birth, his victories in Africa under Augustus, and his unassuming mildness – his nickname was 'The Bell-Wether' – heard that he was accused of plotting against the State, he burst out laughing. Tiberius, already distracted, lost all self-control and said, nearly weeping, to the House: 'If Lentulus too hates me, I am unworthy to live.'

Gallus replied: 'Cheer up, Your Majesty – I beg your pardon, I had forgotten that you dislike the title – I should say, cheer up, Tiberius Caesar! Lentulus was not laughing *at* you, he was laughing *with* you. He was rejoicing with you that for once there should come before the Senate a charge of treason that was absolutely unfounded.' So the charge against Lentulus was dropped. But Tiberius had already been the cause of Lentulus's father's death. He was immensely rich and was so frightened by Tiberius's suspicions of him that he had killed himself, and as a proof of loyalty had left his entire fortune to Tiberius, who thereafter could not believe that Lentulus, now left very poor, harboured no resentment against him.

Tiberius did not enter the Senate again for two whole months: he could not look the senators in the face with the knowledge that their wives had heard Augustus's letters about him. Sejanus suggested that it would be good for his health to leave Rome for a while and stay a few miles away at one of his villas, where he would escape from the daily throng of Palace visitors and the noise and bustle of the City. He followed this advice. The action that he took against his mother was to superannuate her, to omit her name from all public documents, to discontinue her customary birthday honours, and to make it clear that any coupling of her name with his or any praise of her in the Senate would be regarded as little short of treason. More active vengeance he did not dare take. He knew that she still had the letter which he had written from Rhodes promising her his lifelong obedience and that she was quite capable of reading it, even though it might incriminate her as the murderess of Gaius and Lucius.

But this wonderful old woman was not defeated yet, as you shall read. One day I had a note from her. 'The Lady Livia Augusta expects her dear grandson Tiberius Claudius to visit and dine with her on the occasion of her birthday: she hopes that he is in good health.' I could not make it out. I her dear grandson! Tender enquiries after my health! I did not know whether to laugh or be afraid. I had never in my life been allowed to visit her on her birthday. I had never even dined with her. I had not spoken to her, except ceremonially at the Augustan festival, for ten years. What could her motive be? Well, I should know in three days, and meanwhile I must buy her a really magnificent present. I finally bought her something which I was sure she would appreciate – a gracefully-shaped wine-vase in bronze, with serpent-head handles and a complicated design of gold and silver inlay. It was, in my opinion, of far finer workmanship than any of the Corinthian vessels that collectors give such absurd prices for nowadays. It came from China! In the centre of the design had been sunk a gold medallion of Augustus which had somehow strayed to that wonderfully distant land. That vase cost me 500 gold pieces, though it stood no more than eighteen inches high.

But before I tell of my visit and my long interview with her I must clear up a point on which I may perhaps have misled you. From my accounts of the treason-trials and similar atrocities it will probably be deduced that the Empire under Tiberius was intolerably misgoverned in all departments. This was far from being the case. Though he undertook no new public works worth speaking of, merely contenting himself with completing those begun by Augustus, he kept the Army and the Fleet efficient and up to strength, paid his officials regularly and made them send in detailed reports four times a year, encouraged trade, assured a regular supply of corn for Italy, kept the roads and aqueducts in repair, limited public and private extravagance in a variety of ways, stabilized food prices, put down piracy and banditry and built up a considerable reserve of public money in case of any national emergency. He maintained his provincial governors in office for many years at a time, if they were any good, so as not to unsettle matters, keeping a careful watch on them, however. One governor, to show his efficiency and loyalty, sent Tiberius more tribute than was due. Tiberius gave him a reprimand: 'I want my sheep shorn, not shaved.' As a result there were few frontier wars after the German trouble was settled by Maroboduus's welcome to Rome and Hermann's death. Tacfarinas was the chief enemy. He was for a long time known as the 'Laurel-giver' because three generals – my friend Furius, and Apronius, the father of Apronia, and a third, Blaesus, Sejanus's maternal uncle, had each in turn defeated him and been awarded triumphal ornaments. Blaesus, who scattered Tacfarinas's army and captured his brother, was given the unusual honour of being made a field-marshal, an honour reserved in general only for the Imperial family. Tiberius told the Senate that he was glad to honour Blaesus in this way because of his kinship with his trusted friend Sejanus; and when, three years later, a fourth general, Dolabella, put a final end to the African War, which had broken out again with redoubled force, by not only defeating Tacfarinas but killing him, Dolabella was granted only triumphal ornaments 'lest the laurels of Blaesus, uncle of my trusted friend Sejanus, should thereby lose their lustre'.

But I was talking of Tiberius's good deeds, not his weaknesses: and really, from the point of view of the Empire as a whole, he had been for the last twelve years a wise and just ruler. That nobody can deny. The canker in the core of the apple – if the metaphor may be forgiven – did not show on the skin or impair the wholesomeness of the flesh. Of the 5,000,000 Roman citizens, a mere 200 or 300 suffered for Tiberius's jealous fears. A.D. 26 And I do not know how many scores of millions of slaves and provincials, and allies who were subjects in all but name, benefited solidly by the Imperial system as perfected by Augustus and Livia and carried on in this tradition by Tiberius. But I was living in the apple's core, so to speak, and I can be pardoned if I write more about the central canker than about the still unblemished and fragrant outer part.

Once you give way to a metaphor, Claudius, which is rare, you pursue it too far. Surely you remember Athenodorus's injunctions against this sort of thing? Well, call Sejanus the maggot and get it done with; then return to your usual homely style!

Sejanus decided to use Tiberius's sense of shame as a means of keeping him away from the City for a longer time than a mere two months. He encouraged one of his Guards officers to accuse a celebrated wit called Montanus of blackening Tiberius's private character. Whereas hitherto the accusers had been restrained from reporting any but the most general abuse of Tiberius – as haughty, or cruel or domineering – this soldier came forward and credited Montanus with libels of a most particular and substantial kind. Sejanus took care that the libels were as true as they were disgusting; though Montanus, not having Sejanus's knowledge of what went on in the Palace, had not uttered them. The witness, who was the best drill-instructor in the Guards, bawled out Montanus's alleged obscenities at the top of his voice, not slurring over the most obscene words or phrases, and refusing to let himself be cried down by the shocked protests of the senators. 'I swore to tell the whole truth,' he bellowed, 'and for the honour of Tiberius Caesar I shall not omit a single article of the accused's loathsome conversation overheard by me on the said date and in the said circumstances. Accused further declared that our gracious Emperor is fast becoming impotent from said alleged debauches and said over-indulgence in aphrodisiac medicines, and that in order to rally his waning sexual powers he holds private exhibitions every three days or so in a specially decorated underground room of the Palace. Accused declared that the performers at these exhibitions, Spintrians as they are called, come prancing in, three at a time, stark naked ...'

He went on in that strain for half an hour and Tiberius did not dare to stop him – or perhaps he wanted to find out just how much was known – until the witness said one thing too many (never mind what it was). Tiberius, forgetting himself, leaped up suddenly, his face crimson, and declared that he would instantly clear himself of these monstrous charges or establish a judicial investigation. Sejanus tried to calm him down, but he remained on his feet glaring angrily about him, until Gallus rose and gently reminded him that it was Montanus, not he, who was the accused party; that his private character was beyond suspicion; and that if news that such an investigation was about to be held reached the frontier provinces and the allied states, it would be completely misunderstood.

Shortly afterwards Tiberius was warned by Thrasyllus – whether this was arranged by Sejanus I do not know – that he would shortly leave the City and that it would be death for him to re-enter it. Tiberius told Sejanus that he would move to Capri and leave him to look after things at Rome. He attended one more treason-trial – that of my cousin Claudia Pulchra, Varus's widow, who, now that Sosia was banished, was Agrippina's most intimate friend. She was charged with adultery, prostituting her daughters, and witchcraft against Tiberius. She was, I think, completely innocent of all these charges. As soon as Agrippina heard about it she hurried to the Palace and by chance found Tiberius sacrificing to Augustus. Almost before the ceremony was over she came close up to him and said:

'Tiberius, this is illogical behaviour. You sacrifice flamingoes and peacocks to Augustus and you persecute his grandchildren.'

He said slowly: 'I do not understand you. Which grandchildren of Augustus have I persecuted that he did not himself persecute?'

'I am not talking about Postumus and Julilla. I mean myself. You banished Sosia because she was my friend. You forced Silius to kill himself because he was my friend. And Calpurnius because he was my friend. And now my dear Pulchra is doomed too, though her only crime is her foolish fondness for me. People are beginning to avoid me, saying that I am unlucky.'

Tiberius took her by the shoulders and said once more:

> And if you are not queen, my dear,
> Think you that you are wronged?

Pulchra was condemned and executed. The Crown Prosecutor was a man called Afer, engaged because of his eloquence. A few days later Agrippina happened to see him outside the theatre. He appeared ashamed of himself and avoided meeting her eye. She went up to him and said: 'There is no occasion for you to hide from me, Afer.' Then she quoted from Homer, but with alterations to suit the context, Achilles's reassuring answer to the embarrassed heralds who came to him with a humiliating message from Agamemnon. She said:

> He forced you to it. Though you were well fee'd
> It was not yours but Agamemnon's deed.

This was reported to Tiberius (though not by Afer); the word 'Agamemnon' caused him fresh alarm.

Agrippina fell ill and thought that she was being poisoned. She went in her sedan to the Palace to make a last appeal to Tiberius for mercy. She looked so thin and pale that Tiberius was charmed: perhaps she would die soon. He said: 'My poor Agrippina, you look seriously ill. What's wrong with you?'

She answered in a weak voice: 'It may be that I have done you a wrong in thinking that you persecute my friends just because they are my friends. It may be that I am unlucky in my choice of them, or that my judgement is often at fault. But I swear you have done me equal wrong in thinking that I have the least feeling of disloyalty towards you or that I have any ambition to rule either directly or indirectly. All that I ask is to be left alone, and your forgiveness for any injuries that I have unintentionally done you, and ... and ...' She ended in sobs.

'And what else?'

'O Tiberius, be good to my children! And be good to me! Let me marry again. I am so lonely. Since Germanicus died I have never been able to forget my troubles. I can't sleep at night. If you let me marry I'll settle down and lose all my restlessness and be quite a different person, and then perhaps you won't suspect me of plotting against you. I am sure it's only because I look so unhappy that you think I have bad feelings towards you.'

'Who's the man you want to marry?'

'A good, generous, unambitious man, past middle age, and one of your most loyal ministers.'

'What's his name?'

'Gallus. He says that he is ready to marry me at once.'

Tiberius turned on his heel and walked out of the room without another word.

A few days later he invited her to a banquet. He used often to invite people to dine with him whom he particularly mistrusted and stare at them throughout the meal as if trying to read their secret thoughts: which shook the self-possession of all but very few. If they looked alarmed he read it as a proof of guilt. If they met his eye steadily he read it as an even stronger proof of guilt, with insolence added. On this occasion Agrippina, still ill and unable to eat any but the lightest food without nausea, and stared constantly at by Tiberius, had a miserable time. She was not a talkative person, and the conversation, which was about the relative merits of music and philosophy, did not interest her in the least and she found it impossible to contribute anything to it. She made a pretence of eating, but Tiberius, who was watching her attentively, saw that she sent away plate after plate untouched. He thought that she suspected him of trying to poison her, and to test this he carefully picked an apple from the dish in front of him and said: 'My dear Agrippina, you haven't made much of a meal. At any rate, try this apple. It's a splendid one. I had a present of young trees from the King of Parthia three years ago and this is the first time they have borne fruit.'

Now almost everyone has a certain 'natural enemy' – if I may call it that. To some people honey is a violent poison. Others are made ill by touching a horse or entering a stable or even by lying on a couch stuffed with horse-hair. Others again are most uncomfortably affected by the presence of a cat, and going into a room will sometimes say, 'There has been a cat here, excuse me if I retire.' I myself feel an overpowering repugnance to the smell of hawthorn in bloom. Agrippina's natural enemy was the apple. She took the present from Tiberius and thanked him, but with an ill-concealed shudder, and said that she would keep it, if she might, to eat when she reached home.

'Just one bit now, to taste how good it is.'

'Please forgive me, but really I could not.' She handed the apple to a servant and told him to wrap it carefully in a napkin for her.

Why did Tiberius not immediately try her on a treason-charge, as Sejanus urged? Because Agrippina was still under Livia's protection.

Chapter 25

AND so I come to the account of my dinner with Livia. She greeted me very graciously, seeming genuinely delighted with my gift. During the meal, at which nobody else was present but old Urgulania and Caligula, now aged fourteen – a tall, pale boy with a blotched complexion and sunken eyes – she surprised me by the sharpness of her mind and the clearness of her memory. She asked me about my work, and when I began talking about the First Punic War and discrediting certain particulars given by the poet Naevius (he had served in this war) she agreed with my conclusions but caught me out in a misquotation. She said: 'You're grateful to me now, grandson, aren't you, for not letting you write that biography of your father! Do you think that you'd be dining here to-day if I hadn't intervened?'

Every time the slave filled my cup I had drunk it straight up, and now at the tenth or twelfth draught I felt like a lion. I answered boldly: 'Extremely grateful, Grandmother, to be safe among the Carthaginians and Etruscans. But will you tell me just *why* I'm dining here to-day?'

She smiled: 'Well, I admit that your presence at table still causes me a certain amount of ... But never mind. If I have broken one of my oldest rules that is my affair, not yours. Do you dislike me, Claudius? Be frank.'

'Probably as much as you dislike me, Grandmother.' (Could this be my own voice speaking?)

Caligula sniggered, Urgulania tittered, Livia laughed: 'Frank enough! By the way, have you noticed that monster there? He's been keeping unusually quiet during the meal.'

'Who, Grandmother?'

'That nephew of yours.'

'Is he a monster?'

'Don't pretend you don't know it. You *are* a monster, aren't you, Caligula?'

'Whatever you say, Great-grandmother,' Caligula said, with downcast eyes.

'Well, Claudius, that monster there, your nephew – I'll tell you about him. *He's going to be the next Emperor.*'

I thought it was a joke. I said smilingly: 'If you tell me so, Grandmother, it is so. But what are his recommendations? He's the youngest of the family and though he has given evidences of great natural talent ...'

'You mean that they won't any of them stand a chance against Sejanus and your sister Livilla?'

I was astounded at the freedom of the conversation. 'I didn't mean anything of the sort. I never concern myself with high politics. I only meant that he's young yet, much too young to be Emperor; and that as a prophecy it seems rather a long shot.'

'Not a long shot at all. Tiberius will make him his successor. No question of it. Why? Because Tiberius is like that. He has the same vanity as poor Augustus had: he can't bear the idea of a successor who will be more popular than himself. But at the same time he does all he can to make himself hated and feared. So, when he feels that his time's nearly up, he'll search for someone just a little worse than himself to succeed him. And he'll find Caligula. There is one deed that Caligula has already done which puts him in a far higher rank of criminality than Tiberius can ever now attain.'

'Please, Great-grandmother ...' Caligula pleaded.

'All right, monster, your secret's safe with me so long as you behave.'

'Does Urgulania know the secret?' I asked.

'No. It's between the monster and myself.'

'Did he confess it voluntarily?'

'Certainly not. He's not the confessing sort. I found out about it by accident. I was searching his bedroom one night to see if he was trying any schoolboy tricks on me – whether he was doing any amateur black magic, for instance, or distilling poisons or anything of the sort. I came across ...'

'*Please*, Great-grandmother.'

'A green object that told me a very remarkable story. But I gave it back to him.'

Urgulania said, grinning: 'Thrasyllus said I'm going to die this year, so I won't have the pleasure of living in your reign, Caligula, unless you hurry up and murder Tiberius!'

I turned to Livia: 'Is he going to do that, Grandmother?'

Caligula said: 'Is it safe for Uncle Claudius to be told things? Or are you going to poison him?'

She answered: 'Oh, he's quite safe, without any poison. I want you two to know each other better than you do. That's one reason for this dinner. Listen, Caligula. Your uncle Claudius is a phenomenon. He's so old-fashioned that because he's sworn an oath to love and protect his brother's children you can always impose on him – as long as you live. Listen, Claudius. Your nephew Caligula is a phenomenon. He's treacherous, cowardly, lustful, vain, deceitful, and he'll play some very dirty tricks on you before he's done: but remember one thing, he'll never kill you.'

'Why's that?' I asked, draining my cup again. The conversation was like the sort one has in dreams – mad but interesting.

'Because you're the man who's going to avenge his death.'

'I? Who said so?'

'Thrasyllus.'

'Does Thrasyllus never make mistakes?'

'No. Never. Caligula's going to be murdered and you're to avenge his death.'

A gloomy silence suddenly fell and continued until dessert, when Livia said: 'Come, Claudius, the rest of our talk shall be in private.' The other two rose and left us alone.

I said: 'That seemed to me a very odd conversation, Grandmother. Was it my fault? Had I been drinking too much? I mean, some jokes aren't safe, nowadays. It was rather dangerous fooling. I hope the servants ...'

'Oh, they're deaf-mutes. No, don't blame the wine. There's truth in wine, and the conversation was perfectly serious so far as I was concerned.'

'But ... but if you really think him a monster, why do you encourage him? Why not give Nero your support? He's a fine fellow.'

'Because Caligula, not Nero, is to be the next Emperor.'

'But he'll make a marvellously bad one if he's what you say he is. And you, who have devoted your whole life to the service of Rome ...'

'Yes. But you can't fight against Fate. And now that Rome has been ungrateful and mad enough to allow my blackguardly son to put me on the shelf, and insult me – *me*, can you imagine it, perhaps the greatest ruler that the world has ever known, and his mother, too ...' Her voice grew shrill.

I was anxious to change the subject. I said, 'Please calm yourself, Grandmother. As you say, you can't fight against Fate. But isn't there something particular that you want to tell me, Grandmother, connected with all this?'

'Yes, it's about Thrasyllus. I consult him frequently. Tiberius doesn't know that I do, that Thrasyllus has been here often. He told me some years ago what would happen between Tiberius and me – that he'd eventually rebel against my authority and take the Empire wholly into his own hands. I didn't believe it then. He also told me another thing: that though I would die a disappointed old woman I would be acknowledged a Goddess many years after my death. And previously he had said that one who must die in the year which I know now is the year in which I must die will become the greatest Deity the world has ever known and that, finally, no temples at Rome or anywhere in the Empire will be dedicated to anyone else. Not even to Augustus.'

'When are you to die?'

'Three years hence, in the spring. I know the very day.'

'But are you so anxious to become a Goddess? My uncle Tiberius isn't at all anxious, it seems.'

'It is all I think about, now that my work is over. And why not? If Augustus is a God, it's absurd for me to be merely his priestess. I did all the work, didn't I? He no more had it in him to be a great ruler than Tiberius has.'

'Yes, Grandmother. But isn't it enough for you to *know* what you have done without wanting to be worshipped by the ignorant rabble?'

'Claudius, let me explain. I quite agree about the ignorant rabble. It's not so much my fame on earth that I'm thinking about as the position I am to occupy in Heaven. I have done many impious things – no great ruler can do otherwise. I have put the good of the Empire before all human considerations. To keep the Empire free from factions I have had to commit many crimes. Augustus did his best to wreck the Empire by his ridiculous favouritism: Marcellus against Agrippa, Gaius against Tiberius. Who saved Rome from renewed Civil War? I did. The unpleasant and difficult task of removing Marcellus and Gaius fell on me. Yes, don't pretend you haven't ever suspected me of poisoning them. And what is the proper reward for a ruler who commits such crimes for the good of his subjects? The proper reward, obviously, is to be deified. Do you believe that the souls of criminals are eternally tormented?'

'I have always been taught to believe that they are.'

'But the Immortal Gods are free from any fear of punishment, however many crimes they commit?'

'Well, Jove deposed his father and killed one of his grandsons and incestuously married his sister, and ... yes, I agree. ... They none of them have a good moral reputation. And certainly the Judges of the Mortal Dead have no jurisdiction over them.'

'Exactly. You see now why it's all-important for me to become a Goddess. And this, if you must know, is the reason why I tolerate Caligula. He has sworn that if I keep his secret he will make a Goddess of me as soon as he's Emperor. And I want you to swear that you'll do all in your power to see that I become a Goddess as soon as possible, because – oh, don't you see? – until he makes me a Goddess I'll be in Hell, suffering the most frightful torments, the most exquisite ineluctable torments.'

The sudden change in her voice, from cool Imperial arrogance to terrified pleading astonished me more than anything I had yet heard. I had to say something, so I said: 'I don't see what influence poor Uncle Claudius is ever likely to have, either on the Emperor or on the Senate.'

'Never mind about what you see or don't see, idiot! Will you swear to do as I ask? Will you swear by your own head?'

I said: 'Grandmother, I'll swear by my head – for what that's worth now – on one condition.'

'You dare to make conditions to *me*?'

'Yes, after the twentieth cup; and it's a simple condition. After thirty-six years of neglect and aversion you surely don't expect me to do anything for you without making conditions, do you?'

She smiled. 'And what is this one simple condition?'

'There are a lot of things that I'd like to know about. I want to know, in the first place, who killed my father, and who killed Agrippa, and who killed my brother Germanicus, and who killed my son Drusillus. ...'

'Why do you want to know all this? Some imbecile hope of avenging their deaths on me?'

'No, not even if you were the murderess. I never take vengeance unless I am forced to do so by an oath or in self-protection. I believe that evil is its own punishment. All I want now is just to know the truth. I am a professional historian and the one thing that really interests me is to find out how things happen and why. For instance, I write histories more to inform myself than to inform my readers.'

'Old Athenodorus has had a great influence on you, I see.'

'He was kind to me and I was grateful, so I became a Stoic. I

289

never meddled with philosophical argument – that never appealed to me – but I adopted the Stoic way of looking at things. You can trust me not to repeat a word of what you tell me.'

I convinced her that I meant what I said, and so for four hours or more I asked her the most searching questions; and each questions she answered without evasion and as calmly as if she had been some country steward relating the minor casualties of the farm-yard to the visiting owner. Yes, she had poisoned my grandfather, and no, she had not poisoned my father in spite of Tiberius's suspicions – it was a natural gangrene; and yes, she had poisoned Augustus by smearing poison on the figs while they were still on the tree; and she told me the whole Julia story as I have related it, and the whole Postumus story – the details of which I was able to check; and yes, she had poisoned Agrippa and Lucius, as well as Marcellus and Gaius, and yes, she had intercepted my letters to Germanicus, but no, she had not poisoned him – Plancina had done that on her own initiative – but she had marked him out for death as she had marked out my father, and for the same reason.

'What reason was that, Grandmother?'

'He had decided to restore the Republic. No, don't mistake me: not in a way which violated his oath of allegiance to Tiberius, though it meant removing me. He was going to make Tiberius take the step himself voluntarily, and allow him all the credit for it, keeping in the background himself. He nearly persuaded Tiberius. You know what a coward Tiberius is. I had to work hard and forge a lot of documents and tell a lot of lies to keep Tiberius from making a fool of Sejanus. This republicanism is a persistent taint in himself. I even had to come to an understanding with the family. Your grandfather had it.'

'I have it.'

'Still? That's amusing. Nero has it too, I understand. It won't bring him much luck. And it's no use arguing with you republicans. You refuse to see that one can no more reintroduce republican government at this stage than one can reimpose primitive feelings of chastity on modern wives and husbands. It's like trying to turn the shadow back on a sundial: it can't be done.'

She confessed to having had Drusillus throttled. She told me how close I was to death when I first wrote to Germanicus about Postumus. The only reason that she had spared me was that there was a possibility of my writing him information as to Postumus's whereabouts. The most interesting account she gave me was of her poisoning methods. I asked her Postumus's question – whether she favoured slow poisons or quick ones – and she answered without the least embarrassment that she preferred repeated doses of slow tasteless poisons which gave the effect of consumption. I asked how she managed to cover up her traces so well and how she managed to strike at such long distances: for Gaius had been murdered in Asia Minor and Lucius at Marseilles.

She reminded me that she had never contrived a murder which might be held to benefit her directly and immediately. She had not, for instance, poisoned my grandfather until some time after being divorced from him, nor had she poisoned any of her female rivals – Octavia, or Julia, or Scribonia. Her victims were mostly people by whose removal her sons and grand-children were brought closer to the succession. Urgulania had been her only confidant, and she was so discreet and skilful and so devoted that not only was it most unlikely that the crimes they planned together would ever be detected but, even if they were, they would never have been brought home to *her*. The annual confessions made to Urgulania in preparation for the festival of the Good Goddess had been a useful means of removing several people who stood in the way of her plans. She explained this fully. It happened sometimes that confession was made not merely to adultery but to incest with a brother or son. Urgulania would declare that the only possible penance was the death of the man. The woman then pleaded, was there no other possible penance? Urgulania would then say that there was perhaps an alternative that the Goddess would permit. The woman could purify herself by assisting the Goddess's vengeance – with the help of the man who had caused her shame. For, Urgulania would tell her, a similarly detestable confession had been made some time before by another woman, who had however shrunk from killing her ravisher, and so the wretch was still alive, though the woman herself had suffered. The 'wretch' was successively Agrippa, Lucius, and Gaius. Agrippa was accused of incest with his daughter Marcellina – whose unexplained suicide gave colour to the story; Gaius and Lucius of incest with their mother before her banishment – and Julia's reputation gave colour to this story too. In each case the woman was only too glad to plan the murder and the man to execute it. Urgulania assisted with advice and suitable poisons. Livia's safety lay in the remoteness of the agent, who if he were to be suspected or even taken redhanded could not explain his motive for the murder without further incriminating himself. I asked whether she had had no compunction about murdering Augustus and either murdering or banishing so many of his descendants. She said: 'I never for a moment forgot whose daughter I was.' And that explained a great deal. Livia's father, Claudian, had been proscribed by Augustus after the Battle of Philippi and had committed suicide rather than fall into his hands.

In short, she told me everything that I wanted to know except about the haunting of Germanicus's house at Antioch. She repeated that she had not ordered it and that neither Plancina nor Piso had told her anything about it and that I was in as good a position to clear up the mystery as she was. I saw that it was useless to press her further, so I thanked her for her patience with me and at last took the oath by my head to do all in my power to make her a Goddess.

As I was going she handed me a small volume and told me to read it when I was in Capua. It was the collection of rejected Sibylline verses that I have written about in the first pages of this story, and when I came across the prophecy called 'The Succession of Hairy Ones' I thought I knew why Livia had invited me to dinner and made me swear that oath. If I had sworn it. It all seemed like a drunken dream.

Chapter 26

SEJANUS composed a memorial to Tiberius, begging to be remembered if a husband for Livilla was being looked for; saying that he was only a knight, he was aware, but Augustus had once spoken of marrying his only daughter to a knight, and Tiberius at least had no more loyal subordinate than himself. He did not aim at senatorial rank but was content to continue in his present station as sleepless sentinel for his noble Emperor's safety. He added that such a marriage would be a serious blow to Agrippina's party, who recognized him as their most active opponent. They would be afraid to offer violence to Castor's surviving son by Livilla – young Tiberius Gemellus. The recent death of the other twin must be laid at Agrippina's door.

Tiberius answered graciously that he could not yet give a favourable answer to the request, in spite of his great sense of obligation to Sejanus. He thought it unlikely that Livilla, both of whose previous husbands had been men of the highest birth, would be content for him to remain a knight; but if he were advanced in rank as well as being married into the Imperial family this would cause a great deal of jealousy, and so strengthen the party of Agrippina. He said that it was precisely to avoid such jealousies that Augustus had thought of marrying his daughter to a knight, a retired man who was not mixed up with politics in any way.

But he ended on a hopeful note: 'I shall forbear to tell you yet precisely what plans I have for binding you closer to me in affinity. But I shall say this much, that no recompense that I could pay you for your devotion would be too high, and that when the opportunity presents itself I shall have great pleasure in doing what I propose to do.'

Sejanus knew Tiberius too well not to realize that he had made the request prematurely – he had only written at all because Livilla had pressed him – and had given considerable offence. He decided that Tiberius must be persuaded to leave Rome at once, and must appoint him permanent City Warden – a magistrate from whose decisions the only appeal was to the Emperor. As Commander of the Guards he was also in charge of the Corps of Orderlies, the Imperial couriers, so he would have the handling of all Tiberius's correspondence. Tiberius would depend on him, too, for deciding what people to admit to his presence; and the fewer people he had to see the better he would be pleased. Little by little the City Warden would have all the real power, and could act as he pleased without danger of interference by the Emperor.

At last Tiberius left Rome. His pretext was the dedication of a temple at Capua to Jove, and one at Nola to Augustus. But he did not intend ever to return. It was known that he had taken this decision because of Thrasyllus's warning; and what Thrasyllus prophesied was accepted without question as bound to come to pass. It was assumed that Tiberius, now sixty-seven years of age – and an ugly sight he was, thin, stooping, bald, stiff-jointed, with an ulcered face patched with plasters – was to die within a very short time. Nobody could possibly have guessed that he was fated to live eleven years longer. This may have been because he never came nearer the City again than the suburbs. Well, anyway it was how it turned out.

Tiberius took with him to Capri a number of learned Greek professors, and a picked force of soldiers, including his German bodyguard, and Thrasyllus, and a number of painted strange-looking creatures of doubtful sex and, the most curious choice of all, Cocceius Nerva. Capri is an island in the Bay of Naples about three miles from the coast. Its climate is mild in winter and cool in summer. There is only one possible landing-place, the rest of the island being protected by steep cliffs and impassable thickets. How Tiberius spent his leisure time here – when he was not discussing poetry and mythology with the Greeks, or law and politics with Nerva – is too revolting a story even for history. I shall say no more than that he had brought with him a complete set of the famous books of Elephantis, the most copious encyclopaedia of pornography ever gathered together. In Capri he could do what he was unable to do at Rome – practise obscenities in the open air among the trees and flowers or down at the water's edge, and make as much noise as he liked. As some of his field-sports were extremely cruel, the sufferings of his playmates being a great part of his pleasure, he considered that the advantage of Capri's remoteness greatly outweighed the disadvantages. He did not live wholly there: he used to go for visits to Capua, Baiae, and Antium. But Capri was his headquarters.

After a while he gave Sejanus authority to remove the leaders of Agrippina's party by whatever means seemed most convenient. He was in daily touch with Sejanus and approved all his acts in letters to the Senate. One New Year's Festival he cele-

A.D. 28 brated at Capua by speaking the customary prayer of blessing, as High Pontiff, and then suddenly turning on a knight called Sabinus, who was standing near, and accusing him of trying to seduce the loyalty of his freedmen. One of Sejanus's men at once pulled Sabinus's gown up, muffled his head with it, and then threw a noose round his neck, and dragged him away. Sabinus called out in a choking voice: 'Help, friends, help!' But nobody stirred, and Sabinus, whose only crime was that he had been Germanicus's friend and had been tricked by a tool of Sejanus's into privately expressing sympathy for Agrippina, was summarily executed. A letter from Tiberius was read the next day in the Senate, reporting the death of Sabinus and mentioning Sejanus's discovery of a dangerous conspiracy. 'My Lords, pity an unhappy old man, living a life of constant apprehension, with members of his own family plotting wickedly against his life.' It was clear that Agrippina and Nero were meant by this. Gallus rose and moved that the Emperor should be desired to explain his fears to the Senate, and to allow them to be set at rest: as no doubt they could easily be. But Tiberius did not yet feel himself strong enough to revenge himself on Gallus.

In the summer of this year there was an accidental meeting between Livia in a sedan-chair and Tiberius on a cob in the main street of Naples. Tiberius had just landed from Capri and Livia was returning from a visit to Herculaneum. Tiberius wanted to ride past without a greeting but force of habit made him rein up and salute her with formal enquiries after her health. She said: 'I'm all the better for your kind enquiries, my boy. And as a mother my advice to you is: *be very careful of the barbel you eat on your island*. Some of the ones they catch there are highly poisonous.'

'Thank you, Mother,' he said. 'As the warning comes from you I shall in future stick religiously to tunny and mullet.'

Livia snorted and, turning to Caligula, who was with her, said in a loud voice: 'Well, as I was saying, my husband (your great-grandfather, my dear) and I came hurrying along this street one dark night sixty-five years ago, wasn't it, on our way to the docks where our ship was secretly waiting. We were expecting any moment to be arrested and killed by Augustus's men – how strange it seems! My elder boy – we had had only one child so far – was riding on his father's back. Then what should that little beast do but set up a terrific yowl: "Oh, father, I want to go back to Peru-u-u-sia." That gave the show away. Two soldiers came out of a tavern and called after us. We dodged into a dark doorway to let them pass. But Tiberius kept on yowling, "I want to go back to Peru-u-u-sia." I said, "Kill him! Kill the brat! It's our only hope." But my husband was a tender-hearted fool and refused. It was only by the merest chance we escaped.'

Tiberius, who had stopped to hear the end of the story, dug his spurs into his cob and clattered off in a fury. They never saw each other again.

Livia's warning about fish was only intended to make him

295

uncomfortable, to make him think that she had his fishermen or his cooks in her pay. She knew Tiberius's fondness for barbel, and that he would now have a constant conflict between his appetite and his fear of assassination. There was a painful sequel. One day Tiberius was sitting under a tree on a western slope of the island, enjoying the breeze and planning a verse-dialogue in Greek between the hare and the pheasant, in which each in turn claimed gastronomic pre-eminence. It was not an original idea: he had recently rewarded one of his court-poets with 2,000 gold pieces for a similar poem, in which the rivals were a mushroom, a titlark, an oyster, and a thrush. In his introduction to the present piece he brushed all these claims aside as trifling, saying that the hare and pheasant alone had the right to dispute the parsley-crown – their flesh alone had dignity without heaviness, delicacy without paltriness.

He was just searching for a discourteous adjective with which to qualify the oyster when he heard a sudden rustling from the thorn-bushes below him and a tousle-headed, wild-looking man appeared. His clothes were wet and torn to rags, his face bleeding, and an open knife was in his hand. He burst through the thicket, shouting: 'Here you are, Caesar; isn't it a beauty?' From the sack he was carrying over his shoulder he pulled out a monstrous barbel and threw it, still kicking, on the turf at Tiberius's feet. He was only a simple fisherman who had just made this remarkable catch and, seeing Tiberius at the cliff-top, had decided to present it to him. He had moored his boat to a rock, swum to the cliff, struggled up a precipice path to the belt of thorn-bushes, and hacked himself a path through them with his clasp-knife.

But Tiberius had been startled nearly out of his senses. He blew a whistle and shouted out in German: 'Help, help! Come at once! Wolfgang! Siegfried! Adelstan! An assassin! *Schnell!*'

'Coming, all-highest, noblest-born, gift-bestowing Chief,' the Germans instantly replied. They had been on sentry-duty to his left and right and behind him, but there was nobody posted in front, naturally. They came bounding along, brandishing their assegais.

The man did not understand German, and shutting his clasp-knife said cheerfully: 'I caught him by the grotto yonder. What do you guess he weighs? A regular whale, eh? Nearly pulled me out of the boat.'

Tiberius, somewhat reassured, but with his imagination now running on poisoned fish, shouted to the Germans: 'No, don't spear him. Cut that thing in two and rub the pieces in his face.'

Burly Wolfgang from behind clasped the fisherman around the middle so that he could not move his arms, while the other two scrubbed his face with raw fish. The unfortunate fellow called out: 'Hey, stop it! That's no joke! What luck that I didn't first offer the Emperor the other thing in my sack.'

'See what it is,' Tiberius ordered.

Edelstein opened the sack and found in it an enormous lobster. 'Rub his face with that,' said Tiberius. 'Rub it well in!'

The wretched man lost both his eyes. Then Tiberius said: 'That's enough, men. You may let him go!' The fisherman stumbled about screaming and raving with pain, and there was nothing to be done but toss him into the sea from the nearest crag.

I am glad to say that I was never invited to visit Tiberius on his island and have carefully avoided going there since, though all evidences of his vile practices have long ago been removed and his twelve villas are said to be very beautiful.

I had asked Livia's permission to marry Aelia and she had given it with malicious good wishes. She even attended the wedding. It was a very splendid wedding – Sejanus saw to that – and one effect of it was to alienate me from Agrippina and Nero and their friends. It was thought that I would not be able to keep any secrets from Aelia and that Aelia would tell Sejanus all that she found out. This saddened me a great deal, but I saw that it was useless trying to reassure Agrippina (who was now in mourning for her sister Julilla, who had just died after a twenty-years' exile in that wretched little island of Tremerus). So gradually I stopped visiting her house, to avoid embarrassment. I and Aelia were man and wife only in name. The first thing she said to me when we went into our bridal-chamber was: 'Now understand, Claudius, that I don't want you to touch me and that if we ever have to sleep to-gether again in one bed, like to-night, there'll be a coverlet between us, and the least movement you make – out you go. And another thing: you mind your own business, and I'll mind mine. ...'

I said: 'Thank you: you have taken a great load off my mind.'

She was a dreadful woman. She had the loud, persistent eloquence of an auctioneer in the slave-market. I soon gave up trying to answer her back. Of course I still lived at Capua, and Aelia never came to see me there, but Sejanus insisted that whenever I visited Rome I should be seen in her company as much as possible.

Nero had no chance against Sejanus and Livilla. Though Agrippina constantly warned him to weigh every word he spoke, he was of far too open a nature to conceal his thoughts. Among the young noblemen whom he trusted as his friends there were several secret agents of Sejanus, and these kept a register of the opinions he expressed on all public events. Worse still, his wife, whom we called Helen, or Heluo, was Livilla's daughter and reported all his confidences to her. But the worst of all was his own brother, Drusus, to whom he confided even more than to his wife, and who was jealous because Nero was the elder son, and Agrippina's favourite. Drusus went to Sejanus and said that Nero had asked him to sail secretly to Germany with him on the next dark night, where they would throw themselves on the protection of the regiments, as Germanicus's sons, and call for a march on Rome; that he had of course indignantly refused. Sejanus told him to wait a little longer and he would then be called on to tell the story to Tiberius: but the right moment had not yet come.

Meanwhile, Sejanus sent the rumour flying around that Tiberius was about to charge Nero with treason. Nero's friends began to desert him. As soon as two or three of them began excusing themselves from attending his dinners, and returning his greeting coldly when they met him in public, the rest followed their example. After a few months only his real friends remained. Among them was Gallus, who now that Tiberius himself did not visit the Senate any more, concentrated on teasing Sejanus. His method with Sejanus was constantly to propose votes of thanks for his services, and the granting of exceptional honours – statues and arches and titles and prayers and the public celebration of his birthday. The Senate did not dare to oppose these motions, and Sejanus, not being a senator, had no say in the matter; and Tiberius did not wish to go against the Senate by vetoing their vote for fear of antagonizing Sejanus or seeming to have lost confidence in him. Whenever the Senate now wanted anything done they would first send representatives to Sejanus asking for permission to apply to Tiberius about it: and if Sejanus discouraged them the matter would be dropped. Gallus one day proposed that, as the descendants of Torquatus had a golden torque and those of Cincinnatus

298

a curled lock of hair, granted by the Senate as family badges in commemoration of their ancestors' services to the State, so Sejanus and his descendants should be awarded as their badge a golden key, in token of his faithful services as the Emperor's doorkeeper. The Senate unanimously voted this motion and Sejanus, growing alarmed, wrote to Tiberius and complained that Gallus had maliciously proposed all the previous honours in the hope of making the Senate jealous of him, and even perhaps of making the Emperor suspect him of insolent ambitions. The present motion had been still more malicious – a suggestion to the Emperor that access to the Imperial presence was in the hands of someone who had made use of it for his own private enrichment. He begged that the Emperor would find a technical reason for vetoing the decree, and a way to silence Gallus. Tiberius answered that he could not veto the decree without damaging Sejanus's credit, but that he would very soon take steps to silence Gallus: Sejanus need not be anxious about the matter and his letter had shown true loyalty and a fine delicacy of judgement. But Gallus's hint had struck home. Tiberius suddenly realized that while all the goings and comings at Capri were known to Sejanus and could to a great extent be controlled by him, he himself only knew as much as Sejanus cared to tell him about the comings and goings by Sejanus's front door.

And now I have come to a turning-point in my story – the death of my grandmother Livia at the age of eighty-six. She might well have lived many years longer, for she kept her eyesight and hearing and the use of her limbs – not to mention her A.D. 29 mind and memory – unimpaired. But recently she had suffered from repeated colds owing to some infection of the nose, and at last one of these settled on her lungs. She summoned me to her bedside at the Palace. I happened to be in Rome and came immediately. I could see that she was dying. She reminded me of my oath again.

'I'll not rest until it's fulfilled, Grandmother,' I said. When a very old woman lies dying, one's grandmother too, one says whatever one can to please her. 'But I thought Caligula was going to arrange it for you?'

She did not answer for a time. Then she said, raging weakly:

'He was here ten minutes ago! He stood and laughed at me. He said that I could go to Hell and stew there for ever and ever

299

for all he cared. He said that now I was dying he had no need to keep in with me any longer, and that he did not consider himself bound by the oath, because it was forced on him. He said that *he* was going to be the Almighty God that has been prophesied, not I. He said ...'

'That's all right, Grandmother. You'll have the laugh of him in the end. When you're the Queen of Heaven and he's being slowly broken on an eternal wheel by Minos's men in Hell ...'

'And to think that I ever called you a fool,' she said. 'I'm going now, Claudius. Close my eyes and put the coin in my mouth that you'll find under the pillow. The Ferryman will recognize it. He'll pay proper respect. ...'

Then she died and I closed her eyes and put the coin in her mouth. It was a gold coin of a type I had never seen before, with Augustus's head and her own facing each other on the obverse, and a triumphant chariot on the reverse.

Nothing had been said between us about Tiberius. I soon heard that he had been warned about her condition in plenty of time to pay her the last offices. He now wrote to the Senate excusing himself for not having visited her but saying that he had been exceedingly busy and would at all events come to Rome for the funeral. Meanwhile the Senate had decreed various extraordinary honours in her memory, including the title Mother of the Country, and had even proposed to make her a demi-goddess. But Tiberius reversed nearly all these decrees, explaining in a letter that Livia was a singularly modest woman, averse to all public recognition of her services, and with a peculiar sentiment against having any religious worship paid to her after death. The letter ended with reflexions on the unsuitability of women's meddling in politics 'for which they are not fitted, and which rouse in them all those worst feelings of arrogance and petulance to which the female sex is naturally prone'.

He did not of course come to the City for the funeral, though, solely with the object of limiting its magnificence, he made all arrangements for it. And he took so long over them that the corpse, old and withered as it was, had reached an advanced stage of putrefaction before it was put on the pyre. To the general surprise, Caligula spoke the funeral oration, which Tiberius himself should have done, and if not Tiberius, then Nero, as his heir. The Senate had decreed an arch in Livia's memory – the first time in the history of Rome that a woman had been so honoured. Tiberius allowed this decree to stand but promised to build the arch at his own expense: and then neglected to build it. As for Livia's will, he inherited the greater part of her fortune as her natural heir, but she had left as much of it as she was legally permitted to members of her own household and other trusted dependants. He did not pay anybody a single one of her bequests. I was to have benefited to the extent of 20,000 gold pieces.

Chapter 27

I COULD never have thought it possible that I would miss Livia when she died. When I was a child I used secretly, night after night, to pray to the Infernal Gods to carry her off. And now I would have offered the richest sacrifices I could find – unblemished white bulls and desert antelopes and ibises and flamingoes by the dozen – to have had her back again. For it was clear that it had long been only the fear of his mother that had kept Tiberius within bounds. A few days after her death he struck at Agrippina and Nero. Agrippina had by now recovered from her illness. He did not charge them with treason. He wrote to the Senate complaining of Nero's gross sexual depravity, of Agrippina's 'haughty bearing and mischief-making tongue', and suggested that severe steps should be taken for keeping both of them in order.

When the letter was read in the Senate nobody said a word for a long time. Everyone was wondering on just how much popular support Germanicus's family could count now that Tiberius was preparing to victimize them; and whether it would not be safer to go against Tiberius than against the populace. At last a friend of Sejanus's rose to suggest that the Emperor's wishes should be respected and that some decree or other should be passed against the two persons mentioned. There was a senator who acted as official recorder of the Senate's transactions, and what he said carried great weight. He had hitherto voted without question whatever had been suggested in any letter of Tiberius's, and Sejanus had reported that he could always be counted upon to do what he was told. Yet it was this Recorder who rose to oppose the motion. He said that the question of Nero's morals and

Agrippina's bearing should not be raised at present. It was his opinion that the Emperor had been misinformed and had written hastily, and that in his own interest therefore, as well as that of Nero and Agrippina, no decree should be passed until he had been allowed time to reconsider such grave charges against his near relatives. The news of the letter had meanwhile spread all over the City, though all transactions in the Senate were supposed to be secret until officially published by the Emperor's orders, and huge crowds gathered around the Senate House, making demonstrations in favour of Agrippina and Nero, and crying out, 'Long live Tiberius! The letter is forged! Long live Tiberius! It's Sejanus's doing!'

Sejanus sent a messenger at great speed to Tiberius, who had moved for the occasion to a villa only a few miles outside the City, in case of trouble. He reported that the Senate had, on the motion of the Recorder, refused to pay any attention to the letter; that the people were on the point of revolt, calling Agrippina the true Mother of the Country and Nero their Saviour; and that unless Tiberius acted firmly and decisively there would be bloodshed before the day was out.

Tiberius was frightened, but he took Sejanus's advice and wrote a menacing letter to the Senate, putting the blame on the Recorder for this unparalleled insult to the Imperial dignity, and demanding that the whole affair should be left entirely to him to settle since they were so half-hearted in his interests. The Senate gave way. Tiberius, after having the Guards marched through the City with swords drawn and trumpets blowing, threatened to halve the free ration of corn if any further seditious demonstrations were made. He then banished Agrippina to Pandataria, the very island where her mother Julia had been first confined, and Nero to Ponza, another tiny rocky island, half-way between Capri and Rome but far out of sight of the coast. He told the Senate that the two prisoners had been on the point of escaping from the City in the hope of seducing the loyalty of the regiments on the Rhine.

Before Agrippina went to her island he had her before him and asked her mocking questions about how she proposed to govern the mighty kingdom which she had just inherited from her mother (his virtuous late wife), and whether she would send ambassadors to her son, Nero, in *his* new kingdom, and enter into a grand military alliance with him. She did not answer a word. He grew angry

302

and roared at her to answer, and when she still kept silent he told a captain of the guard to strike her over the shoulders. Then at last she spoke. 'Blood-soaked Mud is your name. That's what Theodorus the Gadarene called you, I'm told, when you attended his rhetoric classes at Rhodes.' Tiberius seized the vine branch from the captain and thrashed her about the body and head until she was insensible. She lost the sight of an eye as a result of this dreadful beating.

Soon Drusus too was accused of intriguing with the Rhine regiments. Sejanus produced letters in proof, which he said that he had intercepted, but which were really forged, and also the written testimony of Lepida, Drusus's wife (with whom he had a secret affair), that Drusus had asked her to get in touch with the sailors of Ostia, who, he hoped, would remember that Nero and he were Agrippa's grandsons. Drusus was handed over by the Senate to Tiberius to deal with and Tiberius had him confined in a remote attic of the Palace under Sejanus's supervision.

Gallus was the next victim. Tiberius wrote to the Senate that Gallus was jealous of Sejanus and had done all that he could to bring him into disfavour with his Emperor by ironical praises and other malicious methods. The Senate were so upset by the news of the suicide of the Recorder, which reached them the same day, that they immediately sent a magistrate to arrest Gallus. When the magistrate went to Gallus's house he was told that Gallus was out of the City, at Baiae. At Baiae he was directed to Tiberius's villa and, sure enough, he came on him there at dinner with Tiberius. Tiberius was pledging Gallus in a cup of wine and Gallus was responding loyally, and there seemed such an air of good humour and jollity in the dining-hall that the magistrate was embarrassed and did not know what to say. Tiberius asked him why he had come. 'To arrest one of your guests, Caesar, by order of the Senate.' 'Which guest?' asked Tiberius. 'Asinius Gallus,' replied the magistrate, 'but it seems to be a mistake.' Tiberius pretended to look grave: 'If the Senate have anything against you, Gallus, and have sent this officer to arrest you, I'm afraid our pleasant evening must come to an end. I can't go against the Senate, you know. But I'll tell you what I'll do, now that you and I have come to such a friendly understanding: I'll write to ask the Senate, as a personal favour, not to take any action in your case until they hear from me. That will mean that you will be under simple arrest, in the charge of the Consuls – no fetters or anything degrading. I'll arrange to secure your acquittal as soon as I can.'

Gallus felt bound to thank Tiberius for his magnanimity, but was sure that there was a catch somewhere, that Tiberius was paying back irony with irony; and he was right. He was taken to Rome and put in an underground room in the Senate House. He was not allowed to see anyone, not even a servant, or send any messages to his friends or family. Food was given him every day through a grille. The room was dark except for the poor light coming through the grille and unfurnished except for a mattress. He was told that these quarters were only temporary ones and that Tiberius would soon come to settle his case. But the days drew on into months, and months into years, and still he stayed there. The food was very poor – carefully calculated by Tiberius to keep him always hungry but never actually starving. He was allowed no knife to cut it up with, for fear he might use it to kill himself, or any other sharp weapon, or anything to distract himself with, such as writing materials or books or dice. He was given very little water to drink, none to wash in. If ever there was talk about him in Tiberius's presence the old man would say, grinning: 'I have not yet made my peace with Gallus.'

When I heard of Gallus's arrest I was sorry that I had just quarrelled with him. It was only a literary quarrel. He had written a silly book called: *A Comparison between my Father, Asinius Pollio, and his Friend Marcus Tullius Cicero, as Orators*. If the ground of the comparison had been moral character or political ability or even learning, Pollio would have easily come off the best. But Gallus was trying to make out that his father was the more polished orator. That was absurd, and I wrote a little book to say so; which, coming shortly after my criticism of Pollio's own remarks about Cicero, greatly annoyed Gallus. I would willingly have recalled my book from publication if by doing so I could have lightened Gallus's miserable prison life in the least degree. It was foolish of me, I suppose, to think in this way.

Sejanus was at last able to report to Tiberius that the power of the Leek Green Party was broken and that he need have no further anxieties. Tiberius rewarded him by saying that he had decided to marry him to his granddaughter Helen (whose marriage with Nero he had dissolved) and hinting at even greater favours. It was at this point that my mother, who, you must remember, was Livilla's mother too, interposed. Since Castor's death Livilla had been living with her, and was now careless enough to let her find out about a secret correspondence which she was carrying on with Sejanus. My mother had always been very economical, and in her old age her chief delight was saving candle-ends and melting them down into candles again, and selling the kitchen refuse to pig-keepers, and mixing charcoal-dust with some liquid or other and kneading it into cakes which, when dried, burned almost as well as charcoal. Livilla, on the other hand, was very extravagant and my mother was always scolding her for it. One day my mother happened to pass Livilla's room and saw a slave coming out of it with a basket of waste-paper. 'Where are you going, boy?' she asked.

'To the furnace, Mistress; the Lady Livilla's orders.'

My mother said: 'It's most *wasteful* to stoke the furnace wth perfectly good pieces of paper; do you know what paper costs? Why, three times as much as parchment, even. Some of those pieces seem hardly written on at all.'

'The Lady Livilla ordered most particularly ...'

'The Lady Livilla must have been very preoccupied when she ordered you to destroy valuable paper. Give me the basket. The clean parts will be useful for household lists, and all sorts of things. Waste not, want not.'

So she took the papers to her room and was about to clip the good pieces off one of them when it struck her that she might as well try to remove the ink from the whole thing. Until now she had honourably refrained from reading the writing; but when she began rubbing away at it, it was impossible to avoid doing so. She suddenly realized that these were rough drafts, or unsatisfactory beginnings, of a letter to Sejanus; and once she began reading she could not stop, and before she had done she knew the whole story. Livilla was clearly angry and jealous that Sejanus had consented to marry someone else – her own daughter too! But she was trying to conceal her feelings – each draft of the letter was toned down a little more. She wrote that he must act quickly before Tiberius suspected that he really had no intention of marrying Helen: and if he was not yet ready to assassinate Tiberius and usurp the monarchy had she not better poison Helen herself?

My mother sent for Pallas, who was working for me at the Library, looking up some historical point about the Etruscans, and told him to go to Sejanus and, in my name and as if sent by me, ask his permission to see Tiberius at Capri, in order to present him with my 'History of Carthage'. (I had just finished this work and sent a fair copy to my mother before having it published.) At Capri he was to beg the Emperor, in my name again, to accept the dedication of the work. Sejanus gave permission readily; he knew Pallas as one of our family slaves and suspected nothing. But in the twelfth volume of the history my mother had pasted Livilla's letters and a letter of her own in explanation, and told Pallas not to let anybody handle the volumes (which were all sealed up) but to give them to Tiberius with his own hands. He was to add to my supposed greetings and my request for permission to dedicate the book the following message: 'The Lady Antonia, too, sends her devoted greetings, but is of opinion that these books by her son are of no interest at all to the Emperor, except the twelfth volume which contains a very curious digression which will, she trusts, immediately interest him.'

Pallas stopped at Capua to tell me where he was going. He said that it was strictly against my mother's orders that he was telling me about his errand, but after that all I was his real master, not my mother, though she pretended to own him; and that he would do nothing willingly to get me into trouble; and that he was sure that I had no intention myself of offering the Emperor the dedication. I was mystified, at first, especially when he mentioned the twelfth volume, so while he was washing and changing his clothes I broke the seal. When I saw what had been inserted I was so frightened that for the moment I thought of burning the whole thing. But that was as dangerous as letting it go, so eventually I sealed it up again. My mother had used a duplicate seal of my own, which I had given her for business uses, so nobody would know that I had opened the book, not even Pallas. Pallas then hurried on to Capri and on his way back told me that Tiberius had picked up the twelfth volume and taken it out into the woods to look at. I might dedicate the book to him if I wished, he had said, but I must abstain from extravagant phrases in doing so. This re-assured me somewhat, but one could never trust Tiberius when he seemed friendly. Naturally I was in the deepest anxiety as to what would happen and felt very bitter against my mother for hav-ing put my life into such terrible danger by mixing me up in a quarrel between Tiberius and Sejanus. I thought of running away, but there was nowhere to run to.

The first thing that happened was that Helen became an invalid – we know now that there was nothing wrong with her, but Livilla had given her the choice of taking to her bed as if she were ill or of taking to her bed because she was ill. She was moved from Rome to Naples, where the climate was supposed to be healthier. Tiberius gave leave for the marriage to be postponed indefinitely, but addressed Sejanus as his son-in-law as if it had already taken place. He elevated him to senatorial rank and made him his colleague in the Consulship and a pontiff. But he then A.D. 31 did something else which quite cancelled these favours: he invited Caligula to Capri for a few days and then sent him back armed with a most important letter to the Senate. In the letter he said that he had examined the young man, who was now his heir, and found him of a very different temper and character from his brothers and would, indeed, refuse to believe any accusations that might be brought against his morals or loyalty. He now entrusted Caligula to the care of Aelius Sejanus, his fellow-Consul, begging him to guard the young man from all harm. He appointed him a pontiff too, and a priest to Augustus.

When the City heard about this letter there was great rejoicing. By making Sejanus responsible for Caligula's safety Tiberius was understood to be warning him that his feud with Germanicus's family had now been carried far enough. Sejanus's Consulship was regarded as a bad omen for him: this was Tiberius's fifth time in office and every one of his previous colleagues had died in unlucky circumstances: Varus, Gnaeus Piso, Germanicus, Castor. So new hopes arose that the nation's troubles would soon be over: a son of Germanicus would rule over them. Tiberius might perhaps kill Nero and Drusus but he had clearly decided to save Caligula: Sejanus would not be the next Emperor. Everyone whom Tiberius now sounded on the subject seemed so genuinely relieved at his choice of a successor – for somehow they had persuaded themselves that Caligula had inherited all his father's virtues – that Tiberius, who recognized real evil whenever he saw it and had told Caligula frankly that he knew he was a poisonous snake and had spared him for that very reason, was much amused, and thoroughly pleased. He could use Caligula's rising popularity as a check to Sejanus and Livilla.

He now took Caligula somewhat into his confidence and gave him a mission: to find out by intimate talks with Guardsmen which of their captains had the greatest personal influence in the Guards' camp, next to Sejanus; and then to make sure that he was equally bloody-minded and fearless. Caligula dressed up in a woman's wig and clothes and, picking up with a couple of young prostitutes, began frequenting the suburban taverns where the soldiers drank in the evening. With a heavily made up face and padded figure he passed for a woman, a tall and not very attractive one, but still, a woman. The account that he gave of himself in the taverns was that he was being kept by a rich shop-keeper who gave him plenty of money – on the strength of which he used to stand drinks all round. This generosity made him very popular. He soon came to know a great deal of camp gossip, and the name that was constantly coming up in conversation was that of a captain called Macro. Macro was the son of one of Tiberius's freedmen, and from all accounts was the toughest fellow in Rome. The soldiers all spoke admiringly of his drinking feats and his wenching and his domination of the other captains and his presence of mind in difficult situations. Even Sejanus was afraid of him, they said: Macro was the only man who ever stood up to him. So Caligula picked up with Macro one evening and secretly introduced himself: the two went off for a stroll together and had a long talk.

Tiberius then began writing a queer series of letters to the Senate, now saying that he was in a bad state of health and almost dying, and now that he had suddenly recovered and would arrive in Rome any moment. He wrote very queerly too about Sejanus, mixing extravagant praises with petulant rebukes; and the general impression conveyed was that he had become senile and was losing his senses. Sejanus was so puzzled by these letters that he could not make up his mind whether to attempt a revolution at once or to hold on to his position, which was still very strong, until Tiberius died or could be removed from power on the grounds of imbecility. He wanted to visit Capri and find out for himself just how things stood with Tiberius. He wrote asking permission to visit him on his birthday, but Tiberius answered that as Consul he should stay at Rome; it was irregular enough for himself to be permanently absent. Sejanus then wrote that Helen was seriously ill at Naples and had begged him to visit her: could he not be permitted to do so, just for a day? and from Naples it was only an hour's row to Capri. Tiberius answered that Helen had the best doctors and must be patient; and that he himself was really coming to Rome now and wanted Sejanus to be there to welcome him. At about the same time he quashed an indictment against an ex-Governor of Spain, whom Sejanus was accusing of extortion, on the grounds that the evidence was conflicting. He had never before failed to support Sejanus in a case of the sort. Sejanus began to be alarmed. The term of his Consulship expired.

On the day set by Tiberius for his arrival in Rome, Sejanus was waiting, at the head of a battalion of Guards, outside the temple of Apollo, where the Senate happened to be sitting because of repairs that were being done at the time to the Senate House. Suddenly Macro rode up and saluted him. Sejanus asked him why he had left the Camp. Macro replied that Tiberius had sent him a letter to deliver to the Senate.

'Why *you*?' Sejanus asked suspiciously.

'Why not?'

'But why not me?'

'Because the letter is about you!' Then Macro whispered in his ear, ' My heartiest congratulations, General. There's a surprise for you in the letter. You're to be made Protector of the People. That means you're to be our next Emperor.' Sejanus had not really expected Tiberius to appear, but he had been made very anxious by his recent silence. He now rushed, elated, into the Senate House.

Macro then called the Guards to attention. He said: 'Boys, the Emperor has just appointed me your General in Sejanus's place. Here's my commission. You are to go straight back to the Camp now, excused all guard duties. When you get there tell the other fellows that Macro's in charge now and that there's thirty gold pieces coming to every man who knows how to obey orders. Who's the senior captain? You? March the men off! But don't make too much row about it.'

So the Guards went off and Macro called on the Commander of the Watchmen, who had already been warned, to furnish a guard in their place. Then he went in after Sejanus, handed the letter to the Consuls and came out at once before a word had been read. He satisfied himself that the Watchmen were properly posted and then hurried after the returning Guards to make sure that no disturbance arose in the Camp.

Meanwhile the news of Sejanus's Protectorship had gone round the House and everyone began to cheer him and offer their congratulations. The senior Consul called for order and began reading

309

the letter. It began with Tiberius's usual excuses for not attending the meeting – pressure of work and ill-health – and went on to discuss general topics, then to complain slightly of Sejanus's hastiness in preparing the indictment of the ex-Governor without proper evidence. Here Sejanus smiled because this petulance of Tiberius had always hitherto been a prelude to the granting of some new honour. But the letter continued in the same strain of reproach, paragraph after paragraph, with gradually increasing severity, and the smile slowly left Sejanus's face. The senators who had been cheering him grew silent and perplexed, and one or two who were sitting near him made some excuse and walked across to the other side of the House. The letter ended by saying that Sejanus had been guilty of grave irregularities, that two of his friends, his uncle Junius Blaesus who had triumphed over Tacfarinas, and another, should, in his opinion, be punished and that Sejanus himself should be arrested. The Consul, who had been warned by Macro the night before what Tiberius wanted him to do, then called out 'Sejanus, come here!' Sejanus could not believe his ears. He was waiting for the end of the letter and his appointment to the Protectorship. The Consul had to call him twice before he understood. He said: 'Me? You mean me?'

As soon as his enemies realized that Sejanus had at last fallen they began loudly booing and hissing him; and his friends and relatives, anxious for their own safety, joined in. He suddenly found himself without a single supporter. The Consul asked the question, whether the Emperor's advice should be followed. 'Ay, ay!' the whole House shouted. The Commander of the Watchmen was summoned, and when Sejanus saw that his own Guards had disappeared and that Watchmen had taken their places, he knew that he was beaten. He was marched off to prison. and the populace, who had got wind of what was happening, crowded round him and shouted and groaned and pelted him with filth. He muffled his face with his gown, but they threatened to kill him if he did not show it; and when he obeyed they pelted him all the harder. The same afternoon the Senate, seeing that no Guards were about and that the crowd was threatening to break into the gaol to lynch Sejanus, decided to keep the credit for themselves and condemned him to death.

Caligula sent Tiberius the news at once by beacon signal. Tiberius had a fleet standing by prepared to take him to Egypt if his plans went astray. Sejanus was executed and his body thrown down the Weeping Stairs, where the rabble abused it for three whole days. When the time came for it to be dragged to the Tiber with a hook through the throat, the skull had been carried off to the Public Baths and used as a ball, and there was only half the trunk left. The streets of Rome were littered, too, with the broken limbs of his innumerable statues.

His children by Apicata were put to death by decree. There was a boy who had come of age, and a boy under age, and the girl who had been betrothed to my son Drusillus – she was now fourteen years old. The boy under age could not legally be executed, so, following a Civil War precedent, they made him put on his manly-gown for the occasion. The girl being a virgin was still more strongly protected by law. There was no precedent for executing a virgin whose only crime was being her father's daughter. When she was carried off to prison she did not understand what was happening and called out: 'Don't take me to prison! Whip me if you like and I won't do it again!' She apparently had some girlish naughtiness on her conscience. Macro gave orders that, to avoid the ill-luck that would befall the City if they executed her while still a virgin, the public executioner should outrage her. As soon as I heard of this, I said to myself: 'Rome, you are ruined; there can be no expiation for a crime so horrible,' and I called the Gods to witness that though a relative of the Emperor I had taken no part in the government of my country and that I detested the crime as much as they did, though powerless to avenge it.

When Apicata was told what had happened to her children and saw the crowd insulting their bodies on the Stairs she killed herself. But first she wrote a letter to Tiberius telling him that Castor had been poisoned by Livilla and that Livilla and Sejanus had intended to usurp the monarchy. She blamed Livilla for everything. My mother had not known about the murder of Castor. Tiberius now called my mother to Capri, thanked her for her great services, and showed her Apicata's letter. He told her that any reward within reason was hers for the asking. My mother said that the only reward that she would ask was that the family name should not be disgraced: that her daughter should not be executed and her body thrown down the Stairs. 'How is she to be punished, then?' Tiberius asked sharply. 'Give her to me,' said my mother. '*I* will punish her.'

So Livilla was not publicly proceeded against. My mother locked her up in the room next to her own and starved her to death. She could hear her despairing cries and curses, day after day, night after night, gradually weakening; but she kept her there, instead of in some cellar out of earshot, until she died. She did this not from a delight in torture, for it was inexpressibly painful to her, but as a punishment to herself for having brought up so abominable a daughter.

A whole crop of executions followed as a result of Sejanus's death – all his friends who had not been quick in making the change-over, and a great many of those who had. The ones who did not anticipate death by suicide were hurled from the Tarpeian cliff of the Capitoline Hill. Their estates were confiscated. Tiberius paid the accusers very little; he was becoming economical. On Caligula's advice he framed charges against those accusers who were entitled to benefit most heavily and so was able to confiscate their estates too. About sixty senators, 200 knights, and 1,000 or more of the commons died at this time. My alliance by marriage with Sejanus's family might easily have cost me my life, had I not been my mother's son. I was now allowed to divorce Aelia and to retain an eighth part of her dowry. As a matter of fact I returned it all to her. She must have thought me a fool. But I did this as some compensation for taking our little child Antonia away from her as soon as she was born. For Aelia had allowed herself to become pregnant by me as soon as she felt that Sejanus's position was becoming insecure. She thought that this would be some protection to her if he fell from power: Tiberius could hardly have her executed while she was with child to his nephew. I welcomed my divorce from Aelia, but would not have robbed her of the child if my mother had not insisted on it: my mother wanted Antonia for herself as something to mother of her very own – grandmother-hunger, as it is called.

The only member of Sejanus's family who escaped was his brother, and he escaped for the strange reason that he had publicly made fun of Tiberius's baldness. At the last annual festival in honour of Flora, at which he happened to be presiding, he employed only bald-headed men to perform the ceremonies, which were prolonged to the evening, and the spectators were lighted out of the theatre by 5,000 children with torches in their hands and their heads shaved. Tiberius was informed of this in Nerva's pre-

sence by a visiting senator and just to create a good impression on
Nerva he said, 'I forgive the fellow. If Julius Caesar did not resent
jokes about his baldness, how much less should I?' I suppose that
when Sejanus fell Tiberius decided, by the same kind of whim, to
renew his magnanimity.

But Helen was punished, merely for having pretended to be ill,
by being married to Blandus, a very vulgar fellow whose grandfather, a provincial knight, had come to Rome as a teacher of
rhetoric. This was considered very base behaviour on Tiberius's
part, because Helen was his granddaughter and he was dishonouring his own house by this alliance. It was said that one had not
to go far back in the Blandus line before one came to slaves.

Tiberius realized now that the Guards, to whom he paid a
bounty of fifty gold pieces each, not thirty, as Macro had promised, were his one certain defence against the people and the
Senate. He told Caligula: 'There's not a man in Rome who would
not gladly eat my flesh.' The Guards, to show their loyalty to
Tiberius, complained that they had been wronged by having the
Watchmen preferred to them as Sejanus's prison escort, and as a
protest marched out of Camp to plunder the suburbs. Macro let
them have a good night out, but when the Assembly-call was
blown at dawn the next day, the men who were not back within
two hours he flogged nearly to death.

After a time Tiberius declared an amnesty. Nobody could now
be tried for having been politically connected with Sejanus, and
if anyone cared to go into mourning for him, remembering his
noble deeds now that his evil ones had been fully punished, there would be no objection to this. A good many   A.D. 32
men did so, guessing that this was what Tiberius wanted,
but they guessed wrong. They were soon on trial for their lives,
faced with perfectly groundless charges, the commonest being incest. They were all executed. It may be wondered how it happened that there were any senators or knights left after all this
slaughter: but the answer is that Tiberius kept the Orders up to
strength by constant promotion. Free birth, a clean record, and so
many thousands of gold pieces, were the only qualifications for
admission into the Noble Order of Knights, and there were always plenty of candidates, though the initiation fee was heavy.
Tiberius was becoming more grasping than ever: he expected rich
men to leave him at least half their estates in their wills, and if they

313

were found not to have done so he declared the wills technically invalid because of some legal flaw or other, and took charge of the entire estate himself; the heirs getting nothing. He spent practically no money on public works, not even completing the Temple of Augustus, and stinted the corn-dole and the allowance for public entertainments. He paid the armies regularly, that was all. As for the provinces, he did nothing at all about them any more, so long as the taxes and tribute came in regularly; he did not even trouble to appoint new governors when the old ones died. A deputation of Spaniards once came to complain to him that they had been four years now without a governor and that the staff of the last one were pillaging the province shamefully. Tiberius said: 'You aren't asking for a new governor, are you? But a new governor would only bring a new staff, and then you'd be worse off than before. I'll tell you a story. There was once a badly wounded man lying on the battle-field waiting for the surgeon to dress his wound, which was covered with flies. A lightly wounded comrade saw the flies and was going to drive them away. "Oh, no," cried the wounded man, "don't do that! These flies are almost gorged with my blood now and aren't hurting me nearly so much as they did at first: if you drive them away their place will be taken at once by hungrier ones, and that will be the end of me." '

He allowed the Parthians to overrun Armenia, and the trans-Danube tribes to invade the Balkans, and the Germans to make raids across the Rhine into France. He confiscated the estates of a number of allied chiefs and petty kings in France, Spain, Syria, and Greece, using the most flimsy pretexts. He relieved Vononés of his treasure – you will recall that Vonones was the former king of Armenia, about whom my brother Germanicus had quarrelled with Gnaeus Piso – by sending agents to help him escape from the city in Cilicia where Germanicus had him put under guard and then having him pursued and killed.

The informers about this time began to accuse wealthy men of charging more than the legal interest on loans – one and a half per cent was all that they were allowed to charge. The statute about it had long fallen into abeyance and hardly a single senator was innocent of infringing it. But Tiberius upheld its validity. A deputation went to him and pleaded that everyone should be allowed a year and a half to adjust his private finances to conform with the letter of the law, and Tiberius as a great favour granted the re-

314

quest. The result was that all debts were at once called in, and this caused a great shortage of current coin. Tiberius's great idle hoards of gold and silver in the Treasury had been responsible for forcing up the rate of interest in the first place, and now there was a financial panic and land-values fell to nothing. Tiberius was eventually forced to relieve the situation by lending the bankers 1,000,000 gold pieces of public money, without interest, to pay out to borrowers in exchange for securities in land. He would not even have done this much but for Cocceius Nerva's advice. He still used occasionally to consult Nerva, who, living at Capri, where he was kept carefully away from the scene of Tiberius's debauches and allowed little news from Rome, was perhaps the only man in the world who still believed in Tiberius's goodness. To Nerva (Caligula told me some years later) Tiberius explained his painted favourites as poor orphans on whom he had taken pity, most of them a little queer in the head, which accounted for the funny way they dressed and behaved. But could Nerva really have been so simple as to have believed this, and so short-sighted?

Chapter 28

OF the last five years of Tiberius's reign the less told the better. I cannot bear to write in detail of Nero, slowly starved to death; or of Agrippina, who was cheered by news of Sejanus's fall, but when she saw that it made matters no better for her refused to eat, and was forcibly fed for awhile, and then at last left to die as she wished; or of Gallus, who died of a consumption; or of Drusus, who, removed some time before from his attic in the Palace to a dark cellar, was found dead with his mouth full of the flock from his mattress, which he had been gnawing in his starvation. But I must record at least that Tiberius wrote letters to the Senate rejoicing in the death of Agrippina and Nero – he accused her now of treason and of adultery with Gallus – and regretting, in the case of Gallus, that 'the press of public business had constantly postponed his trial so that he had died before his guilt could be proved'. As for Drusus, he wrote that this young man was the lewdest and most treacherous rascal he had ever encountered. He ordered a record to be publicly read, by the Guards' captain who had been in charge of him, of the treasonable remarks which Drusus had uttered while in prison. Never had such a painful document been read in the House before. It was clear from Drusus's remarks that he had been beaten and tortured and insulted by the captain himself, by common soldiers, and even by slaves, and that he had very cruelly been given every day less and less food and drink, crumb by crumb, and drop by drop. Tiberius even ordered the captain to read Drusus's dying curse. It was a wild but well-composed imprecation, accusing Tiberius of miserliness, treachery, obscene filthiness, and delight in torture, of murdering Germanicus and Postumus, and of a whole series of other crimes (most of which he had committed but none of which had ever been publicly mentioned before); he prayed the Gods that all the immeasurable suffering and distress that Tiberius had caused others should weigh upon him with increasing strength, waking or sleeping, night and day, for as long as he lived, should overwhelm him in the hour of his death, and should commit him to everlasting torture in the day of infernal Judgement. The senators interrupted the reading with exclamations of pretended horror at Drusus's treason, but these 'oh, oh's' and groans covered their amazement that Tiberius should voluntarily provide such a revelation of his own wickedness. Tiberius was very sorry for himself at the time (I heard afterwards from Caligula), tormented by insomnia and superstitious fears; and actually counted on the Senate's sympathy. He told Caligula with tears in his eyes that the killing of his relatives had been forced on him by their own ambition and by the policy that he had inherited from Augustus (he said Augustus, not Livia) of putting the tranquillity of the realm before private sentiment. Caligula, who had never shown the slightest signs of grief or anger at Tiberius's treatment of his mother or brothers, condoled with the old man; and then quickly began telling him of a new sort of vice that he had heard about recently from some Syrians. Such talk was the only way to cheer Tiberius up when he had attacks of remorse. Lepida, who had betrayed Drusus, did not long survive him. She was accused of adultery with a slave, and not being able to deny the charge (for she was found in bed with him), took her own life.

Caligula spent most of his time at Capri but occasionally went to Rome on Tiberius's behalf to keep an eye on Macro. Macro did all Sejanus's work now, and very efficiently, but was sensible enough to let the Senate know that he wanted no honours voted to him and that any senator who proposed any such would soon find himself on trial for his life on some charge of treason, incest, or forgery. Tiberius had indicated Caligula as his successor for several reasons. The first was that Caligula's popularity as Germanicus's son kept the people on their best behaviour for fear that any disturbance on their part would be punished by his death. The next was that Caligula was an excellent servant and one of the few people wicked enough to make Tiberius feel, by comparison, a virtuous man. The third was that he did not believe that Caligula would, as a matter of fact, ever become Emperor. For Thrasyllus, whom he still trusted absolutely (since no event had ever happened contrary to his predictions), had told him 'Caligula can no more become Emperor than he could gallop across yonder bay from Baiae to Puteoli'. Thrasyllus also said:

'Ten years from now Tiberius Caesar will still be Emperor.' This was true, as it turned out, but it was another Tiberius Caesar.

Tiberius knew a great deal, but some things Thrasyllus kept from him. He knew, for instance, the fate of his grandson Gemellus, who was not really his grandson because Castor was not the father, but Sejanus. He said to Caligula one day: 'I am making you my principal heir. I am making Gemellus my second heir in case you die before him, but this is only a formality. I know that you'll kill Gemellus; but then, others will kill you.' He said this expecting to outlive them both. Then he added, quoting from some Greek tragedian or other: 'When I am dead, let Fire the Earth confound.'

But Tiberius was not dead yet. The informers were still busy and every year more and more people were executed. There was hardly a senator left who had kept his seat since the days of Augustus. Macro had a far greater appetite for blood and far less compunction in shedding it than Sejanus. Sejanus was at any rate the son of a knight; Macro's father had been born a slave. Among the new victims was Plancina, who, now that Livia had died, had nobody to protect her. She was accused once more of poisoning Germanicus; for she was quite wealthy. Tiberius had not allowed her to be prosecuted until Agrippina was dead, because if Agrippina had heard the news it would have pleased her greatly. I was not sorry when I heard that Plancina's body had been thrown on the Stairs, though she had anticipated execution by suicide.

One day at dinner with Tiberius, Nerva asked Tiberius's pardon, explaining that he was not feeling hungry and wanted no food. Nerva had been in perfect health and spirits all this time and apparently quite contented with his sheltered life at Capri. Tiberius thought at first that Nerva had taken a purge the night before and was resting his stomach, but when he carried his fast through into the second and third day, Tiberius began to fear that he had decided to commit suicide by starvation. He sat down at Nerva's side and begged him to tell him why he was not eating. But all Nerva would do was apologize again and say that he was not hungry. Tiberius thought that perhaps Nerva was annoyed with him for not having taken his advice sooner about averting the financial crisis. He asked, 'Would you eat with a better appetite if I repealed all laws limiting the interest on loans to a figure which you consider too low?'

Nerva said: 'No, it isn't that. I'm just not hungry.'

The next day Tiberius said to Nerva: 'I have written to the Senate. Someone has told me that two or three men actually make a living by acting as professional informers against wrongdoers. It never occurred to me that by rewarding loyalty to the State I should encourage men to tempt their friends into crime and then betray them, but this seems to have happened in more than one instance. I am telling the Senate immediately to execute any person who can be proved to have made a living by such infamous conduct. Perhaps now you'll take something?'

When Nerva thanked him and praised his decision but said that he had still no appetite at all, Tiberius became most depressed. 'You'll die if you don't eat, Nerva, and then what will I do? You know how much I value your friendship and your political advice. Please, please eat, I beseech you. If you were to die the world would think that it was my doing, or at least that you were starving yourself out of hatred for me. Oh, don't die, Nerva! You're my only real friend left.'

Nerva said: 'It's no use asking me to eat, Caesar. My stomach would refuse anything I gave it. And surely nobody could possibly say such ill-natured things as you suggest? They know what a wise ruler and kind-hearted man you are and I am sure they have no reason for supposing me ungrateful, have they? If I must die, I must die, and that's all there is to it. Death is the common fate of all and at least I shall have the satisfaction of not out-living you.'

Tiberius was not to be convinced, but soon Nerva was too weak to answer his questions: he died on the ninth day.

Thrasyllus died. His death was announced by a lizard. It was a very small lizard and ran across the stone table where Thrasyllus was at breakfast with Tiberius in the sun and straddled across his forefinger. Thrasyllus asked, 'You have come to summon me, brother? I expected you at this very hour.' A.D. 36 Then, turning to Tiberius, he said: 'My life is at an end, Caesar, so farewell! I never told you a lie. You told me many. But beware when *your* lizard gives you a warning.' He closed his eyes and a few moments later was dead.

Now Tiberius had made a pet of the most extraordinary animal ever seen at Rome. Giraffes excited great admiration when first seen, and so did the rhinoceros, but this, though not so large, was far more fabulous. It came from an island beyond India called Java, and it was like a scaly lizard nine feet long with an ugly head and a long darting tongue. When Tiberius first looked at it he said that he would now no longer be sceptical about the monsters said to have been slain by Hercules and Theseus. It was called the Wingless Dragon and Tiberius fed it himself every day with cockroaches and dead mice and such-like vermin. It had a disgusting smell, dirty habits, and a vicious temper. The dragon and Tiberius understood each other perfectly. He thought that Thrasyllus meant the dragon would bite him one day, so he put it in a cage with bars too small for it to poke its ugly head through.

Tiberius was now seventy-eight years old, and constant use of myrrh and similar aphrodisiacs had made him very feeble; but he dressed sprucely and tried to behave like a man not yet past middle age. He had grown tired of Capri, now that Nerva and Thrasyllus were gone, and early in March the next year determined to defy Fate and visit Rome. He went there by easy stages, his last stopping place being a villa on the Appian A.D. 37 Road, within sight of the City walls. But the day after he arrived there the dragon gave him the prophesied warning. Tiberius went to feed it at noon and found it lying in the cage, dead, and a huge swarm of large black ants running all over it, trying to pull away bits of soft flesh. He took this as a sign that if he went any further towards the City he would die like the dragon and the crowd would tear his body to pieces. So he hurriedly turned back. He caught a chill by travelling in an east wind, which he made

319

worse by attending some Games exhibited by the soldiers of a garrison town through which he passed. A wild boar was released in the arena and he was asked to throw a javelin at it from his box. He threw one and missed, and was annoyed with himself for missing, and called for another. He had always prided himself on his skill with the javelin and did not want the soldiers to think that old age had beaten him. So he got hot and excited, hurling javelin after javelin, trying to hit the boar from an impossible distance, and finally had to stop from exhaustion. The boar was untouched and Tiberius ordered it to be released as a reward for its skill in avoiding his shots.

The chill settled on his liver, but he continued travelling back to Capri. He reached Misenum: it lies at the nearer end of the bay of Naples. The Western fleet has its headquarters here. Tiberius was annoyed to find the sea so rough that he could not cross. He had a splendid villa, however, on the promontory of Misenum – it had once belonged to the famous epicure Lucullus. He moved into it with his train. Caligula had accompanied him and so had Macro, and to show that there was nothing seriously amiss with him Tiberius gave a great banquet to all the local officials. The feasting had gone on for some time when Tiberius's private physician asked permission to leave the table and attend to some medical business: certain herbs, you know, have greater virtue when they are picked at midnight or when the moon is in such and such a position, and Tiberius was accustomed to the physician's rising during the meal to see to things of this sort. He took up Tiberius's hand to kiss it, but held it rather longer than necessary. Tiberius thought, quite rightly, that the physician was feeling his pulse to see how weak he was, so he made him sit down again as a punishment and kept the banquet going all night, just to prove that he wasn't ill. The next day Tiberius was in a state of prostration, and the word went round Misenum, and spread from there to Rome, that he was about to die.

Now, Tiberius had told Macro that he wished evidence of treason found against certain leading senators whom he disliked and had given him orders to secure their conviction by whatever means he pleased. Macro wrote them all down as accomplices in a charge that he was preparing against a woman he had a grudge against, the wife of a former agent of Sejanus: she had repelled his advances. They were all accused of adultery with her and of taking

Tiberius's name in vain. By browbeating freedmen and torturing slaves Macro got the evidence that was needed – freedmen and slaves had by now all lost the tradition of fidelity towards their masters. The trial began. But the friends of the accused noticed that though Macro himself had conducted the examination of witnesses and the torture of slaves, the usual Imperial letter approving his actions was not laid on the table: so they concluded that perhaps Macro had added one or two private enemies of his own to the list given him by Tiberius. The chief victim of these obviously absurd charges was Arruntius, the oldest and most dignified member of the Senate. Augustus, a year before his death, had said that he was the only possible choice for Emperor, failing Tiberius; Tiberius had already once tried to convict him of treason, but unsuccessfully. Old Arruntius was the only remaining link with the Augustan age. On the previous occasion sentiment had been so strong against his accusers, though it was believed that they were acting on Tiberius's instigation, that they were themselves tried, convicted of perjury, and put to death. It was known now that Macro had recently had a dispute with Arruntius about money, so the trial was adjourned until Tiberius should have confirmed Macro's commission. Tiberius neglected to reply to the Senate's enquiry, so Arruntius and the rest had been in prison for some time. At last Tiberius sent the necessary confirmation, and the day for the new trial was fixed. Arruntius had determined to kill himself before the trial came off so that his estate should not be confiscated and his grandchildren pauperized. He was saying goodbye to a few old friends when the news arrived of Tiberius's severe illness. His friends begged him to postpone suicide until the last moment, because if the news was true he had a very good chance of surviving Tiberius and being pardoned by his successor. Arruntius said: 'No, I have lived too long. My life was difficult enough in the days when Tiberius shared his power with Livia. It was wellnigh intolerable when he shared it with Sejanus. But Macro has shown himself more of a villain even than Sejanus and, mark my words, Caligula with his Capri education will make a worse Emperor even than Tiberius. I cannot in my old age become the slave of a new master like him.' He took a penknife and severed an artery of his wrist. Everyone was greatly shocked, for Caligula was a popular hero, and was expected to be a second and better Augustus. Nobody thought of blaming him for his pretended loyalty to Tiberius: he was on the contrary greatly admired for his cleverness in surviving his brothers and for concealing so well what were supposed to be his real feelings.

Meanwhile, Tiberius's pulse nearly stopped and he lapsed into a coma. The physician told Macro that two days more, at the outside, were all that he had to live. So the whole Court was in a great bustle. Macro and Caligula were in perfect accord. Caligula respected Macro's popularity with the Guards, and Macro respected Caligula's popularity with the nation as a whole: each counted on the other's support. Besides, Macro was indebted to Caligula for his rise to power, and Caligula was carrying on an affair with Macro's wife, which Macro had been good enough to overlook. Tiberius had already commented sourly on Macro's cultivation of Caligula, saying, 'You do well to desert the setting for the rising sun.' Macro and Caligula began sending off messages to the commanders of different regiments and armies to tell them that the Emperor was sinking fast and had appointed Caligula as his successor: he had given him his signet ring. It was true that Tiberius in a lucid interval had called for Caligula and drawn the ring off his finger. But he had changed his mind and put the ring back on again and then clasped his hands tightly together as if to prevent anyone from robbing him of it. When he relapsed into unconsciousness and gave no further signs of life Caligula had quietly pulled the ring off and was now strutting about, flashing it in the faces of everyone he met and accepting congratulations and homage.

But Tiberius was not dead yet even now. He groaned, stirred, sat up, and called for his valets. He was weak because of his long fast, but otherwise quite himself. It was a trick that he had played before, to seem dead and then to come to life again. He called once more. Nobody heard him. The valets were all in the buttery, drinking Caligula's health. But soon an enterprising slave happened to come along to see what he could steal from the death-chamber in their absence. The room was dark and Tiberius frightened him nearly out of his senses by suddenly shouting: 'Where in Hell's name are the valets? Didn't they hear me call? I want bread and cheese, an omelette, a couple of beef-cutlets, and a drink of Chian wine *at once*! And a thousand Furies! Who's stolen my ring?' The slave dashed out of the room and nearly ran into Macro, who was passing. 'The Emperor's alive, sir, and calling for food and his ring.' The news ran through the Palace and a ludicrous scene followed. The crowd around Caligula scattered in all directions. Cries went up. 'Thank God, the news was false. Long live Tiberius!' Caligula was in a miserable state of shame and terror. He pulled the ring off his finger and looked around for somewhere to hide it.

Only Macro kept his head. 'It's a nonsensical lie,' he shouted. 'The slave must have lost his wits. Have him crucified, Caesar! We left the old Emperor dead an hour ago.' He whispered something to Caligula, who was seen to nod in grateful relief. Then he hurried into Tiberius's room. Tiberius was on his feet, cursing and groaning and tottering feebly towards the door. Macro picked him up in his arms, threw him back on the bed, and smothered him with a pillow. Caligula was standing by.

So Arruntius's fellow-prisoners were released, though most of them later wished that they had followed Arruntius's example. There were, besides, about fifty men and women who had been accused of treason in a separate batch from this. They had no influence in the Senate, being mostly shopkeepers who had baulked at paying the 'protection money' that Macro's captains now levied on all the City wards. They were tried and condemned and were to be executed on the 16th of March. This was the very day that news came of Tiberius's death, and they and their friends went nearly mad with joy to think that now they would be saved. But Caligula was away at Misenum and could not be appealed to in time, and the prison governor was afraid of losing his job if he took the responsibility of postponing the executions. So they were killed and their bodies thrown on the Stairs in the usual way.

This was the signal for an outburst of popular anger against Tiberius. 'He stings like a dead wasp,' someone shouted. Crowds gathered at the street corners for solemn commination-services under the ward-masters, beseeching Mother Earth and the Judges of the Dead to grant the corpse and the ghost of that monster no rest or peace until the day of universal dissolution. Tiberius's body was brought to Rome under a strong escort of Guards. Caligula walked in the procession as a mourner and the whole countryside came flocking to meet him, not in mourning for Tiberius but in holiday clothes, weeping with gratitude that Heaven had preserved a son of Germanicus to rule over them. Old country women cried out, 'O sweet darling, Caligula! Our chicken! Our baby! Our star!' A few miles from Rome he rode ahead to make preparations for the solemn entry of the corpse into the City. But when he had passed, a big crowd gathered and barricaded the Appian Road with planks and blocks of building-stone. When the outriders of the escort appeared there was booing and groaning and cries of 'Into the Tiber with Tiberius!' 'Throw him down the Stairs!' 'Eternal damnation to Tiberius!' The leader shouted: 'Soldiers, we Romans won't allow that evil corpse into the City. It will bring us bad luck. Take it back to Atella and half-burn it in the amphitheatre there!' Half-burning, I should explain, was the usual fate of paupers and unfortunates, and Atella was a town celebrated for a kind of rough country masque or farce which had been performed there at the harvest festival every year from the very earliest times. Tiberius had a villa at Atella and used to attend the festival nearly every year. He had converted the innocent rural bawdry of the masque into a sophisticated vileness. He made the men of Atella build an amphitheatre to present the revised show, which was produced by himself.

Macro ordered his men to charge the barricade, and a number of citizens were killed and wounded, and three or four soldiers were knocked unconscious with paving-stones. Caligula prevented further disorders and Tiberius's body was duly burned on Mars Field. Caligula spoke the funeral oration. It was a very formal and ironical one and much appreciated because there was a good deal in it about Augustus and Germanicus, but very little about Tiberius.

At a banquet that night Caligula told a story which made the whole company weep and gained him great credit. He said that early one morning at Misenum, being as usual sleepless with grief for the fate of his mother and brothers, he had determined, come what might, to be avenged at last on their murderer. He seized the dagger that had been his father's and went boldly into Tiberius's room. The Emperor lay groaning and tossing in nightmare on his bed. Caligula slowly lifted the dagger to strike but a Divine Voice sounded in his ears: 'Great-grandson, hold your hand! To kill him would be impious.' Caligula answered, 'O God Augustus, he killed my mother and my brothers, your descendants. Should I not avenge them even at the price of being shunned by all men as a parricide?' Augustus answered, 'Magnanimous son, who art to be Emperor hereafter, there is no need to do what you would do.

By My orders the Furies nightly avenge your dear ones, while he
dreams.' And so he had laid his dagger on the table beside the bed
and walked out. Caligula did not explain what had happened next
morning when Tiberius woke and saw the dagger on the table;
the presumption was that Tiberius had not dared to mention the
incident.

Chapter 29

CALIGULA was twenty-five years old when he became Emperor.
Seldom, if ever, in the history of the world has a prince been more
enthusiastically acclaimed on his accession or had an easier task
offered him of gratifying the modest wishes of his people, which
were only for peace and security. With a bulging treasury, well-
trained armies, an excellent administrative system that needed
only a little care to get it into perfect order again – for in spite of
Tiberius's neglect the Empire was still running along fairly well
under the impetus given it by Livia – with all these advantages,
added to the legacy of love and confidence he enjoyed as Germanicus's son, and the immense relief felt by Tiberius's removal,
what a splendid chance he had of being remembered in history as
'Caligula the Good', or 'Caligula the Wise', or 'Caligula the
Saviour!' But it is idle to write in this way. For if he had been the
sort of man that the people took him for, he would never have
survived his brothers or been chosen by Tiberius as his successor.
Claudius, remember what scorn old Athenodorus had for such
impossible contingencies: he used to say, 'If the Wooden Horse of
Troy had foaled, horses to-day would cost far less to feed.'

It amused Caligula at first to encourage the absurd misconcep-
tion that everyone but myself and my mother and Macro and one
or two others had of his character, and even to perform a number
of acts in keeping with it. He wanted also to make sure of his position. There were two obstacles to his complete freedom of action.
One was Macro, whose power made him dangerous. The other
was Gemellus. For when Tiberius's will was read (which for
secrecy's sake he had had witnessed by a few freedmen and illiter-
ate fishermen) it was found that the old man, just to make trouble,
had not appointed Caligula his first heir, with Gemellus as a

second choice in case of accidents: he had made them joint-heirs, to rule alternate years. However, Gemellus had not come of age and so was not even allowed yet to enter the Senate, while Caligula was already a magistrate of the second rank, some years before the legal age, and a pontiff. The Senate was therefore very ready to accept Caligula's view that Tiberius had not been of sound mind when he made the will and to give the whole power to Caligula without encumbrance. Except for this matter of Gemellus, from whom he also withheld his share in the Privy Purse, on the ground that the Privy Purse was an integral part of the sovereignty, Caligula observed all the terms of the will and paid every legacy promptly.

The Guards were to receive a bounty of fifty gold pieces a man; Caligula, to ensure their loyalty when the time came for Macro's removal, doubled the amount. He paid the people of Rome the 450,000 gold pieces bequeathed them and added three gold pieces a head; he said that he had intended to give them this when he came of age, but the old Emperor had forbidden it. The armies were awarded the same bounty as under Augustus's will, but this time it was paid promptly. What was more, he paid all the sums owing under Livia's will, which we legatees had long ago written off as bad debts. To me the two most interesting items in Tiberius's will were: the specific bequest to me of the historical books which Pollio had left me but which I had been cheated of, together with a number of other valuable volumes, and the sum of 20,000 gold pieces; and a bequest to the Chief Vestal, the granddaughter of Vipsania, of 100,000 gold pieces to be spent as she pleased, either on herself or on the College. The Chief Vestal, as the granddaughter of the murdered Gallus, melted the coin down and made it into a great golden casket for his ashes.

With these bequests from Livia and Tiberius I was now quite well off. Caligula astonished me by further paying me back the 50,000 that I had found for Germanicus at the time of the mutiny: he had heard the story from his mother. He did not allow me to refuse it and said that if I made any further protest he would insist on paying me the accumulated interest too: it was a debt he owed his father's memory. When I told Calpurnia about my new wealth she seemed more sorry than pleased. 'It won't bring you any luck,' she said. 'Much better be modestly well off, as you have been, than run the risk of having your whole fortune stripped from you by informers on a charge of treason.' Calpurnia was Actë's successor, you remember. She was very shrewd for her years – seventeen.

I said, 'What do you mean, Calpurnia? Informers? There are no such things in Rome now, and no treason-trials.'

She said: 'I didn't hear that the informers were packed off in the same boat with the Spintrians.' (For Tiberius's painted 'orphans' had been banished by Caligula. As a public gesture of pure-mindedness he had sent the whole crew of them off to Sardinia, a most unhealthy island, and told them to labour honestly for their living as road-makers. Some of them just lay down and died when picks and shovels were put into their hands, but the rest were whipped into work, even the daintiest of them. Soon they had a stroke of luck. A pirate vessel made a sudden raid, captured them, and carried them off to Tyre, where they were sold as slaves to rich Eastern profligates.)

'But they wouldn't dare to try their old tricks again, Calpurnia?'

She put down her embroidery. 'Claudius, I'm no politician or scholar, but I can at least use my prostitute's wit and do simple sums. How much money did the old Emperor leave?'

'About twenty-seven million gold pieces. That's a lot of money.'

'And how much has the new one paid out in legacies and bounties?'

'About three million and a half. Yes, at least that amount.'

'And since he has been Emperor how many panthers and bears and lions and tigers and wild bulls and things has he imported for the huntsmen to kill in the amphitheatres and the Circus?'

'About twenty thousand, perhaps. Probably more.'

'And how many other animals have been sacrificed in the temples?'

'I don't know. I should guess between one and two hundred thousand.'

'Those flamingoes and desert antelopes and zebras and British beavers must have cost him something! So what with buying all those animals and paying the huntsmen in the amphitheatres, and then the sword-fighters, of course – sword-fighters get four times what they got under Augustus, I'm told – and all the State banquets and decorated cars and the theatre shows – they say that

327

when he recalled the actors whom the old Emperor banished he paid them for all the years they were out of work – handsome, eh? – and my goodness, the money he has spent on racehorses! Well, what with one thing and the other he can't have much change left out of twenty million, can he?'

'I think you're right there, Calpurnia.'

'Well, seven million in three months! How is the money going to last at that rate, even if all the rich men who die leave him all their money? The Imperial revenue is less now than it used to be when your old grandmother ran the business and went over the accounts.'

'Perhaps he'll be more economical after the first excitement of having money to spend. He's got a good excuse for spending: he says that the stagnation of money in the Treasury under Tiberius had a most disastrous effect on trade. He wants to put a few million into circulation again.'

'Well, you're better acquainted with him than I am. Perhaps he'll know just when to stop. But if he goes on at this rate he won't have a penny left in a couple of years, and then who's going to pay? That's why I spoke of informers and treason-trials.'

I said: 'Calpurnia. I'm going to buy you a pearl necklace while I still have the money. You're as clever as you are beautiful. And I only hope you are as discreet.'

'I'd prefer cash,' she said, 'if you don't mind.' And I gave her 500 gold pieces the next day. Calpurnia, a prostitute and the daughter of a prostitute, was more intelligent and loyal and kind-hearted and straightforward than any of the four noblewomen I have married. I soon began to take her into my confidence about my private affairs and I may say at once that I never regretted having done so.

The moment that Tiberius's funeral was over, Caligula had taken ship, in spite of very bad weather, to the islands where his mother and his brother Nero had been buried; he gathered up their remains, half-burned, and brought them back, burned them properly, and piously interred them in Augustus's tomb. He instituted a new annual festival, with sword-fighting and horse races, in his mother's memory and annual sacrifices to her ghost and that of his brothers. He called the month of September 'Germanicus', as the previous month had been called after Augustus. He also heaped on my mother by a single decree as many honours as

328

Livia had been given in her lifetime, and appointed her High-Priestess of Augustus.

He next pronounced a general amnesty, recalling all banished men and women and releasing all political prisoners. He even brought together a large batch of criminal records covering the cases of his mother and brothers and publicly burned them in the Market Place, swearing that he had not read them and that anyone who had acted as informer or contributed in any other way to the deplorable fate of his loved ones need have no fear: all record of those evil days was destroyed. As a matter of fact what he burned were only copies: he kept the originals. He followed Augustus's example by making a strict scrutiny of the Orders and rejecting all unworthy members of either, and Tiberius's example in refusing all titles of honour except those of Emperor and Protector of the People and in forbidding statues of himself to be set up. I wondered how long this mood of his would last, and how long he would keep by the promise he had made to the Senate on the occasion that they had voted him the Imperial power, to share it with them and be their faithful servant.

After six months of his monarchy, in September, the Consuls in office finished their term and he undertook a Consulship for himself for a while. Whom do you suppose he chose as a colleague? He actually chose me! And I who had twenty-three years before begged Tiberius to be given real honours, not empty ones, would now willingly have resigned my appointment in anyone's favour. It was not that I wanted to go back to my writing (for I had just completed and revised my Etruscan history and had begun on no new work), but that I had quite forgotten all the rules of procedure and legal formulas and precedents that I had once studied so painfully, and that I felt thoroughly ill at ease in the Senate. From being so little at Rome, too, I knew nothing about how to pull strings and get things done quickly, or who were the men with real power. I got into great trouble with Caligula almost at once. He entrusted me with the task of having statues made of Nero and Drusus, to be set up and consecrated in the Market Place, and the Greek firm from whom I commissioned them promised faithfully to have them ready on the day fixed for the ceremony early in December. Three days before I went along to see how the statues looked. The rogues hadn't begun on them. They made some excuse about the right coloured marble having only just come in. I flew into a temper (as I often do on occasions of this sort, but my anger doesn't last long) and told them that if they didn't get workmen busy on the blocks and keep them at the job night and day I would have the whole firm – owner, managers, and men – thrown out of the City. Perhaps I made them nervous, because though Nero was done on the afternoon before the ceremony – it was a good likeness too – a careless sculptor somehow broke Drusus's hand off at the wrist. There are ways of repairing a break of this sort, but the join always shows, and I couldn't present Caligula with a botched piece of work on so important an occasion. All that I could do was to go at once and tell him that Drusus wouldn't be ready. Heavens, how angry he was! He threatened to degrade me from my Consulship and wouldn't listen to any explanation. Fortunately he had decided to resign his own Consulship the next day, and ask me to resign mine, in favour of the men who had originally been chosen for it; so nothing came of his threat and I was even chosen again as Consul with him for four years ahead.

I was expected to occupy a suite of rooms at the Palace and because of Caligula's stern speeches against all sorts of immorality (in the manner of Augustus) I could not have Calpurnia there with me, though I was unmarried. She had to remain at Capua, much to my annoyance, and I was only able to get away occasionally to visit her. His own morals seemed not to come into the scope of his strictures. He was growing tired of Macro's wife, Ennia, whom Macro had divorced at his request and whom he had promised to marry, and used to go out at night in search of gallant adventures with a party of jolly fellows whom he called 'The Scouts'. They consisted usually of three young staff-officers, two famous sword-fighters, Apelles the actor, and Eutychus, the best charioteer in Rome, who won nearly every race in which he competed. Caligula had now come out strong as a partisan of the Leek Greens and sent all over the world in search of the fastest horses. He found a religious excuse for public chariot-racing, with twenty heats a day, almost whenever the sun shone. He made a lot of money by challenging rich men to take his bets against the other colours, which for politeness they did. But what he got by this was a mere drop, as the saying is, in the ocean of his expenses. At all events with these jolly 'Scouts' he used to go out at night, disguised, and visit the lowest haunts of the City, usually coming into conflict with the night-watchmen and having riotous escapades which the Commander of the Watchmen was careful to hush up.

Caligula's three sisters, Drusilla, Agrippinilla, and Lesbia, had all been married to noblemen; but he insisted on their coming to the Palace and living there. Agrippinilla and Lesbia were told to bring their husbands with them, but Drusilla had to leave hers behind; his name was Cassius Longinus and he was sent to govern Asia Minor. Caligula demanded that the three of them should be treated with the greatest respect and gave them all the privileges enjoyed by the Vestal Virgins. He had their names joined with his own in the public prayers for his health and safety, and even in the public oath that officials and priests swore in his name on their consecration ... 'neither shall I value my own life or the lives of my children more highly than His life and the lives of His sisters'. He behaved towards them in a way that puzzled people – rather as if they were his wives than his sisters.

Drusilla was his favourite. Although she was well rid of her husband, she always seemed unhappy now, and the unhappier she grew the more solicitous were Caligula's attentions. He now married her, for appearances only, to a cousin of his, Aemilius Lepidus, whom I have already mentioned as a slack-twisted younger brother of that Aemilia, Julilla's daughter, to whom I was nearly married when I was a boy. This Aemilius Lepidus, who was known as Ganymede because of his effeminate appearance and his obsequiousness to Caligula, was a valued member of the Scouts. He was seven years older than Caligula but Caligula treated him like a boy of thirteen, and he seemed to like it. Drusilla could not bear him. But Agrippinilla and Lesbia were always in and out of his bedroom laughing and joking and playing pranks. Their husbands did not seem to mind. Life at the Palace I found extremely disorderly. I don't mean that I wasn't made very comfortable or that the servants were not well trained or that the ordinary formalities and courtesies were not observed towards visitors. But I never quite knew what tender relations existed between this person and that: Agrippinilla and Lesbia seemed to have exchanged husbands at one time, and at another Apelles seemed somehow intimately connected with Lesbia and the charioteer with Agrippinilla. As for Caligula and Ganymede – but I have said enough to show what I mean by 'disorderly'. I was the only one among them past middle-age, and did not understand the ways of the new generation at all. Gemellus also lived in the Palace: he was a frightened, delicate boy who bit his nails to the quick and was usually to be found sitting in a corner and drawing designs of nymphs and satyrs and that sort of thing for vases. I can't tell you much more about Gemellus than that I got into talk with him once or twice, feeling sorry for him because he was not really one of the party, any more than I was; but perhaps he thought that I was trying to draw him out and force him into saying something against Caligula, for he would only answer in monosyllables. On the day that he put on his manly-gown Caligula adopted him as his son and heir, and appointed him Leader of Cadets; but that wasn't the same thing by any means as sharing the monarchy with him.

Caligula fell ill and for a whole month his life was despaired of. The doctors called it brain-fever. The popular consternation at Rome was so great that a crowd of never less than 10,000 people stood day and night around the Palace, waiting A.D. 38 for a favourable bulletin. They kept up a quiet muttering and whispering together; the noise, as it reached my window, was like that of a distant stream running over pebbles. There were a number of most remarkable manifestations of anxiety. Some men even pasted up placards on their house-doors, to say that if Death held his hand and spared the Emperor, they vowed to give him their own lives in compensation. By universal consent all traffic noises and street cries and music ceased within half a mile or more of the Palace. That had never happened before, even during Augustus's illness, the one of which Musa was supposed to have cured him. The bulletin always read: 'No change'.

One evening Drusilla knocked at my door and said, 'Uncle Claudius! The Emperor wants to see you urgently. Come at once. Don't stop for anything.'

'What does he want me for?'

'I don't know. But for Heaven's sake humour him. He's got a sword there. He'll kill you if you don't say what he wants you to say. He had the point at my throat this morning. He told me that I didn't love him. I had to swear and swear that I did love him. "Kill me, if you like, my darling," I said. O Uncle Claudius, why was I ever born? He's mad. He always was. But he's worse than mad now. He's possessed.'

332

I went along to Caligula's bedroom, which was heavily curtained and thickly carpeted. One feeble oil-lamp was burning by the bedside. The air smelt stale. His querulous voice greeted me. 'Late again? I told you to hurry.' He didn't look ill, only unhealthy. Two powerful deaf-mutes with axes stood as guards, one on each side of his bed.

I said, saluting him, 'Oh, how I hurried! If I hadn't had a lame leg I'd have been here almost before I started. What joy to see you alive and to hear your voice again, Caesar! Can I dare to hope that you're better?'

'I have never really been ill. Only resting. And undergoing a metamorphosis. It's the most important religious event in history. No wonder the City keeps so quiet.'

I felt that he expected me to be sympathetic, nevertheless. 'Has the metamorphosis been painful, Emperor? I trust not.'

'As painful as if I were my own mother. I had a very difficult delivery. Mercifully, I have forgotten all about it. Or nearly all. For I was a very precocious child and distinctly remember the midwives' faces of admiration as they washed me after my emergence into this world, and the taste of the wine they put between my lips to refresh me after my struggles.'

'An astounding memory, Emperor. But may I humbly enquire precisely what is the character of this glorious change that has come over you?'

'Isn't it immediately apparent?' he asked angrily.

Drusilla's word 'possessed' and the conversation I had had with my grandmother Livia as she lay dying gave me the clue. I fell on my face and adored him as a God.

After a minute or two I asked from the floor whether I was the first man privileged to worship him. He said that I was and I burst out into gratitude. He was thoughtfully prodding me with the point of his sword in the back of my neck. I thought I was done for.

He said: 'I admit I am still in mortal disguise, so it is not remarkable that you did not notice my Divinity at once.'

'I don't know how I could have been so blind. Your face shines in this dim light like a lamp.'

'Does it?' he asked with interest. 'Get up and give me that mirror.'

I handed him a polished steel mirror and he agreed that it shone

333

very brightly. In this fit of good humour he began to tell me a good deal about himself.

'I always knew that it would happen,' he said. 'I never felt anything but divine. Think of it. At two years old I put down a mutiny of my father's army and so saved Rome. That was prodigious, like the stories told about the God Mercury when a child, or about Hercules, who strangled the snakes in his cradle.'

'And Mercury only stole a few oxen,' I said, 'and twanged a note or two on the lyre. That was nothing by comparison.'

'And what's more, by the age of eight I had killed my father. Jove himself never did that. He merely banished the old fellow.'

I took this as raving on the same level, but I asked in a matter-of-fact voice, 'Why did you do that?'

'He stood in my way. He tried to discipline me – me, a young God, imagine it! So I frightened him to death. I smuggled dead things into our house at Antioch and hid them under loose tiles; and I scrawled charms on the walls; and I got a cock in my bedroom to give him his marching orders. And I robbed him of his Hecate. Look, here she is! I always keep her under my pillow.' He held up the green jasper charm.

My heart went as cold as ice when I recognized it. I said in a horrified voice: '*You* were the one, then? And it was you who climbed into the bolted room by that tiny window and drew your devices there too?'

He nodded proudly and went rattling on: 'Not only did I kill my natural father but I killed my father by adoption too – Tiberius, you know. And whereas Jupiter only lay with one sister of his, Juno, I have lain with all three of mine. Martina told me it was the right thing to do if I wanted to be like Jove.'

'You knew Martina well, then?'

'Indeed I did. When my parents were in Egypt I used to visit her every night. She was a very wise woman. I'll tell you another thing. Drusilla's divine too. I'm going to announce it at the same time as I make the announcement about myself. How I love Drusilla! Almost as much as she loves me.'

'May I ask what are your sacred intentions? This metamorphosis will surely affect Rome profoundly.'

'Certainly. First, I'm going to put the whole world in awe of me. I won't allow myself to be governed by a lot of fussy old men any longer. I'm going to show ... but you remember your old

334

grandmother, Livia? That was a joke. Somehow she had got the notion that it was she who was to be the everlasting God about whom everyone has been prophesying in the East for the last thousand years. I think it was Thrasyllus who tricked her into believing that she was meant. Thrasyllus never told lies but he loved misleading people. You see, Livia didn't know the precise terms of the prophecy. The God is to be a man not a woman, and not born in Rome, though he is to reign at Rome (I was born at Antium), and born at a time of profound peace (as I was), but destined to be the cause of innumerable wars after his death. He is to die young and to be at first loved by his people and then hated, and finally to die miserably, forsaken of all. "His servants shall drink his blood." Then after his death he is to rule over all the other Gods of the world, in lands not yet known to us. That can only be myself. Martina told me that many prodigies had been seen lately in the near East, which proved conclusively that the God had been born at last. The Jews were the most excited. They somehow felt themselves peculiarly concerned. I suppose that this was because I once visited their city Jerusalem with my father and gave my first divine manifestation there.' He paused.

'It would greatly interest me to know about that,' I said.

'Oh, it was nothing much. Just for a joke I went into a house where some of their priests and doctors were talking theology together and suddenly shouted out: "You're a lot of ignorant old frauds. You know nothing at all about it." That caused a great sensation and one old white-bearded man said: "Oh? And who are you, Child? Are you the prophesied one?" "Yes," I answered boldly. He said, weeping for rapture: "Then teach us!" I answered: "Certainly not! It's beneath my dignity," and ran out again. You should have seen their faces! No, Livia was a clever and capable woman in her way – a female Ulysses, as I called her once to her face – and one day perhaps I shall deify her as I promised, but there's no hurry about that. She will never make an important deity. Perhaps we'll make her the patron goddess of clerks and accountants, because she had a good head for figures. Yes, and we'll add poisoners, as Mercury has thieves under his protection as well as merchants and travellers.'

'That's only justice,' I said. 'But what I am anxious to know at once is this: in what name am I to adore you? Is it incorrect, for instance, to call you Jove? Aren't you someone greater than Jove?'

335

He said: 'Oh, greater than Jove, certainly, but anonymous as yet. For the moment, I think though, I'll call myself Jove – the Latin Jove to distinguish myself from that Greek fellow. I'll have to settle with him one of these days. He's had his own way too long.'

I asked: 'How does it happen that your father wasn't a God too? I never heard of a God without a divine father.'

'That's simple. The God Augustus was my father.'

'But he never adopted you, did he? He only adopted your elder brothers and left you to carry on your father's line.'

'I don't mean that he was my father by adoption. I mean that I am his son by his incest with Julia. I must be. That's the only possible solution. I'm certainly no son of Agrippina: her father was a nobody. It's ridiculous.'

I was not such a fool as to point out that in this case Germanicus wasn't his father and therefore his sisters were only his nieces. I humoured him as Drusilla advised and said: 'This is the most glorious hour of my life. Allow me to retire and sacrifice to you at once, with my remaining strength. The divine air you exhale is too strong for my mortal nostrils. I am nearly fainting.' The room was dreadfully stuffy. Caligula hadn't allowed the windows to be opened ever since he took to his bed.

He said: 'Go in peace. I thought of killing you, but I won't now. Tell the Scouts about my being a God and about my face shining, but don't tell them any more. I impose holy silence on you for the rest.'

I grovelled on the floor again and retired, backwards. Ganymede stopped me in the corridor and asked for the news. I said: 'He's just become a God and a very important one, he says. His face shines.'

'That's bad news for us mortals,' said Ganymede. 'But I saw it coming. Thanks for the tip. I'll pass it on to the other fellows. Does Drusilla know? No? Then I'll tell her.'

'Tell her that she's a Goddess too,' I said, 'in case she hasn't noticed it.'

I went back to my room and thought to myself, 'This has happened for the best. Everyone will soon see that he's mad, and lock him up. And there are no other descendants of Augustus left now of an age to become Emperor, except Ganymede, and he's not got the popularity or the necessary force of character. The Republic will be restored. Caligula's father-in-law is the man for that. He has the most influence of any man in the Senate. I'll back him up. If only we could get rid of Macro, and have a decent commander of the Guards in his place, everything would be easy. The Guards are the greatest obstacle. They know very well that they'd never get bounties of fifty and a hundred gold pieces a man voted them by a Republican Senate. Yes, it was Sejanus's idea of turning them into a sort of private army for my uncle Tiberius that gave monarchy its oriental absoluteness. We ought to break up the Camp and billet the men in private houses again as we used to do.'

But – would you believe it? – Caligula's divinity was accepted by everyone without question. For awhile he was content to let the news of it circulate privately, and to remain officially a mortal still. It would have spoilt his free and easy relations with the Scouts and curtailed most of his pleasure if everyone had had to lie face-down on the floor whenever he appeared. But within ten days of his recovery, which was greeted with inexpressible jubilation, he had taken on himself all the mortal honours that Augustus had accepted in a lifetime and one or two more besides. He was Caesar the Good, Caesar the Father of the Armies, and the Most Gracious and Mighty Caesar, and Father of the Country, a title which Tiberius had steadfastly refused all his life.

Gemellus was the first victim of the terror. Caligula sent for a colonel of the Guards and told him, 'Kill that traitor, my son, at once.' The colonel went straight to Gemellus's rooms and struck his head off. The next victim was Caligula's father-in-law. He was one of the Silanus family – Caligula had married his daughter Junia but she had died in childbirth a year before he became Emperor. Silanus enjoyed the distinction of being the only Senator whom Tiberius had never suspected of disloyalty: Tiberius had always refused to listen to any appeal from his judicial sentences. Caligula now sent him a message, 'By dawn to-morrow you must be dead.' The unfortunate man thereupon said good-bye to his family and cut his throat with a razor. Caligula explained in a letter to the Senate that Gemellus had died a traitor's death: during his own dangerous illness the lad had offered no prayer for his recovery but had tried to ingratiate himself with the officers of the bodyguard. He had moreover taken antidotes against poison whenever he came to dine at the Palace, so his whole person smelt of them. 'But is there any antidote against Caesar?' His father-in-law, Caligula wrote, was another traitor: he had refused to come to sea with him that stormy day when he had sailed to Pandataria and Ponza to collect the remains of his mother and brother, and had stayed behind in the hope of seizing the monarchy if tempests wrecked the ship.

These explanations were accepted by the Senate. The truth of the matter was that Silanus was so bad a sailor that he nearly died of sea-sickness every time he went out in a boat, even in fine weather, and it was Caligula himself who kindly refused his offer to accompany him on that voyage. As for Gemellus he had an obstinate cough and smelt of the medicine that he took to soothe his throat, so as not to be a nuisance at table.

Chapter 30

WHEN my mother heard of Gemellus's murder she was very grieved and came to the Palace asking to see Caligula, who received her sulkily, for he felt that she was about to scold him. She said: 'Grandson, may I speak to you in private? It is about the death of Gemellus.'

'No, certainly not in private,' he answered. 'Say what you wish to say in Macro's presence. I must have a witness by me if what you have to say is as important as all that.'

'Then I prefer to keep silent. It is a family matter, not for the ears of the sons of slaves. That fellow's father was the son of one of my vine-dressers. I sold him to my brother-in-law for forty-five gold pieces.'

'You will please tell me at once what it was you were about to say, without insulting my ministers. Don't you know that I have the power to make anyone in the world do just what I please?'

'It is nothing that you will be glad to hear.'

'Say it.'

'As you wish. I came to say that your killing of my poor Gemellus was wanton murder and I wish to resign all the honours I have had from your wicked hands.'

Caligula laughed and said to Macro: 'I think the best thing that this old lady can do now is to go home and borrow a pruning-knife from one of her vine-dressers and cut her vocal cords with it.'

Macro said: 'I always gave the same sort of advice to *my* grandmother, but the old witch refused to take it.'

My mother came to see me. 'I am about to kill myself, Claudius,' she said. 'You will find all my affairs in order. There will be a few small debts outstanding: pay them punctually. Be good to my household staff; they have been loyal workers, every one of them. I am sorry that your little daughter will have nobody now to look after her: I think that you had better marry again to give her a mother. She's a good child.'

I said: 'What, Mother! Kill yourself? Why? Oh, don't do that!'

She smiled sourly. 'My life's my own, isn't it? And why should you dissuade me from taking it? Surely you won't miss me, will you?'

'You are my mother,' I said. 'A man has only one mother.'

'I am surprised that you speak so dutifully. I have been no very loving mother to you. How could I have been expected to be so? You were always a great disappointment to me – a sick, feeble, timorous, woolly-witted thing. Well, I have been prettily punished by the Gods for my neglect of you. My splendid son Germanicus murdered, and my poor grandsons Nero and Drusus and Gemellus murdered, and my daughter Livilla punished for her wickedness, her abominable wickedness, by my own hand – that was the worst pain I suffered, no mother ever suffered a worse – and my four granddaughters all gone to the bad, and this filthy, impious Caligula. ... But you'll survive him. You'd survive a Universal Deluge, I believe.' Her voice, calm at first, had risen to its usual angry scolding tone.

I said: 'Mother, have you no kindly word to give me even at a time like this? How did I ever intentionally wrong you or disobey you?'

But she did not seem to hear. 'I have been prettily punished,' she repeated. Then: 'I wish you to come to my house in five hours' time. By that time I shall have completed my arrangements. I count on you to pay me the last rites. I don't want you to catch my dying breath. If I am not dead when you arrive, wait in the ante-room until you get the word from my maid Briseis. Don't make a muddle of the valedictory: that would be just like you. You will find full instructions written out for the funeral. You are

339

to be chief mourner. I want no funeral oration. Remember to cut off my hand for separate burial: because this will be a suicide. I want no perfumes on the pyre; it's often done but it's strictly against the law and I have always regarded it as a most *wasteful* practice. I am giving Pallas his freedom, so he'll wear the cap of liberty in the procession, don't forget. And just for once in your life try to carry one ceremony through without a mistake.' That was all, except a formal 'Good-bye.' No kiss, no tears, no blessing. As a dutiful son I carried out her last wishes, to the letter. It was odd her giving my own slave Pallas his freedom. She did the same with Briseis.

Watching her pyre burning, from his dining-room window, a few days later, Caligula said to Macro: 'You stood by me well against that old woman. I'm going to reward you. I'm going to give you the most honourable appointment in the whole Empire. It's an appointment which, as Augustus laid down as a principle of State, must never fall into the hands of an adventurer. I am going to make you Governor of Egypt.' Macro was delighted: he did not quite know, these days, how he stood with Caligula, and if he went to Egypt he would be safe. As Caligula had said, the appointment was an important one: the Governor of Egypt had the power of starving Rome by cutting off the corn-supply, and the garrison could be strengthened by local levies until it was big enough to hold the province against any invading army that could be brought against it.

So Macro was relieved of his command of the Guards. Caligula appointed nobody in his place for a time, but let the nine colonels of battalions each command for a month in turn. He gave out that at the end of this time the most loyal and efficient of them would be given the appointment permanently. But the man to whom he secretly promised it was the colonel of the battalion which found the Palace Guard – none other than the same brave Cassius Chaerea whose name you cannot have forgotten if you have read this story with any attention – the man who killed the German in the amphitheatre, the man who led his company back from the massacre of Varus's army, and who afterwards saved the bridge-head; the man too who cut his way through the mutineers in the camp at Bonn and who carried Caligula on his back that early morning when Agrippina and her friends had to trudge on foot from the camp under his protection. Cassius was white-haired now, though not yet sixty years of age, and stooped a little, and his hands trembled because of a fever that had nearly killed him in Germany, but he was still a fine swordsman and reputedly the bravest man in Rome. One day an old soldier of the Guards went mad and ran amok with his spear in the courtyard of the Palace. He thought he was killing French rebels. Everyone fled but Cassius, who though unarmed stood his ground until the madman charged him, when he calmly gave the parade-ground order, 'Company, halt! Ground arms!' and the crazy fellow, to whom obedience to orders had become second nature, halted and laid his spear flat along the ground. 'Company about turn,' Cassius ordered again. 'Quick march!' So he disarmed him. Cassius, then, was the first temporary commander of the Guards and kept them in order while Macro was being tried for his life.

For Macro's appointment to the governorship of Egypt was only a trick of Caligula's, the same sort of trick that Tiberius had played on Sejanus. Macro was arrested as he went aboard his ship at Ostia and brought back to Rome in chains. He was accused of having brought about the deaths of Arruntius and several other innocent men and women. To this charge Caligula added another, namely that Macro had played the pander, trying to make him fall in love with his wife Ennia – a temptation to which in his youthful inexperience, he admitted, he had nearly succumbed. Macro and Ennia were both forced to kill themselves. I was surprised how easily he got rid of Macro.

One day Caligula as High Pontiff went to solemnize a marriage between one of the Piso family and a woman called Orestilla. He took a fancy to Orestilla, and when the ceremony was completed and most of the high nobility of Rome were gathered at the wedding feast, having great fun, as one does on these occasions, he suddenly called out to the bridegroom: 'Hey, there, Sir, stop kissing that woman! She's my wife.' He then rose and, in the hush of surprise that followed, ordered the guards to seize Orestilla and carry her off to the Palace. Nobody dared to protest. The next day he married Orestilla: her husband was forced to attend the ceremony and give her away. He sent a letter to the Senate to inform them that he had celebrated a marriage in the style of Romulus and Augustus – referring, I suppose, to Romulus's rape of the Sabine women and Augustus's marriage with my grandmother (when my grandfather was present). Within two months he had divorced Orestilla and banished her, and her former husband too, on the grounds that they had been committing adultery when his back was turned. She was sent to Spain and he to Rhodes. He was only allowed to take ten slaves with him: when he asked as a favour to be allowed double that number Caligula said: 'As many as you like, but for every extra slave you take you'll have to have an extra soldier to guard you.'

Drusilla died. I am certain in my own mind that Caligula killed her, but I have no proof. Whenever he kissed a woman now, I am told, he used to say: 'As white and lovely a neck as this is, I have only to give the word, and slash! it will be cut clean through.' If the neck was particularly white and lovely he could sometimes not resist the temptation of giving the word and seeing his boast proved true. In the case of Drusilla I think that he struck the blow himself. At all events nobody was allowed to see her corpse. He gave out that she died of a consumption and gave her a most extraordinarily rich funeral. She was deified under the name of Panthea and had temples built to her, and noblemen and noblewomen appointed her priests, and a great annual festival instituted in her honour, more splendid than any other in the Calendar. A man earned 10,000 gold pieces for seeing her spirit being received into Heaven by Augustus. During the days of public mourning that Caligula ordered in her honour, it was a capital crime for any citizen to laugh, sing, shave, go to the baths, or even have dinner with his family. The law-courts were closed, no marriages were celebrated, no troops performed military exercises. Caligula had one man put to death for selling hot water in the streets, and another for exposing razors for sale. The resulting gloom was so profound and widespread that he could not himself bear it (or it may have been remorse), so one night he left the City and travelled down towards Syracuse, alone except for a guard of honour. He had no business there, but the journey was a distraction. He got no further than Messina, where Etna happened to be in slight eruption. The sight frightened him so much that he turned back at once. When he reached Rome again he soon set things going as usual, particularly sword-fighting, chariot-racing, and wild-beast hunting. He suddenly remembered that the men who had vowed their lives in exchange for his during his illness had not yet committed suicide; and made them do it, not only on general principles to keep them from the sin of perjury, but more particularly to prevent Death from going back on the bargain they had struck with him.

A few days later at supper I happened to be laying down the law, rather drunkenly, about the inheritance of female beauty, and quoting examples of my contention that it usually missed a generation, going from the grandmother to the granddaughter. Unfortunately I wound up by saying, 'The most beautiful woman in Rome when I was a boy has reappeared, feature for feature, and limb for limb, in the person of her granddaughter and namesake Lollia, the wife of the present Governor of Greece. With the sole exception of a certain lady whom I shall not name, because she is present in this room, Lollia is in my opinion the most beautiful woman alive to-day.' I made this exception merely for tactfulness. Lollia was far and away more beautiful than my nieces, Agrippinilla or Lesbia, or than any other member of the company. I was not in love with her, I may say: I had merely noticed one day that she was perfect, and remembered having made exactly the same observation about her grandmother when I was a boy. Caligula grew interested and questioned me about Lollia. I did not realize that I had said too much, and said more. That evening Caligula wrote to Lollia's husband telling him to return to Rome and accept a signal honour. The signal honour turned out to be that of divorcing Lollia and marrying her to the Emperor.

Another chance remark that I made at supper about this time had an unexpected effect on Caligula. Someone mentioned epilepsy and I said that Carthaginian records showed Hannibal to have been an epileptic, and that Alexander and Julius Caesar were both subject to this mysterious disease, which seemed to be an almost inevitable accompaniment of superlative military genius. Caligula pricked up his ears at this, and a few days later he gave a very good imitation of an epileptic fit, falling on the floor in the Senate House and screaming at the top of his voice, his lips white with foam – soap-suds, probably.

The people of Rome were still happy enough. Caligula continued giving them a good time with theatrical shows and sword-fights and wild-beast hunts and chariot-races and largesse thrown from the Oration Platform or from the upper windows of the Palace. What marriages he contracted or dissolved, or what courtiers he murdered, they did not much care. He was never satisfied unless every seat in the theatre or Circus was occupied and all the gangways crowded; so whenever there was a performance he postponed all lawsuits and suspended all mourning to give nobody any excuse for not attending. He made several other innovations. He allowed people to bring cushions to sit on, and in hot weather to wear straw hats, and to come barefooted – even senators, who were supposed to set an example of austerity.

When I eventually managed to visit Capua for a few days, for the first time for nearly a year, almost the first thing Calpurnia asked me was: 'How much is left in the Privy Purse, Claudius, of that twenty million?'

'Less than five million, I believe. But he's been building pleasure-barges of cedar-wood and overlaying them with gold and studding them with jewels and putting baths and flower-gardens in them, and he's started work on sixty new temples and talks of cutting a canal across the isthmus of Corinth. He takes baths in spikenard and oil of violet. Two days ago he gave Eutychus, the Leek Green charioteer, a present of twenty thousand in gold for winning a close race.'

'Does Leek Green always win?'

'Always. Or almost always. Scarlet happened to come in first the other day and the people gave it a big cheer. They were tiring of the monotony of Leek Green. The Emperor was furious. Next day the Scarlet charioteer and his winning team were all dead. Poisoned. The same sort of thing has happened before.'

'By this time next year things will be going badly with you, my poor Claudius. By the way, would you like to look at your accounts? It's been an unlucky year, as I wrote to you. Those valuable cattle dying, and the slaves stealing right and left, and the corn-ricks burned. You're the poorer by two thousand or more gold pieces. It's not the steward's fault, either. He does his best and at least he's honest. It's because you are not here to act as overseer that these things happen.'

'It can't be helped,' I said. 'To be frank, I am more anxious about my life than about money these days.'

'Are you badly treated?'

'Yes. They make a fool of me all the time. I don't like it. The Emperor is my chief tormentor.'

'What do they do to you?'

'Oh, practical jokes. Booby traps with buckets of water suspended over doors. And frogs in my bed. Or nasty pathics smelling of myrrh: you know how I loathe frogs and pathics. If I happen to take a nap after my dinner they flip date-stones at me or tie shoes on my hands or ring the fire-bell in my ears. And I never get time to do any work. If I ever start they upset my inkpot all over it. And nothing that I say is ever treated seriously.'

'Are you the only butt they have?'

'The favourite one. The official one.'

'Claudius, you're luckier than you realize. Guard your appointment jealously. Don't let anyone usurp it.'

'What do you mean, girl?'

'I mean that people don't kill their butts. They are cruel to them, they frighten them, they rob them, but they don't kill them.'

I said: 'Calpurnia, you are very clever. Listen to me now. I still have money. I shall buy you a beautiful silk dress and a gold cosmetic box and a marmoset and a parcel of cinnamon sticks.'

She smiled. 'I should prefer the present in cash. How much were you going to spend?'

'About seven hundred.'

'Good. It will come in handy one of these days. Thank you, kind Claudius.'

When I returned to Rome I heard that there had been trouble. Caligula had been disturbed one night by the distant noise of the people crowding to the amphitheatre just before dawn, and pushing and struggling to get near the gates, so that when these opened they could get into the front rows of the free seats. Caligula sent a company of Guards with truncheons to restore order. The Guards were ill-tempered at being pulled from their beds for this duty and struck out right and left, killing a number of people, including some quite substantial citizens. To show his displeasure at having had his sleep disturbed by the original commotion and by the far louder noise that the people made when they scattered screaming before the truncheon-charge, Caligula did not appear in the amphitheatre until well on in the afternoon when everyone was worn out by waiting for him, and hungry too. When the Leek Greens gave an equestrian display they were hissed and booed. Caligula leaped angrily from his seat: 'I wish you had only a single neck. I'd hack it through!'

The next day there was to be a sword-fight and a wild-beast hunt. Caligula cancelled all the arrangements that had been made and sent in the most wretched set of animals that he could buy up in the wholesale market – mangy lions and panthers and sick bears and old worn-out wild bulls, the sort that are sent to out-of-the-way garrison towns in the provinces where audiences are not particular and amateur huntsmen don't welcome animals of too good quality. The huntsmen whom Caligula substituted for the performers advertised to appear were in keeping with the animals: fat, stiff-jointed, wheezy veterans. Some of them had perhaps been good men in their day – back in Augustus's golden age. The crowd jeered and booed them. This was what Caligula had been waiting for. He sent his officers to arrest the men who were making most noise and put them into the arena to see if they would do any better. The mangy lions and panthers and sick bears and worn-out bulls made short work of them.

He was beginning to be unpopular. That the crowd always likes a holiday is a common saying, but when the whole year becomes one long holiday, and nobody has time for attending to his business, and pleasure becomes compulsory, then it is a different matter. Chariot-races grew wearisome. It was all very well for Caligula, who had a personal interest in the teams and drivers and even used sometimes to drive a car himself. He was not a bad hand with the reins and whip and the competing charioteers took care not to win from him. Theatrical shows grew rather wearisome too. All theatre-pieces are much the same except to connoisseurs: or they are to me at all events. Caligula fancied himself a connoisseur and was also sentimentally attached to Apelles, the Philistine tragic actor, who wrote many of the pieces in which he played. One piece which Caligula admired particuarly – because he had made suggestions which Apelles had incorporated in his part – was played over and over again until everyone hated the sight and sound of it. He had an even stronger liking for Mnester, the principal dancer of the mythological ballets then in fashion. He used to kiss Mnester in full view of the audience whenever he had done anything particularly well. A knight began coughing once during a performance, couldn't stop, and at last had to leave. The noise he made by squeezing along past people's knees, and apologizing and coughing and pushing his way through the crowded aisles to the exit disturbed Mnester, who stopped in the middle of one of his most exquisite dances to soft flute-music and waited for everyone to settle down again. Caligula was furious with the knight, had him brought before him and gave him a good beating with his own hands. Then he sent him off post-haste on a journey to Tangier, with a sealed message for the King of Morocco. (The King, a relative of mine – his mother was my Aunt Selene, Antony's daughter by Cleopatra – was greatly mystified by the message. It read: 'Kindly send bearer back to Rome.') The other knights resented this incident very much: Mnester was only a freedman and gave himself airs like a triumphant general. Caligula took private lessons in elocution and dancing from Apelles and Mnester and after a time frequently appeared on the stage in their parts. After delivering a speech in some tragedy, he used sometimes to turn and shout to Apelles in the wings: 'That was perfect, wasn't it? You couldn't have done better yourself.' And after a graceful hop, skip, and jump or two in the ballet he would stop the orchestra, hold up his hand for absolute silence, and then go through the movement again unaccompanied.

As Tiberius had a pet dragon, so Caligula had a favourite stallion. This horse's original stable name was Porcellus (meaning 'little pig') but Caligula did not consider that grand enough and renamed him 'Incitatus', which means 'swift-speeding'. Incitatus never lost a race and Caligula was so extravagantly fond of him that he made him first a citizen and then a senator and at last put him on the list of his nominees for the Consulship four years in advance. Incitatus was given a house and servants. He had a marble bedroom with a big straw mat for a bed, a new one every day, also an ivory manger, a gold bucket to drink from, and pictures by famous artists on the walls. He used to be invited to dinner with us whenever he won a race, but preferred a bowl of barley to the meat and fish that Caligula always offered him. We had to drink his health twenty times over.

The money went faster and faster and at last Caligula decided to make economies. He said one day, for instance, 'What is the use of putting men in prison for forgery and theft and breaches of the peace? They don't enjoy themselves there and they are a great expense for me to feed and guard; yet if I were to let them go they would only start their career of crime again. I'll visit the prisons to-day and look into the matter.' He did. He weeded out the men whom he considered the most hardened criminals, and had them executed. Their bodies were cut up and used as meat for the wild beasts waiting to be killed in the amphitheatre: which made it a double economy. Every month now he made his round of the prisons. Crime decreased slightly. One day his Treasurer, Callistus, reported only a million gold pieces left in the Treasury and only half a million in the Privy Purse. He realized that economy was not enough: revenue had to be increased. So first he began selling priesthoods and magistracies and monopolies, and that brought him in a great deal, but not enough; and then, as Calpurnia had foreseen, he began using informers to convict rich men of real or imaginary crimes, in order to get their estates. He had abolished the capital charge for treason as soon as he became Emperor, but there were plenty of other crimes punishable with death.

He celebrated his first batch of convictions with a particularly splendid wild-beast hunt. But the crowd was in an ugly temper. They booed and groaned and refused to pay any attention to the proceedings. Then a cry began at the other end of the amphitheatre from the President's Box where Caligula sat: 'Give up the informers! Give up the informers!' Caligula rose to command silence, but they howled him down. He sent Guards with truncheons along to the part where noise was loudest and they whacked a few men on the head, but it began again more violently elsewhere. Caligula grew alarmed. He hurriedly left the amphitheatre, calling on me to take on the presidency from him. I did not welcome this at all and was much relieved, when I rose to speak, that the crowd gave me a courteous hearing and even shouted 'Feliciter' which means 'Good luck to you!' My voice is not strong. Caligula's was very strong: he could make himself heard from one end of Mars Field to the other. I had to find someone to repeat my speech after me. Mnester volunteered, and made it sound much better than it was.

I announced that the Emperor had unfortunately been called away on important State business. That made everyone laugh; Mnester did some beautiful gestures illustrative of the importance and urgency of this State business. Then I said that the President's duties had devolved on my unfortunate and unworthy self. Mnester's hopeless shrug and the little twiddle with a forefinger at his temples expressed this excellently. Then I said: 'Let us go on with the Games, my friends.' But at once the shout rose again, 'Give up the informers!' But I asked, and Mnester repeated the question willingly: 'And if the Emperor does consent to give them up, what then? Will someone inform against them?' There was no answer to this but a confused buzzing. I asked them a further question. I asked them which was the worst sort of criminal – an informer? or an informer against an informer? or an informer against an informer against an informer? I said that the further you took the offence the more heinous it became, and the more people it polluted. The best policy was to do nothing which might give informers any ground for action. If everyone, I said, lived a life of the strictest virtue, the cursed breed would die out for want of nourishment, like mice in a miser's kitchen. You would never believe what a tempest of laughter this sally provoked. The simpler and sillier the joke, the better a big crowd likes it. (The greatest applause I ever won for a joke was once in the Circus when I happened to be presiding in Caligula's absence. The people called out angrily for a sword-fighter called Pigeon who was advertised to perform but had not turned up, so I said, 'Patience, friends! First catch your Pigeon and then pluck him!' Whereas really witty jokes of mine have been quite lost on them.)

'Let's get on with the Games, my friends,' I repeated, and this time the shouting stopped. The Games turned out very good ones. Two sword-fighters killed each other, with simultaneous thrusts in the belly: this is a very rare happening. I ordered the weapons to be brought to me and had little knives made of them; such little knives are the most effective charms known for use in cases of epilepsy. Caligula would appreciate the gift – if he forgave me for quieting the crowd where he had failed. For he had been in such a fright that he had driven out of Rome at full speed in the direction of Antium; and did not reappear for several days.

It turned out all right. He was pleased with the little knives, which gave him an opportunity of enlarging on the splendour of his disease; and when he asked what had happened at the amphitheatre I said that I had warned the crowd of what he would do if they did not repent of their disloyalty and ingratitude. I said that they had then changed their rebellious cries into howls of guilty fear and pleas for forgiveness. 'Yes,' he said, 'I was too gentle with them. I am determined now not to yield an inch. "Immovable rigour" is the watchword from henceforward.' And to keep himself reminded of this decision, he used every morning now to practise frightful faces before a mirror in his bedroom and terrible shouts in his private bathroom, which had a fine echo.

I asked him: 'Why don't you publicly announce your God-head? That would awe them as nothing else would!'

He answered: 'I have still a few acts to perform in my human disguise.'

The first of these acts was to order harbourmasters throughout Italy and Sicily to detain all vessels that were over a certain tonnage, put their cargoes in bond, and send them empty under the convoy of warships to the Bay of Naples. Nobody understood what this order meant. It was supposed that he contemplated an invasion of Britain and wanted the vessels for use as transports. But nothing of the sort. He was merely about to justify Thrasyllus's statement that he could no more become Emperor than ride a horse across the Bay of Baiae. He collected about 4,000 vessels, including 1,000 built especially for the occasion, and anchored them across the bay, thwart to thwart in a double line from the docks of Puteoli to his villa at Bauli. The prows were outward, and the sterns interlocked. The sterns stuck up too high for his purpose, so he had them trimmed flat, sawing off the helmsman's seat and the figurehead from every one; which made the crews very unhappy, because the figurehead was the guardian deity of the ship. Then he boarded the double line across and threw earth on the boards and had the earth watered and rammed flat; and the result was a broad firm road, some 6,000 paces long from end to end. When more ships arrived, just back from voyages to the East, he lashed them together into five islands which he linked to the road, one at every 1,000 paces. He had a row of shops built all the way across and ordered the ward-masters of Rome to have them stocked and staffed within ten days. He installed a drinking-water system and planted gardens. The islands he made into villages.

Fortunately the weather was fine throughout these preparations and the sea glassy smooth. When everything was ready he put on the breastplate of Alexander (Augustus was unworthy to use Alexander's ring, but Caligula wore his very breastplate) and over it a purple silk cloak stiff with jewel-encrusted gold embroidery; then he took Julius Caesar's sword and the reputed battle-axe of Romulus and the reputed shield of Aeneas which were stored in the Capitol (both forgeries in my opinion, but such early forgeries as to be practically genuine) and crowned himself with a garland of oak-leaves. After a propitiatory sacrifice to Neptune – a seal, because that is an amphibious beast – and another, a peacock, to Envy, in case, as he said, any God should be jealous of him, he mounted on Incitatus and began trotting across the bridge from the Bauli end. The whole of the Guards cavalry was at his back, and behind that a great force of cavalry brought from France, followed by 20,000 infantry. When he reached the last island, close to Puteoli, he made his trumpeters blow the charge and dashed into the city as fiercely as if he were pursuing a beaten enemy.

He remained in Puteoli that night and most of the next day, as if resting from battle. In the evening he returned in a triumphal chariot with gold-plated wheels and sides. Incitatus and the mare Penelope to whom Caligula had ritually married him were in the shafts. Caligula was wearing the same splendid clothes as before, except that he had a garland of bay-leaves instead of oak-leaves. A long wagon-train followed heaped high with what were supposed to be battle-spoils – furniture and statues and ornaments robbed from the houses of rich Puteoli merchants. For prisoners he used the hostages which the petty kings of the East were required to send to Rome as earnest of good behaviour and whatever foreign slaves he could lay his hands upon, dressed in their national costumes and loaded with chains. His friends followed in decorated chariots, wearing embroidered gowns and chanting his praises. Then came the army, and last a procession of about 200,000 people in holiday dress. Countless bonfires were alight on the whole circle of hills around the bay and every soldier and citizen in the procession carried a torch. It was the most impressive theatrical spectacle, I should think, that the world has ever seen, and I am sure it was the most pointless. But how everybody enjoyed it! A pine-wood went on fire at Cape Misenum to the southwest and blazed magnificently. As soon as Caligula reached Bauli again he dismounted and called for his gold-pronged trident and his other purple cloak worked over with silver fish and dolphins. With these he entered the biggest of his five cedar-built pleasure-barges which were waiting on the shore-side of the bridge, and was rowed out in it to the middle island of the five, which was by far the biggest, followed by most of his troops in war-vessels.

Here he disembarked, mounted a silk-hung platform and harangued the crowds as they passed along the bridge. There were watchmen to keep them on the move, so nobody heard more than a few sentences, except his friends around the platform – among whom I found myself – and the soldiers in the nearest war-vessels, who had not been permitted to land. Among other things, he called Neptune a coward for allowing himself to be put in fetters without a struggle, and promised, one day soon, to teach the old God an even sharper lesson. (He seemed to forget the propitiatory sacrifice he had made.) As for the Emperor Xerxes who had once bridged the Hellespont in the course of his unlucky expedition against Greece, Caligula laughed at him like anything. He said that Xerxes's famous bridge had been only half the length of the present one and not nearly so solid. Then he announced that he was about to give every soldier two gold pieces to drink his health with, and every member of the crowd five silver pieces.

The cheering lasted for half an hour; which seemed to satisfy him. He stopped it and had the money paid out on the spot. The whole procession had to file past again and bag after bag of coin was brought up and emptied. After a couple of hours the money-supply failed and Caligula told the disappointed late-comers to revenge themselves on the greedy first-comers. This, of course, started a free fight.

There followed one of the most remarkable nights of drinking and singing and horse-play and violence and merry-making that was ever known. The effect of drink on Caligula was always to make him a little mischievous. At the head of the Scouts and the German bodyguard he charged about the island and along the line of shops, pushing people into the sea. The water was so calm that it was only the dead-drunk, the decrepit, the aged, and little children who failed to save themselves. Not more than 200 or 300 were drowned.

About midnight he made a naval attack on one of the smaller islands, breaking the bridge on either side of it and then ramming ship after ship of the island until the inhabitants whom he had cut off were crowded together in a very small space in the middle. The finsl assault was reserved for Caligula's flag-ship. He stood waving his trident in the forecastle top, swept down on the terrified survivors, and sent them all under. Among the victims of this sea-battle was the most remarkable exhibit of Caligula's triumphal procession – Eleazar, the Parthian hostage, who was the tallest man in the world. He was over eleven foot high. He was not, however, strong in proportion to his height: he had a voice like the bleat of a camel and a weak back, and was considered to be of feeble intellect. He was a Jew by birth. Caligula had the body stuffed and dressed in armour and put Eleazar outside the door of his bed-chamber to frighten away would-be assassins.

Chapter 31

THE expense of this two days' entertainment drained the Treasury and the Privy Purse completely dry. To make things worse Caligula, instead of returning the vessels to their masters and crew, ordered the breach in the bridge to be repaired and then, riding back to Rome, busied himself with other affairs. Neptune, to prove himself no coward, sent a heavy storm at the bridge from the west and sank about 1,000 ships. Most of the rest dragged their anchors and were driven ashore. About 2,000 rode the storm or were hauled in on the beach for safety, but the loss of the rest caused a great shortage of ships for the carriage of corn from Egypt and Africa, and so a serious food-shortage in the City. Caligula swore to be revenged on Neptune. His new ways of raising money were most ingenious and amused all but the victims and their friends or dependants. For instance, any young men whom he put so deeply in his debt by fines or confiscations that they became his slaves he sent to the sword-fighting schools. When they were trained he put them into the amphitheatre to fight for their lives. His only expense in this was their board and lodgings: being his slaves they were given no payment. If they were killed, there was an end of them. If they were victorious he auctioned them off to the magistrates whose duty it was to give similar contests – lots were drawn for this distinction – and to any-one else who cared to bid. He ran up the prices to an absurd height by pretending that people had made bids when they had done no more than scratch their heads or rub their noses. My ner-vous toss of the head got me into great trouble: I was saddled with three sword-fighters at an average of 2,000 gold pieces each. But I was luckier than a magistrate called Aponius who fell asleep during the auction. Caligula sold him sword-fighters whom no-body else seemed to fancy, raising the bid every time his head nodded on his breast: when he woke up he found that he had no less than 90,000 gold pieces to pay for thirteen sword-fighters whom he did not in the least want. One of the sword-fighters I had bought was a very good performer, but Caligula betted against him heavily with me. When the day came for him to fight he could hardly stand and was easily beaten. It appears that Caligula had drugged his food. Many rich men came to these auctions and willingly bid large sums, not because they wanted sword-fighters but because if they loosened their purse-strings now Caligula would be less likely to bring some charge against them later and rob them of their lives as well as of their money.

An amusing thing happened on the day that my sword-fighter was beaten. Caligula had betted heavily with me against five net-and-trident men who were matched against an equal number of chasers armed with sword and shield. I was resigned to losing the 1,000 gold pieces that he had made me bet against 5,000 of his own; for as soon as the fight began I could see that the net-men had been bribed to give the fight away. I was sitting next to Caligula and said: 'Well, you seem likely to win, but it's my opinion that those net-men aren't doing their best.' One by one the chasers rounded up the net-men, who surrendered, and finally all five were lying with their faces in the sand and each with a chaser standing over him with a raised sword. The audience turned their thumbs downwards as a signal that they should be killed. Caligula, as the President, had a right to take this advice or not, as he pleased. He took it. 'Kill them!' he shouted. 'They didn't try to win!' This was hard luck on the net-men, to whom he had secretly promised their lives if they allowed themselves to be beaten; for I wasn't by any means the only man who had been forced to bet on them – he stood to win 80,000 if they lost. Well, one of them felt so sore at being cheated that he suddenly grappled with his chaser, overturned him and managed to pick up a trident, which was lying not far off, and a net, and dash away. You wouldn't believe it, but I won my 5,000 after all! First that angry net-man killed two chasers who had their backs to him, and were busy acknowledging the cheers of the audience after dispatching their victims, and then he killed the other three, one by one, as they came running at him, each a few paces behind the other. Caligula wept for vexation and exclaimed, 'Oh, the monster! Look, he's killed five promising young swordsmen with that horrible trout-spear of his!' When I say that I won my 5,000, I mean that I would have won it if I hadn't been tactful enough to call the bet off. 'For one man to kill five isn't fair fighting,' I said.

Up to this time Caligula had always spoken of Tiberius as a thorough scoundrel and encouraged everyone else to do the same. But one day he entered the Senate and delivered a long eulogy on him, saying that he had been a much misunderstood man and that nobody must speak a word against him. 'In my capacity as Emperor I have the right to criticize him if I please, but you have no right. In fact you are guilty of treason. The other day a senator said in a speech that my brothers Nero and Drusus were murdered by Tiberius after having been imprisoned on false charges. What an amazing thing to say!' Then he produced the records which he had pretended to burn, and read lengthy extracts. He showed that the Senate had not questioned the evidence collected against his brothers by Tiberius, but had unanimously voted for them to be handed over to him for punishment. Some had even volunteered testimony against them. Caligula said: 'If you knew that the evidence which Tiberius laid before you (in all good faith) was false, then you are the murderers, not he; and it is only since he has been dead that you have dared to blame your cruelty and treachery on him. Or if you thought at the time that the evidence was true, then he was no murderer and you are treasonauly defaming his character. Or if you thought that it was false and that he knew it was false, then you were as guilty of murder as he was, and cowards too.' He frowned heavily in imitation of Tiberius and made Tiberius's sharp chopping motion of the hand, which brought back frightening memories of treason-trials, and said in Tiberius's harsh voice, 'Well spoken, my Son! You can't trust any one of these curs farther than you can kick him. Look what a little God they made of Sejanus before they turned and tore him to pieces! They'll do the same to you if they get half a chance. They all hate you and pray for your death. My advice to you is, consult no interest but your own and put pleasure before everything. Nobody likes being ruled over, and the only way that I kept my place was by making this trash afraid of me. Do the same. The worse you treat them, the more they'll honour you.'

Caligula then reintroduced treason as a capital crime, ordered his speech to be at once engraved on a bronze tablet and posted on the wall of the House above the seats of the Consuls, and rushed away. No more business was transacted that day: we were all too dejected. But the next day we lavished praise on Caligula as a sincere and pious ruler and voted annual sacrifices to his Clemency. What else could we do? He had the Army at his back, and power of life and death over us, and until someone was bold and clever enough to make a successful conspiracy against his life all that we could do was to humour him and hope for the best. At a banquet a few nights later he suddenly burst into a most extraordinary howl of laughter. Nobody knew what the joke was. The two Consuls, who sat next to him, asked whether they might be graciously permitted to share in it. At this Caligula laughed even louder, the tears starting from his eyes. 'No,' he choked, 'that's just the point. It's a joke that you wouldn't think at all funny. I was laughing to think that with one nod of my head I could have both your throats cut on the spot.'

Charges of treason were now brought against the twenty reputedly wealthiest men in Rome. They were given no chance of committing suicide before trial and all condemned to death. One of them, a senior magistrate, proved to have been quite poor. Caligula said: 'The idiot! Why did he pretend to have money? I was quite taken in. He need not have died at all.' I can only remember a single man who escaped with his life from a charge of treason. That was Afer, the man who had prosecuted my cousin Pulchra, a lawyer famous for his eloquence. His crime was having put an inscription on a statue of Caligula in the hall of his house, to the effect that the Emperor in his twenty-seventh year was already Consul for the second time. Caligula found this treasonable – a sneer at his youth and a reproach against him for having held the office before he was legally capable of doing so. He composed a long, careful speech against Afer and delivered it in the Senate with all the oratorical force at his command, every gesture and tone carefully rehearsed beforehand. Caligula used to boast that he was the best lawyer and orator in the world, and was even more anxious to outshine Afer in eloquence than to secure his condemnation and confiscate his money. Afer realized this and pretended to be astonished and overcome by Caligula's genius as a prosecutor. He repeated the counts against himself, point by point, praising them with a professional detachment and muttering 'Yes, that's quite unanswerable' and 'He's got the last ounce of weight out of that argument' and 'A very real dilemma' and 'What extraordinary command of language!' When Caligula had finished and sat down with a triumphant grin, Afer was asked if he had anything to say. He answered: 'Nothing except that I consider myself most unlucky. I had counted on using my oratorical gifts as some slight offset against the Emperor's anger with me for my inexcusable thoughtlessness in the matter of that cursed inscription. But Fate has weighted the dice far too heavily against me. The Emperor has absolute power, a clear case against me, and a thousand times more eloquence than I could ever hope to achieve even if I escaped sentence and studied until I was a centenarian.' He was condemned to death, but reprieved the next day.

Speaking of weighted dice – when rich provincials came to the City they were always invited to dinner at the Palace and a friendy gamble afterwards. They were astonished and dismayed by the Emperor's luck: he threw Venus every time and skinned them of all they had. Yes, Caligula always played with weighted dice. For instance, he now removed the Consuls from office and fined them heavily on the ground that they had celebrated the usual festival in honour of Augustus's victory over Antony at Actium. He said that it was an insult to his ancestor Antony. (By the way, he appointed Afer to one of the vacant Consulships.) He had told us at dinner a few days before the festival that whatever the Consuls did he would punish them: for if they refrained from celebrating the festival they would be insulting his ancestor Augustus. It was on this occasion that Ganymede made a fatal mistake. He cried: 'You *are* clever, my dear! You catch them every way. But the poor idiots will celebrate the festival, if they have any sense; because Agrippa did most of the work at Actium and he was your ancestor too, so they will at least be honouring two of your ancestors out of three.'

Caligula said: 'Ganymede, we are no longer friends.'

'Oh,' said Ganymede, 'don't tell me that, my dear! I said nothing to offend you, did I?'

'Leave the table,' ordered Caligula.

I knew at once what Ganymede's mistake was. It was a double one. Ganymede, as Caligula's cousin on the maternal side, was descended from Augustus and Agrippa, but not from Antony. All his ancestors had been of Augustus's party. So he should have been careful to avoid the subject. And Caligula disliked any reminder of his descent from Agrippa, a man of undistinguished family. But he took no action against Ganymede yet.

357

He divorced Lollia, saying that she was barren, and married a woman called Caesonia. She was neither young nor good-looking and was the daughter of a captain of the Watchmen, and married to a baker, or some such person, by whom she already had three children. But there was something about her that attracted Caligula in a way that nobody could explain, himself least of all. He used often to say that he would fetch the secret out of her, even if he had to do it with the fiddle-string torture, why it was that he loved her so entirely. It was said that she won him with a love-philtre, and further that it sent him mad. But the love-philtre is only a guess, and he had begun to go mad long before he met her. In any case, she was with child by him, and he was so excited at the thought of being a parent that, as I say, he married her. It was shortly after his marriage with Caesonia that he first publicly declared his own Divinity. He visited the temple of Jove on the Capitoline Hill. Apelles was with him. He asked Apelles, 'Who's the greater God – Jove or myself?' Apelles hesitated, thinking that Caligula was joking, and not wishing to blaspheme Jove in Jove's own temple. Caligula whistled two Germans up and had Apelles stripped and whipped in sight of Jove's statue. 'Not so fast,' Caligula told the Germans. 'Slowly, so that he feels it more.' They whipped him until he fainted, and then revived him with holy water and whipped him until he died. Caligula then sent letters to the Senate announcing his divinity and ordered the immediate building of a great shrine next door to the temple of Jove, 'in order that I may dwell with my brother Jove'. Here he set up an image of himself, three times the size of life, made of solid gold and dressed every day in new clothes.

But he soon quarrelled with Jove and was heard to threaten him angrily: 'If you can't realize who's master here I'll pack you off to Greece.' Jove was understood to apologize, and Caligula said: 'Oh, keep your wretched Capitoline Hill. I'll go to the Palatine. It's a much finer situation. I'll build a temple there worthy of myself, you shabby old belly-rumbling fraud.' Another curious thing happened when he visited the temple of Diana in company with a former governor of Syria called Vitellius. Vitellius had done very well out there, having surprised the King of Parthia, who was about to invade the province, by a forced march across the Euphrates. Caught on ground unfavourable for battle, the Parthian king was obliged to sign a humiliating peace and give his sons up

358

as hostages. I should have mentioned that Caligula had the eldest son as a prisoner with him in his chariot when he drove across the bridge. Well, Caligula was jealous of Vitellius and would have put him to death if Vitellius had not been warned by me (he was a friend of mine) what to do. A letter from me was waiting for him at Brindisi when he arrived, and as soon as he reached Rome and was admitted to Caligula's presence he fell prostrate and worshipped him as a God. This was before the news of Caligula's divinity was officially known, so Caligula thought it was a genuine tribute. Vitellius became his intimate friend and showed his gratitude to me in many ways. As I was saying, Caligula was in Diana's temple talking to the Goddess – not the statue but an invisible presence. He asked Vitellius whether he could see her too, or only the moonlight. Vitellius trembled violently, as if in awe, and keeping his eyes fixed on the ground said: 'Only you Gods, my Lord, are privileged to behold one another.'

Caligula was pleased. 'She's very beautiful, Vitellius, and often comes to sleep with me at the Palace.'

It was about this time that I got into trouble again. I thought at first that it was a plot of Caligula's to get rid of me. I am still not so sure that it was not. An acquaintance of mine, a man I used to play dice with a good deal, forged a will and took the trouble to forge my seal to it as witness. Luckily for me he had not noticed a tiny chip on the edge of the agate seal-gem, which always left its mark on the wax. When I was suddenly arrested for conspiracy to defraud and brought to Court, I bribed a soldier to carry a secret plea to my friend Vitellius, begging him to save my life as I had saved his. I asked him to hint about the chip to Caligula, who was judging the case, and to have a genuine seal of mine ready for Caligula to compare with the forged one. But Caligula must be encouraged to find the difference for himself and to take all the credit. Vitellius managed the affair very tactfully. Caligula noticed the chip, boasted of his quickness of eye, and absolved me with a stern warning to be more careful in future about my associates. The forger had his hands cut off and hung around his neck as a warning. If I had been found guilty I would have lost my head. Caligula told me so at supper that night.

I replied: 'Most merciful God, I really don't understand why you trouble so much about my life.'

It is the nature of nephews to enjoy an uncle's flattery. He unbent a little and asked me, with a wink to the rest of the table, 'And what precise valuation would you put on your life to-night, may I ask?'

'I have worked it out already: one farthing.'

'And how do you arrive at so modest a figure?'

'Every life has an assessable value. The ransom that Julius Caesar's family actually paid the pirates who had captured him and threatened to kill him – though they asked a great deal more than this at first – was no more than twenty thousand in gold. So Julius Caesar's life was actually worth no more than twenty thousand. My wife Aelia was once attacked by footpads, but persuaded them to spare her life by handing over an amethyst brooch worth only fifty. So Aelia was worth only fifty. *My* life has just been saved by a chip of agate weighing, I should judge, no more than the fortieth part of a scruple. That quality of agate is worth perhaps as much as a silver-piece a scruple. The chip, if one could find it, which would be difficult, or find a buyer, which would be still more difficult, would therefore be worth one fortieth part of a silver piece or exactly one farthing. So my life is also worth exactly one farthing – –'

'– *If you could find a buyer*,' he roared, delighted with his own wit. How everybody cheered, myself included! For a long time after this was I was called 'Teruncius' Claudius at the Palace, instead of Tiberius Claudius. Teruncius is Latin for farthing.

For his worship he had to have priests. He was his own High Priest and his subordinates were myself, Caesonia, Vitellius, Ganymede, fourteen ex-Consuls, and his noble friend the horse Incitatus. Each of these subordinates had to pay 80,000 gold pieces for the honour. He helped Incitatus to raise the money by imposing a yearly tribute in his name on all the horses in Italy: if they did not pay they would be sent to the knackers. He helped Caesonia to raise the money by imposing a tax in her name on all married men for the privilege of sleeping with their wives. Ganymede, Vitellius, and the others were rich men; though in some instances they had to sell property at a loss to get the 80,000 in cash at short notice, they still remained comfortably off. Not so poor Claudius. Caligula's previous tricks in selling me sword-fighters, and charging me heavily for the privilege of sleeping and boarding at the Palace, had left me with a mere 30,000 in cash, and no property to sell except my small estate at Capua and the house left me by my mother. I paid Caligula the 30,000 and told him the same night at dinner that I was putting up all my property for sale at once to enable me to pay him the remainder when I found a buyer. 'I've nothing else to sell,' I said. Caligula thought this a great joke. 'Nothing at all to sell? Why, what about the clothes you're wearing?'

By this time I had found it wisest to pretend I was quite half-witted. 'By heaven,' I said, 'I forgot all about them. Will you be good enough to auction them for me to the company? You're the most wonderful auctioneer in the world.' I began stripping off all my clothes until I had on nothing but a table-napkin which he hastily wrapped round my loins. He sold my sandals to someone for 100 gold pieces each, and my gown for 1,000, and so on, and each time I expressed my boisterous delight. He then wanted to auction the napkin. I said, 'My natural modesty would not prevent me from sacrificing my last rag, if the money it brought in helped me to pay the rest of the fee. But in this case, alas, something more powerful even than modesty prevents me from selling.'

Caligula frowned. 'What's that? What's stronger than modesty?'

'My veneration for yourself, Caesar. It's your own napkin. One that you had graciously set for my use at this excellent meal.'

This little play only reduced my debt by 3,000. But it did convince Caligula of my poverty.

I had to give up my rooms and my place at table and lodged for a time with old Briseis, my mother's former maid, who was caretaker of the house until it found a buyer. Calpurnia came to live with me there, and would you believe it, the dear girl still had the money which I had given her instead of necklaces and marmosets and silk dresses, and offered to lend it to me. And what was more, my cattle hadn't really died as she pretended, nor had the ricks burned. It was just a trick to sell them secretly at a good price and put the money aside for an emergency. She paid it all over to me – 2,000 gold pieces – together with an exact account of the transactions signed by my steward. So we managed pretty well. But to keep up the pretence of absolute poverty I used to go out with a jug every night, using a crutch instead of a sedan chair, and buy wine from the taverns.

Old Briseis used to say, 'Master Claudius, people all think that I was your mother's freedwoman. It isn't so. I became your slave when you first grew up to be Master, and it was you who gave me my freedom, not she, wasn't it?'

I would answer, 'Of course, Briseis. One day I'll nail that lie in public.' She was a dear old thing and entirely devoted to me. We lived in four rooms together, with an old slave to do the porter's work, and had a very happy time, all considered.

Caesonia's child, a girl, was born a month after Caligula married her. Caligula said that this was a prodigy. He took the child and laid her on the knees of the statue of Jove – this was before his quarrel with Jove – as if to make Jove his honorary colleague in fatherhood, and then put her in the arms of Minerva's statue and allowed her to suck at the Goddess's marble breast for awhile. He called her Drusilla, the name that his dead sister had discarded when she became the Goddess Panthea. This child was made a priestess too. He raised the money for the initiation fee by making a pathetic appeal to the public, complaining of his poverty and the heavy expenses of fatherhood, and opening a fund, called the Drusilla Fund. He put collecting boxes in every street marked 'Drusilla's Food', 'Drusilla's Drink', and 'Drusilla's Dowry', and nobody dared pass by the Guards posted there without dropping in a copper or two.

Caligula dearly loved his little Drusilla, who turned out as precocious a child as he had himself been. He took delight in teaching her his own 'immovable rigour', beginning the lessons when she was only just able to walk and talk. He encouraged her to torture kittens and puppies and to fly with her sharp nails at the eyes of her little playmates. 'There can be no reasonable doubt as to your paternity, my pretty one,' he used to chuckle when she showed particular promise. And once in my presence he bent down and said slyly to her: 'And the first full-sized murder you commit, Precious, if it's only your poor old granduncle Claudius, I'll make a Goddess of you.'

'Will you make me a Goddess if I kill Mamma?' the little fiend lisped. 'I hate Mamma.'

The gold statue for his temple was another expense. He paid for it by publishing an edict that he would receive New Year's gifts at the main gate of the Palace. When the day came he sent parties of Guards out to herd the City crowds up the Palatine Hill at the sword-point and make them shed every coin they had on them into great tubs put out for the purpose. They were warned that if they tried to dodge the Guards or hold back a single farthing of money they would be liable to instant death. By evening 2,000 huge tubs had been filled.

It was about this time that he said to Ganymede and Agrippinilla and Lesbia: 'You ought to be ashamed of yourselves, you idle drones. What do you do for your living? You're mere parasites. Are you aware that every man and woman in Rome works hard to support me? Every wretched baggage-porter gladly pays me one-eighth of his wage, and every poor prostitute the same.'

Agrippinilla said: 'Well, brother, you have stripped us of practically all our money on one pretext or another. Isn't that enough?'

'Enough? Indeed it isn't. Money inherited is not the same as money honestly earned. I'm going to make you girls and boys work.'

So he advertised in the Senate, by distributing leaflets, that on such and such a night a most exclusive and exquisite brothel would be opened at the Palace, with entertainment to suit all tastes provided by persons of the most illustrious birth. Admission, only 1,000 gold pieces. Drinks free. Agrippinilla and Lesbia, I am sorry to say, did not protest very strongly against Caligula's disgraceful proposal, and indeed thought that it would be great fun. But they insisted that they should have the right of choosing their own customers and that Caligula should not take too high a commission on the money earned. Much to my disgust I was dragged into this business, by being dressed up as the comic porter. Caligula, wearing a mask and disguising his voice, was the bawd-master, and played all the usual bawd-master tricks for cheating his guests of their pleasure and their money. When they protested, I was called upon to act as chucker-out, I am strong enough in the arms, stronger than most men, I may say, though my legs are very little use to me: so I caused a great deal of amusement by my clumsy hobbling and by the unexpectedly heavy drubbing I gave the guests when I managed to get hold of them. Caligula declaimed in a theatrical voice the lines from Homer:

> Vulcan with awkward grace his office plies
> And unextinguished laughter shakes the skies.

This was the passage in the First Book of the *Iliad* where the lame God goes hobbling about Olympus and the other Gods all laugh at him. I was lying on the floor pounding Lesbia's husband with my fists – it wasn't often that I got such a chance of paying back old scores – and raising myself up I said:

> Then from his anvil the lame craftsman rose.
> Wide, with distorted legs, oblique he goes,

and staggered over to the refreshment table. Caligula was delighted and quoted another couple of lines which occur just before the 'unextinguished laughter' passage:

> If you submit, the Thunderer stands appeased,
> The Gracious God is willing to be pleased.

This was how he came to call me Vulcan, a title that I was glad to win, because it gave me a certain protection against his caprices.

Caligula then quietly left us, removed his disguise, and reappeared as himself, coming in from the Palace courtyard by the door where he had posted me. He pretended to be utterly surprised and shocked at what was going on and stood declaiming Homer again – Ulysses's shame and anger at the behaviour of the palace-women:

> As thus pavilioned in the porch he lay,
> Scenes of lewd loves his wakeful eyes survey,
> Whilst to nocturnal joys impure repair
> With wanton glee, the prostituted fair.
> His heart with rage this new dishonour stung,
> Wavering his thought in dubious balance hung.
> Or, instant should he quench the guilty flame
> With their own blood, and intercept the shame;
> Or to their lust indulge a last embrace,
> And let the peers consummate the disgrace;
> Round his swoln heart the murmurous fury rolls;
> As o'er her young the mother-mastiff growls,
> And bays the stranger groom: so wrath compress'd
> Recoiling, mutter'd thunder in his breast.
> 'Poor, suffering heart,' he cried, 'support the pain
> Of wounded honour and thy rage restrain!
> Not fiercer woes thy fortitude could foil
> When the brave partners of thy ten-year toil
> Dire Polypheme devoured: I then was freed
> By patient prudence from the death decreed.'

'For "Polypheme" read "Tiberius",' he explained. Then he clapped his hands for the Guard, who came running up at the double. 'Send Cassius Chaerea here at once!' Cassius was sent for and Caligula said: 'Cassius, old hero, you who acted as my war-horse when I was a child, my oldest and most faithful family-friend, did you ever see such a sad and degrading sight as this? My two sisters prostituting their bodies to senators in my very Palace, my uncle Claudius standing at the gate selling tickets of admission! Oh, what would my poor mother and father have said if they had lived to see this day!'

'Shall I arrest them all, Caesar?' asked Cassius eagerly.

> No, to their lust indulge a last embrace
> And let the peers consummate the disgrace,

Caligula replied resignedly, and made mother-mastiff noises in his throat. Cassius was told to march the Guard off again.

It was not the last orgy of this sort at the Palace and thereafter Caligula made the senators who had attended the show bring their wives and daughters to assist Agrippinilla and Lesbia. But the problem of raising money was becoming acute again and Caligula decided to visit France and see what he could do there.

He first gathered an enormous number of troops, sending for detachments from all the regular regiments, and forming new regiments, and raising levies from every possible quarter. He marched out of Italy at the head of 150,000 men and increased them, in France, to 250,000. The expense of arming and equipping this immense force fell on the cities through which he passed: and he commandeered the necessary food supplies from them too. Sometimes he went forward at a gallop and made the army march forty-eight hours or more on end to catch up with him, sometimes he went forward at the rate of only a mile or two a day, admiring the scenery from a sedan-chair carried on eight men's shoulders and frequently stopping to pick flowers.

He sent letters ahead ordering the presence at Lyons, where he proposed to concentrate his forces, of all officials in France and the Rhine provinces who were over the rank of captain. Among those who obeyed the summons was Gaetulicus, one of my dear brother Germanicus's most valued officers, who had been in command of the four regiments of the Upper Province for the last few years. He was very popular among the troops because he kept up the tradition of mild punishments and of discipline based on love rather than on fear. He was popular with the regiments in the

Lower Province too, commanded by his father-in-law Apronius – for Gaetulicus had married a sister of that Apronia whom my brother-in-law Plautius was supposed to have thrown out of the window. At the fall of Sejanus he would have been put to death by Tiberius because he had promised his daughter in marriage to Sejanus's son, but he escaped by writing the Emperor a bold letter. He said that *so long as he was allowed to retain his command* his allegiance could be counted on, and so could that of the troops. Tiberius wisely let him alone. But Caligula envied him his popularity and almost as soon as he arrived had him arrested.

Caligula had not invited me on this expedition, so I missed what followed and cannot write about it in detail. All I know is that Ganymede and Gaetulicus were accused of conspiracy – Ganymede with designs on the monarchy, Gaetulicus with abetting him, and that both were put to death without trial. Lesbia and Agrippinilla (the latter's husband had lately died of dropsy) were also supposed to be in the plot. They were banished to an island off the coast of Africa near Carthage. It was a very hot, very arid island where sponge-fishing was the only industry, and Caligula ordered them to learn the trade of diving for sponges, for he said that he could not afford to support them longer. But before being sent to their island they had a task laid on them: they had to walk to Rome, all the way from Lyons, under an armed escort, and take turns at carrying in their arms the urn in which Ganymede's ashes had been put. This was a punishment for their persistent adultery with Ganymede, as Caligula explained in a loftily styled letter he sent the Senate. He enlarged on his own great clemency in not putting them to death. Why, they had proved themselves worse than common prostitutes: no honest prostitute would have had the face to ask the prices they asked, and got, for their debaucheries!

I had no reason to feel sorry for my nieces. They were as bad as Caligula, in their way, and treated me very spitefully. When Agrippinilla's baby was born three years before, she had asked Caligula to suggest a name for it. Caligula said, 'Call it Claudius and it will be sure to turn out a beauty.' Agrippinilla was so furious that she nearly struck Caligula; instead she turned quickly round and spat towards me – and then burst into tears. The baby was called Lucius Domitius.* Lesbia was too proud to pay attention to me or acknowledge my presence in any way. If I happened

* Afterwards the Emperor Nero. – R. G.

to meet her in a narrow passage she used to walk straight on down the middle without slackening her pace, making me squeeze against the wall. It was difficult for me to remember that they were the children of my dear brother and that I had promised Agrippina to do my very best to protect them.

I had the embarrassing duty assigned to me of going to France, at the head of an embassy of four ex-Consuls, to congratulate Caligula on his suppression of the conspiracy. This was my first visit to France since my infancy and I wished I was not making it. I had to take money from Calpurnia for travelling expenses, for my estate and home had not yet found a buyer, and I could not count on Caligula's being pleased to see me. I went by sea from Ostia, landing at Marseilles. It appears that after banishing my nieces Caligula had auctioned the jewellery and ornaments and clothes they had brought with them. These fetched such high prices that he also sold their slaves and then their freedmen, pretending that these were slaves too. The bids were made by rich provincials who wanted the glory of saying, 'Yes, such and such belonged to the Emperor's sister. I bought it from him personally!' This gave Caligula a new idea. The old Palace where Livia had lived was now shut up. It was full of valuable furniture and pictures and relics of Augustus. Caligula sent for all this stuff to Rome and made me responsible for its safe and prompt arrival at Lyons. He wrote 'Sent it by road, not by sea. I have a quarrel with Neptune.' The letter arrived only the day before I sailed, so I put Pallas in charge of the job. The difficulty was that all the surplus horses and carts had already been commandeered for the transport of Caligula's army. But Caligula had given the order, and horses and conveyances had somehow to be found. Pallas went to the Consuls and showed them Caligula's orders. They were forced to commandeer public mail-coaches and bakers' vans and the horses that turned the corn-mills, which was a great inconvenience to the public.

So it happened that one evening in May just before sunset, Caligula, sitting on the bridge at Lyons engaged in imaginary conversation with the local river-god, saw me coming along the road in the distance. He recognized my sedan A.D. 40 by the dice-board I have fitted across it: I beguile long journeys by throwing dice with myself. He called out angrily: 'Hey, you sir, where are the carts? Why haven't you brought the carts?'

I called back: 'Heaven bless your Majesty! The carts won't be here for a few days yet, I fear. They are coming by land, through Genoa. My colleagues and I have come by water.'

'Then back by water you'll go, my man,' he said. 'Come here!'

When I reached the bridge I was pulled out of my sedan by two German soldiers and carried to the parapet above the middle arch, where they sat me with my back to the river. Caligula rushed forward and pushed me over. I turned two back-somersaults and fell what seemed like 1,000 feet before I struck the water. I remember saying to myself: 'Born at Lyons, died at Lyons!' The river Rhône is very cold, very deep, and very swift. My heavy robe entangled my arms and legs, but somehow I managed to keep afloat, and to clamber ashore behind some boats about half a mile downstream, out of sight of the bridge. I am a much better swimmer than I am a walker: I am strong in the arms and being rather fat from not being able to take exercise and from liking my meals I float like a cork. By the way, Caligula couldn't swim a stroke.

He was surprised, a few minutes later, to see me come hobbling up the road, and laughed hugely at the stinking, muddy mess I was in. 'Where have you been, my dear Vulcan?' he called.

I had the answer pat:

> 'I felt the Thunderer's might,
> Hurled headlong downward from th' ethereal height.
> Tost all the day in rapid circles round
> Nor till the sun descended touch'd the ground.
> Breathless I fell, in giddy motions lost;
> The Sinthians raised me on the Lemnian coast.

'For "Lemnian" read "Lyonian",' I said.

He was sitting on the parapet with my three fellow-envoys lying on the ground face-downwards in a row before him. He had his feet on the necks of two and his swordpoint balanced between the shoulders of the third, Lesbia's husband, who was sobbing for mercy. 'Claudius,' he groaned, hearing my voice, 'beseech the Emperor to set us free: we only came to offer him our loving congraulations.'

'I want carts, not congratulations,' said Caligula.

It seemed as if Homer had written the passage from which I had just quoted on purpose for this occasion. I said to Lesbia's husband:

> 'Be patient and obey,
> Dear as you are, if Jove his arm extend,
> I can but grieve, unable to defend.
> What soul so daring in your aid to move
> Or lift his hand against the might of Jove?'

Caligula was delighted. He said to the three suppliants: 'What are your lives worth to you? Fifty thousand gold pieces each?'

'Whatever you say, Caesar,' they answered faintly.

'Then pay poor Claudius that sum as soon as you get back to Rome. He's saved your lives by his ready tongue.' So they were allowed to rise and Caligula made them sign a promise then and there, to pay me 150,000 gold pieces in three months' time. I said to Caligula: 'Most gracious Caesar, your need is greater than mine. Will you accept one hundred thousand gold pieces from me, when they pay me, in gratitude for my own salvation? If you condescend to take that gift, I would still have fifty thousand left, which would enable me to pay my initiation fee in full. I have worried a great deal about that debt.'

He said, 'Anything that I can do that will contribute to your peace of mind!' and called me his Golden Farthing.

So Homer saved me. But Caligula a few days later warned me not to quote Homer again. 'He's a most overrated author. I am going to have his poems called in and burned. Why shouldn't I put Plato's philosophical recommendations into practice? You know *The Republic*? An admirable piece of argument. Plato was for keeping all poets whatsoever out of his ideal state: he said that they were all liars, and so they are.'

I asked: 'Is your Sacred Majesty going to burn any other poets beside Homer?'

'Oh, indeed, yes. All the overrated ones. Virgil for a start. He's a dull fellow. Tries to be a Homer and can't do it.'

'And any historians?'

'Yes, Livy. Still duller. Tries to be a Virgil and can't do it.'

Chapter 32

HE called for the most recent official property-census and after examining it summoned all the richest men in France to Lyons, so that when the Palace-stuff arrived there from Rome he would be sure to get good prices for it. Just before the auction started, he made a speech. He said that he was a poor bankrupt with enormous liabilities, but trusted that, for the sake of the Empire, his affectionate provincial friends and grateful allies would not take advantage of his financial plight. He begged them not to offer less than the true value of the family heirlooms which, much to his grief, he was being forced to put up for sale.

There was no ordinary auctioneer's trick that he had not learned, and he invented a great many new ones, too, beyond the scope of the market-place cheap-jacks from whom he borrowed so much of his patter. For instance, he sold the same article several times over to different buyers with each time a different account of its quality and usefulness and history. And by 'true value' he expected bidders to understand 'sentimental value' which always turned out to be a hundred times greater than the intrinsic value. For instance he would say: 'This was the favourite easy-chair of my great-grandfather Mark Antony' – 'the God Augustus drank out of this wine-cup at his marriage feast' – 'this dress was worn by my sister, the Goddess Panthea, at a reception given to King Herod Agrippa in celebration of his release from prison' – and so forth. And he sold what he called 'blind bargains', small articles wrapped up in cloth. When he had inveigled a man into buying an old sandal or a piece of cheese for 2,000 gold pieces, he was tremendously pleased with himself.

Bidding always started at the reserve price; for he would nod at some rich Frenchman and say, 'I think you said forty thousand gold pieces for that alabaster casket? Thank you. But let's see if we can't do better. Who'll say forty-five thousand?' You can imagine that fear made the bidding brisk. He skinned the whole lot of all they had and celebrated the skinning by a magnificent ten-day festival.

He then continued his progress to the Rhine Provinces. He swore that he was about to fight a war against the Germans that would only end in their total extermination. He would piously complete the task begun by his grandfather and father. He sent a couple of regiments over the river to locate the nearest enemy. About 1,000 prisoners were brought back. Caligula reviewed them and after picking out 300 fine young men for his bodyguard he lined up the remainder against a cliff. A bald-headed man was at either end of the line. Caligula gave Cassius the order: 'Kill them, from bald head to bald head, in vengeance for the death of Varus.' The news of this massacre reached the Germans and they withdrew into their thickest forests. Caligula then crossed the river with his entire army and found the entire countryside deserted. The first day of his march, just to make things more exciting, he ordered some of his German bodyguard into a neighbouring wood, and then had news brought to him at supper that the enemy was at hand. At the head of his 'Scouts' and a troop of Guards Cavalry he then dashed out to the attack. He brought back the men as prisoners, loaded with chains, and announced a crushing victory against overwhelming odds. He rewarded his comrades-in-arms with a new sort of military decoration called 'The Scouts' Crown', a golden coronet decorated with the Sun, Moon, and stars in precious stones.

On the third day the road lay through a narrow pass. The army had to move in column instead of in skirmishing order. Cassius said to Caligula, 'It was in a place rather like this, Caesar, that Varus got ambushed. I shall never forget that day so long as I live. I was marching at the head of my company and had just reached a bend in the road, as it might be this one we are coming to, when suddenly there was a tremendous war-cry, as it might be from that clump of firs yonder, and three or four hundred assegais came whizzing down on us. ...'

'Quick, my mare!' called Caligula in a panic. 'Clear the road.' He sprang from his sedan, mounted Penelope (Incitatus was at Rome, winning races) and galloped back down the column. In four hours' time he was at the bridge again, but found it so choked with baggage-wagons and was in such a hurry to cross that he dismounted and made soldiers hand him in a chair from wagon to wagon until he was safely on the other side. He recalled his arms at once, announcing that the enemy were too cowardly to meet him in battle, and that he would therefore seek new conquests elsewhere. When the whole force had reassembled at Cologne he

371

marched down the Rhine and then across to Boulogne, the nearest port to Britain. It so happened that the heir of Cymbeline, the King of Britain, had quarrelled with his father and, hearing of Caligula's approach, he fled across the Channel with a few followers and put himself under Roman protection. Caligula, who had already informed the Senate of his total subjugation of Germany, now wrote to say that King Cymbeline had sent his son to acknowledge Roman suzerainty over the entire British archipelago from the Scilly Islands to the Orkneys.

I was with Caligula throughout this expedition and had a very difficult time trying to humour him. He complained of sleeplessness and said that his enemy Neptune was plaguing him all the time with sea-noises in his ears, and used to come by night and threaten him with a trident. I said: 'Neptune? I wouldn't allow myself to be browbeaten by that saucy fellow if I were you. Why don't you punish him as you punished the Germans? You threatened him once before, I remember, and if he continues to flout you, it would be wrong to stretch your clemency any further.'

He looked at me, uncomfortably, through narrowed eyelids. 'Do you think I'm mad?' he asked, after a time.

I laughed nervously. '*Mad*, Caesar? You ask whether I think you *mad*? Why, you set the standard of sanity for the whole habitable world.'

'It's a very difficult thing, you know, Claudius,' he said confidentially, 'to be a God in human disguise. I've often thought I was going mad. They say that the hellebore cure at Anticyra is very good. What do you think of it?'

I said: 'One of the greatest Greek philosophers, but I can't remember now which of them it was, took the hellebore cure just to make his clear brain still clearer. But if you are asking me to advise you, I should say, "Don't take it! Your brain is as clear as a pool of rock-water."'

'Yes,' he said, 'but I wish I could get more than three hours' sleep at night.'

'Those three hours are because of your mortal disguise,' I said. 'Undisguised Gods never sleep at all.'

So he was comforted and the next day drew up his army in order of battle on the sea-front: archers and slingers in front, then the auxiliary Germans armed with assegais, then the main Roman forces, with the French in the rear. The cavalry were on the wings and the siege-engines, mangonels, and catapults planted on sand-dunes. Nobody knew what on earth was going to happen. He rode forward into the sea as far as Penelope's knees and cried: 'Neptune, old enemy, defend yourself. I challenge you to mortal fight. You treacherously wrecked my father's fleet, did you? Try your might on me, if you dare.' Then he quoted from Ajax's wrestling match with Ulysses, in Homer:

> Or let me lift thee, Chief, or lift thou me.
> Prove we our force ...

A little wave came rolling past. He cut at it with his sword and laughed contemptuously. Then he coolly retired and ordered the 'general engagement' to be sounded. The archers shot, the slingers slung, the javelin-men threw their javelins; the regular infantry waded into the waters as far as their arm-pits and hacked at the little waves, the cavalry charged on either flank and swam out some way, slashing with their sabres, the mangonels hurled rocks, and the catapults huge javelins and iron-tipped beams. Caligula then put to sea in a war-vessel and anchored just out of range of the missiles, uttering absurd challenges to Neptune and spitting far out over the vessel's side. Neptune made no attempt to defend himself or to reply, except that one man was nipped by a lobster, and another stung by a jelly-fish.

Caligula finally had the rally blown and told his men to wipe the blood off their swords and gather the spoil. The spoil was the sea-shells on the beach. Each man was expected to collect a helmet-full, which was added to a general heap. The shells were then sorted and packed in boxes to be sent to Rome in proof of this unheard-of victory. The troops thought it great fun, and when he rewarded them with four gold pieces a man cheered him tremendously. As a trophy of victory he built a very high lighthouse, on the model of the famous one at Alexandria, which has since proved a great blessing to sailors in those dangerous waters.

He then marched us up the Rhine again. When we reached Bonn Caligula took me aside and whispered darkly: 'The regiments have never been punished for the insult they once paid me by mutinying against my father, during my absence from this Camp. You remember, I had to come back and restore order for him.'

'I remember perfectly,' I said. 'But that's rather long ago, isn't it? After twenty-six years there can't be many men still serving in the ranks who were then there. You and Cassius Chaerea are probably the only two veteran survivors of that dreadful day.'

'Perhaps I shall only decimate them, then,' he said.

The men of the First and Twentieth Regiments were ordered to attend a special assembly and told that they might leave their arms behind, because of the hot weather. The Guards cavalry were also ordered to attend but instructed to bring their lances as well as their sabres. I found a sergeant who looked as though he might have fought at Philippi, he was so old and scarred. I said, 'Sergeant, do you know who I am?'

'No, sir. Can't say that I do, sir. You seem to be an ex-Consul, sir.'

'I am the brother of Germanicus.'

'Indeed, sir. Never knew that there was such a person, sir.'

'No, I'm not a soldier or anyone important. But I've got an important message for you fellows. *Don't leave your swords too far away when you go to this afternoon's assembly!*'

'Why, sir, if I may ask?'

'Because you may need them. Perhaps there will be an attack by the Germans. Perhaps by someone else.'

He stared hard at me and then saw that I really meant it.

'Much obliged to you, sir; I'll pass the word around,' he answered.

The infantry were massed in front of the tribunal platform and Caligula spoke to them with an angry, scowling face, stamping his feet and sawing with his hands. He began reminding them of a certain night in early autumn, many years before, when under a starless and bewitched sky. ... Here some of the men began sneaking away through a gap between two troops of cavalry. They were going to fetch their swords. Others boldly pulled theirs out from under their military cloaks where they had been hiding them. Caligula must have noticed what was happening, for he suddenly changed his tone, in the middle of a sentence. He began drawing a happy contrast between those bad days, happily forgotten, and the present reign of glory, wealth, and victory. 'Your little playfellow grew to manhood,' he said, 'and became the mightiest Emperor this world has ever known. No foeman, however fierce, dares challenge his unconquerable arms.'

My old sergeant rushed forward. 'All is lost, Caesar,' he shouted. 'The enemy has crossed the river at Cologne – three hundred thousand strong. They're out to sack Lyons – then they'll cross the Alps, and sack Rome!'

Nobody believed this nonsensical story but Caligula. He turned yellow with fear, dived from the platform, grabbed hold of a horse, tumbled into the saddle, and was out of the camp like a flash. A groom galloped after him and Caligula called back to him, 'Thank God I still hold Egypt. I'll be safe there at least. The Germans aren't sailors.'

How everyone laughed! But a colonel went after him on a good horse and caught him before very long. He assured Caligula that the news was exaggerated. Only a small force, he said, had crossed the river and had been beaten back: the Roman bank was now quite clear of the enemy. Caligula stopped at the next town and wrote a dispatch to the Senate, informing them that all his wars were now successfully over and that he was coming back at once with his laurel-garlanded troops. He blamed those cowardly stay-at-homes most severely for having, from all accounts, lived life in the City just as usual – theatres, baths, supper-parties – while he had been undergoing the severest hardships of campaign. He had eaten, drunk, and slept no better than a private soldier.

The Senate was puzzled how to pacify him, being under strict orders from him to vote him no honours on their own initiative. They sent him an embassy, however, congratulating him on his magnificent victories and begging him to hasten back to Rome where his presence was so sadly missed. He was dreadfully angry that no triumph had been decreed him even in spite of his orders, and that he was not referred to as Jove in the message but merely as the Emperor Gaius Caesar. He rapped his hand on his sword-pommel and shouted: 'Hasten back? Indeed I will, and with this in my hand.'

He had made preparations for a triple triumph: over Germany, over Britain, and over Neptune. For British captives he had Cymbeline's son and his followers, to which were added the crews of some British trading vessels whom he had detained at Boulogne. For German captives he had 300 real ones and all the tallest men he could find in France, wearing yellow wigs and German clothes and talking together in a jargon supposed to be German. But, as I say, the Senate had been afraid to vote him a formal triumph, so he had to be content with an informal one. He rode into the

City in the same style as he had ridden across the bridge at Baiae, and it was only on the intercession of Caesonia, who was a sensible woman, that he refrained from putting the entire Senate to the sword. He rewarded the people for their alms-giving generosity to him in the past by showering gold and silver from the Palace roof. But he mixed red-hot discs of iron with this largesse, to remind them that he had not yet forgiven them for their behaviour in the amphitheatre. His soldiers were told that they could make as much disturbance as they pleased and get as drunk as they liked at the public expense. They took full advantage of this licence, sacking whole streets of shops and burning down the prostitutes' quarter. Order was not restored for ten days.

This was in September. While he was away the workmen had been busy on the new temple on the Palatine Hill at the other side of the Temple of Castor and Pollux from the New Palace. An extension had been made as far as the Market Place. Caligula now turned the Temple of Castor and Pollux into a vestibule for the new temple, cutting a passage between the statues of the Gods. 'The Heavenly Twins are my doorkeepers,' he boasted. Then he sent a message to the Governor of Greece to see that all the most famous statues of Gods were removed from the temples there and sent to him at Rome. He proposed to take off their heads and substitute his own. The statue he most coveted was the colossal one of Olympian Jove. He had a special ship built for its conveyance to Rome. But the ship was struck by lightning just before it was launched. Or this, at least, was the report – I believe, really, that the superstitious crew burned it on purpose. However, Capitoline Jove then repented of his quarrel with Caligula (or so Caligula told us) and begged him to return and live next to him again. Caligula replied that he had now practically completed a new temple; but since Capitoline Jove had apologized so humbly he would make a compromise – he would build a bridge over the valley and join the two hills. He did this: the bridge passed over the roof of the Temple of Augustus.

Caligula was now publicly Jove. He was not only Latin Jove but Olympian Jove, and not only that but all the other Gods and Goddesses, too, whom he had decapitated and re-headed. Sometimes he was Apollo and sometimes Mercury and sometimes Pluto, in each case wearing the appropriate dress and demanding the appropriate sacrifices. I have seen him go about as Venus in a long gauzy silk robe with face painted, a red wig, padded bosom, and high-heeled slippers. He was present as the Good Goddess at her December festival: *that* was a scandal. Mars was a favourite character with him, too. But most of the time he was Jove: he wore an olive-wreath, a beard of fine gold wires, and a bright blue silk cloak, and carried a jagged piece of electrum in his hand to represent lightning. One day he was on the Oration Platform in the Market Place dressed as Jove and making a speech. 'I intend shortly,' he said, 'to build a city for my occupation on the top of the Alps. We Gods prefer mountain-tops to unhealthy river-valleys. From the Alps I shall have a wide view of my Empire – France, Italy, Switzerland, the Tyrol, and Germany. If I see any treason hatching anywhere below me, I shall give a warning growl of thunder so! [He growled in his throat.] If the warning is disregarded I shall blast the traitor with this lightning of mine, so!' [He hurled his piece of lightning at the crowd. It hit a statue and bounced off harmlessly.] A stranger in the crowd, a shoemaker from Marseilles on a sight-seeing visit to Rome, burst out laughing. Caligula had the fellow arrested and brought nearer to the platform, then bending down he asked, frowning: 'Who do I seem to you to be?' 'A big humbug,' said the shoemaker. Caligula was puzzled. 'Humbug?' he repeated. '*I* a humbug!' 'Yes,' said the Frenchman. 'I'm only a poor French shoemaker and this is my first visit to Rome. And I don't know any better. If anyone at home did what you're doing he'd be a big humbug.'

Caligula began to laugh too. 'You poor half-wit,' he said. 'Of course he would be. That's just the difference.'

The whole crowd laughed like mad, but whether at Caligula or at the shoemaker was not clear. Soon after this he had a thunder-and-lightning machine made. He lit a fuse and it made a roar and a flash and catapulted stones in whatever direction he wanted. But I have it on good authority that whenever there was a real thunderstorm at night he used to creep under the bed. There is a good story about that. One day a storm burst when he was parading about dressed as Venus. He began to cry: 'Father, Father, spare your pretty daughter!'

The money he had won in France was soon spent and he invented new ways of increasing the revenue. His favourite one now was to examine judicially the wills of men who had just died and had left him no money: he would then give evidence of the benefits that the testators had received from him and declare that they had been either ungrateful or of unsound mind at the time of drawing their wills and that he preferred to think that they had been of unsound mind. He cancelled the wills and appointed himself principal heir. He used to come into Court in the early morning and write up on a blackboard the sum of money that he intended to win that day, usually 200,000 gold pieces. When he had won it, he closed the Court. He made a new edict one morning about the hours of business permitted in various sorts of shops. He had it written in very small letters on a tiny placard posted high on a pillar in the Market Place where nobody troubled to read it, not realizing its importance. That afternoon his officers took the names of several hundred tradesmen who had unwittingly infringed the edict. When they were brought to trial he allowed any of them who could do so to plead in mitigation of sentence that they had named him as co-heir with their children. Few of them could. It now became customary for men with money to notify the Imperial Treasurer that Caligula was named in their wills as the principal heir. But in several cases this proved unwise. For Caligula made use of the medicine chest that he had inherited from my grandmother Livia. One day he sent round presents of honied fruits to some recent testators. They all died at once. He also summoned my cousin, the King of Morocco, to Rome and put him to death, saying simply: 'I need your fortune, Ptolemy.'

During his absence in France there had been comparatively few convictions at Rome and the prisons were nearly empty: this meant a shortage of victims for throwing to the wild beasts. He made the shortage up by using members of the audience, first cutting out their tongues so that they could not call out to their friends for rescue. He was becoming more and more capricious. One day a priest was about to sacrifice a young bull to him in his aspect of Apollo. The usual sacrificial procedure was for a deacon to stun the bull with a stone axe, and for the priest then to cut its throat. Caligula came in dressed as a deacon and asked the usual question: 'Shall I?' When the priest answered 'Do so,' he brought the axe down smash on the priest's head.

I was still living in poverty with Briseis and Calpurnia, for though I had no debts, neither had I any money except what little income came to me from the farm. I was careful to let Caligula know how poor I was and he graciously permitted me to remain in the Senatorial Order though I no longer had the necessary financial qualifications. But I felt my position daily more insecure. One midnight early in October I was awakened by loud knocking at the front door. I put my head out of the window. 'Who's there?' I asked.

'You're wanted at the Palace immediately.'

I said: 'Is that you, Cassius Chaerea? Am I going to be killed, do you know?'

'My orders are to fetch you to him immediately.'

Calpurnia cried and Briseis cried and both kissed me good-bye very tenderly. As they helped me to dress I hurriedly told them how to dispose of my few remaining possessions, and what to do with little Antonia, and about my funeral, and so on. It was a most affecting scene for all of us, but I did not dare prolong it. Soon I was hopping along at Cassius's side to the Palace. He said gruffly, 'Two more ex-Consuls have been summoned to appear with you.' He told me their names and I was still more alarmed. They were rich men, just the sort whom Caligula would accuse of a plot against him. But why me? I was the first to arrive. The two others came rushing in almost immediately after, breathless with haste and fear. We were taken into the Hall of Justice and made to sit on chairs on a sort of scaffold looking down on the tribunal platform. A guard of German soldiers stood behind us, muttering together in their own language. The room was in complete darkness but for two tiny oil lamps on the tribunal. The windows behind were draped, we noticed, with black hangings embroidered with silver stars. My companions and I silently clasped hands in farewell. They were men from whom I had had many insults at one time or another, but in the shadow of death such trifles are forgotten. We sat there waiting for something to happen until just before daybreak.

Suddenly we heard a clash of cymbals and the gay music of oboes and fiddles. Slaves filed in from a door at the side of the tribunal, each carrying two lamps, which they put on tables at the side; and then the powerful voice of a eunuch began singing the well-known song *When the long watches of the night*. The slaves retired. A shuffling sound was heard and presently in danced a tall ungainly figure in a woman's pink silk gown with a crown of imitation roses on its head. It was Caligula.

The rosy-fingered Goddess then
Will roll away the night of stars ...

379

Here he drew away the draperies from the window and disclosed the first streaks of dawn, and then, when the eunuch reached the part about the rosy-fingered Goddess, blowing out the lamps one by one, brought this incident into the dance too. Puff. Puff. Puff.

> And where clandestine lovers lie
> Entangled in sweet passion's toils ...

From a bed which we had not noticed, because it was in an alcove, the Goddess Dawn then pulled out a girl and a man, neither of them with any clothes on, and in dumb show indicated that it was the time for them to part. The girl was very beautiful. The man was the eunuch who was singing. They parted in opposite directions as if profoundly distressed. When the last verse came:

> O Dawn, of Goddesses most fair,
> Who with thy slow and lovely tread
> Dost give relief to every care ...

I had the sense to prostrate myself on the ground. My companions were not slow in following my example. Caligula capered off the stage and soon afterwards we were summoned to breakfast with him. I said, 'O God of Gods, I have never in my life witnessed any dance that gave me such profound spiritual joy as the one I have just witnessed. I have no words for its loveliness.'

My companions agreed with me and said that it was a million pities that so matchless a performance had been given to so tiny an audience. He said, complacently, that it was only a rehearsal. He would give it one night soon in the amphitheatre to the whole City. I didn't see how he would manage the curtain-drawing effect in an open-air amphitheatre hundreds of yards long, but I said nothing about that. We had a very tasty breakfast, the senior ex-Consul sitting on the floor alternately eating thrush-pie and kissing Caligula's foot. I was just thinking how pleased Calpurnia and Briseis would be to see me back when Caligula, who was in a very pleasant humour, suddenly said: 'Pretty girl, wasn't she, Claudius, you old lecher?'

'Very pretty indeed, God.'

'And still a virgin, so far as I know. Would you like to marry her? You can if you like. I took a fancy to her for a moment, but it's a funny thing, I don't really like immature women any more. ... Or any mature woman, for that matter, except Caesonia. Did your recognize the girl?'

'No, Lord, I was only watching you, to tell the truth.'

'She's your cousin Messalina, Barbatus's daughter. The old pander didn't utter a word of protest when I asked for her to be sent along to me. What cowards they are, after all, Claudius!'

'Yes, Lord God.'

'All right, then, I'll marry you two to-morrow. I'm going to bed now, I think.'

'A thousand thanks and homages, Lord.'

He gave me his other foot to kiss. Next day he kept his promise and married us. He accepted a tenth of Messalina's dowry as a fee but otherwise behaved courteously enough. Calpurnia had been delighted to see me alive again and had pretended not to mind about my marriage. She said in a businesslike way: 'Very well, my dear, I'll go back to the farm and look after things for you there again. You won't miss me, with that pretty wife of yours. And now you have money you'll have to live at the Palace again.'

I told her that the marriage was forced on me and that I would miss her very much indeed. But she pooh-poohed that: Messalina had twice her looks, three times her brains, and birth and money into the bargain. I was in love with her already, Calpurnia said.

I felt uncomfortable. Calpurnia had been my only true friend in all those four years of misery. What had she not done for me? And yet she was right: I *was* in love with Messalina, and Messalina was to be my wife now. There would be no place for Calpurnia with Messalina about.

She was in tears as she went away. So was I. I was not in love with her, but she was my truest friend and I knew that if ever I needed her she would be there to help me. I need not say that when I received the dowry money I did not forget her.

Chapter 33

MESSALINA was an extremely beautiful girl, slim and quick moving, with eyes as black as jet and masses of curly black hair. She hardly spoke a word and had a mysterious smile which drove me nearly crazy with love for her. She was so glad to have escaped from Caligula and so quick to realize the advantages that marriage with me gave her, that she behaved in a way which made me quite sure that she loved me as much as I loved her. This was practically the first time I had been in love with anyone since my boyhood; and when a not very clever, not very attractive man of fifty falls in love with a very attractive and very clever girl of fifteen it is usually a poor look-out for him. We were married in October. By December she was pregnant by me. She appeared very fond of my little Antonia, who was aged about ten, and it was a relief to me that the child now had someone whom she could call mother, someone who was near enough to her in age to be a friend and could explain the ways of society to her and take her about, as Calpurnia had not been able to do.

Messalina and I were invited to live at the Palace again. We arrived at an unfortunate time. A merchant called Bassus had been asking questions of a captain of the Palace Guards about Caligula's daily habits – was it true that he walked about the cloisters at night because he could not sleep? At what time did he do this? Which cloisters did he usually choose? What Guard did he have with him? The captain reported the incident to Cassius and Cassius reported it to Caligula. Bassus was arrested and cross-examined. He was forced to admit that he had intended to kill Caligula but denied even under torture that he had any associates. Caligula then sent a message to Bassus's old father, ordering him to attend his son's execution. The old man, who had no notion that Bassus had been planning to assassinate Caligula or even that he had been arrested, was greatly shocked to find his son groaning on the Palace floor, his body broken by torture. But he controlled himself and thanked Caligula for his graciousness in summoning him to close his son's eyes. Caligula laughed. 'Close his eyes indeed! He's going to have no eyes to close, the assassin! I'm going to poke them out in a moment. And yours too.'

Bassus's father said: 'Spare our lives. We are only tools in the hands of powerful men. I'll give you all the names.'

This impressed Caligula, and when the old man mentioned the Guards' Commander, the Commander of the Germans, Callistus the Treasurer, Caesonia, Mnester, and three or four others, he grew pale with alarm. 'And whom would they make Emperor in my place?' he asked.

'Your uncle Claudius.'

'Is he in the plot too?'

'No, they were merely going to use him as a figure-head.'

Caligula hurried away and summoned the Guards' Commander, the Commander of the Germans, the Treasurer, and myself to a private room. He asked the others, pointing to me: 'Is that creature fit to be Emperor?'

They answered in surprised tones, 'Not unless you say so, Jove.'

Then he gave them a pathetic smile and exclaimed, 'I am one and you are three. Two of you are armed and I am defenceless. If you hate me and want to kill me, do so at once and put that poor idiot into my place as Emperor.'

We all fell on our faces and the two soldiers handed him their swords from the floor, saying, 'We are innocent of any such treacherous thought, Lord. If you disbelieve us, kill us!'

Do you know, he was actually about to kill us! But while he hesitated I said: 'Almighty God, the colonel who summoned me here told me of the charge brought against these loyal men by Bassus's father. Its falsity is evident. If Bassus had really been employed by them, would it have been necessary for him to question the captain about your movements? Would he not have been able to get all the necessary information from these generals themselves? No, Bassus's father has tried to save his own life and Bassus's by a clumsy lie.'

Caligula appeared to be convinced by my argument. He gave me his hand to kiss, made us all rise, and handed the swords back. Bassus and his father were thereupon hewn to pieces by the Germans. But Caligula could not rid his mind of the dread of assassination, which was presently increased by a number of unlucky omens. First the porter's lodge at the Palace was struck by lightning. Then Incitatus, when he was brought in to dinner one evening, reared up and cast a shoe which broke an alabaster cup that had belonged to Julius Caesar, spilling the wine on the floor. The worst omen of all was what happened at Olympus, when, in accordance with Caligula's orders, the temple workmen began to take the statue of Jove to pieces for conveyance to Rome. The head was to come off first, to be used as a measure for the new head of Caligula that would be substituted when the statue was reassembled. They had got the pulley fixed to the temple roof and a rope knotted around the neck and were just about to haul, when suddenly a thunderous peal of laughter roared out through the whole building. The workmen rushed away in panic. Nobody could be found bold enough to take their places.

Caesonia now advised him, since by his immovable rigour he had made everyone tremble at the very sound of his name, to rule mildly and earn the people's love instead of their fear. For Caesonia realized how dangerously he was placed and that if anything happened to him she would certainly lose her life too, unless she was known to have done her best to dissuade him from his cruelties. He was behaving in a most imprudent way now. He went in turn to the Guards' Commander, the Treasurer, and the Commander of the Germans and pretended to take each of them into his confidence, saying, 'I trust *you*, but the others are plotting against me and I want you to regard them as my deadliest enemies.' They compared notes; and that is why when a real plot was formed they shut their eyes to it. Caligula said that he approved Caesonia's advice and thanked her for it; he would certainly follow it when he had made his peace with his enemies. He called the Senate together and addressed us in this strain: 'Soon I shall grant you all an amnesty, my enemies, and reign with love and peace a thousand years. That is the prophecy. But before that golden time comes heads must roll along the floor of this House and blood spurt up to the beams. A wild five minutes that will be.' If the 1,000 years of peace had come first, and then the wild five minutes, we should have preferred it.

The plot was formed by Cassius Chaerea. He was an old-fashioned soldier, accustomed to blind obedience to the orders of his superiors. Things have to be extraordinarily bad before a man of this stamp can think of plotting against the life of his Commander-in-Chief, to whom he has sworn allegiance in the most solemn terms imaginable. Caligula had treated Cassius extremely badly. He had definitely promised him the command of the Guards and then without a word of explanation or apology had given it to a captain of short service and no military distinction as a reward for a remarkable drinking feat at the Palace: he had volunteered to drain a three-gallon jar of wine without removing it from his lips, and had really done so – I was watching – and kept the wine down into the bargain. Caligula had also made this man a senator. And Caligula employed Cassius on all his most unpleasant errands and tasks – collection of taxes that were not really due, the seizure of property for offences never committed, the execution of innocent men. Recently he had made him torture a beautiful girl, well born too, called Quintilia. The story was as follows. Several young men had wanted to marry her, but the one whom her guardian had proposed, a member of the Scouts, she did not like at all. She begged him to let her choose one of the others; he consented, and the day for the marriage was fixed. The rejected Scout went to Caligula and brought an accusation against his rival, saying that he had blasphemed, speaking of his August Sovereign as 'that bald-headed madame'. He cited Quintilia as a witness. Quintilia and her betrothed were brought before Caligula. Both denied the charge. Both were sentenced to the rack. Cassius's face revealed his disgust, for only slaves could legally be put to torture. So Caligula ordered him to supervise Quintilia's racking and turn the screws with his own hands. Quintilia did not utter a word or a cry throughout her ordeal and afterwards said to Cassius, who was so affected that he was weeping, 'Poor Colonel, I bear you no grudge. Sometimes it must be hard to obey orders.' Cassius said bitterly: 'I wish I had died that day with Varus in the Teutoburger Forest.'

She was taken again into Caligula's presence, and Cassius reported that she had made no confession and not allowed a cry to escape her. Caesonia said to Caligula, 'That was because she was in love with the man. Love conquers all. You might cut her in pieces but she would never betray him.'

Caligula said: 'And would you too be so gloriously brave on my account, Caesonia?'

'You know that I would,' she said.

So Quintilia's betrothed was not tortured but given a free pardon, and Quintilia was awarded a dowry of 8,000 gold pieces from the estate of the Scout, who was executed for perjury. But Caligula heard that Cassius had wept during Quintilia's torture and jeered at him for an old cry-baby. 'Cry-baby' was not the worst name he found. He pretended that Cassius was an effeminate old pathic, and was always making dirty jokes about him to the other Guards officers, who were obliged to laugh heartily at them. Cassius used to come to Caligula for the watchword every day at noon. It had always been 'Rome' or 'Augustus' or 'Jove' or 'victory' or something of the sort; but now to annoy Cassius, Caligula would give him absurd words like 'Staylaces' or 'Lots of Love' or 'Curling-irons' or 'Kiss me, Sergeant', and Cassius had to take them back to his brother-officers and stand their chaff. He decided to kill Caligula.

Caligula was madder than ever. He came into my room one day and said without any introductory remark: 'I shall have three Imperial cities, and Rome won't be one of them. I shall have my city on the Alps, and I shall rebuild Rome at Antium because that's where I was born and it deserves the honour, and because it's on the sea, and then I shall have Alexandria in case the Germans capture the other two. Alexandria is a very cultivated place.'

'Yes, God,' I said humbly.

He then suddenly remembered that he had been called a bald-headed madame – his hair was certainly very thin on top now – and shouted out, 'How dare you go about with a great ugly bush of hair in my presence? It's blasphemy.' He turned to his German guard. 'Cut his head off!'

Once more I thought I was done for. But I had the presence of mind to say sharply to the Guard who was running at me with his sword, 'What are you doing, idiot? The God didn't say "head", he said "hair"! Run off and fetch the shears at once!' Caligula was taken aback and perhaps really thought that he had said 'hair'. He allowed the German to fetch the shears. My crown was shorn clean. I asked permission to dedicate the clippings to his Deity and he graciously gave consent. So now he had everyone in the Palace shorn, except the Germans. When it came to Cassius's turn Caligula said, 'Oh, what a pity! Those darling little ringlets that the Sergeant loves so much!'

That evening Cassius met Lesbia's husband. He had been Ganymede's best friend and from something that Caligula had said that morning was not likely to live much longer. He said, 'Good evening, Cassius Chaerea, my friend. What's the watchword to-day?'

Cassius had never been called 'my friend' before by Lesbia's husband and looked intently at him.

Lesbia's husband – his name was Marcus Vinicius – said again, 'Cassius, we have much in common and when I call you "friend", I mean it. What's the watchword?'

Cassius answered, 'The watchword to-night is "Little Ringlets". But, my friend Marcus Vinicius, if I may indeed call you friend, give me the watchword "Liberty" and my sword is at your service.'

Vinicius embraced him. 'We are not the only two who are ready to strike for Liberty. The Tiger is also with me.' The Tiger – his real name was Cornelius Sabinus – was another Guards colonel, who relieved Cassius whenever he went off duty.

The great Palatine Festival started the next day. This festival in honour of Augustus had been instituted by Livia at the beginning of Tiberius's monarchy and was held annually in the Southern Court of the Old Palace. It began with sacrifices to Augustus and a symbolic procession, and continued for three A.D. 41 days with theatrical pieces, dancing, singing, juggling, and the like. Wooden stands were erected with seating for 60,000 people. When the festival ended the stands were taken down and stored away until the following year. This year Caligula had prolonged the three days to eight, interspersing the performances with chariot-races in the Circus and sham naval-fights in the Basin. He wanted to be continuously amused until the day he sailed for Alexandria, which was to be the twenty-fifth of January. For he was going to Egypt to see the sights, to raise money by immovable rigour and the same sort of trickery he had used in France, to make plans for the rebuilding of Alexandria and, lastly, so he boasted, to put a new head on the Sphinx.

The Festival started. Caligula sacrificed to Augustus, but in a somewhat perfunctory and disdainful way – like a master who in some emergency or other has to perform some menial service for one of his slaves. When this was over he proclaimed that if any citizen present asked a boon that it was in his power to grant he would graciously grant it. He had been angry with the people lately for their lack of enthusiasm at the last wild-beast show and had punished them by shutting the city granaries for ten days; but perhaps he had forgiven them now, because he had just scattered largesse from the Palace roof. So a glad shout went up. 'More bread, less taxes, Caesar! More bread, less taxes!' Caligula was very angry. He sent a platoon of Germans along the benches and 100 heads were chopped off. This incident disturbed the conspirators; it was a reminder of the barbarity of the Germans and the marvellous devotion that they paid Caligula. By this time, there can hardly have been a citizen in Rome who did not long for the death of Caligula, or would not willingly have eaten his flesh, as the saying is; but to these Germans he was the most glorious hero the world had ever known. And if he dressed as a woman; or galloped suddenly away from his army on the march; or made Caesonia appear naked before them and boasted of her beauty; or

387

burned down his most beautiful villa at Herculaneum on the ground that his mother Agrippina had been imprisoned there for two days on her way to the island where she died – this inexplicable sort of behaviour only made him the more worthy of their worship as a divine being. They used to nod wisely to each other and say, 'Yes, the Gods are like that. You can't tell what they are going to do next. Tuisco and Mann, at home, in our dear, dear Fatherland, are just the same.'

Cassius was reckless and did not care what happened to him personally, so long as Caligula was assassinated, but the other conspirators, who did not feel so strongly, began to wonder what vengeance the Germans would take on the murderers of their wonderful hero. They began making excuses and Cassius could not get them to agree on a proper plan of action. They suggested leaving it to chance. Cassius grew anxious. He called them cowards and accused them of playing for time. He said that they really wanted Caligula to get safe away to Egypt. The last day of the festival came, and Cassius had with great difficulty persuaded them to agree to a workable plan, when Caligula suddenly gave out that the festival would go on for another three days. He said that he wanted to act and sing in a masque which he had himself composed for the benefit of the Alexandrians, but which he thought it only fair to show his own countrymen first.

This change of plans gave the more timorous of the conspirators a new opportunity for hedging. 'Oh, but Cassius, this quite alters matters. It makes everything much easier for us. We can kill him on the last day, just as he comes off the stage. That's a far better plan. Or as he goes on. Whichever you prefer.'

Cassius answered: 'We've made a plan and sworn to keep it, and keep it we must. It's a very good plan too. Not a flaw in it.'

'But we have plenty of time now. Why not wait another three days?'

Cassius said: 'If you won't carry that plan out to-day as you all swore you would, I shall have to work single-handed. I won't have much of a chance against the Germans – but I'll do my best. If they are too strong for me I'll call out, "Vinicius, Asprenas, Bubo, Aquila, Tiger, why aren't you here as you promised?"'

So they agreed to carry out the original plan. Caligula was to be persuaded by Vinicius and Asprenas to leave the theatre at noon for a plunge in the swimming pool and a quick lunch. Just before this Cassius, The Tiger, and the other captains who were in the plot were to slip out unobtrusively by the stage-door. They were to go round to the entrance of the covered passage which was the short cut from the theatre to the New Palace. Asprenas and Vinicius would persuade Caligula to take this short cut.

The play that day had been announced as *Ulysses and Circe* and Caligula had promised to scatter fruit and cakes and money at the end of it. He would naturally do this from the end nearest the gate, where his seat was, so everyone came as early as possible to the theatre to secure seats at that end. When the gates were opened the crowd rushed in and raced for the nearest seats. Usually all the women sat together in one part, and there were seats reserved for knights, and for senators, and for distinguished foreigners, and so on. But to-day everyone was muddled up together. I saw a senator who had come in late forced to sit between an African slave and a woman with saffron-dyed hair and the dark-coloured gown that common prostitutes wear as their professional dress. 'So much the better,' said Cassius to The Tiger. 'The more confusion there is, the better chance we have.'

Apart from the Germans and Caligula himself almost the only person at the Palace who had not by now heard of the plot was poor Claudius. This was because poor Claudius was going to be killed too, as Caligula's uncle. All Caligula's family were to be killed. The conspirators were afraid, I suppose, that I would make myself Emperor and avenge his death. They had determined to restore the Republic. If only the idiots had taken me into their confidence this story would have had a very different ending. For I was a better Republican than any of them. But they mistrusted me, and very cruelly doomed me to death. Even Caligula knew more about the plot than I did, in a sense, for he had just been sent a warning oracle from the Temple of Fortune at Antium: 'Beware of Cassius.' He misunderstood it, and recalled Drusilla's first husband, Cassius Longinus, from Asia Minor, where he was Governor. He thought that Longinus was angry with him for murdering Drusilla and remembered that he was a descendant of that Cassius who helped to assassinate Julius Caesar.

I came into the theatre that morning at eight o'clock and found that a place had been reserved for me by the ushers. I was between the Guards' Commander and the Commander of the Germans.

The Guards' Commander leant across me and asked: 'Have you heard the news?'

'What news?' asked the Commander of the Germans.

'They are playing a new drama to-day.'

'What is it?'

'*The Tyrant's Death.*'

The Commander of the Germans gave him a quick look and quoted frowning:

> 'Brave comrade, hold thy peace
> Lest someone hear thee, of the men of Greece.'

I said: 'Yes, there is a change in the programme. Mnester is to give us *The Tyrant's Death*. It hasn't been played for years. It's about King Cinyras, who wouldn't come into the war against Troy, and got killed for his cowardice.'

The play began and Mnester was at the top of his form. When he died at the hands of Apollo he spurted blood all over his clothes from a little bladder concealed in his mouth. Caligula sent for him and kissed him on both cheeks. Cassius and The Tiger escorted him to his dressing-room as if to protect him from his admirers. Then they went out by the stage-door. The captains followed during the confusion of the largesse-throwing. Asprenas said to Caligula: 'That was marvellous. Now what about a plunge in the bath and a little light luncheon?'

'No,' said Caligula. 'I want to see those girl acrobats. They're said to be pretty good. I think I'll sit the show out. It's the last day.' He was in an extremely affable mood.

So Vinicius rose. He was going to tell Cassius, The Tiger, and the rest, not to wait. Caligula pulled at his cloak. 'My dear fellow, don't run away. You must see those girls. One does a dance called the fish-dance which makes you feel as if you were ten fathoms under water.'

Vinicius sat down and saw the fish-dance. But first he had to sit through a short melodramatic interlude called *Laureolus*, or *The Robber Chief*. There was a lot of slaughter in it and the actors, a second-rate lot, had all found blood-bladders to put in their mouths in imitation of Mnester. You never saw such an ill-omened mess as they made of the stage! When the fish-dance was over Vinicius rose again: 'To tell the truth, Lord, I would love to stay but Cloacina calls me. It's some confounded thing I ate.

       'Soft but cohesive let my offerings flow,
       Not roughly swift, nor impudently slow ...'

Caligula laughed. 'Don't blame it on me, my dear fellow. You're one of my best friends. I wouldn't doctor your food for the world.'

Vinicius went out by the stage-door and found Cassius and The Tiger in the court. 'You'd better come back,' he said. 'He's sitting it out to the end.'

Cassius said: 'Very well. Let's go back. I'm going to kill him where he sits. I expect you to stand by me.'

Just then a Guardsman came up to Cassius and said, 'The boys are here at last, sir.'

Now, Caligula had lately sent letters to the Greek cities of Asia Minor ordering them each to send him ten boys of the noblest blood to dance the national sword-dance at the festival and sing a hymn in his honour. This was only an excuse for getting the boys in his power: they would be useful hostages when he turned his fury against Asia Minor. They should have arrived several days before this, but rough weather in the Adriatic had held them up at Corfu. The Tiger said, 'Inform the Emperor at once.' The Guardsman hurried to the theatre.

Meanwhile I was beginning to feel very hungry. I whispered to Vitellius who was sitting behind me, 'I do wish that the Emperor would set us the example of going out for a little luncheon.' Then the Guardsman came up with the message about the boys' arrival and Caligula said to Asprenas: 'Splendid! They'll be able to perform this afternoon. I must see them at once and have a short rehearsal of the hymn. Come on, friends! The rehearsal first, then a bathe, luncheon, and back again!'

We went out. Caligula stopped at the gate to give orders about the afternoon performance. I walked ahead with Vitellius, a senator named Sentius, and the two generals. We went by the covered passage. I noticed Cassius and The Tiger at the entrance. They did not salute me, which I thought strange, for they saluted the others. We reached the Palace. I said, 'I *am* hungry. I smell venison cooking. I hope that rehearsal won't take too long.' We were in the ante-room to the banqueting-hall. 'This is odd,' I thought. 'No captains here, only sergeants.' I turned questioningly to my companions but – another odd thing – found that they had all silently vanished. Just then I heard distant shouting and screams, then more shouting. I wondered what on earth was happening. Some-one ran past the window shouting, 'It's all over. He's dead!' Two minutes later there came a most awful roar from the theatre, as if the whole audience was being massacred. It went on and on but after a time there was a lull followed by tremendous cheering. I stumbled upstairs to my little reading-room where I collapsed trembling on a chair.

The pillared portrait-busts of Herodotus, Polybius, Thucydides, and Asinius Pollio stood facing me. Their impassive features seemed to say: 'A true historian will always rise superior to the political disturbances of his day.' I determined to comport myself as a true historian.

Chapter 34

WHAT had happened was this. Caligula had come out of the theatre. A sedan was waiting to take him the long way round to the New Palace between double ranks of Guards. But Vinicius said: 'Let's go by the short cut. The Greek boys are waiting there at the entrance, I believe.' 'All right, then, come along,' said Cali-gula. The people tried to follow him out but Asprenas dropped behind and forced them back. 'The Emperor doesn't want to be bothered with you,' he said. 'Get back!' He told the gate-keepers to close the gates again.

Caligula went towards the covered passage. Cassius stepped for-ward and saluted. 'The watchword, Caesar?'

Caligula said, 'Eh? Oh, yes, the watchword, Cassius. I'll give you a nice one to-day – "Old Man's Petticoat".'

The Tiger called from behind Caligula, 'Shall I?' It was the agreed signal.

'*Do so!*' bellowed Cassius, drawing his sword, and striking at Caligula with all his strength.

He had intended to split his skull to the chin, but in his rage he missed his aim and struck him between the neck and the shoul-ders. The upper breastbone took the chief force of the blow. Cali-gula was staggered with pain and astonishment. He looked wildly around him, turned, and ran. As he turned Cassius struck at him again, severing his jaw. The Tiger then felled him with a badly-aimed blow on the side of his head. He slowly rose to his knees. 'Strike again!' Cassius shouted.

Caligula looked up to Heaven with a face of agony. 'O Jove,' he prayed.

'Granted,' shouted The Tiger, and hacked off one of his hands.

A captain called Auila gave the finishing stroke, a deep thrust in the groin, but ten more swords were plunged into his breast and belly afterwards, just to make sure of him. A captain called Bubo dipped his hand in a wound in Caligula's side and then licked his fingers, shrieking, 'I swore to drink his blood!'

A crowd had collected and the alarm went round, 'The Germans are coming.' The assassins had no chance against a whole battalion of Germans. They rushed into the nearest building, which happened to be my old home, lately borrowed from me by Caligula as guest-apartments for foreign ambassadors whom he did not want to have about in the Palace. They went in at the front door and out at the back door. All got away in time but The Tiger and Asprenas. The Tiger had to pretend that he was not one of the assassins and joined the Germans in their cries for vengeance. Asprenas ran into the covered passage, where the Germans caught him and killed him. They killed two other senators whom they happened to meet. This was only a small party of Germans. The rest of the battalion marched into the theatre and closed the gate behind them. They were going to avenge their murdered hero by a wholesale massacre. That was the roar and screaming I had heard. Nobody in the theatre knew that Caligula was dead or that any attempt had been made against his life. But it was quite clear what the Germans intended because they were going through their curious performance of patting and stroking their assegais and speaking to them as if they were human beings, which is their invariable custom before shedding blood with those terrible weapons. There was no escape. Suddenly from the stage the trumpet blew the Attention, followed by the six notes which mean Imperial Orders. Mnester entered and raised his hand. And at once the terrible din died down into mere sobs and smothered groans, for when Mnester appeared on the stage it was a rule that nobody should utter the least sound on pain of instant death. The Germans, too, stopped their patting and stroking and incantations. The Imperial Orders stiffened them into statues.

Mnester shouted: 'He's not dead, Citizens. Far from it. The

assassins set on him and beat him to his knees, so! But he presently rose again, so! Swords cannot prevail against our Divine Caesar. Wounded and bloody as he was, he rose, so! He lifted his august head and walked, so! with divine stride through the ranks of his cowardly and baffled assassins. His wounds healed, a miracle! He is now in the Market Place loudly and eloquently haranguing his subjects from the Oration Platform.'

A mighty cheer arose and the Germans sheathed their swords and marched out. Mnester's timely lie (prompted, as a matter of fact, by a message from Herod Agrippa, King of the Jews, the only man in Rome who kept his wits about him that fateful afternoon) had saved 60,000 lives or more.

But the real news had by now reached the Palace, where it caused the most utter confusion. A few old soldiers thought that the opportunity for looting was too good to be missed. They would pretend to be looking for the assassins. Every room in the Palace had a golden door-knob, each worth six months' pay, easy enough to hack off with a sharp sword. I heard the cries, 'Kill them, kill them! Avenge Caesar!' and hid behind a curtain. Two soldiers came in. They saw my feet under the curtain. 'Come out of there, assassin. No use hiding from us.'

I came out and fell on my face. 'Don't k-k-k-k-kill me, Lords,' I said. 'I had n-nothing to d-d-d-d-do with it.'

'Who's this old gentleman?' asked one of the soldiers who was new at the Palace. 'He doesn't look dangerous.'

'Why! Don't you know? He's Germanicus's invalid brother. A decent old stick. No harm in him at all. Get up, sir. We won't hurt you.' This soldier's name was Gratus.

They made me follow them downstairs again into the banqueting-hall where the sergeants and corporals were holding a council-of-war. A young sergeant stood on a table waving his arms and shouting, 'Republic be hanged! A new Emperor's our only hope. Any Emperor so long as we can persuade the Germans to accept him.'

'Incitatus,' someone suggested, guffawing.

'Yes, by God! Better the old nag than no Emperor at all. We want someone immediately, to keep the Germans quiet. Otherwise they'll run amok.'

My two captors pushed their way through the crowd dragging me behind them. Gratus called out, 'Hey, Sergeant! Look whom we have here! A bit of luck, I think. It's old Claudius. What's wrong with old Claudius for Emperor? The best man for the job in Rome, though he do limp and stammer a bit.'

Loud cheers, laughter, and cries of 'Long live the Emperor Claudius!' The Sergeant apologized. 'Why, sir, we all thought you were dead. But you're our man, all right. Push him up, lads, where we can all see him!' Two burly corporals caught me by the legs and hoisted me on their shoulders. 'Long live the Emperor Claudius!'

'Put me down,' I cried furiously. 'Put me down! I don't want to be Emperor. I refuse to be Emperor. Long live the Republic!'

But they only laughed. 'That's a good one. He doesn't want to be Emperor, he says. Modest, eh?'

'Give me a sword,' I shouted. 'I'll kill myself sooner.'

Messalina came hurrying towards us. 'For my sake, Claudius, do what they ask of you. For our child's sake. We'll all be murdered if you refuse. They've killed Caesonia already. And they took her little girl by the feet and bashed out her brains against a wall.'

'You'll be all right, sir, once you get accustomed to it,' Gratus said, grinning. 'It's not such a bad life, an Emperor's isn't.'

I made no more protests. What was the use of struggling against Fate? They hurried me out into the Great Court, singing the foolish hymn of hope composed at Caligula's accession, '*Germanicus is come Again, To Free the City from her Pain.*' For I had the surname Germanicus too. They forced me to put on Caligula's golden oak-leaf chaplet, recovered from one of the looters. To steady myself I had to cling tightly to the corporals' shoulders. The chaplet kept slipping over one ear. How foolish I felt. They say that I looked like a criminal being hauled away to execution. Massed trumpeters blew the Imperial Salute.

The Germans came screaming towards us. They had just heard for certain of Caligula's death, from a senator who came to meet them in deep mourning. They were furious at having been tricked and wanted to go back to the theatre, but the theatre was empty now, so they were at a loss what to do next. There was nobody about to take vengeance on except the Guards, and the Guards were armed. The Imperial Salute decided them. They rushed forward shouting: 'Hoch! Hoch! Long live the Emperor Claudius!' and began frantically dedicating their assegais to my service and struggling to break through the crowd of Guardsmen to kiss my feet. I called to them to keep back, and they obeyed, prostrating themselves before me. I was carried round and round the Court.

And what thoughts or memories, would you guess, were passing through my mind on this extraordinary occasion? Was I thinking of the Sibyl's prophecy, of the omen of the wolf-cub, of Pollio's advice, or of Briseis's dream? Of my grandfather and liberty? Of my father and liberty? Of my three Imperial predecessors, Augustus, Tiberius, Caligula, their lives and deaths? Of the great danger I was still in from the conspirators, and from the Senate, and from the Guards battalions at the Camp? Of Messalina and our unborn child? Of my grandmother Livia and my promise to deify her if ever I became Emperor? Of Postumus and Germanicus? Of Agrippina and Nero? Of Camilla? No, you would never guess what was passing through my mind. But I shall be frank and tell you what it was, though the confession is a shameful one. I was thinking, 'So, I'm Emperor, am I? What nonsense! But at least I'll be able to make people read my books now. Public recitals to large audiences. And good books too, thirty-five years' hard work in them. It won't be unfair. Pollio used to get attentive audiences by giving expensive dinners. He was a very sound historian, and the last of the Romans. My *History of Carthage* is full of amusing anecdotes. I'm sure they'll enjoy it.'

That was what I was thinking. I was thinking, too, what opportunities I should have, as Emperor, for consulting the secret archives and finding out just what happened on this occasion or on that. How many twisted stories still remained to be straightened out! What a miraculous fate for an historian! And as you will have seen, I took full advantage of my opportunities. Even the mature historian's privilege of setting forth conversations of which he knows only the gist is one that I have availed myself of hardly at all.

TREE OF THE
IMPERIAL FAMILY AND CONNEXIONS
TO THE YEAR A.D. 41

GIVING NAMES AS ABBREVIATED
IN THIS BOOK

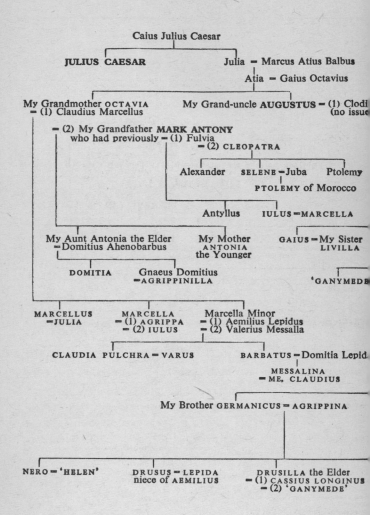

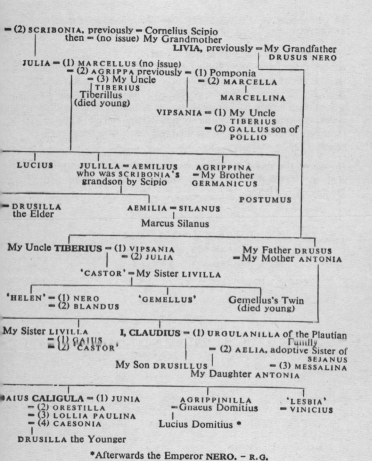

— (2) SCRIBONIA, previously = Cornelius Scipio
  then = (no issue) My Grandmother
                              LIVIA, previously = My Grandfather
                                                  DRUSUS NERO

JULIA = (1) MARCELLUS (no issue)
      = (2) AGRIPPA previously = (1) Pomponia
      = (3) My Uncle   = (2) MARCELLA
           TIBERIUS
      Tiberillus   MARCELLINA
      (died young)

                    VIPSANIA = (1) My Uncle
                                   TIBERIUS
                             = (2) GALLUS son of
                                   POLLIO

LUCIUS   JULILLA = AEMILIUS   AGRIPPINA
              who was SCRIBONIA'S   = My Brother
              grandson by Scipio   GERMANICUS

                                                  POSTUMUS

— DRUSILLA   AEMILIA = SILANUS
  the Elder
                        Marcus Silanus

My Uncle TIBERIUS = (1) VIPSANIA   My Father DRUSUS
                  = (2) JULIA   = My Mother ANTONIA

              'CASTOR' = My Sister LIVILLA

'HELEN' = (1) NERO   'GEMELLUS'   Gemellus's Twin
        = (2) BLANDUS   (died young)

My Sister LIVILLA   I, CLAUDIUS = (1) URGULANILLA of the Plautian
  = (1) GAIUS   Family
  = (2) 'CASTOR'   = (2) AELIA, adoptive Sister of
                                          SEJANUS
              My Son DRUSILLUS   = (3) MESSALINA
                        My Daughter ANTONIA

GAIUS CALIGULA = (1) JUNIA   AGRIPPINILLA   'LESBIA'
             = (2) ORESTILLA   = Gnaeus Domitius   = VINICIUS
             = (3) LOLLIA PAULINA
             = (4) CAESONIA   Lucius Domitius *

DRUSILLA the Younger

                *Afterwards the Emperor NERO. – R.G.

Also by Robert Graves —

CLAUDIUS THE GOD

In the sequel to *I, Claudius* a republican Roman Emperor writes the inside story of his reign.

Men classed Claudius as a pitiful fool. But the reign he describes is far from folly. Reluctantly launched into the purple, he emerges as a man who erred on the side of good nature and credulity. It is the common people and the common soldiers who sustain him in his efforts to repair the damage of Caligula's reign, his relations with the Jewish King, Herod Agrippa, his conquest of Britain, and his final reckoning with his promiscuous wife, Messalina.

In one of the finest historical reconstructions of the century Robert Graves has created a character to compare with Dostoyevsky's *Idiot*.

and

GOODBYE TO ALL THAT
GREEK MYTHS VOL. 1
GREEK MYTHS VOL. 2